Common Values and
the Public-Private Divide

Law in Context

Editors: William Twining (University College, London) and
Christopher McCrudden (Lincoln College, Oxford)

Common Values and the Public-Private Divide

Dawn Oliver
Faculty of Laws, University College London

Butterworths
London, Edinburgh, Dublin
1999

United Kingdom	Butterworths, a Division of Reed Elsevier (UK) Ltd, Halsbury House, 35 Chancery Lane, LONDON WC2A 1EL and 4 Hill Street, EDINBURGH EH2 3JZ
Australia	Butterworths, a Division of Reed International Books Australia Pty Ltd, CHATSWOOD, New South Wales
Canada	Butterworths Canada Ltd, MARKHAM, Ontario
Hong Kong	Butterworths Asia (Hong Kong), HONG KONG
India	Butterworths India, NEW DELHI
Ireland	Butterworth (Ireland) Ltd, DUBLIN
Malaysia	Malayan Law Journal Sdn Bhd, KUALA LUMPUR
New Zealand	Butterworths of New Zealand Ltd, WELLINGTON
Singapore	Butterworths Asia, SINGAPORE
South Africa	Butterworths Publishers (Pty) Ltd, DURBAN
USA	Lexis Law Publishing, CHARLOTTESVILLE, Virginia

 A member of the Reed Elsevier plc group

A CIP Catalogue record for this book is available from the British Library.

ISBN   0 406 98303 8

Printed and bound by Hobbs the Printers Ltd, Totton, Hampshire

Visit us at our website: http://www.butterworths.co.uk

Preface

In this book I have sought to make some sense of difficulties in establishing an acceptable basis for the judicial review jurisdiction, of the exclusivity rule introduced by the House of Lords in the decision in *O'Reilly v Mackman*, and of the many parallels that can be drawn between public and private law, in relation to decision making and tortious and other obligations. It seems to me to be obvious that the distinctions between public and private law are artificial, and that it is more productive to concentrate on the similarities between the two kinds of law rather than the differences. I have come to the conclusion that both public and private law are concerned, and concerned in similar if not identical ways, with three projects: to protect the interests of individuals in their autonomy, dignity, respect, status and security; to control exercises of power; and to promote democracy and citizenship both in the public or political sphere and in the private sphere. In effect, systems of civil and civic democracy have been evolving in Britain for many decades, as a matter of public policy. This evolution is in effect a joint enterprise between Parliament, the common law and equity, with some help from the European Community and the European Convention on Human Rights.

I found that there was more material on the public-private divide, the control of power, the protection of individual interests and public interests and the democratic theories inherent in the law on these matters than I could possibly include in this work, and so I have been selective. I am conscious in particular of the rich veins of untapped material in, for instance, restitution, land law and criminal law. However, my hope is that the material I have chosen will make out the thesis, even if it is not comprehensive.

I owe considerable debts of gratitude to many people. In writing this book I have drawn on articles that I have previously published,[1] and I am grateful to colleagues who gave me advice and feedback on those pieces. I have also received very valuable feedback on earlier drafts of these chapters from other colleagues, including the following: Roger Errera, Conseiller d'Etat very kindly advised me on French administrative law; Andrew Lewis helped on legal history; Jeffrey Jowell and Andrew le Sueur gave me helpful critical feedback on the chapters on public law; without the help of Gillian Morris and Roger Rideout on employment law that section could not have been written; Alison Clarke and Paul Kohler gave me guidance on property law, especially matrimonial property; Richard O'Dair and Roger Halson gave me very helpful assistance on contract and tort and remedies; Sir John Vinelott was very helpful in relation to discretionary decision making in equity and equitable remedies; Ben Pettet tried to put me right on company law; LLM student Jonathan Foster researched the field of private law controls on decision making for an essay 'Reviewing the exercise of regulatory power – supervisory jurisdiction in public and private law' and dug up useful material which I would not have found on my own; Christopher Himsworth was most helpful in enabling me to compare English and Scots law on supervisory jurisdictions. The discussions at a Conference held at the Cambridge Centre for Public Law in May 1999 on the Foundations for Judicial Review also helped to resolve some issues in my own mind.

As always I owe a lot to those who have gone before and have enriched the literature and opened up new avenues of inquiry and ideas which would not be possible if one was working without other people's wisdom to build on.

None of this would have been possible without the support and encouragement of my family, Stephen, Beccy, Adam and Rosie.

I am conscious that there must be many failings in this final product, and I take entire responsibility for them. Colleagues have done their best, and so have I, but it would not surprise me to know that my best was not good enough.

Dawn Oliver

University College London

May 1999

1   'Is the ultra vires rule the basis for judicial review?' [1987] Public Law 543; 'The underlying values of public and private law' in M Taggart (ed) *The Province of Administrative Law* (1997); 'Common Values of Public and Private Law and the Public Private Divide' [1997] Public Law 630.

Contents

Table of statutes

List of cases

PAGE

F

G

H

Decisions of the European Court of Justice are listed below numerically. These
    decisions are also included in the preceding alphabetical list.

Chapter One

Public Law, Private Law: Problematic Concepts

This book is about the relationship between public law and private law. Three themes will weave their way through the chapters. First, the fact that public and private law have in common that they are concerned with controlling exercises of power, whether by the state or by private bodies. Secondly, the fact that both public law and private law are concerned to protect certain vital interests of individuals and public interests against abuses of state and private power; and thirdly, that similar theories of government, democracy and citizenship underpin these roles of the courts in controlling power and protecting individual and public interests. Let us consider these three themes briefly before passing on to what is known as the public private divide.

The relationship between public law and private law has both legal and political – democratic – dimensions. They are both about the control of power. Public law is primarily about the exercise and control of state power. Private law is about the control of private power. Public law is political in that it determines the extent of the power of state bodies – Parliament, the government, the courts, local authorities, the police and other institutions – to discharge their functions, and it determines the limits of the powers of those bodies to interfere with the liberties of individuals. Public law has what Harlow and Rawlings have called 'green light' and 'red light' functions.[1] It is the courts which determine both the extent of state power (often showing green lights to state bodies) and its limitations (which may mean displaying a red light); in doing so, the courts sometimes apply statutes; at other times they apply and develop the common law. It will be shown in the chapters that follow that there

---

1   C Harlow and R Rawlings *Law and Administration* (2nd edn, 1998) chapters 2 and 3.

are parallels between public and private law in each of these respects: private law constitutes and controls private power too, for example in employment and family relationships, contractual relationships, trusts and company law, to mention some of the topics that will be explored later.

Public law is also about protecting individuals against actions and decisions that might interfere with their vital interests – in their livelihoods, their access to benefits and so on. This is largely what the rules of natural justice and principles of *Wednesbury* reasonableness are designed to do. But private law too is often concerned with these matters, and principles of procedural fairness and rationality can be found operating in, for instance, employment law, trusts, contract and so on. Public law is not as different and separate from private law as it is often assumed to be.

THEORIES OF GOVERNMENT, DEMOCRACY AND CITIZENSHIP IN PUBLIC LAW

Underlying the functions of the courts as red lights and green lights in public law are a number of parallel strands of constitutional and citizenship theory. It will be helpful to summarise these briefly here, since in the chapters which follow the ways in which these theories are reflected in various subdivisions of both public and private law will be noted. A consequence of the evolutionary nature of constitutional law and theory, and of public and private law in the common law system, is that elements of past non-democratic theories about the position of the state and of individuals in their relationships with the state and with private bodies survive the processes of democratisation that have been taking place for at least three centuries.

Positivist authoritarianism

There is a (diminishingly important) positivist-authoritarian strand in public law, which is in effect a *non-democratic* strand. In former times – broadly until the Glorious Revolution of 1688 transferred the sovereignty of the monarch to Parliament – this positivist-authoritarian strand found expression in the very considerable common law prerogatives at the disposal of the monarch. These included the prerogatives of making and changing, suspending and dispensing with, the law, imposing taxation, spending public revenues. But by 1688 these legally recognised prerogatives had already been considerably eroded. This had been partly achieved by political processes, in particular negotiation between the monarch and Parliament, resulting in instruments such as Magna Carta

(1215), the Petition of Right (1628) and other measures, which cumulatively reduced the monarch's power to raise taxation without the consent of Parliament, or to act in ways that were beyond the reach of the courts. But the erosion of a positivist-authoritarian approach to government was also contributed to in very substantial ways by the courts, in decisions which, for instance, removed the power of the monarch to change the law affecting the liberties of individuals without the consent of Parliament,[2] and excluded the monarch from sitting in his own courts, thus establishing a separation of powers between the judiciary and the other arms of the state.[3] In 1688 the Bill of Rights transferred most of the royal prerogatives – and the legal sovereignty that previously belonged to the monarch – to Parliament, for instance by providing that there should be no taxation without the consent of Parliament and that the exercise of suspending and dispensing powers was, generally, unlawful.

However, there remain important royal prerogatives – exercisable formally by the monarch, but in practice by ministers – to this day, including the powers relating to the conduct of foreign and defence policy and the declaration and waging of war, prerogatives relating to the system of justice such as mercy and pardon, and miscellaneous other powers including the management of the civil service. These powers remain essentially authoritarian, positivist and non-democratic from a legal point of view, although they are politically encrusted with conventions of ministerial responsibility to Parliament which expose ministers exercising these powers to some, though not very effective, democratic accountability. Thus, this strand of authoritarian-positivist theory still surfaces in cases where the courts find decisions of government taken under prerogative powers to be non-justiciable.[4]

Positivist authoritarianism may also be found operating in the present system where the courts refuse to impose duties of, for instance, fairness and rationality, on decision making on grounds that to intervene would be to undermine the authority of the decision maker. The circumstances in which the courts take this view are rare but in the relatively recent past the courts have regarded decisions taken in disciplinary proceedings in prisons, for instance, as not subject to duties of natural justice on this ground.[5]

---

2   *Case of Proclamations* (1611) 12 Co Rep 74.
3   *Case of Prohibitions Del Roy* (1607) 12 Co Rep 63.
4   See for instance *Council of Civil Service Unions v Minister for the Civil Service* [1985] AC 374; and see discussion of this case in chapters 4 and 5.
5   See for instance the principles relating to disciplinary proceedings in *R v Metropolitan Police Comr, ex p Parker* [1953] 1 WLR 1150; *Ex p Fry* [1954] 1 WLR 730; *R v Board of Visitors of Hull Prison, ex p St. Germain* [1978] QB 678, 690 (reversed on appeal); De Smith, Woolf and Jowell, *Judicial Review of Administrative Action* (5th edn, 1995) chapter 24.

Liberal majoritarianism

In parallel to this essentially authoritarian constitutional theory runs a second strand, a theory of liberal-majoritarian democracy. Despite the apparent contradiction in putting these two terms together, they do in fact operate in partnership in much of our constitutional law. The theory is liberal in the sense that the liberties or freedoms of individuals may only be interfered with under parliamentary authority and not, for instance, by executive diktat.[6] It is also pluralist, since the tolerance of individual liberty necessarily involves that private associations will form, providing outlets for a variety of activities, religious practices, political opinions and so on. However, the theory is fundamentally majoritarian. Given that there is no written constitution for the United Kingdom which limits the legislative power of the sovereign – the Queen in Parliament – either absolutely or by procedural means (such as requirements for special majorities or referenda before particular measures can be passed), the theory of representative democracy as applied in United Kingdom courts is in practice a majoritarian theory: the majority in Parliament can pass whatever laws it wishes, however substantively illiberal or undemocratic they may be.[7] And Parliament can protect the government from being held even politically accountable for its actions (save at election time), by uniting behind a minister or an administration that is subject to criticism on the ground, for instance, that its policies are illiberal. Liberal majoritarianism generally entails, on the one hand (save, for instance, where European law is concerned[8]) that Parliament's consent is required for legislation, and on the other hand, that any legislation passed by Parliament must be given effect by the courts. It is the fact that the Commons are elected which legitimates their exercise of legislative power and thus attracts the label 'democratic' to this liberal-majoritarian theory, and requires the courts to give effect to Acts of Parliament as the highest form of law.

This liberal-majoritarian theory illustrates both 'green light' and 'red light' aspects of the constitution. It illustrates the former in that (subject to European Community law) the courts will give effect to any Act of Parliament, regardless of whether it is compatible with human rights instruments, international law, common sense or any other standards; and it illustrates 'red light' theory in that without statutory authorisation government will not be permitted to interfere with the liberties of individuals, raise taxation and so on.

6   *Case of Proclamations* (1611) 12 Co Rep 74; *Entick v Carrington* (1765) 19 State Tr 1029.
7   See *Cheney v Conn* [1968] 1 All ER 779; *Edinburgh and Dalkeith Rly v Wauchope* (1842) 8 Cl & Fin 710. And see A W Bradley and K D Ewing *Constitutional and Administrative Law* (12th edn, 1997) chapter 4.
8   See chapter 5.

Liberal-majoritarian theory can be seen being applied by the courts in judicial review where the doctrine of legislative intent[9] is taken both to justify actions or decisions taken under statutory authority, and to justify the courts imposing duties of, broadly, procedural fairness and rationality in the exercise of statutory discretions: Parliament is taken to have intended that the powers it grants be exercised fairly and rationally. However, sometimes, as we shall see in the next chapter, the majoritarian strand of this theory is said to make it illegitimate for the courts to impose any kind of constraint on those exercising statutory powers such as ministers and local authorities, even by requiring that they conform to the requirements of procedural propriety or reasonableness in their decision making.[10]

Considerate altruism

A third strand of democratic theory that may be found operating in public law is what may be termed considerate altruism: according to this theory public bodies have no rights or interests of their own and must exercise their powers altruistically, and for the general good. They are also under responsibilities – duties of consideration – towards individuals affected by their decisions.[11] These are not only responsibilities to hear them and take their interests into account before exercising a discretion, but also duties to act considerately towards them, to place their interests in the balance, not to act 'unreasonably' or arbitrarily or capriciously.

This strand of theory can be found operating in cases in which the courts have struck down decisions where a minister or other body has acted in a partisan way or to protect its own interests, or '*Wednesbury* unreasonably'[12]; it also operates where activity – as opposed to a decision – has been held to be unlawful or tortious, as in the tort of misfeasance in a public office and other 'public' torts (considered in chapters 8 and 9).

Participative communitarianism

The fourth strand in democratic theory which may be seen to be at work in public law is what might be termed participative communitarianism. On this theory individuals – and groups – affected by public decisions ought to have the opportunity to participate in those decisions, for instance

9   See discussion of this doctrine in chapter 2.
10 M Elliott 'The demise of parliamentary sovereignty? The implications for justifying judicial review' (1999) 115 LQR 119.
11 See discussion of the interests of state bodies in chapter 3.
12 See the seminal decision of Lord Greene MR in *Associated Provincial Picture Houses v Wednesbury Corpn* [1948] 1 KB 223.

by being given a hearing before the decision is made, having opportunities to put their own case and arguments, or being given reasons for the eventual decision and having the right to apply for judicial review if decision makers have not complied with these requirements.[13] On this theory the importance to individuals (and to the common good) of the involvement of members of the public in government ought to be recognised and such involvement ought to be encouraged through rights to be consulted and heard, even where a decision does not directly affect the organisation that is being consulted.

This strand of democratic theory may be seen operating in cases where the courts have laid down duties of procedural propriety – consultation, hearings, the giving of reasons, both for the benefit of individuals who are directly affected by the decision and for groups with something to say on the matter, where the rules of standing in judicial review have been substantially liberalised in recent years to permit challenge on the basis of failure to consult, or to provide a court forum for the ventilation of issues.[14] The emphasis on participation in this strand focuses on the importance of securing 'good' decisions which will take fully into account the interests of individuals and the detriment that may be caused to them by a possible decision, and arguments about the public interest; it also focuses attention on the learning experience which individuals will benefit from through being able to participate in decisions, a form of 'developmental democracy' which facilitates community activity, commitment and involvement,[15] and also enables people to develop shared standards.[16] Another strand in this theory is 'dignitarian', claiming that respect for the dignity of individuals requires that they be heard when decisions that affect them are in contemplation, even (in its strong form) if the hearing will not affect the outcome of the decision-making process.[17] Communitarianism also involves the idea that the various communities in society ought to be able to influence and participate in government, and to govern themselves, giving effect to

13 See for instance T R S Allan 'Fairness, equality, rationality: Constitutional theory and judicial review' in C Forsyth and I Hare, (eds) *The Golden Metwand and the Crooked Cord* (1998); R Cotterrell 'Judicial review and legal theory' in G Richardson and H Genn *Administrative Law and Government Action* (1994). For discussion of the rationales for this kind of participation see D J Galligan *Due Process and Fair Procedures: A Study of Administrative Procedures* (1996) chapter 4.

14 On standing see *IRC v National Federation of Self Employed and Small Businesses* [1982] AC 617; De Smith, Woolf and Jowell *Judicial Review of Administrative Action* (5th edn, 1994) chapter 2; and discussion in chapter 5.

15 See for instance C B Macpherson *The Life and Times of Liberal Democracy* (1977) chapters III and V.

16 See D J Galligan *Due Process and Fair Procedures: A Study of Administrative Procedures* (1996) pp 152-153.

17 See *Galligan*, supra, chapter 4.

values rooted in the community rather than values imposed from above or outside. On this approach one value of participation is that it facilitates the development of values.[18]

Citizenship theories

Each of the four strands of constitutional theory identified above focuses on public action or decision making. Implicit in these theories are assumptions about citizenship, the relationship between the individual and the state. Positivist authoritarianism places little importance on the individual and the effects of state action upon individual interests, and treats individuals as subjects rather than citizens.[19] Liberal-majoritarian theory gives individuals a political role in at least electing and dismissing their law makers; and the theory requires that the civil and political rights or liberties of individuals may only be interfered with through legislation duly passed by Parliament.[20] But Parliament may pass legislation on any subject matter. Thus this theory does provide some protection for civil and political rights as against the state, though it does not envisage a participative role for the citizen outside the right to vote and to stand for election and the exercise, within legally prescribed limits, of freedom of expression and association – which may, of course, have political aspects.[1] This democratic theory envisages a 'liberal' form of citizenship, which retains a clear sphere of 'private' activity with which the state cannot interfere save through statutory authority, alongside the 'public' roles of individuals. The purpose of political rights on this model is primarily to enable individuals to protect themselves against state interference.

Considerate altruism emphasises the position of the citizen as the considered beneficiary of state action. By 'considered' is meant that public bodies, when deciding on actions and policies, should weigh in the balance the interests not only of particular individuals who may be affected by their actions, but also of the collectivities or groups of individuals who might be so affected. Individuals, on this basis, are not to be treated as subjects, objects or as means to ends. This aspect of citizenship theory reflects Kant's principle that individuals are to be treated as ends and not means. Considerate altruism is also reflected in Marshall's idea of social

18 See *Galligan*, supra, chapter 1.
19 See discussion of the sovereign subject relationship in chapter 6.
20 See discussion of the development of civil rights in the eighteenth century and of political rights in the nineteenth century in T H Marshall *Citizenship and Social Class* (1950).
1 See for instance discussion of human rights in chapter 10.

rights[2] as forming part of citizenship, though in contemporary conditions the notion that the state should *provide* benefits and services as opposed to facilitating their provision[3] represents a rejection of some of the assumptions that Marshall made in his discussion of citizenship. We can see this model of citizenship at work in judicial review, where duties of altruism, procedural propriety and rationality – considerate decision making – are imposed on public decision makers,[4] as well as in the imposition of tort liability on public bodies, for instance in negligence in the exercise of a power or function.[5]

By contrast with liberal-majoritarian theory, participative communitarianism does envisage the participation by individuals and groups in public decision making, and to that extent it involves a model of citizenship of a 'civic republican' kind, which emphasises involvement in politics as being of central importance, not only for particular individuals but also in the general public interest. It therefore has a different focus from the 'liberal' model with its emphasis on a divide between the public and private lives of individuals; it focuses on the social involvement or integration of individuals and institutions of civil society in public life, rather than establishing a fence between public and private life.

Civil democracy and citizenship

Each of the theories of democracy and citizenship sketched in the previous paragraphs is pre-eminently concerned with relationships between individuals and the state. We shall see in subsequent chapters, especially as we focus on developments in the law of (private) relationships and private law, that parallel thought patterns and concepts can be identified in private law. An authoritarian-positivist theory is influential in the employment relationship when the authority of the employer is held to outweigh the interests of the employee;[6] this theory was also, until relatively recently, influential in marriage and parent-child relationships;[7] there are traces of it in relationships between membership associations and their members or aspiring members, such

2   T H Marshall *Citizenship and Social Class* (1950).
3   See D Osborne and T Gaebler *Reinventing Government: How the Entrepreneurial Spirit is Transforming the Public Sector* (1992) on the facilitative role of the state.
4   See chapter 5.
5   See for instance *East Suffolk Rivers Catchment Board v Kent* [1941] AC 74; *Dutton v Bognor Regis UDC* [1971] 2 All ER 462; *Home Office v Dorset Yacht Co Ltd* [1970] 2 All ER 294; *Anns v London Borough of Merton* [1978] AC 728; *Baccett v London Borough of Enfield* [1999] 3 WLR 79.
6   Discussed in chapter 6.
7   See chapter 7.

as professional and sporting bodies and trade unions, when the courts accede to their claims to the right to exercise authority free from duties of either natural justice or rationality.[8]

A liberal-majoritarian theory is at work in company law, especially where the interests of minority shareholders are adversely affected by the decisions of directors or majority shareholders and are overridden by the majority.[9] Considerate altruism is mirrored in private law where private bodies in positions of power are required to act altruistically and with a sense of responsibility and consideration for those who might be affected by their acts or decisions, as for example in tort, trusts, restraint of trade and private monopoly situations.[10] Communitarian-participative theory can be seen at work in some private situations, notably where private bodies are required to allow those affected by decisions to participate in them, as in some dismissals from employment[11] and expulsions from institutions of civil society such as trade unions, professional bodies, pension arrangements.[12]

In such private situations, it will be suggested, what is emerging is a model of 'civil democracy' alongside the models of 'civic democracy' that operate in public law and in relations between individuals and the state. Civil democracy involves that those in positions of private power allow individuals to participate in decisions that affect them, and that they should act considerately, not selfishly, arbitrarily or capriciously towards others, and that the vulnerable are entitled to be treated with consideration not only by the state but by other private bodies.

THE PUBLIC-PRIVATE DIVIDE IN ENGLISH LAW

A major focus in this book will be on the problematic nature of the public-private divide as it has developed since the landmark House of Lords' decision in *O'Reilly v Mackman*[13] in 1983. Here the House of Lords struck out a civil action to declare decisions of a Prison Board of Visitors disciplining a prisoner for his participation in a prison riot to be void on the grounds that it was an abuse of process to seek a remedy by ordinary action and in such a case judicial review was the only procedure open to a complainant.[14] That decision (which will be considered in detail in chapter 4) raised complex and challenging

8   See chapters 8 and 9.
9   See chapter 8.
10 See discussion in chapters 8 and 9.
11 See chapter 6.
12 See chapters 8 and 9.
13 [1983] 2 AC 237.
14 For full discussion of the case see chapter 4.

issues to do with the conflicting needs, as perceived by the courts, to give the state protection against litigation which undermines the interests of good administration, and yet to protect individuals and public interests against abuses of state power.

The first point to confront here is that the terms 'public law' and 'private law' are ambiguous and are liable to be used in conflicting and misleading ways. Cane[15] shows that they may be used either descriptively or prescriptively: used descriptively the terms indicate that 'according to some norm or set of norms, the term "public" or "private" is appropriately applied to a body,' or a function. This may open up an argument about the appropriateness of the norms, or of the descriptive terms. Used prescriptively the terms may be used to suggest that it is right that certain bodies or functions, when actions or decision making are at issue, should enjoy special immunities[16] or privileges[17] or be subject to special burdens.[18] This may open up discussion about such matters as the appropriateness of the present position, and whether the privileges or burdens might be differently distributed, or whether there should be increased rights of public participation in the decision making.[19]

Cane also notes that there are some counter-intuitive uses of the terms. Some theorists tend to categorise judicial review as 'private' because it is available at the suit of individuals and because courts purport to decide cases according to rules, not political considerations. For such commentators only 'political' modes and standards of control of public bodies are 'public'. For the courts, on the other hand (and for most lawyers), judicial review is 'public', and political mechanisms are extra-legal, not falling into the category of public law at all.

One of the arguments that will be presented in the following chapters will be that the particular distinctions the courts have sought to maintain

15 P Cane 'Public law and private law: A study of the analysis and use of a legal concept' in J Eekelaar and J Bell *Oxford Essays in Jurisprudence*, Third series (1987) p 56.

16 As, for example, the immunity of the police from negligence actions for failing to arrest identified suspects before they commit an offence on an identifiable prospective victim: *Osman v Ferguson* [1993] 4 All ER 344, CA. See also *Hill v Chief Constable of West Yorkshire* [1989] AC 53, HL for police immunity from negligence for failing to arrest a serial murderer before he killed his next victim.

17 Such as the procedural privileges in applications for judicial review under section 31 of the Supreme Court Act 1981 and Order 53 of the Rules of the Supreme Court, by way of short time limits, the requirement for permission to apply, limitations on disclosure and cross examination and discretion in the award of remedies. See chapters 4 and 5 below.

18 Such as duties of legality, fairness and rationality imposed under *Council of Civil Service Unions v Minister for the Civil Service* [1985] AC 374. See chapters 4 and 5 below.

19 P Cane, supra, at p 56.

since *O'Reilly* between public law and private law, between public or governmental functions and private functions, and between public and private rights are essentially unsound. It is more constructive to focus on what public law and private law have in common than on what are supposed to be the differences between them. There are strong common features in both substantive and procedural aspects of public and private law. The parallels in democratic and citizenship theory were sketched in at the start of this chapter. Both public law and private law are concerned, among other things, with the control of power and protecting individuals against abuses of power (the meanings of power will be considered in chapter 2); they are both about upholding important common values of respect for the interests of individuals (these values are discussed in chapter 3); this is done either by proscribing activity that interferes with those interests, or imposing duties of reasonableness, as in much of the law of tort; equity, especially in fiduciary relationships, imposes very similar controls on certain exercises of private power to those imposed on public bodies in judicial review; many aspects of private law controls of discretionary decision making rest on the same principles as judicial review. But the control of power and protection of individuals are not the only concerns of public and private law: both are also concerned to uphold authority and protect the interests of good administration, and in this endeavour they have to achieve a balance between conflicting considerations.[20]

These commonalities between public and private law undermine the separation of public and private law which the decision in *O'Reilly* sought to achieve. This book then is concerned to explore the common concerns of public and private law, and to put forward ways in which the difficulties experienced in operating the public-private divide – or operating with a more subtle set of distinctions and considerations – might be solved, principally by integrating public and private law rather than seeking to divide them. This conclusion raises issues about our theories of democracy, discussed briefly at the start of this chapter, extending as it does the traditional concern to control the use and abuse of state power across the divide so as to embrace concerns about the abuse of private power.

The state and public sector reform

The need to question the public-private divide is the greater in the light of the radical changes in the delivery of public services that have been

---

20 See discussions of judicial review in chapter 5, of the employment relationship in chapter 6, and of family law in chapter 7.

taking place in the United Kingdom and other countries over the last quarter century.[1] Many formerly state-owned utilities and other industries have been transferred to private ownership, thus removing them from political and democratic control and raising issues as to how the exercise of power by those bodies which affects individuals – our principal concern in this book – and the general public interest may be controlled. One response is regulation of the private sector.[2] But can private law impose controls on these industries that are analogous to those previously imposed by public law?

On one approach privatised or contracted out activities should be regarded as retaining the quality of publicness which means that they are subject to 'public law' standards. On another approach – the one preferred in this work – what have been assumed to be 'public law' standards are not unique to public law, indeed they derive from private law, and private law can, and should, impose standards not only of considerate action but of considerate decision making, of, broadly, legality, fairness and rationality,[3] on the actions and decision making of these – and other – private bodies. A strong example of considerate action – a duty of care – being imposed on private bodies was the House of Lords' decision in *Donoghue v Stevenson*[4] which introduced product liability and wider duties of care towards 'neighbours' across a wide range of 'private' activity. Our argument here will be that it is entirely appropriate for private bodies in positions of power to be under legally enforceable duties of consideration in many (but not all) of their activities.

It is not part of our argument that there is no difference between state bodies and others – individuals, commercial companies for instance. Differences include the following. Many – but not all – state bodies are elected, or accountable to elected bodies; this gives them, if no greater degree of wisdom than the unelected, at least the legitimacy to inflict their mistakes on the country which the unelected lack. It may be that the fact that a state body is *politically* accountable could be taken as a justification for not imposing *legal* controls upon them – though this argument for judicial restraint is not nowadays commonly accepted by

---

1   See D Oliver and G Drewry *Public Service Reforms. Issues of Accountability and Public Law* (1996); I Harden *The Contracting State* (1992); D Osborne and T Gaebler *Reinventing Government: How the Entrepreneurial Spirit is Transforming the Public Sector* (1992) (United States); G Palmer *Unbridled Power* (1987) (New Zealand).

2   See T Prosser *Law and the Regulators* (1997); J Black, P Muchlinski and P Walker (eds) *Commercial Regulation and Judicial Review* (1998); Sir Gordon Borrie 'The Regulation of Public and Private Power' [1989] Public Law 552.

3   For explanation of these terms see discussion of supervisory jurisdictions below.

4   [1932] AC 562, HL.

the judiciary. State bodies often have legal coercive powers – the fact that they are politically and legally accountable is regarded as legitimating such powers and providing protection to individuals against their abuse. These state coercive powers generally have no parallel in the private sector (though the running of prisons by private companies in effect gives the latter coercive restraining powers). It is a function of state bodies to determine and then to promote the common or public interest: their political accountability provides checks and balances that should minimise errors and misjudgments in this function. It is commonly understood in the United Kingdom that state bodies should act in the general public interest, altruistically – election or accountability to elected bodies is supposed to ensure that this is the case – while private bodies are entitled, though to greater and lesser extents, to pursue self-regarding interests.

Nor will it be suggested that there are no differences between some of the activities in which the state engages and functions in which the private sector is involved. Some of what state bodies do could be done by the private or voluntary sector – the provision of education, health care and pensions are examples – and the fact that something is done by the state signifies, in a democracy, that a choice has been made that the state should undertake the activity, thus giving the activity, as well as the state, legitimacy it might not otherwise have. State bodies are often engaged – and the law permits them to be engaged – in activities which would not be tolerated if engaged in by the private sector – conducting foreign policy, defence of the realm, maintenance of law and order, imposing and collecting taxation and so on.

But it would be wrong to infer that very clear dividing lines can be drawn, even here. The state engages in many activities which have clear parallels in the private sector – contracting, building and so on. And private bodies often work in areas where they are expected to pursue public, not private, interests. Charities and other organisations operating in the voluntary sector are acting altruistically, often in ways very similar to government, as where charities provide medical care, education for disabled children, university education, and the like. In effect principles of considerate action, altruism and public service apply not only to state, but also to some private, organisations.

Private bodies also take part in activities which, it might be assumed, are 'state' activities. The Red Cross and other relief agencies engage in 'foreign policy' type matters, often negotiating for the delivery of aid or the care of refugees. Private security firms and store detectives commonly carry out a policing function. Private associations impose levies – private taxes – on their members and collect them for the purpose of providing services such as medical treatment, insurance, pensions and the like.

Can public and private law be separated?

It is part of the thesis of this book that, although it may be convenient, especially for pedagogical purposes, to draw a distinction between public and private law, in practice public and private law cannot be separated, and indeed that it is not possible to define one or the other in ways that can be of wide or general application. This is because 'public law' is shorthand for a whole collection of ideas – about particular bodies that are regarded as 'public' (though some of what they do may be private[5]), about particular functions that are, for the time being, 'public'[6] (though in the past they may have been regarded as only 'private', like banking, and nursery education, and they may be discharged by the private sector), about liabilities of a 'public' kind (such as in the tort of misfeasance in a public office,[7] which might be regarded as a private law tort action but in some respects is public[8]), and about special 'public' interests,[9] and special court procedures and remedies.[10] As these examples show, it is not easy to separate public and private in such areas.

It is worth noting at this point some of the definitions of public law that have been advanced and the purposes for which they are advanced. University law courses include subjects entitled 'public law' or 'administrative law' or 'constitutional law', and these are generally concerned with the distribution of powers between public or governmental institutions such as Parliament, the government, local authorities, the police and a range of quasi-autonomous non-governmental organisations. They are also concerned with relations between the individual and these state bodies. It is convenient for pedagogical purposes to divide the law into subjects and this particular division fits in well with the other divisions of the law – obligations, property, and so on. But in practice much of public law on the above definition could be covered in private law courses – public contracting and procurement, relations between public servants and their employers, interferences by state bodies with the rights or liberties of individuals could all fall to be covered in private law subjects taught at law schools. And much of the law taught in obligations and property courses could be regarded as 'public' and could be taught in public law courses –

5   See discussion of this issue in chapter 4.
6   See discussion in chapter 4.
7   See *Three Rivers District Council v Bank of England (No 3)* [1996] 3 All ER 558, Clarke J. The claim was struck out by the Court of Appeal: (1998) Times, 10 December.
8   See discussion in chapter 8.
9   See for instance the discussion of common callings in chapter 9.
10 Such as the procedure for application for judicial review, and the prerogative orders, discussed in chapter 5.

consumer protection, safety at work legislation, planning law, all of which impinge on private law subjects, are examples.

Defining public law

There are other ways of defining public law. On some approaches activity is 'public' if it is regulated, even if the activity is undertaken by a non-state body. But it is far from clear whether calling a regulated activity 'public' adds much to 'regulated.' In the United States there is a debate about the desirability of regulating the employment relationship which assumes that if it is regulated it is public,[11] but in English usage this relationship is regarded as private, even though it is extensively regulated.[12]

Loughlin suggests that public law is 'simply a sophisticated form of political discourse; … controversies within the subject are simply extended political disputes.'[13] Perhaps a particular meaning attaches to 'political' here, but on the face of it issues in public law such as who is subject to judicial review and who is not need not be 'political.' They are about power and the control of power, including essentially private power that is beyond the reach of political control, such as the power of regulatory bodies in the city.[14] But perhaps by 'political' Loughlin means 'to do with power' in which case much of what we regard as private law (for instance the control of regulatory bodies in sport[15]) is 'political' too. Public and private law are united rather than divided by this characteristic.

The legal control of power will be a major theme in the chapters that follow.[16] In fact, as we shall see, private law is increasingly concerned to control exercises of power by non-state bodies in private law proceedings (ie proceedings other than applications for judicial review under Order 53 of the Rules of the Supreme Court), in ways that are similar to those that have been developed by the courts in judicial review in the last forty years or so. And much of private law, notably tort, aspects of contract law, trusts, company law, restraint of trade and the law of common callings has for a long time been concerned to control abuses of power in the interests of individuals and on public policy grounds.

Interestingly more attention is paid to defining public law than to defining private law. The general assumption seems to be that public

11 See K Klare 'The public-private distinction in labor law' (1982) 130 U Pa L Rev 1358.
12 See discussion of employment in chapter 6.
13 M Loughlin *Public Law and Political Theory* (1992) at p 4.
14 See for instance *R v Panel on Take-overs and Mergers, ex p Datafin* [1987] QB 815.
15 See discussion in chapter 4.
16 See especially chapter 2 below.

law is a special area carved out of the rest – the private rest – of the law. Private law is a residual category. Yet, as we shall see, much of what is generally regarded as private law has heavy layers of what is regarded as 'public law' in it. For instance, duties of legality, fairness and rationality on the part of decision makers, which are often assumed to be 'public law duties', in fact arise in private law. On one view even what we commonly regard as private law, such as contract, tort and property law, is constituted by the state, in the sense that the norms which produce law in this area have been developed by the state in the form of the judiciary or in Acts of Parliament, and these norms are enforceable through the state – the courts and their enforcement mechanisms; on this approach it is artificial to seek to separate out such 'private' areas of law from the state or public sphere.[17]

The public-private divide has also been influenced by public opinion about what are matters of public concern which ought to be regulated in some way, and what matters are of purely private import which should not therefore be subject to legal regulation. The decriminalisation of homosexual activity between consenting males by the Sexual Offences Act 1967, section 1, and the criminalisation of marital rape by the House of Lords in 1991[18] illustrate the point. The first measure deregulated activity and thus moved it from the public to the private sphere, the second regulated previously unregulated activity and thus moved it from the private to the public sphere. The public-private divide is an area in which the law has been influenced by, and has influenced, thinking in other disciplines. The literature from other disciplines will be referred to in passing where appropriate in this book, but the focus of the thesis here is narrower, being on the way in which the law defines and then treats the two categories of public law and private law.

THE PUBLIC-PRIVATE DIVIDE IN CIVIL LAW SYSTEMS

The application of distinctive substantive and procedural rules in relation to administrative law is widespread in Western jurisdictions. Civil law systems operating in most Western European countries have developed separate systems of administrative law and they maintain – or try to maintain – both procedural and substantive distinctions between

---

17   See C Sunstein *The Partial Constitution* (1993) chapter 2; A S Butler 'Constitutional rights in private litigation: A critique and comparative analysis' (1993) 22 Anglo-American LR 1; M Hunt 'The "horizontal effect" of the Human Rights Act' [1998] Public Law 423, pp 424-426.
18   *R v R* [1992] 1 AC 599, HL.

administrative law and private law.[19] Many Western European states
have equivalents to the French Conseil d'Etat, an administrative court
or tribunal with exclusive jurisdiction over administrative law. In many
countries (notably France and Germany) the higher administrative courts
have been the source of a case law which has laid the foundations of
modern administrative law. This continues to be the case, despite the
fact that much modern administrative law is statute based. The rules of
law applicable in these tribunals have been developed with the particular
objective of providing appropriate controls on the use of public power,
and they are not applicable outside these councils or tribunals. For these
purposes public power is power exercised by public bodies, and in strict
theory there is no scope in those systems for powerful non-state bodies
to be supervised by the administrative courts or tribunals. However, in
practice other courts also apply what we might regard as 'administrative
law'. The nature and content of administrative law, as distinct from
private law, needs to be considered irrespective of the existence or absence
of separate courts.

In Germany, Habermas tells us, in the nineteenth century: 'private
law, by organizing a depoliticized economic society withdrawn from
state intrusion, guaranteed the *negative* freedom of legal subjects and
therewith the principle of legal freedom. Public law, on the contrary, was
allocated by a division of labor to the sphere of the authoritarian state in
order to keep a rein on an administration that reserved to itself the right
to intervene.'[20] At the same time, public law came to guarantee the
citizens' *positive* legal status via individual legal protection. However,
German law has moved on, and since the second world war there has
been a 'now-wavering division between private and public law'.[1]

Even in France, the mother of the Conseil d'Etat concept,[2] a public-
private divide is proving difficult to sustain. Indeed French administrative
law has been typified by a variety of hybrid institutions since the Third
Republic, which 'rendered the state and its administration less distinct
and the application of the terms public and private more problematic.'[3]
Brown and Bell summarise the position broadly as follows.[4] The principal
criterion applied by the Conseil d'Etat in determining whether a
particular case falls within its jurisdiction is whether it is a 'service
public',[5] which means 'any activity of a public authority aimed at

19 See generally J Schwarze *European Administrative Law* (1992).
20 J Habermas *Between Facts and Norms* (1997), at p 396.
1   *Habermas* at p 397.
2   See Schwarze, pp 110-114; Allison *A Continental Distinction in the Common Law*
     (1996), chapter 4; L N Brown and J S Bell *French Administrative Law* (1993).
3   Allison, supra, at pp 64-65.
4   L N Brown and J S Bell, at pp 125-131. See also *Allison* chapter 4.
5   *Blanco*, Tribunal des Conflits, 8 February 1873.

satisfying a public need.' This is one of the basics, even the basis, of 'droit administratif' in France. It is a concept with both institutional and functional dimensions. For instance, it embraces the notion of 'public agents' going beyond that of career civil servants; it extends to administrative contracts, and, in relation to property, to the 'domaine public', as well as to a special regime of public liability. Satisfying a public need includes providing a camping ground, and organising a firework display on 14 July, for instance. As far as 'service public' is concerned, it has been held that the activity of a charitable foundation providing student residential accommodation was a 'service public' and by implication the charity was a public authority. A 'service public' does not have to be provided by a public body – so *caisses* (the equivalent of provident societies) generally administer the social-insurance system in France, but in so doing they are nonetheless a 'service public': despite the fact that these have always been regarded as private law, not public law, bodies, the Conseil d'Etat has held that they were engaged in providing a 'service public' and thus fell within the jurisdiction of the administrative courts. A wide variety of sporting bodies is subject to review in the administrative courts, on the basis that they have received, by their statutes, power from (ie delegated by) the minister to organise their activities and this carries with it certain powers. It is for this reason that the administrative courts have jurisdiction over their acts.

But an additional element is also required in the concept of 'service public' in France, namely that the authority must have recourse to methods and prerogatives which would be excluded in relations between private parties, that is 'des prérogatives exorbitantes du droit commun.' Brown and Bell give by way of example that the body may operate the service as a monopoly or may finance it by compulsory contributions from those it benefits. There are strong echoes here of the English law of common callings, restraint of trade and monopoly, which will be discussed in chapter 9.

On the other hand there have been some decisions in France to the effect that if a 'service public' is being operated commercially it falls within the jurisdiction of the civil courts – even if the business is, for instance, a transport enterprise owned or operated by the government. The fact that a service is a 'service public' (for instance, a utility) does not preclude the possibility that it may be governed to some extent by private law, for instance, in its labour relations, or relations with customers, or in relations with third parties: a 'service public' may be private, and it may then be subject to normal civil (for instance tort or consumer) law. But such a body may also be subject to a special regime of public liability in administrative law. Thus a syndicate of private firms undertaking schemes of redevelopment for the administration has been held to be subject to the administrative courts. And a motorway construction company entitled to collect tolls was also within the jurisdiction. As Brown and Bell comment: 'This change of thought and the flexibility of the meaning of the concept of "public service" have made the line between the two jurisdictions very difficult to draw with any precision.'[6]

The distinction between 'droit administratif' and 'droit privé' is less wide that it used to be in France. EC law and the European Convention of Human Rights apply equally to both, as does the jurisprudence of the Conseil constitutionnel: constitutional law, by definition, ignores such distinctions and boundaries.

The French equivalents of British 'Quangos' are also subject to judicial review – perhaps 'supervisory jurisdiction' is a better phrase: this may take place before the ordinary courts, if the relevant statute so provides. For instance, the decisions of the Conseil de la Concurrence (Competition and Concentration [monopoly] authority) may be challenged before the Paris Court of Appeal. The same applies to penalties inflicted by the French Stock Exchange Authority. They may also be challenged before the Conseil d'Etat, as is the case with the Broadcasting Authority, sporting bodies etc.

In practice, then, there is no safe and established definition of what is a 'service public' in France. The problems experienced with any idea of a clear 'divide' between public law and private law, with which much of this book will be concerned, are by no means unique to the United Kingdom.

THE DEVELOPMENT OF ENGLISH PUBLIC LAW: REMEDIES AND SUBSTANCE

The great early writers including Blackstone,[7] Hale[8] and Austin,[9] devoted sections of their works to 'The Law of Persons', grouping together the relationships of individual-state, employment and marriage. But, until *O'Reilly v Mackman*,[10] the common law had not developed the idea that the relationship between the individual and the state was a matter of a separate category of public law, with the implication that there were or should be separate procedures and separate substantive rules for this relationship. This development, culminating in *O'Reilly v Mackman*, was connected with the law of remedies.

---

6   *Brown and Bell* at p 130.
7   See Sir William Blackstone *Commentaries on the Laws of England* (1765) vol 1.
8   See Sir Matthew Hale *An Analysis of the Civil Part of the Law* (4th edn 1779).
9   J Austin *Lectures on Jurisprudence* (5th edn 1995) pp 404-405, 744-759.
10   [1983] 2 AC 237.

Remedies

Atiyah has commented on how, in public law, remedies are emphasised as central, while until recently relatively little attention has been paid to legal rights and principles.[11] The decision in *O'Reilly v Mackman* was taken against the background of the reform of the procedure in judicial review in 1977, which permitted an applicant for one of the prerogative orders of certiorari, mandamus or prohibition to seek in the same proceedings other remedies, notably injunctions, declarations and damages. Before then the only way in which a remedy by way of a prerogative order, previously 'writ', could be obtained was by a special procedure in the Divisional Court of the Queen's Bench Division, and it was not possible to obtain other remedies in the same proceedings. Until 1977 there had been two ways of 'judicially reviewing' the decisions of public bodies, either by way of prerogative order obtainable in the Divisional Court of the Queen's Bench, or in the Chancery or Queen's Bench Division of the High Court in actions for declarations or injunctions. Outside the prerogative order procedures there was no leave requirement (now requirement for 'permission'[12]) and the normal civil limitation periods applied. In the procedure for prerogative orders there was a six month limitation period for certiorari (but not for the other orders), and, since 1936, a leave requirement.[13] Thus it was possible for people who did not wish to obtain leave to proceed and who were out of the certiorari time limit nevertheless to seek remedies outside the Divisional Court. As we shall see in chapter 4, it came to be regarded as an abuse of process to proceed outside the application for judicial review procedure, thus getting round the leave requirement and time limit (and other procedural disadvantages for applicants or plaintiffs) and hence the House of Lords in *O'Reilly* decided that all applications in respect of public law rights should be by way of judicial review.

The significance of the prerogative orders, originally 'prerogative writs'[14], was that they had opened up the possibility of the courts of common law controlling the decisions of bodies taken outside contract and other causes of action such as tort giving rise to a remedy in damages. In the period before the reform of the judicial review procedure in 1977 and *O'Reilly* the courts had developed principles for the review of decision making by public bodies and, very significantly for our purposes, by

11   P S Atiyah *Pragmatism and Theory in English Law* (1987) (Hamlyn Lectures, 39th series).
12   See Civil Procedure Rules 1999, Part 50, RSC Order 53, rule 3(1).
13   This was recommended by the Hanworth Committee on the Business of the Courts, Third Report Cmnd 5066.
14   See next chapter for an account of the development of the prerogative writs and the public-private divide.

private bodies in positions of power, which governed the award of remedies such as injunctions and declarations. As we shall see in chapter 4, one of the questions arising from *O'Reilly* is whether it instituted a substantive divide between public and private law which had not previously existed.

Substantive public law

In awarding prerogative remedies the Court of King's Bench applied from early times substantive principles of ultra vires, improper purpose and natural justice.[15] In modern terminology these are duties of legality, rationality and procedural propriety.[16] A question arises whether these were – and are – uniquely common law (as opposed to equitable or statutory) principles, and whether they are applicable only to broadly public decision making? Here useful comparisons may be made with the grounds on which discretionary decision making is controlled in other areas of the law, for instance equity – notably in the case of trustees and company directors, employment law,[17] the law of contract in relation to membership associations, and restraint of trade.[18]

The relationship between equitable principles and judicial review is illustrated by the classic statement of the grounds for judicial review by Lord Greene MR in *Associated Provincial Picture Houses v Wednesbury Corpn:*[19]

'The court is entitled to investigate the action of a local authority with a view to seeing whether it has taken into account matters which it ought not to take into account, or, conversely, has refused to take into account or neglected to take into account matters which it ought to take into account. Once that question is answered in favour of the local authority, it may still be possible to say that the local authority nevertheless have come to a conclusion so unreasonable that no reasonable authority could ever have come to it. In such a case, again, I think the court can interfere.'

Lord Greene was a great trust and equity lawyer, and as we shall see in later discussion of supervisory jurisdictions in equity, these *Wednesbury* principles are drawn clearly from the principles applied by equity in

---

15 See for instance *Bagg's case* (1615) 11 Co Rep 93b, discussed in chapter 2.
16 Per Lord Diplock in *Council of Civil Service Unions v Minister for the Civil Service* [1985] AC 374, discussed in chapters 4 and 5 below.
17 See discussion in chapter 6.
18 These are considered in chapters 8 and 9 below.
19 [1948] 1 KB 223, CA.

controlling the exercise of discretion by trustees and company directors. Indeed, Sir Anthony Mason has suggested that administrative law is founded on equitable principles: '… administrative law … from its earlier days, has mirrored the way in which equity has regulated the exercise of fiduciary powers.'[20] But the common law courts also developed their own principles, in what we now regard as contract and tort, under which certain private enterprises, notably those in common calling, monopolies, utilities and prime necessities,[1] were required to act rationally and not arbitrarily and capriciously. As already noted, *Donoghue v Stevenson* imposed duties of care (considerateness) on other 'neighbours'. In other words, administrative law is largely about consideration for those affected by decisions or actions and in this respect it has its roots in private law, as discussion in later chapters will show.

FROM STATUS TO CONTRACT: PUBLIC LAW, PRIVATE LAW AND THE IMPOSITION OF LEGAL OBLIGATIONS

Maine suggested that the mark of an advanced legal system is the move from status to contract, meaning that as a system advances the law no longer imposes particular non-negotiable roles on individuals by reason of their membership of a group – notably of a family – but permits individuals to negotiate for themselves the way they live their lives.[2] This insight has been partly responsible for the development of the view that it is not, or should not be, the role of private law to impose obligations on – to regulate the activities of – individuals. This is reflected in the law of tort with its reluctance to impose liability for omissions save in exceptional and strictly limited situations: this has been said to be the product of 'values of an era in which private selfishness was elevated to the rank of public virtue'.[3] Thus the imposition of duties is commonly regarded as the role of public law, which will generally only impose obligations in the public interest. From this position it is a short step to use the criterion of whether obligations are imposed or voluntarily undertaken as a determinant of whether a matter falls into the category of public or private law, and thus judicial review.

At the time that Maine was writing (1861) the law of tort and restitution were far less developed than they are now and it would have been more or less accurate to generalise in terms of the movement away from the

---

20   Sir Anthony Mason QC 'The place of equity and equitable remedies in the contemporary common law world' (1994) 110 LQR 238 at p 238.
1   See chapter 9.
2   Sir Henry Maine *Ancient Law* (1861), reprinted (1959) p 149.
3   B Markesinis 'Negligence, nuisance and affirmative duties of action' (1989) 105 LQR 104 at p 112.

imposition of obligations on persons towards contract as the principal source of obligation. However, even at that period the common law imposed non-contractual duties on those in common calling or in positions of monopoly,[4] and equity imposed duties – on trustees and others in fiduciary relationships,[5] for instance. Since then, the law of tort, and of negligence in particular, has developed so as to impose duties of care and consideration on those with whom individuals have, broadly, relationships of 'neighbours',[6] or with whom they are in proximity, where it would be fair, just and reasonable to impose liability.[7]

The relevance of Maine's points about the move from status to contract, from imposed obligations to voluntarily undertaken obligations, for the public-private divide is that one indicator sometimes put forward for determining whether a matter is within the bounds of public law or private law is the question whether legal obligations – especially obligations of consideration towards others – are voluntarily undertaken, or imposed. In other words, this distinction is reflected in the exclusion from judicial review after *O'Reilly v Mackman* of cases where power derives from a consensual submission to jurisdiction, or contract.[8] If obligations are imposed, on this approach, then they are governed by public law, if not, they are not. And the corollary of this approach is that it is not, or should not be, the function of private law to impose obligations on individuals.

This view, it is suggested, is misconceived. The question whether 'private' activity ought to be regulated is separable from the question – essentially a matter of fact – whether it is regulated. We have long passed the point where as a matter of principle the law does not regulate at all what is still commonly regarded as essentially private activity. Intimate relationships of marriage and parenthood, which most people would regard as 'private' are regulated in a range of ways, including matters to do with financial support, ownership of property, and the upbringing, care and education of children during the continuation of the relationship[9] and adjustment to these obligations and the rights of the parties on divorce. The employment relationship too is extensively regulated, both during its continuance and on its termination;[10] relationships between trustees and beneficiaries, between directors and their companies and shareholders, and other fiduciary relationships are also regulated in

---

4   See chapter 9.
5   See chapter 8.
6   *Donoghue v Stevenson* [1932] AC 562.
7   *Caparo Industries v Dickman* [1990] 2 AC 605.
8   See chapter 4.
9   See chapter 7.
10 See chapter 6.

various ways.[11] Even contractual activity is subject to much regulation.[12] Much of this regulation is imposed by statute, but the common law and equity have also contributed substantially to the regulation of private activity.

The question that arises is whether the fact that a relationship is subject to legal regulation of itself brings it within the scope of public law. This in turn raises issues about the meaning of public law. Clearly regulation of employment, trusts and marriage do not bring them within public law in the sense of judicial review. If the definition of public law were to extend to all matters where the law imposes duties on people, then there would be very little of the law or life that was private and any idea of a 'divide' between public and private life would be of marginal interest.

A separate question is the extent to which it is *appropriate* for the law to regulate private activity. As we shall see in subsequent chapters, there is a range of arguments against regulation, or for light-touch-only regulation. For instance, employment relationships and the activity of governing bodies in sport, the universities and the professions may be regarded as 'mini-legal systems' which should be permitted to regulate themselves without the intervention of statutory provisions or the common law.[13] The 'regulated' party in these relationships, normally the more powerful party, will claim its own interests in autonomy against regulation,[14] or will argue that the efficacy of its activity will be hampered if there is any or too much legal regulation, or that pluralism requires a law-free zone in social activity. The vulnerable parties in these relationships, by contrast, will assert the need for regulation in order to prevent abuse of power against them. There will also be public interest arguments, not related to detriment to particular individuals, but to matters such as the protection of the environment, in favour of the regulation of private activity.

In practice, as we shall see in later chapters, the discretionary decision-making of bodies such as employers, self-regulatory bodies, the universities and the professions, is commonly required by the courts to conform to standards with strong parallels with judicial review – legality,

11 See chapter 8.
12 See chapter 8.
13 See for instance H Arthurs 'Rethinking administrative law: A slightly Dicey business' (1979) 17 Osgoode Hall LR 1; Julia Black 'Constitutionalising Self-regulation' (1996) 59 MLR 24. On mini-legal systems and self-regulation is sport, see discussion in chapters 9 and 11; and see also James A R Nafziger 'International sports law as a process for resolving disputes' (1994) 45 ICLQ 130. On the employment relationship as a mini-legal system and generally regulation in labour law see chapter 6 and Karl E Klare 'The public-private distinction in labor law' (1982) 130 U Pa LR 1358 at p 1417.
14 See discussion of imbalances of power in chapter 2 and of autonomy in chapter 3.

fairness and rationality – as are the decisions of, for instance, trustees of private trusts, directors of companies, and contracting parties enjoying discretionary decision-making power under the terms of the contract. Generally the decisions of the courts which impose these obligations have been welcomed because they operate to control exercises of power that would otherwise be detrimental to individuals or wider public interests.

The obligations in contracts are supposedly voluntarily undertaken by the parties, placing contract law squarely in the private sphere. Some non-consensual forms of liability are close to contract – for instance those based on reliance and voluntary assumption of responsibility. This factor has given rise to debates about the foundations of contract law and where contract ends and tort or restitution begin.[15] As Atiyah has put it: 'This entire problem, concerning the relationship of consensual and non-consensual liabilities, is obviously a matter of great importance, not only because it is such a pressing problem in practical terms today as the courts are flooded with tort claims in circumstances where there is no liability in contract law, but also because it does very vividly illustrate the profound importance of some overall theoretical structure to the law of obligations.'[16] There are also a number of intermediate situations which do not fall within recognisable 'causes of action' in contract, tort or trusts, where the common law or equity – or both – impose obligations and provide remedies for wrongs. Examples include restraints of trade, and fiduciary relationships imposing non-contractual obligations of trust and confidence, and confidentiality.[17]

SUPERVISORY JURISDICTIONS

In judicial review the courts are exercising a supervisory jurisdiction. By this is meant that they are identifying the limits of the powers of bodies, especially those which interfere with the liberties of individuals or with broad public interests, and laying down the rules for the exercise of decision-making powers. Typically in exercising supervisory jurisdictions the courts are requiring that decision makers act within their powers, that they act responsibly in the sense of exercising discretions personally and not fettering their discretions or delegating them, that they follow appropriate procedures, and that their reasoning processes conform to certain requirements of consideration for those

---

15 See P Atiyah *Pragmatism and Theory in English Law* (1987) chapter 1; C Fried *Contract as Promise* (1981); and see discussion in chapter 8.
16 *Atiyah* at p 385.
17 See chapter 9.

affected or the public interest – irrelevant considerations should be excluded, all relevant considerations should be taken into account, the decision maker should act in good faith, and should not act perversely, arbitrarily or capriciously. Not all of these requirements will be imposed in all cases where the courts exercise supervisory jurisdictions, and the exact content of these requirements will vary, but as we shall see they are common requirements. The shorthand adopted for these duties since the House of Lords' decision in *Council of Civil Service Unions v Minister for the Civil Service*[18] has been 'legality, procedural propriety or fairness, and rationality', and this shorthand will be adopted in the chapters which follow.

It is obvious that judicial review under section 31 of the Supreme Court Act 1981 and Order 53 of the Rules of the Supreme Court is only one of a number of public law supervisory jurisdictions exercised by the courts. There are statutory rights of appeal, for instance from planning and compulsory purchase decisions, in which the courts have the power to quash decisions for illegality or procedural impropriety of various kinds, usually specified in the statute.[19] In value added tax law, the VAT Tribunal has a review jurisdiction similar to but not identical with *Wednesbury* unreasonableness in judicial review.[20] The grounds for quashing decisions under these statutory jurisdictions are often similar to those in applications for judicial review. Indeed many of the principles of judicial review have been formulated in statutory appeals to the High Court against planning decisions or compulsory purchase orders.

It is often forgotten that there are also supervisory jurisdictions in private law, in which the legality, fairness and rationality of decisions may be challenged. In later chapters we shall note supervisory jurisdictions in relation to discretionary decision making by employers relating to dismissal of employees,[1] by trustees and company directors,[2] by monopolistic or self-regulatory bodies, and by those acting in restraint of trade or in pursuit of contractual powers affecting individuals' membership of pension or insurance schemes and the like.[3] In each of these jurisdictions the courts impose one or more of the duties of legality, fairness or rationality in decision making which are normally associated with judicial review. In effect both private law and public law impose a

---

18 [1985] AC 374, HL. See chapters 4 and 5 for further discussion of this case.
19 See for instance the Compulsory Purchase Acts, Town and Country Planning Acts. And see (Law Comn no 226) *Administrative Law: Judicial Review and Statutory Appeals* (1994).
20 See *John Dee v Customs and Excise Comrs* [1995] STC 941; *Customs and Excise Comrs v Corbitt (Numismatists) Ltd* [1981] AC 22, HL; *Mr Wishmore Ltd v Customs and Excise Comrs* [1988] STC 723.
1   See chapter 6.
2   See chapter 8.
3   See chapters 8 and 9.

range of what might be conveniently referred to as duties of considerate decision making.

It is a characteristic of many supervisory jurisdictions that the court will not substitute its own view of what the decision maker should have decided to do; if the decision was taken in breach of the duties of legality, procedural propriety and rationality, the court may quash the decision or hold it to be void, so that the decision maker may not act upon it, and require that the decision be retaken in accordance with the law. This is the position in judicial review and many other public law jurisdictions. However, in some supervisory jurisdictions the court may substitute its own view of what should be done for that of the decision maker: in the exercise of its supervision of decisions taken by trustees of discretionary trusts, for instance the Court of Equity may itself execute the trust.[4] In other supervisory jurisdictions the court may award compensation for breach of a duty of considerate decision making and is not limited to declaring a decision to be void and requiring it to be retaken: breach of contractual duties of natural justice provide an example.[5]

WHERE PUBLIC AND PRIVATE LAW MEET AND MIX

There are many areas where laws which might be regarded as 'public' mingle with private law.[6] We shall not be seeking to establish a firm definition of 'public law' here, but whichever of the common criteria are applied it is clear that the two very frequently mix, and that there is no particular requirement that a special procedure – the application for judicial review or any other special procedure – be followed, or that special rules are applied to the award of remedies, simply because a statutory or public interest point arises in a case. An integrated approach is adopted. This point serves to highlight how exceptional the exclusivity rule in *O'Reilly v Mackman* is in requiring cases involving certain public law issues to be litigated by way of application for judicial review, imposing short time limits and leave (now permission) requirements. For instance, where a plaintiff is suing a public authority for negligence, issues will often arise as to whether the fact that the body was 'public' or that it was exercising 'public functions' affects the question of its civil liability, or whether the body enjoyed immunity from what would otherwise be tortious liability.[7] This sort of point is dealt with by the

---

4   See chapter 8.
5   See chapter 8.
6   For discussion see for instance *Cane* at pp 75-6. G Samuel 'Public and private law: A private lawyer's response' (1983) 46 MLR 558.
7   See chapter 8.

trial court which will apply public and private law concurrently, giving precedence to statutory provisions over case law, to reach a decision on the issue, rather than separating them.[8]

There will often be a mix of public and private law, statutory and common law rules in contract cases too, especially where one of the parties to a contract is a local authority or a government department.[9] Here the statutory provisions, for instance limiting the powers of the public body to enter into a contract, operate in parallel to the normal private law rules. But the existence of relevant statutory provisions of a public law nature does not result in the parties being required to proceed by way of judicial review or to resolve the public law issues in judicial review proceedings before an action can be brought in contract; nor does it impose short time limits or leave (permission) requirements. The public law issues and contract issues are resolved alongside each other in the same proceedings.[10]

Restitution is another area in which an integrated approach is adopted – although there is room for further integration. Where taxes have been paid in response to an unlawful demand from the Inland Revenue or Customs and Excise a private law remedy in restitution is available.[11] If the plaintiff's case is that the regulations under which the tax demand was made were ultra vires then it will be necessary to succeed in an application for judicial review to quash the regulations before the action in restitution can succeed,[12] but once the regulations are quashed the right to repayment and interest will be regarded as having existed from the moment the payment was made by the taxpayer. Where tax has been paid in response to an unlawful demand and it is not necessary for the taxpayer to have regulations quashed before a claim for restitution to succeed, then the case will be a straightforward private law action for restitution, although the court will have to determine the legality of the demand by interpreting and construing the statutory provisions. These are matters which could be regarded as public law issues appropriate for solution in an application for judicial review, but in the *British Steel* case

---

8 See discussion of tort in chapter 8.

9 See C C Turpin *Government Procurement and Contracts* (1989); S Arrowsmith *Civil Liability and Public Authorities* (1992), 'Government contracts and public law'(1990) 10 LS 231, *Government Procurement and Judicial Review* (1988), and 'Judicial Review and the Contractual Powers of Public Authorities' (1990) 106 LQR 277.

10 See for instance *Crédit Suisse v Allerdale Borough Council* [1995] 1 Lloyd's Rep 315; *Morgan Grenfell v London Borough of Sutton* (1995) 93 LGR 554.

11 *Woolwich Building Society v IRC (No 2)* [1992] AC 70, HL See also *British Steel v Customs and Excise Comrs* [1997] 2 All ER 366, CA.

12 See chapter 4 for discussion of the disadvantages of this need to take separate proceedings to quash such instruments.

the Court of Appeal accepted that they could be resolved in the claim for restitution.[13]

In each of these causes of action the public law/private law questions arise in ordinary actions, and there is no suggestion that short time limits, permission requirements or special procedures should be observed. The important point here is that the mere fact that 'public law' issues arise in a case does not necessarily determine the procedure that should be followed. The exclusivity rule introduced by *O'Reilly* is unique in seeking to separate out public and private law points in certain kinds of case.

THE NEXT STEPS

In this chapter we have sought to place the public-private divide in the context of theories of democracy and citizenship, to explain the concepts of public and private law and to outline some of the difficulties posed by a public-private divide. This has set the framework for our consideration in the chapters which follow of what public and private law have in common, namely the control of power for the protection of public and individual interests, and versions of four democratic theories and theories of citizenship. In the next chapter the meanings of power in relation to democracy, and to individuals and the protection of their interests will be explored, and the ways in which the law has developed controls on the exercise of power will be considered. The discussion will include theories about the democratic basis of judicial review and the prerogative orders. Chapter 3 considers, in the light of theories of citizenship, what is meant by 'values' and interests and then explores five values which, it is suggested, are commonly protected by both public and private law, namely individual dignity, autonomy, respect, status and security. The significance of these common values is that they provide the rationales for the courts to develop principles for the protection of individuals against exercises of power by others that might damage these interests, whether or not the others are public bodies. This will lay the foundation for discussion in later chapters of the ways in which these common values and a policy in favour of the control of power in both public and private law have led the courts to develop principles of consideration for individuals both in actions and in decision making when those in

---

13 *British Steel plc v Customs and Excise Comrs* [1997] 2 All ER 366, CA. Cf at first instance, when the claim for restitution was struck out on the ground that an application for judicial review should be made first and only if it succeeded could the restitution claim proceed: [1996] 1 All ER 1002, Laws J.

positions of power are proposing to act in ways that might be detrimental to the interests of their neighbours, or ways that might be detrimental to public interests in, for instance, the rule of law and good administration.

Chapter Two

Democracy, Power and its Control

The point was made in chapter 1 that traditionally public law has been concerned with the distribution and control of state power. Much of constitutional law has been the product of decisions by the courts, and these have reflected the constitutional and democratic theories sketched in that chapter. For instance, the doctrine of the legislative supremacy of Parliament is essentially judge-made, and shows the judges adopting a liberal-majoritarian theory which gives priority to the power of Parliament over other considerations or other sources of power such as the Crown and the royal prerogative. But the judges continue to recognise a number of royal prerogatives, suggesting a positivist-authoritarian approach to government in some areas. This approach has weakened since the *CCSU* case,[1] in which the judges were prepared to subject exercises of prerogative powers that are in principle justiciable to the same tests in judicial review as statutory powers are subjected to. Where the rules of procedural propriety or natural justice are applied to decision making, a participative-communitarian theory of democracy is implied; where principles of rationality are applied, a model of considerate altruism is suggested. In later chapters these principles will be explored, but for the time being the interest in them lies in the implications for the control of power that flow from the willingness – and sometimes the unwillingness – of the courts to control the actions and decision-making processes of government and in some circumstances of private bodies, and the parallels between the control of state power and private power.

The importance of power for public law and constitutional theory is highlighted by McCormick: '… a constitutional theory which focuses exclusively on rights and which ignores the principles and rules

---

1   *Council of Civil Service Unions v Minister for the Civil Service* [1985] AC 374.

regulating powers is a partial and one sided theory.' Thus 'It is an important task for public lawyers and legal theorists to explicate and elaborate principles of reasonableness governing the pursuit of public policy'.[2] It is recognition of the imbalance in power between public bodies and private individuals which justifies in large part the imposition of higher order duties of, broadly, procedural propriety and rationality[3] on public bodies and other organisations exercising public functions. Another justification is promotion of the public or common interest in the rule of law and good administration, which arises even where a particular decision or action does not affect the interests of individuals, as was the case in the *Pergau Dam* case[4] for instance (in which the government's policy in awarding overseas aid did not adversely affect the interests of any individuals, and was held to be unlawful).

In this chapter the orthodox basis of the judicial review jurisdiction, that public bodies should not exceed the powers delegated to them – the ultra vires rule – will be explored.[5] The discussion will then broaden to the possible other justifications for judicial review, and this will lead into a consideration of the justifications for the control by the courts of exercises of power by private bodies, and remedies. But first the nature and meanings of power, so far as it is relevant to the role of the courts in controlling its exercise and protecting individuals from having their interests overridden unnecessarily, will be considered.

THE MEANINGS AND NATURE OF POWER

There is a substantial philosophical literature on the meanings and nature of power, especially state power.[6] Our particular concern here, however, is limited, being concerned with the ways in which power, whether in state or private hands, can be used to influence the behaviour of others, whether individuals or corporate bodies, and ways in which power can pose threats to the interests of individuals.

---

2 N McCormick 'Jurisprudence and the Constitution; (1983) Current legal Problems, 13-30, at p 20.

3 See chapter 5 for discussion of these concepts.

4 *R v Secretary of State for Foreign and Commonwealth Affairs, ex p World Development Movement* [1995] 1 WLR 386, DC.

5 The ultra vires rule also causes problems in private law, with which we are not concerned here: see C Clarke and C Otton-Goulder 'The need for wholesale reform on vires issues in public and private law' in J Black, P Muchlinski and P Walker eds (*Commercial Regulation and Judicial Review*) 1998 p 110.

6 See for instance M Foucault 'Disciplinary power and subjection' in S Lukes (ed) *Power* (1986) at p 229; J Habermas *Between Facts and Norms* trans W Rehg (1996) at p 148.

Weber's definition of power is helpful here, highlighting the relevance of relationships, one of the themes of this study. For Weber, power is 'the probability than an actor in a social relationship will be in a position to carry out his own will despite resistance, regardless of the basis on which this probability rests'[7] and later 'the chance of a man or a number of men to realize their own will even against the resistance of others who are participating in the action.'[8] Robert Dahl also focuses on relationships, suggesting that 'A has power over B to the extent that he can get B to do something that B would not otherwise do'.[9]

Power in this sense is to an extent natural and almost inevitable – any person who has the charge of a newborn baby has de facto power over it. But power is also granted or constituted or recognised by law, as where a person is allowed in law to do things or forbear from doing things that will have what another individual would regard as an adverse impact on that individual's interests. It is the role of the law in constituting and controlling power in relationships that is our main concern here.

In practice power can be analysed in various ways and it can take different forms in the hands of public and private bodies. Public bodies – and private bodies exercising public or governmental functions[10] – possess many kinds of power, which do not have direct parallels normally in purely private relationships. For instance, public bodies have a virtual monopoly on the right to use coercion to enforce their will.[11] Public bodies have the power to distribute largesse in the form of cash benefits, licences and so on (much of this would fall within Reich's concept of 'new property'[12]) and thus they have opportunities to influence the behaviour of those who might receive this largesse; they have de facto or de jure power to punish, either through the criminal justice system or

7   Max Weber *Economy and Society* (trans G Roth and Wittich 1978) at p 53.
8   *Weber* at p 926.
9   'The concept of power' (1957) *Behavioural Scientist* 2, pp 201-215
10 Judicial review extends to such bodies and functions: *R v Panel on Take-overs and Mergers, ex p Datafin* [1987] QB 815, CA; *R v Disciplinary Committee Jockey Club, ex p Aga Khan* [1993] 1 WLR 909, CA. See Wade and Forsyth *Administrative Law* (7th edn, 1994) pp 659-667; De Smith, Woolf and Jowell *Judicial Review of Administrative Action* (5th edn, 1995) paras 3-023 – 3.054; P P Craig *Administrative Law* (3rd edn, 1994) pp 562-577.
11 The residual powers of parents to discipline their children are an exception to the monopoly of coercive power of the state. The use of corporal punishment against children is being progressively eroded as a result of decisions of the European Court of Human Rights: see S Cretney and J Masson *Principles of Family Law* (6th edn., 1997) pp 617-618.
12 C Reich 'The New Property' (1964) 73 Yale Law J 733.

other means – the withdrawal of cooperation or benefits, for instance;[13] and they have power to win cooperation through persuasion and the authority and legitimacy that they derive from their elected status or their public status. But, with the exception of the right to use physical force, many private bodies have broadly similar powers to those of state bodies. For instance, many private bodies have wealth or resources of various kinds at their disposal. This may take the form of money to spend, or offers of employment or the right to dismiss from employment, or the power to award or refuse licences to practice an occupation, for instance. Private bodies can punish people by withdrawal of benefits or cooperation. Such bodies can influence the behaviour of others and damage their interests in the ways in which they dispense these resources, and can thus exercise power over them.

Galbraith's anatomy of power

Helpful ways of analysing power that are not constrained by a strict public-private, state/non-state power divide, are to be found in the work of Galbraith and Daintith. Galbraith in *The Anatomy of Power* (1983), separates sources and instruments of power. He does not distinguish in this between public and private power, and he adopts Weber's definition of power as 'the possibility of imposing one's will upon the behaviour of other persons'.[14]

The sources of power, on Galbraith's analysis, are three – property, personality and organisation. By personality – leadership – Galbraith means 'the quality of physique, mind, speech, moral certainty, or other personal trait that gives access to one or more of the instruments of power.'[15] Property – income, wealth – provides the wherewithal to secure submission or cooperation. It also often carries with it an element of authority which induces submission. Organisation, according to Galbraith, is 'the most important source of power in modern societies'.[16] This is increasingly recognised, especially in labour relations where the bureaucracy at the disposal of employers puts them at advantages over

---

13 See for example *Wheeler v Leicester City Council* [1985] AC 1054, in which the council withdrew access to a sports practice ground from a rugby club to punish it for not endorsing the council's policy on apartheid. Lord Roskill held the decision to be unlawful because it punished the club when it had done nothing wrong. See also *R v London Borough of Lewisham, ex p Shell UK* [1988] 1 All ER 938; *R v London Borough of Ealing, ex p Times Newspapers* (1986) 85 LGR 316; *De Smith, Woolf and Jowell* at para 3-042.

14 Max Weber *Law in Economy and Society* (1954) p 323.

15 J K Galbraith *The Anatomy of Power* (1983) at p 6.

16 *Galbraith*; see also Galbraith 'Power and organisation' in S Lukes (ed) *Power* (1986).

employees and unions in collective bargaining. (It has been suggested that the way to counteract this advantage would be to enable employees to participate in the bureaucratic process, thus democratising it by introducing a participative-communitarian element into it.[17])

On Galbraith's analysis, the instruments of power are also three – condign, compensatory and conditioned instruments. Condign power – the power to punish – wins submission by inflicting or threatening to inflict appropriately adverse consequences for failure to submit. Compensatory power – the power to grant benefits – in contrast, wins submission by the offer of affirmative reward. Conditioned power is exercised by changing belief – whether by persuasion, education or 'the social commitment to what seems natural, proper, or right'. Each of these causes the individual to submit to the will of another.[18] In other words, a person with power may impose his or her will on others by punishing them or threatening them with punishment if they do not cooperate, offering inducements or rewards for cooperation, 'conditioning' or persuading them to cooperate, or refusing to cooperate with those who seek a relationship. In later chapters consideration will be given to the power of, for instance, private regulatory bodies in sport and other associations, to refuse admission, an example of a situation in which refusal of cooperation and access to a benefit – membership – can affect individuals adversely in serious ways.

The linkages between the sources and instruments of power are many. For instance, a person with the quality of 'personality' – perhaps charisma – may be in a good position to 'condition' or persuade another to cooperate. A person with plenty of money may be able to buy cooperation, though with a reluctant partner strength of personality may also be needed. Many businesses derive their power from the fact that they own property, and have supporting organisations. When they impose their will on those with whom they wish to deal in business they are often using compensatory power: they will pay for services and goods. Or they will offer the customer a good deal. If a potential business partner is unwilling to cooperate even when offered a 'compensatory' reward, the business may seek to use condign power – to punish the potential partners by withdrawing cooperation or other benefits from them or acting in various unpleasant and damaging ways.

Galbraith deliberately sidesteps the role of the courts in the regulation of power, but by enabling us to understand the nature of power his

---

17 See discussion of employment relationships in chapter 5; and H Collins 'Market power, bureaucratic power, and the contract of employment' (1986) 15 Industrial Law Journal 1; E Jaques *A General Theory of Bureaucracy* (1976); R Edwards *Contested Terrain: The Transformation of the Workplace in the Twentieth Century* (1979).

18 *Galbraith* 1983 at pp 5-6.

framework brings out how, in many areas of their activity, the courts are involved in its regulation. For instance, the criminal courts use condign power – the power to punish – as an instrument for the enforcement of the control of individuals. But this power to punish is only effective because the state has control of an organisation – the bureaucracy – without which punishments could not be enforced. In practice nowadays personality is a relatively minor source of power, since the exercise of power depends increasingly on the existence of an organisation. Organisations and the complex activities which they support generally make it impossible for a single personality to control activity; increasingly organisations operate according to predetermined processes and procedures. These can enable members of organisations to share in the exercise of power – though Galbraith suggests that the sense of sharing this power by members of an organisation is often an illusion. But it is also the case that the processes and procedures adopted by organisations are designed to secure rational decision making and to respond to those who are likely to be affected by the exercise of power: the requirements laid down either voluntarily by organisations, or by legislation or the common law, for the consultation of or the giving of hearings to those who will be adversely affected by decisions of an organisation, and requirements of rationality in decision making are examples.[19]

Daintith's analysis of power: 'imperium' and 'dominium'

Daintith's analysis of power does focus on public power, and seeks to explore the ways in which the courts control what Galbraith called condign and compensatory power. Daintith's terms are 'imperium' and 'dominium'.[20] By imperium he means 'the government's use of the command of law in aid of its policy objectives'; and by 'dominium' he means 'the employment of the wealth of government for this purpose.'[1] Dominium is often grounded in property rights. The courts control imperium, firstly by denying the government the right to make laws which affect the liberties of the individual without statutory authority;[2] secondly by requiring that exercises of 'condign' power, such as punishment through the criminal justice system, or subjection to coercion as through compulsory purchase of land or the exercise of powers to stop and search and seize property, be subject to judicial appeal and

19 See chapters 6 (employment), 7 (children), 8 (contractual relationships) and 9 (public policy).
20 T C Daintith 'The Techniques of Government' in J Jowell and D Oliver (eds) *The Changing Constitution* (3rd. edn, 1994) chapter 8.
1   Daintith, supra, at p 213.
2   *The Case of Proclamations* (1611) 12 Co Rep 74.

scrutiny; and thirdly by requiring those exercising discretionary powers to comply with requirements of legality, rationality and fairness,[3] and by interpreting statutory provisions narrowly in favour of individuals.

The courts control exercises of 'dominium' by public bodies less consistently. Where dominium is exercised under statutory powers, such as governmental powers to make grants of financial assistance in the welfare system, or powers to grant licences or other privileges, then a combination of statutory provisions and common law requirements enables the courts to provide protection for individuals against unfair or irrational decision making. But where 'dominium' is exercised under common law contracting powers then in principle, as we shall see in chapter 4, judicial review is not available, though there may be a supervisory jurisdiction in private law over these activities, which will be considered in chapters 8 and 9.

It will be obvious how the state relies on the use of imperium and dominium on Daintith's analysis. But there are parallels in private law, in situations which are not judicially reviewable. For instance, private regulatory bodies – sporting bodies, membership associations, for example – make rules regulating their activities which are not judicially reviewable,[4] but which are nevertheless legally binding on those wishing to engage in the activity, since without membership of the body or compliance with the rules they will not be permitted to engage in the activity.[5] The same is true of many domestic tribunals, in universities, trade unions, and other bodies which exercise in effect legislative functions. What these activities often have in common is that third parties are reliant on the cooperation of the domestic body, and yet the terms on which cooperation may be granted or withheld are not generally regulated by statute (save to the extent that anti-discrimination legislation does so). In later chapters we shall be considering how, if at all, the exercise of this kind of power, lying between imperium and dominium, is regulated by the courts.

POWER, POWERS AND THE JUSTIFICATIONS FOR JUDICIAL REVIEW

Having sketched in some of the ways in which power is exercised, ways in which it can impact on individuals, ways in which it can be analysed, and how the courts control it, let us turn to how the courts, in the exercise

3   See chapters 1 and 5 for accounts of these concepts.
4   See discussion of the position of sporting bodies in private law in chapter 9 and in judicial review in chapter 5.
5   The positions of membership associations and regulatory bodies in sport are discussed, respectively, in chapters 8 and 9.

of their supervisory jurisdiction in public law, justify that activity. This will be of relevance for the argument to be presented in later chapters in that it raises issues as to the legitimacy – the democratic theory or theories – which justify this role of the courts in judicial review, and it raises issues as to the justification for the courts imposing, as they commonly do, responsibilities on private bodies wielding power.

To the extent that the courts have at their disposal the machinery to enforce their judgments by coercion, they are exercising state power, against other state bodies. What justification do they have for that jurisdiction? In many cases they have been specifically granted power to control the activities of others by Act of Parliament, as under planning and compulsory purchase legislation. But commonly, as in judicial review, there is no specific statutory basis for the courts' jurisdiction, and they rely on powers developed by the courts themselves in the common law.

The ultra vires rule

Until relatively recently the general assumption has been that the jurisdiction of the courts in judicial review rests on the ultra vires rule: the courts are entitled, indeed bound, to investigate whether public bodies have exceeded the powers democratically delegated to them (usually by Parliament or under powers delegated by Parliament) and they may grant remedies if such powers have been exceeded.[6] This supervisory activity by the courts is justified as giving effect to the legislative intent of Parliament. It represents a positivist, *imperium*-based, image of the role of the courts,[7] and forms part of what Allan has called a majoritarian view of democracy.[8]

According to this approach, Parliament, being democratic, is assumed not to have wished ministers and others exercising statutory powers to interfere with the rights or liberties of citizens without clear legislative authority.[9] The courts will assume that Parliament did not intend a body exercising statutory powers to act illegally, unfairly or irrationally, both in order to protect individuals' interests and to further the public interest

---

6   For an account of the history of administrative law theory including the ultra vires rule see P P Craig *Administrative Law* (3rd edn, 1994) chapter 1.

7   See R Cotterrell 'Judicial review and legal theory' in G Richardson and H Genn *Administrative Law and Government Action* (1994).

8   T R S Allan, 'Fairness, equality, rationality: Constitutional theory and judicial review' in C Forsyth and I Hare (eds) *The Golden Metwand and the Crooked Cord* (1998).

9   See the *Case of Proclamations* (1611) 12 Co Rep 74.

in lawful, fair and rational government decision making. A reformulation of this approach is that Parliament delegates to the courts the task of determining the precise scope of executive discretion.[10] Thus all that the courts are doing when they judicially review decisions is to give effect to Parliament's (assumed) will. As Wade and Forsyth have put it:

> 'The courts have only one weapon, the doctrine of ultra vires. …the judge must in every case be able to demonstrate that he is carrying out the will of Parliament as expressed in the statute conferring the power. …The only way in which he can do this in the absence of an express provision, is by finding an implied term or condition in the Act, violation of which then entails the condemnation of ultra vires.'[11]

This rationalisation of the judicial review jurisdiction has until recently been generally accepted, and recognised as providing a democratic justification for review. Most judicial review cases are about challenges to the decisions of elected bodies, either ministers or local authorities, taken under statutory powers. The courts would have been seen to be usurping the roles of politicians in an anti-democratic way if they had taken it upon themselves to impose restrictions on decision making by those elected bodies, as opposed to giving effect to the express or implied intentions of Parliament. In effect, the argument goes, in giving effect to the intentions of Parliament the courts are sustaining, not undermining, democratic government. It is this same desire on the part of the courts not to usurp the functions of executive bodies which accounts for the fact that the courts will not normally substitute their own views of the *merits* of decisions for those of the duly authorised – and usually democratically accountable – decision maker.

However, the doctrine of legislative intent is becoming increasingly difficult to believe in as the basis for judicial review even of statutory powers. The Human Rights Act 1998 exhorts the courts to interpret legislation whenever passed so far as possible so as to be compatible with Convention rights.[12] This represents a major inroad into the doctrine of legislative intent. Further where European law is at issue the courts must give it primacy, regardless of the legislative intent of the United Kingdom Parliament.

---

10 M Elliott, 'The ultra vires doctrine in a constitutional setting: still the central principle of administrative law' (1999) 58 Camb LJ 129 at p 144.
11 Wade and Forsyth *Administrative Law* (7th edn, 1994) p 44.
12 See discussion in chapter 10.

Judicial review of non-statutory powers

The rationalisation of the judicial review jurisdiction as being based on legislative intent and the ultra vires rule has become difficult to sustain, both on the basis of decisions of the courts, and in terms of democratic theory, over the last thirty years or so, particularly since the decisions in *Lain*,[13] *CCSU*[14] and *Datafin*.[15] In none of those cases were the courts asked to review exercises of statutory powers; in the first two the powers under scrutiny derived from a common law source (the prerogative), in the latter it was non-statutory de facto power. So the theory that the courts are simply giving effect to the intentions of Parliament when exercising judicial review powers could not justify their intervention in these cases. (In *CCSU* the House of Lords refused to intervene on grounds of national security, but the important point for this argument is that the case decided that exercises of the royal prerogative – a non-parliamentary set of powers – will be reviewable if they are justiciable.) In the seventh edition of *Administrative Law* the authors – Wade and Forsyth – admit that 'The technique by which the courts have extended the judicial control of powers is that of stretching the doctrine of ultra views ... [A]rtificiality becomes a problem'.[16]

Forsyth has argued that the existence of cases such as *Lain*, *CCSU* and *Datafin* in which the courts have reviewed the exercise of non-statutory powers need not be taken to undermine the position that when statutory powers are subject to judicial review the jurisdiction rests on the courts' role in giving effect to the intentions of Parliament.[17] This approach tries to maintain the constitutional or democratic legitimacy of judicial review, at least in relation to statutory powers. But, as Craig has pointed out, the argument is unconvincing: the grounds for judicial review are the same whether the power being reviewed is statutory or not. So are the remedies, and so is the procedure that has to be adopted, the application

13 *R v Criminal Injuries Compensation Board, ex p Lain* [1967] 2 QB 864.
14 *Council of Civil Service Unions v Minister for the Civil Service* [1985] AC 374.
15 *R v Panel on Take-overs and Mergers, ex p Datafin plc* [1987] QB 815.
16 *Wade and Forsyth* at pp 42, 43.
17 C Forsyth 'Of Fig Leaves and Fairy Tales: The Ultra Vires Doctrine, the Sovereignty of Parliament and Judicial Review' (1996) 55 CLJ 122. See also M Elliott 'The demise of parliamentary sovereignty. The implications for justifying judicial review' (1999) 115 LQR 119 and 'The ultra vires doctrine in a constitutional setting: still the central principle of administrative law' (1999) 58 Camb LJ 129. For critiques of this theory see Sir John Laws 'Illegality: the Problem of Jurisdiction' in M Supperstone and J Goudie (eds) *Judicial Review* (2nd edn, 1997) pp 4.13-4.19. P P Craig 'Ultra vires and the foundations of judicial review' (1998) 57 Camb LJ 63 and 'Competing models of judicial review' [1999] Public Law 428.

for judicial review. Craig argues that 'This dichotomy does little service to a rational system of public law'.[18]

As we shall see, the grounds for judicial review owe much to developments in equity and the common law, in cases – many of them private law cases[19] – decided before the grounds for judicial review were crystallising in the *Wednesbury*[20] case and the line of cases in the 1960s which so rapidly developed the subject.[1] Very similar principles to those used in judicial review are used in many private law supervisory jurisdictions, whether statutory, as in unfair dismissal in employment, or equitable as in trusts and other fiduciary relationships, or at common law as in contracts where discretionary decision making is permitted and controlled by the courts. In such cases the notion of giving effect to the intentions of a donor of a power seldom finds a place, and duties akin to those applied in judicial review are *imposed* by the courts. The circumstances in which they are imposed are varied, but it will be shown in subsequent chapters that they have in common a policy in favour of protecting the interests of individuals or public interests against abuses of power. This set of considerations seems to undermine Forsyth's idea that in the case of judicial review of statutory powers the only justification for requiring decision makers to comply with requirements of, for instance, natural justice or rationality, is legislative intent, and that it would be inappropriate for equity or the common law to impose such obligations on the exercise of statutory discretions. A response to this point might be that imposing duties of fairness and rationality on public and private bodies exercising non-statutory powers is different from imposing such duties on public bodies and others exercising public functions under statutory authority. It is hard to see what justification there might be for such a distinction, especially when, as we have seen in chapter 1, private bodies often perform public functions, public functions are difficult to define or separate from private functions, and the trend in the last century and more has been to remove immunities and privileges from public bodies and to subject them to at least the same obligations as are imposed on private bodies.

The sovereignty of Parliament

Forsyth's defence of the ultra vires as the true basis for judicial review of statutory powers is based on the view that this is the only democratically

---

18 Craig, supra, (1998) at pp 77-78.
19 See chapters 8 and 9 below.
20 [1948] 1 KB 223.
1   For instance *Ridge v Baldwin* [1964] AC 40 on natural justice; *Padfield v Minister of Agriculture, Fisheries and Food* [1968] AC 997.

legitimate rationale for the jurisdiction.[2] Elliott has put forward a second defence of the ultra vires rule, arguing that to reject it would be to reject also the doctrine of parliamentary supremacy.[3] Here two different strands of thinking are unnecessarily conflated: the suggestion made by Craig[4] and others that duties of fairness and rationality in decision making are imposed by the common law, and the separate idea that the courts may have the power to strike down legislation that was seriously undemocratic, floated by Lord Woolf[5] and Sir John Laws[6] in extra-judicial comments.

Elliott seems to assume that abandonment of the ultra vires rule as the basis of judicial review would mean that the courts were assuming a common law jurisdiction to override express terms in Acts of Parliament that they found to be contrary to the common law's requirements of decision making. He states of the view that these requirements are imposed by the common law that: 'In this manner, the essence of the doctrine of Parliamentary sovereignty, namely Parliament's legislative omnicompetence, is displaced by the imposition of fetters on the legislative freedom of Parliament.'[7] This however is to misunderstand the case against the ultra vires rule. The argument that the common law imposes on decision makers duties, broadly of legality (in the sense that powers must not be used for an improper purpose, they must not be delegated, discretions must not be fettered, for instance) and duties of procedural propriety and rationality, to adopt Lord Diplock's shorthand in the *CCSU* case, does not entail a claim that the courts are entitled to disapply a statutory provision that seeks to exclude these duties, or indeed any other statutory provision. All that is claimed is that as a matter of common law, and *subject to any express statutory provisions to the contrary*, where the court has a supervisory jurisdiction, discretions must be exercised in accordance with these common law requirements. Given that these requirements of legality, procedural propriety and rationality apply to non-statutory decision making as a matter of common law, it would be extraordinary if the position was that they did not apply in relation to statutory discretions and that exercises of statutory discretions were subject only to the implied intention of Parliament – especially since the substantive requirements of legality, procedural propriety and rationality are the same whether the power in question is statutory or non-statutory.

---

2   See 'Collateral challenge and the foundations of judicial review: orthodoxy vindicated and procedural exclusivity rejected' [1998] Public Law 364.

3   M Elliott 'The demise of parliamentary sovereignty? The implications for justifying judicial review' (1999) 115 LQR 119.

4   Op cit (1998) at pp 77-78.

5   Lord Woolf, 'Droit public – English style' [1995] Public Law 57 at p 69.

6   Sir John Laws 'Law and Democracy' [1995] Public Law 72 at pp 84-90.

7   Supra, at p 124.

It is suggested that the assumption that ultra vires is the basis for judicial review is simply not convincing, especially when the courts exercise their judicial review jurisdiction over the exercise of non-statutory powers such as the royal prerogative, as in the *CCSU* case, and de facto power in the hands of private bodies, as in *Datafin*. Sir John Laws, writing extra-judicially, considers that the ultra vires rule is a 'figleaf'.[8] This raises the question, what justification – what basis – is there for the judicial review jurisdiction, if it is not the ultra vires rule and giving effect to the legislative intent of Parliament? And how, if at all, does the jurisdiction accord with democratic theory?

The equitable and common law roots of judicial review

An alternative view of the basis for the exercise of supervisory jurisdictions, whether in judicial review or in private law, is emerging: in practice the common law is performing a function that it has performed for many years, *both in public and private law*, namely controlling the exercises of power (not 'powers') and doing justice where the legislature has failed to do so; the justification for the common law – and equity[9] – to exercise that control does not depend upon the power being derived from statute or upon legislative intent (though according to the doctrine of parliamentary sovereignty such jurisdiction may be excluded or displaced by statute).[10] This justification for the intervention of the courts represents a move away from the majoritarian democratic theory that the ultra vires rule represents, and opens up the question what other theory of democracy – if any – is promoted by a 'control of power' model for judicial review and for judicial activity generally, including in private law.[11] It will be suggested in chapter 12 that in fact judicial review and

---

8   Sir John Laws 'Illegality: The problem of jurisdiction' in M Supperstone and J Goudie (eds) *Judicial Review* (2nd edn, 1997) para 4.34 and 'Law and Democracy' [1995] Public Law 72 at 79.
9   See discussion of supervisory jurisdictions in equity in chapter 8 (trustees' duties and company directors) and chapter 9 (restraint of trade and public policy).
10 See for instance D Oliver 'Is the ultra vires rule the basis for judicial review?' [1987] PL 543; B V Harris 'The "third source" of authority for government action' (1992) 108 LQR 626; P P Craig op cit (1998); Sir John Laws 'Illegality: The problem of jurisdiction' in Supperstone and Goudie (eds) *Judicial Review* (1997) p 4.34 and 'Law and Democracy' [1995] Public Law 72 at 79; Sir Stephen Sedley 'The common law and the constitution' in *The Making and Remaking of the British Constitution* (1997) chapter 2.
11 See R Cotterrell 'The Law of Property and Legal Theory' in W L Twining (ed) *Legal Theory and Common Law* (1986); T R S Allan 'Fairness, equality, rationality: Constitutional theory and judicial review' in C Forsyth and I Hare (eds) *The Golden Metwand and the Crooked Cord* (1998); and discussion in chapter 12.

the exercises of supervisory jurisdictions in private law, and indeed much of the law of contract and tort, represent moves towards a 'civil' version of democracy which requires that private bodies, as well as public bodies, in positions of power should exercise their power with consideration for those affected by it and public interests.

The true basis of the jurisdiction in judicial review, it is suggested, is the common law's ancient function in putting injustices right.[12] Judicial review as exercised from about the early seventeenth century in the Court of King's Bench via the prerogative writs was not originally founded on the idea of effectuating legislative intent. This only became a central focus in the nineteenth century, with the growth of the democratic idea. Sedley, noting that in the seminal case of *Cooper v Wandsworth Board of Works*[13] Byles J justified the imposition of a duty of natural justice on the ground that, although the statute had not imposed such a duty, 'the justice of the common law will supply the omission of the legislature,' observes that in such cases 'the common law would speak in its own right.'[14] He suggests that 'the modern reach of public law is expressed in the concept of the abuse of power rather than in a formalistic delineation of its limits.'[15] As will be shown in chapters 6 and 7, this has been a feature of the development of the common law and statute in private relationships of employment, marriage and parenthood; in chapters 8 and 9 it will be shown that this is also a concept in other areas of private law.

Craig, arguing in favour of this justification for judicial review, quotes from the decision in *Bagg's case*[16]: the Court of Kings Bench had the authority:

'not only to correct errors in judicial proceedings, but other errors and misdemeanours extra-judicial, tending to the breach of the peace, or oppression of the subjects, or to the raising of faction, controversy, debate or to any manner of misgovernment; so that no wrong or injury, either public or private, can be done but that it shall be (here) reformed or punished by due course of law.'[17]

This decision, Craig suggests, lends support to the view that another, older justification, quite different in its roots and purpose from legislative intent and the ultra vires rule, provides an explanation of the evolution

12 Craig op cit (1998).
13 (1863) 14 CB NS 180.
14 Sedley, op cit (1997) at p 17.
15 'Public law and contractual employment' (1994) 23 ILJ 201 at p 205.
16 (1615) 11 Co Rep 93b.
17 Ibid at 98a.

of the prerogative remedies and the jurisdiction in judicial review, and one which better explains and justifies the modern jurisdiction. Let us explore this decision.

Bagg's case, 1615[18]

The story of *Bagg's case* has the ring of a Shakespearean comedy to it. James Bagg had been made one of twelve chief burgesses or magistrates of the borough of Plymouth. The Mayor and commonalty of the Borough 'amoved' or disfranchised him because of his history of showing disrespect towards them. Bagg issued a writ of certiorari out of the King's Bench. The way in which the Mayor and commonalty put their defence was as follows: Bagg, as was the custom, had taken a corporal oath that he would carry himself well and honestly, as well towards the mayor of the borough aforesaid as towards the other twelve chief burgesses, and would show reverence towards them. Because Plymouth was a port it was frequented by 'many ill-minded men, as well aliens as within born, of evil and perverse conversations, contemners of good government, and disturbers of the peace, ... who can hardly be there brought to the obedience of good rule and government, unless the authority of the mayor of the borough ... and of the other chief burgesses ... with due reverence of the other burgesses and inhabitants of the said borough, be fortified, and the persons of the said chief burgesses, and of the mayor, from the contempt of the vulgar be preserved.'[19] Bagg, however, had 'contemptuously and malapertly' treated successive mayors over a number of years. He had called one Mayor – in the presence of many inhabitants of the borough – 'a cozening knave'. He had called a later one 'an insolent fellow' in the Guildhall. On another occasion Bagg, 'turning the hinder part of his body in an inhuman and uncivil manner towards the [Mayor] scoffingly, contemptuously, and uncivilly, with a loud voice, said to the [Mayor], these words following, that is to say, ("come and kiss")'.[20]

Bagg was given a chance by his fellow burgesses to agree to behave in future, did not do so, and after a number of subsequent confrontations he was voted out of office. He had, inter alia, stirred up inn keepers and the like to disobey the king's order not to serve meat during Lent, and challenged a local custom requiring taverners to pay custom to the borough.

18 Supra.
19 Ibid at 94.
20 Ibid at 95b.

The King's Bench (Sir Edward Coke, CJ presiding) resolved that there was not any just cause to remove Bagg. It was in this context that the court resolved in the terms quoted above.[1]

On the particular question of the powers of the burgesses to disfranchise one of their number, it was held that disfranchisement was only permitted by conduct which is against the duty of a citizen or burgess and to the prejudice of the public good of the city and against his oath; but words of contempt or contra bonos mores, although they be against the chief officer or his brethren, are not good causes to disfranchise him. 'And the reason and cause thereof is, that when a man is a freeman of a city or borough he has a freehold in his freedom for his life, and with others, in their political capacity, has an inheritance in the lands of the said corporation, and interest in their goods, and perhaps it concerns his trade and means of living, and his credit and estimation'.[2] A further objection to the action of the burgesses was that 'it appears ... that they have proceeded against without hearing him answer to what was objected, or that he was not reasonably warned, such removal is void, and shall not bind the party, ... and such removal is against justice and right'.[3]

Further, Coke said, if a person were wrongly disfranchised the justices would have power to award a writ of restitution, and, if the return to the writ were false in substance, he would have an action on the case – what we would now regard as a private law remedy.[4]

It is worth reflecting on how the court resolved the balance between Bagg's interests and the upholding of the authority of the Mayor and commonalty in this case. It is of particular interest that the Mayor and burgesses put their case in terms of the need to uphold their own authority. It is clear from the way their case was put that in those days there was great concern that civilised life would collapse if the forces of good order were not held in respect and authority maintained. (In chapters 6 and 7, where the relationships of employment, marriage and parenthood are considered, it will be seen how concern to uphold the authority of the superior in those relationships also has been responsible in the past for the legal sanctioning of invasions of the dignity, autonomy and respect of the weaker parties to these relationships on the part of the superiors.) But nearly five hundred years after *Bagg's case* we can view with more equanimity the possible consequences of airing criticisms of those in authority, and indeed, we are less inclined to accept that relationships need to be hierarchical with one party in a position of authority over others.

---

1   *Bagg's case* at 98a.
2   Ibid at 98b.
3   Ibid at 99a.
4   Ibid.

In *Bagg's case*, then, the King's Bench rejected the blanket claims to be protected from criticism and disrespect put forward on behalf of the Mayor and the other burgesses, and favoured Bagg's interests in his property (his office), his security (as his living might be affected) and his status (his credit and estimation) in the borough. Such interests were protected by the court's rejection of the claim by the Mayor and burgesses to be entitled to disfranchise him unless he was actually in breach of his legal duties; stirring up criticism and acting disrespectfully were not considered to be breaches (though they might give rise to him being bound over by the justices). Bagg's interests were also, significantly, entitled to be protected by requirements of natural justice.

Bagg's case also shows how the courts were concerned with the impact of decisions on individuals; and how illegality and unfairness are ancient grounds for intervention by the court in the exercise of a supervisory jurisdiction through the writ of certiorari: they have nothing to do with legislative intent or the ultra vires rule. The jurisdiction of the King's Bench in this case rested on the basis that the court was doing justice, righting a wrong and an injury, by upholding Bagg's interests and controlling the exercise of power by the Mayor and burgesses.

The case was controversial when it was decided and thereafter for many years. It was regarded as claiming too much for the King's Bench, particularly in regard to the control of public power.

The English Reports' commentary on the case notes that Lord Ellesmere took exception to the decision as being an overstatement of the power of the Court of Kings Bench:

> 'for if the King's Bench may reform any manner of misgovernment (as the words are) it seemeth that there is little or no use either of the King's Royal care and authority exercised in his person and by his proclamations, ordinance, and immediate directions, nor of the council-table, which under the King is the chief watch-tower for all points of government.'[5]

THE DEVELOPMENT OF THE COMMON LAW JURISDICTION TO CONTROL EXERCISES OF POWER

The writs of mandamus, certiorari and prohibition[6] are, historically, important remedies for the abuse of public – and in some cases private –

---

5   Ellesmere Observations p 11, noted at 77 ER at 1278.
6   *De Smith, Woolf and Jowell* chapter 14 gives a history of the prerogative remedies. A fuller history was included in appendix I of previous editions, entitled 'The Prerogative Writs: The Historical Origins.' See also S A de Smith 'The Prerogative Writs' (1951) 11 Camb LJ 40; L L Jaffe and E G Henderson 'Judicial review and

power. But, as we shall see in later chapters, private law, particularly the law of tort, also served to control the exercise of public power, for instance in the tort of misfeasance in a public office. The prerogative orders originated in the Court of King's Bench. They were regarded as special common law remedies which enabled the court most closely linked to the King to regulate possible excess of power by other, subordinate bodies. From early on, as *Bagg's case* shows, the grounds for award of the writs included excess of power or jurisdiction, acting for an improper purpose, and breach of natural justice.

A particular point of significance is that the common law courts did not have jurisdiction to award non-pecuniary remedies apart from the prerogative writs. This is in contrast with the courts of equity which had developed non-pecuniary remedies of, for instance, injunctions and specific performance, and rarely awarded damages – when they did so it was for legal rather than equitable wrongs, as in the case of specific performance.[7] So the prerogative orders may be regarded in some respects as the common law adopting a parallel approach to that of the Courts of Equity in specifically enforcing certain legal obligations. Nowadays these prerogative orders are only available in respect of public or governmental functions, but as we shall see in the past certiorari and mandamus have also been available in respect of private activity in certain circumstances. The current remedial public-private divide is of relatively recent origin.

Mandamus

By the early eighteenth century the writ of mandamus had become a comprehensive remedy – more so than its contemporary, the writ of restitution.[8] 'It would go, on the application of a party aggrieved, to compel the performance of a wide range of public or quasi-public duties, performance of which had been wrongfully refused'.[9]

The point is illustrated by *R v Barker*:[10] mandamus was granted to enforce what was regarded as the legal right of a man who had been

---

the rule of law: historical origins' (1956) 72 LQR 345 at p 361; E G Henderson *Foundations of English Administrative Law* (1963); J H Baker *An Introduction to English Legal History* (3rd edn, 1990); G Drewry 'Judicial review: the historical background' in M Supperstone and J Goudie (eds) *Judicial Review* (2nd edn, 1997).

7   *Phelps v Prothero* (1855) 44 ER 280; I C F Spry *The Principles of Equitable Remedies* (5th edn, 1997) pp 625-632. And see chapter 9.

8   See Craig op cit (1998) at pp 81-84; Henderson *Foundations of English Administrative Law* (1963).

9   De Smith *Judicial Review of Administrative Action* (4th edn), Appendix I, p 515.

10 (1762) 3 Burr 1265.

elected to be the pastor of the Presbyterians of Plymouth to be allowed to preach in the meeting-house of the congregation. Lord Mansfield held that this prerogative writ:

> 'was introduced, to prevent disorder from a failure of justice, and defect of police. Therefore it ought to be used upon all occasions where the law has established no specific remedy, and where in justice and good government ought to be one. ... Within the last century, it has been liberally interposed for the benefit of the subject and the advancement of justice. The value of the matter, or the degree of its importance to the public policy, is not scrupulously weighed. If there be a right, and no other specific remedy, this should not be denied. Writs of mandamus have been granted, to admit, lecturers, clerks, sextons, and scavengers, etc and to restore an alderman to the precedency, an attorney to practice in an inferior court, etc. Since the Act of Toleration, it ought to be extended to protect an endowed pastor of Protestant Dissenters; from analogy and the reason of the thing.' [11]

Lord Mansfield later added: 'Here is a function, with emoluments, and no specific legal remedy. The right depends upon election' which interests all the voters. 'The question is of a nature to inflame men's passions. ... Should the Court deny this remedy, the congregation may be tempted to resist violence by force ... To deny this writ, would be putting Protestant Dissenters and their religious worship, out of the protection of the law...'[12]

Mr Justice Foster in that case said 'Here is a legal right. Their ministers are tolerated and allowed: their right is established, therefore is a legal right, and as much as any other legal right.'[13]

Despite the generality of Lord Mansfield's proposition, mandamus was not in practice so widely granted. For instance it was not available in employment cases, since a remedy in breach of contract would be possible, and nor was it available to establish rights of fellowship or membership of colleges or inns of court, because these were domestic bodies under the control of their 'visitor.' But the implication of Lord Mansfield's dictum is quite clear: if there were no alternative specific remedy, mandamus would have been available in what we would now regard as private law cases where in justice there ought to be a remedy.[14]

11 Ibid at 1267.
12 Ibid at 1269.
13 At 1268.
14 See J H Baker *An Introduction to English Legal History* (3rd edn, 1990) at pp 169-170.

R v Barker then is a strong illustration of the way in which mandamus was regarded as a remedy for legal wrongs, which might be available in the absence of a cause of action that would be remediable in damages, and one that might be available against private bodies exercising private functions where public interests such as the upholding of statutorily guaranteed freedoms were at stake, or where public order might be at risk from a sense of injustice. The case is also interesting in that it assumed that a *legal* (as opposed to an equitable) right could arise independently of contract, in this case from the fact of the election of a minister, and that this was a right which would be binding on third parties, in this instance on the trustees of land held for dissenting religious purposes. The court drew support for this approach from the Act of Toleration, which gave expression to a public policy in favour of religious toleration.[15]

Certiorari and prohibition

Certiorari was developed to control inferior tribunals – notably justices of the peace – and correct their errors, as was prohibition, though this last remedy was largely used to limit the jurisdiction of ecclesiastical courts. By the mid-seventeenth century, Sir Edward Coke CJ wrote that: 'This court [the Court of King's Bench] hath not only jurisdiction to correct errors in judicial proceedings, but other misdemeanours extrajudicial tending to the breach of the peace, or oppression of the subject... or any other manner of misgovernment; so that no wrong or injury, either publick or private, can be done but that this shall be reformed or punished'.[16] This was a very expansive view of the jurisdiction of the court in certiorari and prohibition, resembling the approach to mandamus. Other commentators at the time disagreed and did not feel the jurisdiction to correct errors could be used for all manner of misgovernment as this would usurp the king's functions to the courts.[17] This point was based on an assumption that the undertaking by the courts of a function of reforming and punishing wrongs or injuries would involve the courts in actual government. Nowadays it is possible to separate conceptually administration from the supervision of administrative decision making, and an assertion by the courts of a power to reform and correct wrongs and injuries does not carry with it the

---

15   See also *R v Blooer* (1760) 2 Burr 1043, in which mandamus was granted to restore one William Langley to the office of curate of a chapel; the rule was made absolute upon the principle that where there was a temporal right the Court of King's Bench would assist by mandamus.

16   Co Inst, iv, 71. Very similar words were used in *Bagg's case*, supra.

17   *De Smith* 4th edn p 516.

implication of an assumption by them of administrative or executive functions.

By the early 1900s, it was well settled that certiorari would not issue only to a court or in respect of 'judicial acts'. The term 'judicial act' had been used in contrast with purely ministerial acts: in general a judicial act was one which involved 'the exercise of some right or duty to decide' a question affecting individual rights. De Smith, Woolf and Jowell comment: 'It did not follow, however, that every act affecting individual rights was necessarily "judicial" because it was not ministerial'.[18] There might be duties to act judicially even where the decision-maker was not a judge. In the *Electricity Comrs* case[19] the view was taken that certiorari went to bring up and quash decisions of 'any body of persons having legal authority to determine questions affecting the rights of subject, and having the duty to act judicially.'[20] (This phrase had a more limited meaning than it appears to, for certiorari would not lie against private arbitrators.[1]) It was only gradually that the availability of certoirari came to be restricted to where public or governmental functions were exercised.

Procedural protections in judicial review

When the Court of King's Bench was developing the prerogative writs there were far fewer procedural protections for respondents to applications for these than there are now in judicial review. Under the Crown Office Rules 1886, for instance, as far as the writ of certiorari was concerned, evidence was given by affidavit, but there was power to order attendance for cross-examination;[2] application for the writ was to be made by motion for an order to show cause,[3] though there was power to issue the writ forthwith. In those days the issue of the writ was not the same as the granting of a remedy, for it was open to the respondent to establish to the satisfaction of the court that the writ should not be followed up by an order for, for instance, restitution. There was no leave or permission requirement before the writ would issue. There was a six-month limitation period for special cases where there were statutory provisions, but not otherwise. The applicant for the writ had to enter

---

18 *De Smith, Woolf and Jowell* para 14-024. And see *R v Woodhouse* [1906] 2 KB 501, 535, per Fletcher Moulton LJ.
19 *R v Electricity Comrs, ex p London Electricity Joint Committee Co (1920) Ltd* [1924] 1 KB 171.
20 Ibid at 204-205.
1 Contrast the position in Scotland where arbiters are subject to the supervisory jurisdiction of the Court of Session: see Annex, below.
2 Crown Office Rules 1886, rule 5.
3 These writs were not writs of course which could be had for the asking, but proper cause had to be shown to the satisfaction of a court why they should issue: S A de Smith 'The Prerogative Writs' (1951) 11 Camb LJ 40, at p 42.

into recognisances to prosecute the certiorari without delay if the case was for removal of indictments or decisions of inferior tribunals.

As far as mandamus was concerned, under the 1886 rules application was to be made by motion for an order nisi; notice was given to the other parties; any person affected by the proceedings could show cause against; the order absolute for mandamus need not be served. It was also clear at that time that the order was available against private bodies: rule 66 of the Crown Office Rules 1886 provided that 'When a writ of mandamus is directed to companies, corporations, justices or public bodies, service shall be made ....' in certain ways. The court could order that any writ of mandamus be peremptory in the first instance.[4]

It is suggested that, given the absence of any real historical divide between public and private law, and given that many of the bodies subject to the prerogative writs in the past (Plymouth Corporation in *Bagg's case*, trustees of a meeting-house in *R v Barker*[5] for instance) did not have democratic credentials, there is nothing surprising in the fact that judges in the seventeenth and eighteenth centuries did not distinguish between public and private law in developing principles for the control of power.[6] Their concern, as it emerges from *Bagg's case* and *R v Barker*, for instance, was with upholding rights, and avoiding in particular the kinds of injustice that might lead to civil disorder by providing remedies. In today's terms, given that many private acts and decisions are subject to requirements of legality, fairness and rationality that are similar to those that are imposed in judicial review,[7] and given that many bodies subject to judicial review lack democratic credentials (the Take-over Panel, the police, National Health Service Trusts spring to mind), it is hard to see why it should be objectionable for controls over exercises of public (or private) power to be imposed by the common law (or equity) as part of the courts' ancient function in the control of power. But, objectionable or not, it is suggested that this is in fact the basis for the common law's control of exercises of power. The questions to be asked, as Craig suggests, are 'whether there is a reasoned justification which is acceptable in normative terms for the controls which are being imposed'.[8] Much of the discussion in the following chapters is designed to answer these questions in the affirmative.

---

4   Prohibition was dealt with only briefly, in rule 81 of the Crown Office Rules 1886.
5   (1762) 3 Burr 1265.
6   See also Craig (1998) pp 86-89.
7   See discussion of supervisory jurisdictions in chapter 1 and discussions of the control of private power in chapters 6 to 9.
8   Craig (1998) at p 90.

THE ULTRA VIRES RULE RECONSIDERED

As we have seen at the time of *Bagg's case* there was no substantive public-private divide. In the same judgment Coke was discussing the King's Bench's power to issue certiorari, the powers of justices to award writs of restitution, and the powers of the court to give remedies in actions on the case and in trespass, false imprisonment, assault and battery as appropriate in a case where a person has been wrongly disfranchised.[9] Craig notes that: 'The absence of any formal divide between public and private law helps us to understand why it would not have appeared at all odd to a Coke, Heath, Holt or a Mansfield to base judicial review on the capacity of the common law to control public power. It is the very same absence of a formal divide which can help us to understand the willingness of the courts to extend common law created doctrine to bodies which possessed a de facto monopoly.'[10] (This last comment is directed to the control of common callings and other monopolistic powers, which will be discussed in chapter 9, below.) In practice, however, the common law has extended duties of legality, fairness and rationality beyond monopolies, to a wide range of bodies in positions of power over individuals or power that may be used contrary to public policy and the public interest.

In summary, it is obvious that the ultra vires rule and legislative intent do not explain all exercises of judicial review. There is nothing new in the common law seeking to control abuses of power – especially monopoly power, whether public or private. The control of private monopoly power can best be explained, as can many instances of the control of private power, as equivalents of the courts asking 'whether certain constraints imposed on the exercise of private power in, for example contract and tort, are sensible, warranted and justified in the light of the aims of the particular doctrinal area in question.'[11]

It is becoming increasingly widely recognised that the need to control the abuse of power is a thread running through both private and public law. This is no doubt in part due to the fact that we are becoming increasingly conscious of the existence of concentrations of private power, and the need to subject them to judicial control.[12] In effect a theory of

---

9   (1615) 11 Co Rep at 99b.
10 Craig at p 87.
11 Craig at p 87.
12 See for instance Sir Harry Woolf 'Public law – private law: Why the divide?' [1986] Public Law 220; G Borrie 'The control of public and private power' [1989] Public Law 552; Sir John Laws 'Public law and employment law: Abuse of power' [1997] Public Law 455; Sir Stephen Sedley 'The common law and the constitution' in *The Making and Remaking of the British Constitution* (1997) and 'Public law and contractual employment' (1994) 23 ILJ 201.

civil and community obligation – civil democracy – is developing, which provides the democratic justification for the exercise of control over power by the courts.

In other common law jurisdictions too it is coming to be recognised that the common law is concerned with the control of both public and private power. Mr Justice Paul Finn, Judge of the Federal Court of Australia, has examined how the exercise of power is controlled by the common law 'on a broad front.'[13] He argues that a routine function of the common law is to mediate between the possessors of power and those affected by its exercise. He identifies patterns in the manner in which the exercise of power is regulated and suggests that understanding those patterns helps explain the nature and inspiration of some of the more recent shifts in the law in areas as diverse as criminal procedure, statutory interpretation, the implication of contractual terms and unconscionability-based doctrines.[14]

And yet the extent to which power is controlled in private law is often not recognised. The assumption is that the only mechanisms for controlling exercises of power are via judicial review and that any form of control of power is to be categorised as 'public law.' The chapters which follow will seek to establish that this is not the case.

13 'Controlling the exercise of power' 7 Public Law Review (1996) 86.
14 Op cit.

Chapter Three

The Values of Public and Private Law

As indicated in chapter 1 it is part of the thesis of this book that common values underlie both public and private law. The significance of the operation of common values in public and private law is that it undermines the notion that there is a division between the two categories of law. Later chapters will explore this issue further. Our main purpose here is to clarify the meaning of 'values' in this context, and to explain the particular values which, in my view, are key to the legal system.

Values exist at varying levels of generality in the legal system and in various sectors within it. Values familiar to public lawyers, for instance, include openness, fairness and impartiality in the working of tribunals,[1] and fairness and rationality in administrative decision making.[2] Values of importance to private lawyers include trust and confidence, reliability, good faith.

It would clearly not be possible to draw parallels in values across all the subdivisions of law – or other related disciplines – at all levels. For instance, the values implicit in the maxim that he who comes to equity must come with clean hands have little in common with the concept that I owe a duty of care to my neighbour, or with the rules of natural justice in administrative law. Each of these tenets expresses a value, but each value is of limited and rather local applicability in the legal system.

However, it is suggested that important common key values are being developed at a high level of abstraction in public and private law. These values emerge from the common law, equity and statutory developments, and European influences, particularly in the field of human rights.

---

1   See Franks Committee Report *Administrative Tribunals and Inquiries* (1957) Cmnd 218.
2   See *Council of Civil Service Unions v Minister for the Civil Service* [1985] AC 374.

Common law and statutes have also been influenced by European Community law – as in measures to prevent discrimination in employment[3] and in the requirements of legal certainty and proportionality in state action.[4]

The values which span the legal system can be summarised as autonomy – in the sense of freedom of action – dignity, equal respect, status and security. These are 'key' values in the thesis being developed here. As discussion in subsequent chapters will show, these terms are used repeatedly by the courts and by academic commentators on both sides of the public-private division; although these concepts are seldom explored by judges, they underlie many decisions, sometimes explicitly and sometimes implicitly. It might be said that these values are so obviously part of the law that it is superfluous to make of them a central pillar of the thesis being put forward here. It is indeed the case that they are widely accepted as self-evidently basic and pervasive in any democratic system. But this has not always been the case. As discussion of the evolution of the law of public and private relationships in chapters 6 and 7 will show it is only in the last century that the importance of their interests in these values has received legal acknowlegement and protection in the case of, for instance, individuals in their relations with the government, employees in their dealings with employers, wives and children in relationships with husbands and parents respectively. And, it will be shown, it is still the case that these values come into conflict with countervailing values and interests, such as the needs of the market, and the perceived public interest in upholding those in positions of authority, whether public or private.

Before proceeding to elaborate these values, a word of explanation of what is meant by 'values' is required.

THE CONCEPT OF 'VALUES'

Much of the discussion in this and later chapters will be of the ways in which the interests of individuals are weighed against other considerations with which they may conflict in various areas of the law, from family law to employment, contract, tort, equity, restraint of trade and other relationships. Often the terms 'values' and 'individuals' interests' are used interchangeably, but in some contexts values are separate from the interests of individuals. The public law values of openness, fairness and impartiality, for instance, operate in the general public interest and not solely for the protection of particular individuals.

3   See chapter 6.
4   See chapter 5.

The Shorter Oxford English Dictionary definition of value is helpful here: 'That which is worthy of esteem for its own sake; that which has intrinsic worth.' On this definition values are deontological.[5] There are of course many things that could be regarded as values – respect for life, concern for others, courage, truth, beauty, health ... However, our aim is to try to identify the ultimate and most pervasive underlying values in public – and private – law, of which in my view there are very few.[6]

These common, ultimate values are close to the 'background rights' Dworkin refers to, 'rights that provide a justification for political decisions by society in the abstract'.[7] But values, as the term will be used here, are not themselves rights, though rights are reflections of values.[8] For instance, the right to due process – in English terms the rules of procedural propriety and natural justice – provides protection for a person's dignity, autonomy and so on[9] – but it does not of itself treat those values or interests as rights. Justice Paul Finn of the Federal Court of Australia, writing extra-judicially, has neatly drawn the distinction between rights and values: 'Is not the concern of the law less with the rights it assigns to individuals and more with values basic to our civil order which we should assume Parliament will respect unless for good and declared reason?'[10]

Nor are values the same as principles.[11] Jowell defines principles as involving 'normative moral standards by which rules might be evaluated'.[12] Dworkin in *Taking Rights Seriously*[13] uses 'principle' to mean 'a standard that is to be observed, not because it will advance or secure an economic, political, or social situation deemed desirable, but because it is a requirement of justice or fairness or some other dimension of morality.

5   But compare Habermas' comparison of principles and values, below.
6   For a very lucid discussion of the meanings of values see W L Twining and D Miers *How to do Things with Rules* 3rd edn (1991) pp 138-140. And see L Fuller *The Morality of Law* (1969).
7   R Dworkin *Taking Rights Seriously* (1977) p 93.
8   However Dworkin argues that the most fundamental of rights is the right to equal concern and respect (*Taking Rights Seriously*, chapter 6). Here is the concept of a right to the benefit of one of the ultimate and pervasive values which I consider to underlie public – and private – law. But a right in these terms would be too vague and general to be enforceable.
9   See D J Galligan *Due Process and Fair Procedures: A Study of Administrative Procedures* (1996) chapters 1 and 4; G Richardson 'The legal regulation of process' in G Richardson and H Genn *Administrative Law and Government Action* (1994).
10 P Finn 'Controlling the Exercise of Power' 7 Public Law Review 86 at p 89 (1996).
11 For a discussion of the different meanings of 'principle' and related terms see B Simpson 'The common law and legal theory' in W L Twining (ed) *Legal Theory and Common Law* (1986).
12 J L Jowell 'The legal control of administrative discretion' [1973] Public Law 178, 201.
13 (1977) especially chapters 2 and 4.

Thus, ...the standard that no man may profit by his own wrong [is] a principle.'[14] Dworkin's principles are *applications* of values in the sense used here, but these values operate at a lower level on the ladder of abstraction[15] than the levels we are aiming at. For instance, Dworkin refers to the case of *Riggs v Palmer:*[16] a man named in the will of his grandfather was held not entitled to inherit, because he had murdered the testator. On one level, as Dworkin states, the case illustrates the maxim or principle that a man may not profit from his own wrong; on another, more abstract, level it may be taken to illustrate the operation of high level values, for example autonomy and respect, which the heir had denied his grandfather.[17]

The point was made earlier that the *Shorter Oxford English Dictionary* definition of values treats them as deontological. By contrast Habermas, drawing distinctions between values and principles, suggests that: 'Principles or higher-level norms, in the light of which other norms can be justified, have a deontological sense, whereas values are teleological.'[18] Because principles are deontological, he suggests, they can 'claim to be universally binding and not just specially preferred', and so they possess a greater justificatory force than values. 'Values must be brought into a transitive order with other values from case to case. Because there are no rational standards for this, weighing takes place either arbitrarily or unreflectively according to customary standards and hierarchies.'[19] Valid norms have to fit together into a coherent legal system, whereas values, operating at different levels of importance and often being in conflict with one another, have to be weighed against one another to determine what would be good or best or least worst in a given situation.[20]

Values do operate at many levels of a system, and some are teleological. For instance, what have been called the *sigma* values of economy and parsimony, *theta* values of integrity and equity, and *lambda* values of security and reliability[1] are a mixture of teleological and deontological values. Economy and parsimony are not, it is suggested, inherently deontological, whereas equity and security are. We shall be concerned

---

14 *Dworkin* p 22.
15 A ladder of abstraction is 'a continuing sequence of categorizations from a low level of generality up to a high level of generality': W L Twining and D Miers, op cit at p 56.
16 115 NY 506, 22 NE 188 (1889).
17 See Sir John Laws 'Public law and employment law: Abuse of power' [1997] Public Law 455 at p 465 for an insightful brief discussion of differences between principles, rules and values.
18 J Habermas *Between Facts and Norms* trans W. Rehg, (1996) at p 255; and see generally at pp 253-261.
19 *Habermas* at p 259.
20 *Habermas* at p 261.
1   C Hood 'A public management for all seasons' (1991) Public Administration 3.

in what follows with values which are deontological – values such as autonomy, dignity, for instance. That is not to deny that some values can be teleological.

Values have to contend with other considerations in the law and legal policy, and this is one of the reasons why they are not rights. For instance, upholding the autonomy of an individual in the sense of freedom of expression may involve weighing up the competing claims of another person to dignity and respect in privacy.[2] A choice will often have to be made between such claims. Values will often conflict with wider interests and then consideration will also need to be given to the wider implications of giving precedence to such values. For instance, upholding the security and status of all employees could have detrimental effects on the management of enterprises, which could in turn undermine the viability of the enterprise and thus threaten the well-being of the workforce and others with interests in the enterprise.[3] Clearly it will not be appropriate to allow the possibility of damage to the security and status of employees to prevent necessary changes in the operations of enterprises. But requiring employers to take the interests of employees into account before making decisions would secure that considerations of these values influence decision making, without elevating them to rights.

Values, then, are part of the climate, the 'background' in which judges operate. Perhaps Neil McCormick's 'background moral view of how life in an organised society ought to be for individuals' is the nearest to my concept of underlying values.[4] Raz uses the term 'value' at one point to mean something that constitutes or implies the existence of reasons for action.[5] This is a helpful contribution, but of course some reasons for action are bad, and would not merit being given the name 'value', especially in the sense of values that are fundamental to the human condition.

Before turning to explore the particular 'key' values with which this book is principally concerned, it should be noted that consideration of rights is deliberately excluded from the theory that is being put forward. There is a vast literature on rights and it would be superfluous to seek to add to it here. The key values are far more pervasive than rights and it would detract from the argument to focus on rights. Hence in later discussion of the Human Rights Act the focus will be on the values that find expression in the European Convention on Human Rights and the

---

2 See discussion of privacy in chapter 10.
3 See *Boychuk v H J Symons Holdings Ltd* [1977] IRLR 395 at 396, discussed in chapter 6.
4 N McCormick 'Jurisprudence and the Constitution' [1983] Current Legal Problems 13-30 at p 22.
5 J Raz *The Morality of Freedom* (1986) at p 397.

Act.[6] As already noted, values underlie rights. But they also underlie many other matters: principles, the notion of relevant considerations in judicial review cases, the law of confidence and restraint of trade, legal concepts of public policy. These are matters which the courts, the legislature and executive bodies take into account when making decisions on matters ranging from the development of the private law of contract, tort, trusts and property – much of which has little to do with human rights but much to do with the interests of individuals – to embarking on the Citizen's Charter initiative, legislating in the field of employment law, family law, education law and other areas. So the focus on values and not on rights in what follows is deliberate.

THE FIVE 'KEY' VALUES

The point has been made earlier that five values pervade public and private law and are referred to frequently both by the courts and by those commenting on decisions and provisions of European law or statutes. A legitimate question might be, why select these particular values? Where do they come from? That second question will be considered later in this chapter. As far as the question why these particular values provide the focus for discussion here is concerned, the reason is that they are in practice the actual values that can be found operating in both public and private law, as discussion of particular topics in chapters 4 to 10 will show.

The five words dignity, autonomy, respect, status and security, the values with which we are concerned, are terms of art and do not have a fixed or very concrete meaning. Indeed, they are seldom analysed explicitly by the courts, and they seldom appear in terms in legislation. Yet it will be suggested that in practice respect for these values, often unarticulated, influences much of public and private law. In the discussion in later chapters attempts will be made to draw out the various aspects of these values that can be detected in judicial decisions and the texts of statutes and other norms. But at this point it may be helpful to outline broadly what these five words seem to mean in those legal sources and illustrate points with a few examples. In practice, inevitably, they mesh together.

Autonomy, dignity and respect

First, autonomy. This means, strictly, living under one's own laws, or self-government. Raz defines autonomy as the idea that people should

6   See chapter 10.

make their own lives.[7] He argues that autonomous life is 'self-authored'[8] and that subjection to coercion is an invasion of autonomy.[9] Hence control of the ways in which individuals may be subjected to power or coercion by others, whether the state or private bodies, is a relevant consideration in the protection of autonomy, and it is commonly in the context of power imbalances that autonomy is discussed.

Often autonomy is assumed to mean, and mean only, freedom to operate in the market. Such a narrow view would miss the point we are trying to make, for it does not link with our other key values. It does not, for instance, take account of issues of what might be termed 'relational autonomy' which are raised by the law of relationships – marriage, parents and children – where developments over the last century have increased the autonomy of the more vulnerable parties to those relationships, but not to any great degree by reference to market activity.[10]

Where issues of autonomy arise in litigation they are generally to do with the immediate freedom of action of a party – the freedom to move around and not be subject to physical restraint, freedom of speech, freedom to engage in a profession or occupation of one's choice, for instance – and whether and how another party is entitled to restrict that freedom – by physical coercion, withdrawal of cooperation, contract or other means. It is this 'freedom of action' aspect of autonomy that will be the main focus of discussion in what follows.

The values of autonomy and dignity are often considered to be complementary, or are referred to together. Allan, for instance, identifies two interpretations of British democracy, the majoritarian theory and communitarian theory, and suggests that 'On either interpretation ..., the rule of law, conceived as the precepts of formal legality, is an important safeguard of human dignity and liberty'.[11] He goes on to suggest that 'Freedom of conscience and religion are ... of fundamental importance to the values of human dignity and individual autonomy which lie at the heart of our political culture ...'[12] and argues that, in what he calls the 'communitarian' conception of British government

---

7   *Raz* op cit at p 369. Raz argues that 'Ultimately those who live in an autonomy-enhancing culture can prosper only by being autonomous' (at p 394); and see generally *Raz* chapters 14, 15. A new term for autonomy is 'self-ownership' but I do not propose to use it here: see A Reeve 'The theory of property. Beyond private versus common property' in D Held (ed) *Political Theory Today* (1991); see also D Held *Models of Democracy* (1987), chapter 9.

8   *Raz* at p 155.

9   *Raz* at p 154, and pp 377 et seq.

10 See chapters 6 and 7 for consideration of the development of relational autonomy and other key values in these relationships.

11 T R S Allan 'Fairness, Equality, Rationality: Constitutional Theory and Judicial Review' in C Forsyth and I Hare (eds) *The Golden Metwand and the Crooked Cord* (1998) 15, at p 18.

12 Op cit at p 24.

'the individual's dignity and moral autonomy constitute essential components of the common good.'[13]

Just as autonomy and dignity are close relations, so the two values of dignity and respect are closely related. The Latin, 'dignus' means worthy, implying honour and reputableness. Often dignity is to do with how people feel about themselves. In this context, dignity and self-respect are synonymous. A sick person can suffer alone and with dignity. A person can feel humiliated even if there is no witness to the humiliation. But how people feel about themselves may be affected by how they are treated by others. This is where respect (as compared to self-respect) and dignity are linked. An aspect of dignity as linked to respect is expressed in Kant's practical imperative: 'Act in such a way that you always treat humanity, whether in your own person or in the person of any other, never simply as a means, but always at the same time as an end.'[14]

The meanings, among many, of respect in the *Shorter Oxford English Dictionary*, include 'regard, consideration'.[15] These broadly express what 'respect' means in the context of consideration of common values in public and private law. The respect in which a person is held by others affects that person's relations with others. It involves equal treatment and non-discrimination – both examples of considerate altruism on the part of those in positions of power. Recognition of these linkages is found in Dworkin's argument that individuals are entitled to equal concern and respect,[16] though for the reasons given earlier, this is to be regarded as a set of legal values rather than, strictly, a legal right.

There is of course no way in which the law can compel others to 'respect' a person in their own minds, subjectively. But the law can itself treat individuals with respect, for instance by giving them a chance to be heard in their own defence before decisions about them are made, and responding in a reasoned way to their points. And it can – and does – compel others to do the same, especially state bodies. This is in large part what the requirements of fairness and natural justice are for.[17]

The ways in which the common law acknowledges the importance of respect for individuals, including the idea that individuals and corporations should treat individuals with respect, can be illustrated in

---

13 Op cit at p 17.
14 I Kant *The Moral Law (Groundwork of the Metaphysic of Morals)* trans H J Paton, (1965). See discussion of Kant's views on this by Sir John Laws in 'The Constitution: Morals and rights' [1996] Public Law 622.
15 I do not adopt for these purposes the Shorter English Dictionary meaning '*deferential* regard or esteem felt or shown towards a person ...'.
16 *Dworkin* chapter 6.
17 See chapters 6 to 9 for discussion of requirements of fair procedures in public and private decision making. And see D J Galligan, supra.

a number of ways. For present purposes a couple of examples should suffice. In the field of contract the doctrine of unconscionable bargains applies where the advantaged party to a contract has not treated the other party with respect.[18] In *Fry v Lane* Kay J summarised the effect of nineteenth century cases as follows: '… where a purchase is made from a poor and ignorant man at a considerable undervalue, the vendor having no independent advice, a Court of Equity will set aside the transaction.'[19] The point is that in such situations the law imposes an indirect duty of respect, consideration and altruism on the stronger party to the transaction, the remedy for breach of which may be relief for the weaker party. Hence respect is linked to consideration, requiring considerate action in many situations and considerate decision making in relation to those affected by actions, in ways which are explored in later chapters.

Equality is part of dignity and respect. Discrimination is an affront to a person's dignity and irrationally discriminatory behaviour evinces lack of equal respect for a person. Of course some discrimination is justifiable – children require special protections, the disabled may need special provision to be made for them by employers to enable them to work. Affirmative action is an issue into which we shall not plunge here, but clearly there are debates about the appropriate limits of either positive or negative discrimination.

The principal concept of the equality principle in employment is that equal (ie non-discriminatory) treatment is part of the individual worker's right to respect for their personal dignity; this is why it finds a place in employment law.[20] Equality is associated with citizenship (as are the other values with which we are concerned). Allan suggests that 'equality before the law is regarded as an aspect of *equal citizenship*, an ideal of the moral equality or equal dignity of all those subject to governmental power …'[1].

Although equality in the sense of non-discrimination is a common underlying value in both public and private law,[2] it is clearly the case

---

18 Note that Capper discusses the 'sacred *values* and common understandings' between the doctrines of inequality of bargaining power and unconscionability: D Capper 'Undue influence and unconscionability: a rationalisation' (1998) 114 LQR 479 at p 482.

19 (1888) 40 Ch D 312 at 322.

20 See Deakin and Morris, Labour Law (1998) at para 6.2.2.

1 Op cit, Allan p 17.

2 On this see M Taggart 'The province of administrative law determined?' in M Taggart (ed) *The Province of Administrative Law* (1997); C McCrudden 'Racial discrimination' in C McCrudden and G Chambers (eds) *Individual Rights and the Law in Britain* (1994); J L Jowell 'Is equality a constitutional principle?' (1994) 47 Current Legal Problems 1; and see discussion in chapters 6 to 9 below. On the American position on the common law and equality see Note, 'The anti-discrimination principle in the common law' (1989) 102 Harv LR 1193; C M Haar and D W Fessler *The Wrong Side of the Tracks: A Revolutionary Discovery of the Common Law Tradition of Fairness in the Struggle Against Inequality* (1986).

that substantial discrimination is tolerated both by the common law and under statutory provisions. This provides an illustration of the points that values are not the same as rights, and that values often come into conflict with one another. For instance, generally in private law to discriminate on grounds not yet covered by legislation – for instance sexual orientation, political or religious allegiance, age, appearance or personal animosity or friendship – is regarded as part of the freedom – the autonomy – of individuals and companies.[3] But it is nevertheless the case that the law is developing in the direction of recognising the importance of treating all individuals with respect and respecting their dignity, and indirectly this is influencing the development of both public and private law via statutes, European law,[4] and common law developments so that equality in the sense of non-discrimination is creeping into the system as part of the common underlying values of dignity and respect, in both public[5] and private law.[6]

Finally, a word about the origins of these values of dignity, autonomy and respect. They have their roots in liberal theory dating from the seventeenth and eighteenth centuries.[7] In public law they form part of what Loughlin has called 'the normativist style',[8] and in particular its liberal strand. 'The values of classical liberalism assert the dignity of the individual, the primacy of individual freedom, the virtues of markets, and the requirement of limited government operating under the rule of law'.[9] On the face of it, then, these are individualist values. However, the values of dignity and respect are also civil or communitarian, since they require the position of the individual in society and in relation to others to be protected. And the fact that all five of the values here identified find support in public and private law involves that they need to be balanced against one another. Autonomy, with its individualistic associations, is but one of a set of values; communitarian or civil values are also strongly reflected in the areas of law with which we shall be concerned.

The ways in which these values have infiltrated aspects of public and private law are very well illustrated in the law of relationships, discussed in chapters 6 and 7. From a position in the late seventeenth century

---

3   See for instance *Allen v Flood* [1898] AC 1. Compare *Nagle v Feilden* [1966] 2 QB 633, and discussion in chapter 9.
4   Including provisions against discrimination on grounds of race, sex or disability: see chapter 6. And see C Barnard 'The principle of equality in the Community context. *P Grant, Kalanke* and *Marshall*: Four uneasy bedfellows' 57 Camb LJ (1998) 352.
5   J L Jowell, 'Is equality a constitutional principle?' (1994) 47 Current Legal Problems 1.
6   See chapter 9.
7   J Locke *Two Treatises of Government* (1690).
8   M Loughlin *Public Law and Political Theory* (1992) chapter 5.
9   *Loughlin* at p 84.

where relationships between the sovereign and the subject, master and servant, husband and wife and parent and child were hierarchical, with the superior party having complete authority over, and in some respects almost ownership of, the inferior party, developments in statute, the common law and equity have produced the position that the autonomy, dignity and respect of the inferior party receive extensive protection against abuse of power by the superior, and the authority of the superior party has been considerably eroded. In effect the underlying relationship model has shifted from one of positivist authoritarianism to a more participative and altruistic model.

Status

Status has different meanings for sociologists, political scientists and lawyers. It is not used here only in the conventional legal sense, which embraces the special legal disabilities or privileges which are imposed on or granted to certain classes of people – spouses, children, lunatics, aliens, for instance. Legal status involves 'the condition of belonging to a particular class of persons to whom the law assigns certain peculiar legal capacities or incapacities.'[10] Entry to some legal statuses is involuntary – infancy and lunacy for instance. Other legal statuses are voluntary, notably marriage and employment. But once even a voluntary status has come into being many of its incidents are imposed by law. Legal status may impose certain legal rights and duties on individuals which bind not only the parties to a relationship such as marriage but also third parties. The range of special legal statuses of those kinds has reduced considerably over the last century.

Until the late nineteenth century their legal status was of central importance to many individuals. As we shall see in chapter 7, the married woman suffered considerable legal disabilities by virtue of her married status; but she also acquired social standing from her husband together with rights to support and social recognition for her children by him. Illegitimacy was a recognised undesirable status; legitimacy was a privileged status giving the child the social status of the father and the possibility of inheritance and benefit under trusts which would generally be denied to illegitimate children. Infants were under many legal disabilities and enjoyed certain legal privileges and immunities – and still do. These legal statuses reflected social norms and economic realities and as those norms and realities changed, so the law was brought into line with reality, generally moving in the direction of treating all individuals equally so far as practicable.

10   Sir Carlton Allen 'Status and capacity' (1930) 46 LQR 277, 288.

The term 'status' is used for the purposes of the argument being developed in this book in a broadly sociological sense – although some of the incidents of legal statuses coincide with the social aspects of status. Weber regarded status as a form of *social* recognition usually enjoyed by individuals by virtue of their membership of a group. The group need not be legally sanctioned or recognised. For instance membership (in a non-contractual sense) of churches, or of ethnic or professional or sporting groups, or of workforces, or political parties, or families and dynasties, can give rise to status; the membership affects the way other members of the group view the member, and how outsiders view the members.

The courts have come to recognise that status in this 'social' sense is a value worthy of legal protection. It is essentially a communitarian value. In this respect the law promotes civil theories of democracy and concepts of citizenship, protecting the individual's position in civil society.

A person's position in society may depend on reputation, and this is recognised in a number of different legal rules. The tort of defamation is clearly designed to protect status.[11] The obligation of trust and confidence in the employment relationship is designed partly to protect employees from having their characters damaged by the fact of being employed by a corrupt or dishonest employer, and compensation may be awarded for pecuniary damages suffered by reason of damage to reputation from wrongful dismissal or breach of the trust and confidence term.[12] A person's reputation is protected in judicial review[13] and in some private law situations[14] by the requirement that where a decision is likely to result in a slur on the character of the object of the decision that person should be informed of the case against him and have an opportunity to meet it.

Status in the sense in which we are considering it here may also depend upon the possession of professional qualifications, membership of professional or social organisations such as trade unions, clubs, churches and so on. Acceptance of the importance of these institutions to individuals is reflected in the growing body of case law about the membership of and exclusions and expulsion from social organisations. For instance the rules of fairness and natural justice must be observed before a person can be expelled from a body such as a trade union, an

---

11 See chapter 8 below.
12 *Malik v BCCI* [1997] 3 All ER 1 at 9-12, per Lord Nicholls. And see discussion in chapter 8.
13 See for instance *R v Gaming Board of Great Britain, ex p Benaim and Khaida* [1970] 2 QB 417.
14 For instance see *McInnes v Onslow Fane* [1978] 1 WLR 1520.

insurance society or a club of which he or she is a member.[15] These rules imply a participative communitarian theory about the exercise of power.

Security

And finally, the value of security. By this is meant an ability to rely on or trust those with whom one deals – including public bodies – and the condition of being protected from or not exposed to danger or risk.[16] Security is linked to status, because the fact of being held in high regard itself provides some security, as does membership of certain groups that confer status, such as professions.

Security was a strong concern of legal and political commentators in the eighteenth and nineteenth centuries. The Declaration of Rights by the Representatives of the good People of Virginia of 12 June 1776 stated in article III that 'The government is, or ought to be, instituted for the common benefit, protection, and security of the people, nation or community.' The French Declaration of the Right of Man of 1789 included the following: 'II. The end of all political associations is the preservation of the natural and imprescriptible rights of man; and these rights are liberty, property, security, and resistance of oppression'; and later in that Declaration 'XII A public force being necessary to give security to the rights of men and of citizens, that force is instituted for the benefit of the community and not for the particular benefit of the persons to whom it is intrusted'.[17]

Bentham saw security as the most important of the objects of legislative policy and the primary source of utility.[18] It found expression in his 'security-providing principle' and 'the disappointment-prevention principle', the latter of which constituted the sole reason for constituting many criminal offences;[19] he further suggested that 'the practice of compelling the fulfilment of contracts has for its sole reason ... the disappointment produced by the non-fulfilment.'[20] He considered that 'each man's labour looks for security from the Law against calamity, or

---

15 See chapter 9.
16 Shorter Oxford English Dictionary.
17 For discussion of these documents and the philosophy of liberal democracy which they represented see E Kamenka 'The Anatomy of an Idea' in E Kamenka and A E Tay *Human Rights* (1978).
18 See P J Kelly *Utilitarianism and Distributive Justice. Jeremy Bentham and the Civil Law* (1990) p 73. The other objects were subsistence, abundance and equality.
19 Jeremy Bentham *Official Aptitude Maximized; Expense Minimized* ed P Schofield (1993), Appendix B 'On Retrenchment', pp 342-346.
20 *Bentham*, supra, p 346.

hostility from foreigners, fellow subjects or rules'.[1] Bentham did not consider status in so many words, but he suggested that: 'Security considered as applied to individuals has for its objects four distinguishable possessions: person, reputation, property, condition in life'.[2] Reputation and condition in life readily fall into the category of status in this elaboration of common values in public and private law.

For Bentham security was linked with the idea of trust. Kelly suggests:

> '… what underlies Bentham's argument is the view that most of the significant sources of interest, particularly those which give rise to the complex patterns of social interaction which characterize modern societies, are developed within the context of elaborate patterns of belief about how other individual will act… Beliefs about how others will act are indispensable in the formation of particular conceptions of well-being which depend on how an action will affect others' behaviour.'[3]

Kelly argues that security is the most important source of utility because it is a necessary condition of personal continuity and of interest formation.[4] J S Mill also considered security to be a fundamental value – he referred to '… security, to every one's feelings the most vital of all interests. … security no human being can possibly do without; … this most indispensable of all necessaries, after physical nutriment …'[5]

Blackstone saw security as the justification for the surrender by each person of his absolute freedom of action:

> 'For no man that considers for a moment would wish to retain the absolute and uncontrouled power of doing whatever he pleases; the consequence of which is, that every other man would also have the same power; and then there would be no security to individuals in any of the enjoyments of life.'[6]

In contemporary terms security involves, for instance, being entitled to have one's legitimate expectations[7] fulfilled – a right to considerate

1   J Bentham *First Lines of a Proposed Code of Law* ed P Schofield (1998) chapter 2, para 1.
2   *Bentham*, supra, chapter 2, para 1.
3   P J Kelly, op cit at pp 78–79.
4   *Kelly*, supra, at p 73.
5   J S Mill *Utilitarianism, On Liberty and Representative Government* (1910) (ed) at p 50.
6   Sir William Blackstone *Commentaries on the Laws of England* vol I, chapter 1, p 126.
7   See discussion of legitimate expectations in judicial review in chapter 5, and in relation to contracts and trusts in chapter 8.

altruism on the part of those in positions of power. It is notable that Bentham used the term 'expectation' frequently in his discussion of security, especially in relation to the disappointment-prevention principle: 'For disappointment to take place, and consequently for the pain which it is of the nature of disappointment to produce, it must have been preceded by expectation'.[8]

Both in the common law and in many statutes security and trust remain as important as ever. Honoré explored the statutory trends in the fields of landlord and tenant, employment and marriage in his Hamlyn lectures of 1982, and brings out the common thread of a desire to provide security for weaker parties in these relationships.[9] The importance of security is also illustrated by the obligation of trust and confidence in the employment relationship, designed to protect the security – and status – of the employee as well as the employer's interests.[10] And provisions such as the Misrepresentation Act 1967 aim to protect a person's security by imposing duties of trustworthiness on those with whom they deal. Fiduciary duties and duties of good faith and confidentiality[11] aim to promote trust in society and thereby to promote security.

Security is also important in providing protection against risk and danger. Legal arrangements for this are found in private insurances such as life insurance, personal injury and accident insurance, insurance against unemployment and so on, as well as in the provisions of the welfare state, including health services, education, and benefits for the unemployed and redundant.[12]

In summary, security – like status – is a value which promotes not only individualistic interests but also social or civil interests, by underpinning the ways in which an individual is knitted into the social circles in which he or she moves. It is, in other words, a democratic value reflecting participative communitarianism and considerate altruism.

8   J Bentham *Comment* in J H Burns and H L A Hart (eds) *A Comment on the Commentaries and A Fragment on Government* (1977); and see *Kelly*, op cit at p 77.
9   Tony Honoré *The Quest for Security: Employees, Tenants, Wives* (1982). He focuses on the vulnerability of the dependant parties to these relationships and explores the extent to which society gives them greater security.
10   See *Malik v BCCI* [1997] 3 All ER 1, HL, and further discussion in chapter 6 of the employment relationship.
11   For example, confidences, once reposed in another, should be respected: *Stephens v Avery* [1988] Ch 449 at 482.
12   T H Marshall *Citizenship and Social Class* (1950) considered that the introduction of social rights protected by statute in the twentieth century enabled individuals to participate in society as citizens. Marshall meant by this 'social element' of citizenship 'the whole range from the right to a modicum of economic welfare and *security* to the right to share to the full in the social heritage and to live the life of a civilised being according to the standards prevailing in society.': at p 11, emphasis added. See also *Honoré* at p 117.

Competing values

The five common values explored above will often be in conflict with one another in a particular case. In defamation cases the freedom of speech – autonomy – of one individual may be limited by the interests of another in their status, dignity and respect. It will be suggested in what follows in this book that the courts are increasingly explicitly weighing up the interests of parties in litigation in terms of these values and deciding on the relative weight to be given them. In later chapters it will be shown that the trends in the courts in cases where these common values conflict with one another are to give particular weight to the interests of individuals over corporate bodies, not to accept that state bodies have interests in these values for their own benefit, and to seek to redress imbalances of power between parties in favour of the vulnerable party.

These values often come into conflict with other values. These include, for instance, a perceived need for those in authority to be treated with respect,[13] the interests of good administration,[14] of the market and of national security.[15] Parliament and governmental bodies will commonly take the position that these competing values outweigh the common values explored here. But it will be shown in subsequent chapters that our common values are weighty considerations in the balance when the courts are having to decide between them and these other competing values. This is a major shift from the position in the early nineteenth century, for instance, where precedence was commonly given to upholding authority and the interests of good administration – a positivist authoritarian approach – as discussion of developments in the law of relationships in chapters 6 and 7 will show. This brings us back to the strands in constitutional and citizenship theory that were sketched in chapter 1: in effect, as the common values increase in importance on the legal system, the positivist authoritarian model is being replaced by principles of liberalism, participative communitarianism and considerate altruism, in both public and private law.

---

13 See for instance the discussions of *Bagg's case* in chapter 2, of the evolution of employment in chapter 6 and of marriage and parent/child relationships in chapter 7.
14 See discussion of judicial review in chapters 4 and 5.
15 See discussion in chapter 5.

Chapter Four

Public Law 1: *O'Reilly v Mackman*

In this chapter the focus is on the public-private divide as it operates in judicial review since the decision of the House of Lords in *O'Reilly v Mackman*.[1] The next chapter will consider the ways in which public law recognises the importance of the common values that were explored in the previous chapter to individuals, and controls exercises of, broadly, state power.

BEFORE *O'REILLY v MACKMAN*

To place the issues on the exclusivity rule introduced by *O'Reilly* in context, the position before this decision will be summarised. There were two principal kinds of procedure available to a litigant wishing to allege that a public body or a body performing a public function had breached the requirements for the exercise of decision-making powers. First, applications in the Divisional Court of the Queen's Bench Division for what had come to be called judicial review. In these proceedings the court had power to grant any of the old prerogative orders, notably for our purposes certiorari, mandamus and prohibition, and, since 1977 when the rules of court were changed, injunctions, declarations and even damages. Applications for certiorari had to be started within six months of the matter complained of, leave to apply had to be obtained, and at the hearing evidence was normally received only by way of affidavit. Discovery was seldom awarded. Respondents to such cases were in a privileged position because of the very short time limit for certiorari, and the need for the applicant to obtain leave to proceed. Broadly the

1   [1983] 2 AC 237.

prerogative orders were only available against public bodies and those exercising public functions, but the extent of their applicability was not often tested, as alternative remedies were available in proceedings in the Queen's Bench or Chancery Divisions.

The other kind of proceeding available to complainants was in the Queen's Bench or Chancery Division. Applications could be made by writ or originating summons for declarations or injunctions to challenge the decision-making processes of public and private bodies. Here the normal private law limitation periods applied and there was no requirement of leave before a plaintiff or applicant could proceed. It followed that plaintiffs might prefer this procedure to judicial review. The grounds for these applications were to be found in the case law, and broadly the case law did not distinguish substantively between applications for the prerogative orders and applications for declarations or injunctions.

Thus before *O'Reilly v Mackman* no substantive divide between Order 53 and other proceedings was thought to exist. The question whether duties of legality, fairness (in the sense of procedural propriety) or rationality (this categorisation of grounds of review was introduced by Lord Diplock in the post-*O'Reilly* case of *Council for Civil Service Unions v Minister for the Civil Service*[2]) applied in a particular case did not depend on the question whether the body in question was public or private, or whether the function being challenged was public or private. Substantive rules had developed to the effect that bodies that were public did normally have to conform to these requirements, but many of these rules also applied to 'private' bodies or bodies exercising private functions.[3]

Then came the decision in *O'Reilly v Mackman*.

O'REILLY v MACKMAN

It will be recalled that the applicants in *O'Reilly v Mackman* were prisoners who had been disciplined by the Board of Visitors after the Hull prison riots. They started proceedings by originating summons in one case, and by writ in others in 1980, nearly four years after the riots and many months after the disciplinary proceedings had taken place. The reason for the delay was that it was not until the decision in *R v Board of Prison Visitors of Hull, ex p St Germain*[4] that the prisoners realised that they might have grounds for judicial review of the way in which disciplinary

2   [1985] AC 374. See chapter 5 for further discussion of this case.
3   See discussion in chapters 8 and 9 of the existence of such duties in private law.
4   [1979] QB 425, CA and *(No 2)* [1979] 1 WLR 1401, DC.

proceedings against them had been conducted. It was conceded in *O'Reilly v Mackman* that the prisoners would in principle have had a remedy in an application for judicial review under Order 53, but they would have required leave to apply, and leave would not have been granted because they were out of time. Hence their decision to commence private law proceedings instead of applying for judicial review.

The Board of Visitors in *O'Reilly* contended that proceedings to challenge their decisions ought not to be entertained by the court unless they were taken by way of application for judicial review. Lord Diplock for the House of Lords accepted this point, and decided that:

> 'It would in my view as a general rule be contrary to public policy, and as such an abuse of the process of the court, to permit a person seeking to establish that a decision of a public authority infringed rights to which he was entitled to protection under public law to proceed by way of an ordinary action and by this means to evade the provision of Order 53 for the protection of such authorities.'[5]

Lord Diplock elaborated on the public interests which were served by this exclusivity rule: it was necessary that the judge should decide at the outset of a case whether it could proceed and it was not enough to point out that at the end of a case begun by writ or originating summons a judge could exercise a discretion to refuse a remedy.

> 'So to delay the judge's decision as to how to exercise his discretion would defeat the public policy that underlies the grant of those protections: viz the need, in the interests of good administration and of third parties who may be indirectly affected by the decision, for speedy certainty as to whether it has the effect of a decision that is valid in public law ... The period of uncertainty as to the validity of a decision that has been challenged on allegations that may eventually turn out to be baseless and unsupported by evidence on oath, may thus be strung out for a very lengthy period, as the actions of the first three appellants in the instant appeals show. Unless such an action can be struck out summarily at the outset as an abuse of the process of the court the whole purpose of the public policy to which the change in Order 53 was directed would be defeated.'[6]

It is to be noted, however, that so far as the issues in *O'Reilly v Mackman* were concerned, there was no problem over prejudice to the interests of

5 [1983] 2 AC 237 at 284-285.
6 Ibid at 284.

third parties or of good administration to weigh in favour of denying the prisoners the right to raise their grievances in court. It is also to be noted that considerations of good administration or management and prejudice to third parties also arise in private law cases,[7] where they may affect the substantive duties of defendants and the rights of plaintiffs; but in these private law situations such considerations are not regarded as reasons to deny the right of a plaintiff to initiate and pursue proceedings.

To summarise, the arguments in favour of the exclusivity rule are that the rule protects public bodies or those exercising public functions from having their decisions challenged more than a short time after the event, thus enabling them to get on with their jobs, promoting the interests of good administration and protecting them from having their authority challenged.[8] There are strong authoritarian and majoritarian influences at work here. Lord Woolf defends the rule on the basis that the task of the courts in judicial review 'is to ensure that bodies which perform public functions should do so in accordance with the requirements of the law. Many of those functions affect, to differing degrees, a great many people. This gives rise to a need to avoid the uncertainty that the existence of proceedings can cause, so as to protect not only the workings of government and other public bodies, but also all those members of the public whom the decision affects.'[9] This echoes the line of reasoning adopted by Lord Diplock in *O'Reilly*. Overall the Law Commission, when it considered remedies in administrative law, believed that the present position 'whereby a litigant is required to proceed by way of order 53 only when (a) the challenge is on public law and no other grounds; ie where the challenge is solely to the validity or legality of a public authority's act or omissions and (b) the litigant does not seek either to enforce or defend a completely constituted private law right' was satisfactory.[10] As we shall see in future chapters very similar arguments could be put in favour of protecting private decision making, but in practice private decision making is rarely (but not absolutely never[11]) provided with such protections.

---

7   See for instance discussions of employment in chapter 6, and of the duties of company directors in chapter 8.

8   For an account of the arguments in favour of RSC Order 53 and the Supreme Court Act section 30, see *Administrative Law: Judicial Review and Statutory Appeals* (1994) Law Com 225.

9   'Droit public – English style' [1995] PL 57.

10 *Administrative Law: Judicial Review and Statutory Appeals* (Law Com) no 226 (1994) at para 3.15.

11 For instance complaints of discrimination or unfair dismissal under the employment rights legislation must be made within three months of the matter complained of – see chapter 6.

THE CASE AGAINST PROCEDURAL EXCLUSIVITY

The judgment in *O'Reilly* contemplated 'public authorities' benefitting from the considerable protections of Order 53. The availability of these procedural privileges to public bodies is controversial. On one view such privileges are necessary in the interests of good public administration; public interests are more important than those of individuals affected by decisions who have not challenged them promptly; we can be confident that procedural privileges will not be abused because public authorities are generally directly or indirectly democratically accountable and political checks will prevent abuse. This line of defence is essentially a reliance on positivist-authoritarian and liberal-majoritarian theories.[12] However, as we shall see, the protections of Order 53 also apply to bodies that are not democratically or politically accountable at all, such as the Take-over Panel.[13] In such cases there are no political safeguards against abuse of these privileges through the reliance on short time limits in order to avoid having decisions scrutinised for their legality, fairness and rationality by the courts, or through non-disclosure of evidence or the avoidance of cross-examination of witnesses. We may ask why private bodies, even if they are exercising public functions, should enjoy these privileges. A case could be made that such bodies should be subject to particularly rigorous judicial scrutiny rather than that they should enjoy these adjectival law advantages.

Other principled objections to the exclusivity rule are that the requirement for promptness in applying for judicial review, and in any event for the application to be made within three months, is unfair to would-be applicants. They undermine the rule of law by allowing public bodies to get away with unlawful activity unless they are challenged within a very short time. Similar short time limits in civil actions against public bodies were removed by the Limitation Act 1936 so that now 'public' bodies are under the same limitation periods as private bodies in tort litigation. And, as was seen in chapter 1, tort litigation may well raise issues to do with statutory duties or discretionary decision making. In short, the short time limit in judicial review is anomalous.

The requirement for leave (now permission[14]) to apply for judicial review denies applicants access to the courts[15] in ways that are without parallel in civil actions. There has also been unacceptable inconsistency

---

12 See chapter 1 for discussion of these theories.
13 *R v Panel on Take-overs and Mergers, ex p Datafin* [1987] QB 815.
14 See Civil Procedure Rules 1999, Part 50, RSC, rule 3(1).
15 See A Le Sueur and M Sunkin 'Applications for judicial review: The requirement of leave' [1992] Public Law 102; M Sunkin, L Bridges and G Meszaros *Judicial Review in Perspective*, (1993), Public Law Project, London.

between judges in decisions on applications for leave (now permission).[16] Public interests could be protected in less draconian ways, for instance, by provisions along the lines of those in civil actions for striking out cases for failure to disclose a cause of action, through the costs rules, by statutory time limits in specific kinds of case, and by awards of damages instead of injunctions or other mandatory orders.[17]

The principal practical objection to the exclusivity rule is that the distinction between public and private law is difficult to apply, and it is inefficient in that it imposes unnecessary costs on the parties. A whole string of cases has followed *O'Reilly v Mackman* in which the courts have either applied, or developed exceptions to, the rule.[18] This is not the place for a detailed analysis of the ways in which the court has sought to resolve these problems, but examples of the court's approach will illustrate the problems.

The decision in *Cocks v Thanet DC*[19] was delivered on the same day as *O'Reilly*. The plaintiff sought damages in the county court on the ground that he was entitled to be provided with housing by the local authority under the provisions of the Housing (Homeless Persons) Act 1977. This right depended upon the lawfulness of the authority's decision that he was not entitled to be housed. That decision was held to be a public law decision, and challengeable therefore only in an application for judicial review.[20] De Smith, Woolf and Jowell regard the logic of the decision as 'impeccable' but point out the burden that it imposes on a plaintiff or applicant in an area of law such as housing which requires expedition.

The burden on applicants is also illustrated by the *Woolwich* litigation:[1] the applicants had to apply for judicial review to have regulations quashed before they could pursue their restitution claims. The question needs to be asked, what benefits ensue to the respondents or to the interests of justice or good administration by such a requirement? It is hard to see

---

16   See A Le Sueur and M Sunkin supra, M Sunkin, L Bridges and G Meszaros supra.

17   See discussion of remedies in chapter 9.

18   A number of attempts have been made to summarise or rationalise the exceptions to the exclusivity rule or to reformulate the rule so as to take account of the exceptions. See for instance, M Supperstone 'The ambit of judicial review' in M Supperstone and J Goudie (eds) *Judicial Review* (2nd edn, 1998) at pp 3.25-3.31; *Administrative Law: Judicial Review and Statutory Appeals* Law Com no 226 (1994) at paras 3.11, 3.14.

19   [1983] 2 AC 286.

20   Note that on the substantive issue in *Cocks*, namely whether an action for damages could lie for refusal to provide housing when a right to housing did exist under the legislation, the House of Lords decided in *O'Rourke v London Borough of Camden* [1998] AC 188 that no such private law right exists. See Sir Robert Carnwath 'The *Thornton* heresy expose: Financial remedies for breach of public duties' [1998] Public Law 407.

1   *Woolwich Building Society v IRC (No 2)* [1993] AC 70, HL, discussed a p 28 supra.

why in such a case one action could not be taken for (a) the quashing of the regulations and (b) restitution, in which the courts could adopt an 'integrated' approach, first determining the question of the validity of the regulations, and then proceeding to decide upon the remedy in restitution. If there were statutory time limits or permission requirements then these could be observed in such an action, but the requirement for two actions seems quite unnecessary.

UNDERLYING VALUES AND PROCEDURAL EXCLUSIVITY

It may be helpful to relate the *Cocks*[2] decision to some of the themes of this book, notably the legal recognition of the importance of the values explored in the previous chapter (dignity, autonomy, respect, status and security) for individuals, and the way in which the countervailing interests of public bodies or those exercising public functions in being able to get on with the job without being unduly hampered by the courts are weighed in the balance. In *Cocks* the public authority's interests trumped those of the defendant. Underlying the decision were the competing considerations of, on the one hand, the needs of the plaintiff for housing, and consequently for access to the courts to assert his entitlements in order to protect his needs for security and dignity; and, on the other hand, the sense that it should not be too easy for challenges to the decisions of public authorities to be mounted. Another, implicit, assumption in the case was that it was in some way inappropriate for an 'inferior' court such as the county court to determine issues to do with the legality of decisions taken by local authorities. It is to be noted, however, that since this decision the county court has been given jurisdiction to hear appeals on any point of law in homelessness cases (after an internal review has taken place in the local authority[3]), and may confirm, quash or vary the local authority's decision.[4] Thus the two objections set out above have been overridden to an extent in the field of housing.

Since *O'Reilly* and *Cocks v Thanet District Council* the trend has been very much in the opposite direction, and a succession of exceptions to the strict exclusivity rule have been made. In *Wandsworth London Borough Council v Winder*[5] the court decided that if a defendant to a civil action (in this case an action for possession) needed to rely on a public law

---

2   *Cocks v Thanet District Council* [1983] 2 AC 286.
3   Housing Act 1996, section 202.
4   Housing Act 1996, section 204. And see *Warsame v London Borough of Hounslow* (1999) Times, 21 July, CA. However, an applicant for housing may apply for judicial review of a local authority's exercise of discretion, since the appeal to the county court is on a point of law only: *Ali v Westminster City Council* [1999] 1 WLR 384 at 389, per Otton LJ.
5   [1985] AC 461.

issue, then he was entitled to raise that point in the civil action as a collateral issue and was not caught by the *O'Reilly* rule that in principle such matters could only be raised in an application for judicial review. Again the relevance of this decision to our themes should be noted. In *Wandsworth* the defendant's security – continued occupation of his home – was at stake, and the decision effectively gave that interest additional protection by permitting him to raise the substantive public law issue at the earliest possible stage in the litigation. Although the ratios of this and other cases do not note these interests, it is suggested that without taking such interests and values into account it is not possible to make sense of decisions in this line of cases.

Similar points about collateral challenge by defendants to litigation have arisen in criminal cases where a defendant seeks to rely on a challenge to the 'public law' validity of regulations or a decision by way of defence. The position has been reached by the House of Lords, after a series of decisions going the other way,[6] in *Boddington*[7] that a person charged with a byelaw offence may raise the validity of the byelaw and of any decision made under it at the trial.

Relating these criminal cases to the broader themes in this argument, the interests at stake for the defendant will often be his or her autonomy, if a prison sentence is possible, and status to the extent that a criminal conviction affects the attitude of others in society to the person convicted. The liberalisation of the exclusivity rule in the area of criminal law, it is suggested, recognises the claims of individuals to respect for these values as being superior to the claim by public authorities to be permitted to get on with the job of regulation or law enforcement, and their claim to have their authority protected by the court by placing obstacles in the path of those wishing to challenge their decisions.

EXCEPTIONS TO PROCEDURAL EXCLUSIVITY

In a number of cases since *O'Reilly* (including *Wandsworth v Winder*, above) the courts have exercised a supervisory jurisdiction over decisions of public bodies in ordinary actions, on the basis that a flexible approach is desirable. Thus in *Mercury Communications Ltd v Director General of Telecommunications*[8] it was held that Mercury's action challenging the director's imposition of terms in a (contractual) licence by way of

---

6   See *Bugg v DPP* [1993] QB 473; *R v Crown Court at Reading, ex p Hutchinson* [1988] QB 384; *Quietlynn Ltd v Plymouth City Council* [1988] QB 144; *R v Wicks* [1998] AC 92, HL.
7   [1998] 2 WLR 639.
8   [1996] 1 WLR 48.

originating summons was at least as well suited to deal with the issue of construction of a licence as judicial review would be. The overriding question was whether a private action constituted an abuse of process. This approach was followed in *Dennis Rye Pension Fund Trustees v Sheffield City Council:*[9] where the case involved issues largely of fact and did not require the special expertise of a nominated judge, and where the remedy sought, payment of a sum of money, was not available in judicial review, it was not an abuse of process to initiate private law proceedings.[10]

In *Roy v Kensington and Chelsea and Westminster Family Practitioner Committee*[11] Roy, a general medical practitioner, took civil proceedings to recover from the committee the amount he claimed was due to him – his full practice allowance – either under a contract or by way of a statutory entitlement. The committee contended that he was entitled to a lesser sum because he was devoting a substantial amount of time to his private practice. The House of Lords permitted his civil action to proceed on the basis either that this was an entirely private law matter, or that his private law rights dominated the proceedings and that he would not have been able to recover the sum owed to him, the remedy he sought, in an application for judicial review. In this case part of the plaintiff's livelihood, and therefore his security, was at issue and this factor may explain why the court favoured enabling him to raise the point in one set of civil proceedings rather than having to take two sets of proceedings, one in public law in which he could not obtain the necessary remedy, followed possibly by a second civil action to recover the sums due to him.

Public employment and the exclusivity rule

Cases about public employment have caused special difficulties for the exclusivity rule. Office holders will be entitled to judicial review of decisions relating to their 'employment', as will employees whose contracts have a public law overlay,[12] whereas in cases where there is no such overlay disputes will be regarded as contractual and judicial review will not be available.[13] But it is by no means easy to predict what view the

9   [1997] 4 All ER 747, CA.
10 See also *Mayer Parry Recycling Ltd v Environment Agency* [1999] 1 CMLR 963, Carnwath J.
11 [1992] 1 AC 624. See also *Andreou v Institute of Chartered Accountants of England and Wales* [1998] 1 All ER 14 and *Trustees of the Dennis Rye Pension Fund Trustees v Sheffield City Council* [1997] 4 All ER 747.
12 See *Ridge v Baldwin* [1964] AC 40; *Malloch v Aberdeen Corpn* [1971] 1 WLR 1578, HL.
13 See for instance *R v East Berkshire Health Authority, ex p Walsh* [1985] QB 152; *R v BBC, ex p Lavelle* [1983] ICR 99. See further discussion in chapter 6.

court will take of a particular employment relationship. There is also a sense that public employers should not be entitled to the same freedom of action as private employers, and that they ought to be subject to higher order duties of fairness and rationality in their relations even with their 'ordinary' employees. In other words, public employers do not have a claim to autonomy, and in this respect they differ from private employers, a point which illustrates the operation of the perspective noted in chapter 5, that public bodies do not have interests; this factor may affect the extent to which they are subject to duties of legality, fairness and rationality. Fredman and Morris have suggested that there should be a unified procedure in employment cases, as this would give the courts greater flexibility to impose constraints on the exercise of power where this is deemed appropriate, regardless of whether that power lies with public or private bodies.[14] With the advent of the Human Rights Act,[15] which binds public authorities in all their actions, even 'private' activity, it will be even more difficult to operate a public private divide in employment cases.

Overall, then, the exclusivity rule, having initially proved extremely difficult to operate in practice, largely because many cases raise mixed questions of public and private law, has been considerably watered down and a more flexible approach based on whether it would be an abuse of process[16] to proceed by way of private law proceedings has been adopted. Nevertheless, the strict time limit and requirement for permission place applicants for judicial review in a disadvantageous position as compared with plaintiffs in private law proceedings.

A SUBSTANTIVE PUBLIC-PRIVATE DIVIDE?

In the first section of this chapter the point was made that, until *O'Reilly*, there was no substantive divide between public and private law. Duties of legality, fairness and rationality were imposed in certain cases on

---

14 See S Fredman and G Morris 'The costs of exclusivity. Public and private re-examined' [1994] Public Law 69, esp p 84; and 'Public or private? State employees and judicial review' (1991) 107 LQR 298.

15 See chapter 10.

16 J A Jolowicz criticises the resort to 'abuse of process' in *O'Reilly* as the reason to strike out the action on the basis that 'The power to put a stop to an abuse of process exists to protect the administration of justice, and its exercise is not justified by a general appeal to public policy. ... Lord Diplock's somewhat cavalier approach to the power to strike out or dismiss ... ignores the innumerable warnings against use of the power save in extreme cases and it pays inadequate regard to the need to protect the litigant's right to be heard.' See 'Abuse of the process of the court: Handle with care' 1990 CLP 77 at p 92.

private bodies taking private decisions[17] as well as on public bodies. Since then, however, the divide established by Lord Diplock in *O'Reilly* has operated so that the answers to the questions: 'What rights does an applicant or plaintiff have?' or: 'What duties does the respondent or defendant owe to the respondent?' have come to be assumed to depend on whether the respondent or defendant is a public body or is exercising public or governmental functions. (The word 'assumed' is used advisedly, as we shall see in chapters 8 and 9 that in practice this is not the case.) In other words, an assumption that there is a substantive public-private divide has crept into our legal system. The position now is that if a body is public or is exercising public or governmental functions, then generally he or she or it will be under special duties of legality, fairness and rationality (the exact content of which varies from case to case) – duties of considerate decision making to adopt the phrase used in earlier chapters – which, it is assumed, would not rest on that body if it were private or exercising purely private functions.

Lord Woolf has maintained that '… there can be no dispute as to the dramatic nature of the changes which have occurred in the principle or substance of public law since the introduction of the new procedure for judicial review'.[18] De Smith, Woolf and Jowell observe that 'the principles of judicial review can have the effect of extending the rights of the individual; for instance, it can give an individual a right to be consulted *which he would not have in private law*' (my italics).[19] However, this comment fails to take account of the range of situations in private law in which private bodies will be bound by duties of procedural fairness in their decision making.[20]

It was not envisaged at the time that the reforms to Order 53 in 1977 and the Supreme Court Act 1981, giving statutory force to the reforms, were introduced, that they would result in a substantive divide. Lord Scarman stated that the new procedure under Order 53 and the Supreme Court Act 1981 'neither extends nor diminishes the substantive law.'[1] Beatson, however, commented with prescience that 'Consideration of what is a public law case at the remedial level could, in the long run, have

---

17 See, for example, *Lee v Showmen's Guild of Great Britain* [1952] 2 QB 329 (chapter 8); *Re Baden's Deed Trusts (McPhail v Doulton)* [1971] AC 424; *Nagle v Feilden* [1966] 1 All ER 689; *Wood v Woad* (1874) LR 9 Exch 190; *Breen v Amalgamated Engineering Union* [1971] 2 QB 175 (chapter 9).
18 See 'Droit public – English style' [1995] PL 57, at p 58.
19 *Judicial Review of Administrative Action*, para 3-029.
20 See for instance *De Smith, Woolf and Jowell*, paras 3-016, 7-012. This issue will be explored in chapters 6 to 9.
1   *IRC v National Federation of Self Employed and Small Businesses* [1982] AC 617 at 647.

effects at the level of substantive principle.'[2] He welcomed this possibility on the basis that it might lead to a more principled approach to administrative law, with more sensitivity for the legitimate needs of administrative bodies and less emphasis on the 'control' model of administrative law which sees the role of the courts as a counterweight to the interventionist state.[3] However, the trend in the last twenty years has been increasingly for many functions that were formerly performed by state bodies to be transferred to private bodies; and the trend in both statute and the common law has been to extend duties of legality, fairness and rationality into private law relationships.[4] Thus it has become increasingly difficult to distinguish between 'administrative bodies' and others or to define the 'state' for the purposes of determining what their legal obligations and privileges are.

Lord Woolf has welcomed the development of a substantive public law/private law divide. He maintains that '... there is the need for there to be different, that is higher, standards to which public, but not private, bodies should be required to conform by the courts when performing public functions. I do believe that these features provide a solid foundation for the procedural divide.'[5] . And:

'The importance of the distinction between public and private law issues goes far beyond the correctness of the procedure by which a challenge to an activity should be brought. For example, it determines who can bring the proceedings. At one time it was thought that only those who are affected in some way which goes beyond the effect which the activity has on the public as a whole could bring proceedings, but now it is generally accepted that a much more generous approach to an issue as to standing needs to be adopted. This is necessary to ensure that there is never a situation where a public wrong can be committed without anyone having the right to seek redress. The courts should welcome the publicly interested litigant. ... The division is also necessary because of the separate principles and standards which the courts will require of public as opposed to private bodies. The courts can and do require of those who perform public functions higher standards of behaviour than those which are required when what is being performed is a private activity. This is what public law is all about. What judicial review does is to provide a remedy, usually when no

2   J Beatson '"Public" and "Private" in English administrative law' 103 LQR (1987) at p 38.
3   Here Beatson was referring to Harlow and Rawlings *Law and Administration* (1st edn, 1984) pp 39-51. See now (2nd edn, 1997) chapter 2.
4   These will be considered in chapters 6 to 9.
5   'Droit public – English style' [1995] PL 57 at p 61.

other remedy is available, to ensure that bodies adhere to those standards when performing public functions.'[6]

The existence of important distinctions between judicial review and private law controls over exercises of power was also noted by Simon Brown LJ in *R v IRC, ex p Unilever plc*:

'It may no doubt be helpful to consider whether a person could in private law act with impunity in the manner complained of as unfair in public law proceedings; people's conduct and relationships are, after all, generally regulated in private law according to accepted tenets of fairness. But one must beware of placing too great reliance upon any suggested parallels: they may mislead more than assist. ... Public authorities in general ... are required to act in a high-principled way, on occasions being subject to a stricter duty of fairness than would apply as between private citizens.'[7]

Simon Brown LJ went on to refer to Lord Mustill's reference in *Matrix Securities* to 'the spirit of fair dealing which should inspire the whole of public life'.[8]

Thus procedure and substance have become linked in judicial review. For instance, the distinction between public and private law has come to play a crucial role in determining not only when it is necessary to proceed by way of application for judicial review, and by and against whom proceedings raising public law issues can be brought, and the remedies which can be granted, but also, significantly the principles which the court will apply in order to determine these issues.[9] This development runs counter to the trend before the decision in *O'Reilly* outlined at the start of this chapter. In chapters 8 and 9 the position in private law, including the extent to which duties of considerate decision making may be imposed on a private decision maker making a private decision, will be considered, to start to build up an alternative approach to the problems posed by the exclusivity principle which integrates public and private law. Meanwhile we shall continue with our focus on public law.

One of the tests for whether a decision or action is subject to judicial review has been the source of the power. In principle if a power is statutory,

---

6 Op cit. at p 62.
7 [1996] STC 681, 695.
8 *R. v IRC, ex p Matrix Securities* [1994] 1 WLR 334 at 358.
9 De Smith, Woolf and Jowell *Judicial Review of Administrative Action* (5th edn, 1995) at para 3-002.

or derives from the royal prerogative,[10] it may be judicially reviewable – subject to justiciability issues. However, this 'source of a power' test is not determinative of whether a decision is challengeable only by judicial review. Decisions taken because de facto power exists[11] may also be judicially reviewable under Order 53. But of course only decisions taken under de facto power that is public or governmental rather than contractual or purely private are so reviewable.

Under the Human Rights Act 1998 all actions by public authorities will have to be compatible with Convention rights, and this includes 'private activity'[12] (though it is not clear to what extent this will give rise to remedies in private law or in judicial review). The relevant point for present purposes is that when issues of human rights arise, the source of the power will be irrelevant and the determinative point will be whether the activity complained of was undertaken by a public authority. (However, even the distinction between public and private activity undertaken by private bodies will become less important as the courts develop the (private) common law in line with the Convention, as they will be required to do by section 6 of the Human Rights Act 1998.[13])

Rights protected by public law

The exclusivity rule depends on a distinction between 'rights protected by public law', in Lord Diplock's words in *Council of Civil Service Unions v Minister for the Civil Service*,[14] and rights protected by private law. It is not at all clear what 'rights' Lord Diplock had in mind in the *CCSU* case. *CCSU* was about 'rights' to be consulted, and 'rights' to belong to a trade union. If by 'rights protected by public law' Lord Diplock meant 'rights' to procedural propriety and rationality in decision making, then, as chapters 6 to 9 will show, such rights also exist in private law situations. They are not peculiarly 'rights protected by public law'. For instance, employers must follow fair procedures before dismissing certain employees, trustees must act legally and rationally when making discretionary decisions, membership associations must act fairly before expelling a member, regulatory bodies in sport must act rationally in their decisions relating to members and applicants for benefits. These are not essentially public law rights or duties.

---

10 *R v Criminal Injuries Compensation Board, ex p Lain* [1967] 2 QB 864; *Council of Civil Service Unions v Minister for the Civil Service* [1985] AC 374.
11 *R v Panel on Take-overs and Mergers, ex p Datafin plc* [1987] QB 815.
12 See chapter 10.
13 See chapter 10.
14 [1985] AC 374.

If Lord Diplock had in mind substantive rights such as a right or liberty to belong to a trade union, an entitlement to be housed, or to receive suitable education, to be admitted to this country as a refugee, or to receive a certain welfare benefit, it would be hard to classify these as 'rights' in any meaningful way. In *CCSU* all that was at stake was a residual freedom to belong to a trade union. If 'rights' implies that remedies are available as of right the term is meaningless in judicial review: in most judicial review cases only remedies by way of prerogative order or injunction or declaration will be available, and these are not granted as of right.

Lord Diplock's distinction between rights protected by public law and those protected by private law is, it is suggested, virtually impossible to press very far. The Justice-All Souls Report *Administrative Justice. Some Necessary Reforms* concluded that 'We do not believe that any such clear-cut distinction can consistently be drawn. The term "public law" has been useful to remind courts and practitioners that in many administrative law cases there are values and interests to be upheld which transcend the private rights normally the subject of litigation between individuals, but it is, in our view, dangerous to suppose that there is a category of right which can be clearly identified as a public law right'.[15]

Saville LJ put the position neatly when he observed in *British Steel plc v Customs and Excise Comrs* '... over the last decade or so there has been a stream of litigation on this subject, much of it proceeding to the House of Lords. The cases raise and depend upon the most sophisticated arguments, such as the distinction and difference between what is described as "public" as opposed to "private" law, whether rights are of a "private" or "public" nature, whether "private" rights depend upon the exercise of "public" obligations and so on; ... Such litigation brings the law and our legal system into disrepute, and to my mind correctly so.'[16]

Justiciability

The *CCSU* case decided that exercises of power derived from the royal prerogative are judicially reviewable if the function in question is justiciable. In this respect the case marks a dramatic shift away from a positivist-authoritarian approach to the use of prerogative power, under which the exercise of this kind of power had been reviewable only on the question whether the power existed, and not as to the fairness or

---

15 (1988) para 6.20. The report pointed to the difficulties in *Cocks v Thanet District Council* [1983] 2 AC 286, discussed above; see also *Davy v Spelthorne Borough Council* [1984] AC 262.

16 [1997] 2 All ER 366 at 379.

rationality of its exercise. The *CCSU* decision substituted for this a combination of participative communitarianism (where procedural propriety is required) and considerate altruism (where rationality is required). Many functions exercised under the royal prerogative *are* in principle justiciable, notably those relating to the civil service. But many are not – in *CCSU* examples of non-justiciable powers were given and included treaty making and foreign relations.[17] Lord Diplock maintained in *CCSU* that in principle contractual powers are excluded from judicial review. But even that rule is not immutable: in local government cases involving the exercise of contractual powers the courts have been willing to exercise the judicial review jurisdiction.[18] It is to be noted that in many contract cases alternative private law remedies may be available for breach of duties in decision making, under the contract.[19]

Public or governmental functions

A test for whether a matter should be dealt with in judicial review is whether the power or function or activity being challenged is of a public or governmental kind. This test was formulated in *Datafin*, mainly to exclude from review bodies whose powers derived from contract.[20] The 'public element' test in *Datafin* was refined in *Aga Khan* to 'governmental' but this has not proved much easier to apply. In *R v Chief Rabbi of the United Hebrew Congregation of Great Britain and the Commonwealth, ex p Wachmann*[1] Simon Brown J noted that:

> 'To say of decisions of a given body that they are public law decisions with public law consequences means something more than that they are decisions which may be of great interest or concern to the public or, indeed, which may have consequences for the public. To attract the court's supervisory jurisdiction there must be not merely

---

17 On these, see also *R v Secretary of State for Foreign and Commonwealth Affairs, ex p Rees-Mogg* [1994] QB 552.

18 See *Wheeler v Leicester City Council* [1985] AC 1054; *R v London Borough of Lewisham, ex p Shell UK Ltd* [1988] 1 All ER 938; *R v London Borough of Ealing, ex p Times Newspapers* (1986) 85 LGR 316. In *R v BBC, ex p Referendum Party* [1997] EMLR 605 there were obiter observations on the possibility that an obligation contractually undertaken to the government to treat subjects of, inter alia, political controversy with impartiality would be regarded as 'governmental' and therefore subject to judicial review: Times 29 April 1997. For further discussion see Murray Hunt 'Constitutionalism and Contractualisation' in M Taggart (ed) *The Province of Administrative Law* (1997) at pp 27-33.

19 See discussion in chapters 8 and 9.

20 On contract and the supervisory jurisdictions of the court see chapter 8.

1 [1993] 2 All ER 249.

a public but potentially a governmental interest in the decision-making power in question... where non-governmental bodies have hitherto been held reviewable, they have generally been operating as an integral part of a regulatory system which, although itself non-statutory, is nevertheless supported by statutory powers and penalties clearly indicative of government concern'.[2]

R v Wear Valley District Council, ex p Binks[3] is a case in which it is very hard to see what was public or governmental about the local authority's decision. The authority owned the land in the town's market square on which the applicant regularly parked her hot dog stall. She had a licence to do so, but the local authority withdrew the licence. It was held that the local authority should have given Mrs Binks a hearing before removing the licence. In order to found the jurisdiction in the application for judicial review the judge had to be satisfied that there was a public or governmental element and he indicated that he was so satisfied.

This, it is suggested, is not at all a convincing finding. That is not to say that it was wrong to find that a duty of fairness was owed to Mrs Binks. It will be suggested in due course that the basis exists for the imposition of such duties in both public and private law, because the decision would have a serious impact on her livelihood and thus on her security: the step of finding a public or governmental element in decision making is superfluous to the question of whether a duty of natural justice exists.

Case law since *O'Reilly*, notably in *Datafin*[4] has produced the position that bodies which are not public in the orthodox sense – and are not at all democratically accountable – now enjoy the procedural protections of Order 53 and are subject to the higher order duties of legality, fairness and rationality – considerate decision making. Their subjection to Order 53 is not necessarily because of the nature of the bodies, but rather because of the functions they perform. The Takeover Panel in *Datafin* was an unincorporated association with no legal personality, and with no statutory, common law or prerogative powers. It was not in contractual relationship with the applicants. In effect, in the words of Sir John Donaldson MR, the panel had no 'visible means of legal support'. Yet it exercised immense de facto power, in that it could withdraw the benefit of recognition and 'membership' in the City, and withhold cooperation.[5] It is true that its functions were statutorily underpinned and it had the support of the Secretary of State, but it was not actually accountable to

2   Ibid at 254.
3   [1985] 2 All ER 699.
4   *R v Panel on Take-overs and Mergers, ex p Datafin* [1987] QB 815.
5   See discussion of power and cooperation in chapter 2.

him or to Parliament.[6] The upshot in such a case is that, on the one hand the higher order duties of considerate decision making are imposed on the private body, and on the other hand it is entitled to the privileges offered by Order 53, notably the tight time limit and the requirement for permission.

Since the *Datafin* decision, there has been a number of further instances in which non-statutory regulatory bodies which are not directly or indirectly democratically accountable have been found to be judicially reviewable and entitled to the adjectival law privileges offered by Order 53 RSC. These include LAUTRO (the Life Assurance and Unit Trust Regulatory Organisation), the Advertising Standards Authority, and professional associations and their committees.[7]

However, there is also a line of cases in which the courts have declined to control the decision-making processes of powerful private bodies exercising regulatory power in the exercise of the supervisory jurisdiction in judicial review. But that has not necessarily precluded their control in private law. Most of these have been in the field of sport, to which we now turn.

BODIES EXCLUDED FROM JUDICIAL REVIEW: REGULATORY BODIES IN SPORT AND THE SUBSTANTIVE PUBLIC-PRIVATE DIVIDE

The seminal case on the non-reviewability of sporting bodies is *Law v National Greyhound Racing Club* (1983), started in the Chancery Division.[8] The club, the regulatory body for greyhound racing, had decided to deprive the plaintiff of his licence. The Court of Appeal decided that the decision was not judicially reviewable, because the club's authority derived wholly from a contract between the parties and therefore there was no public element – a necessary requirement for the exercise of

---

6 See also *R v Panel on Take-overs and Mergers, ex p Guinness plc* [1990] 1 QB 146.
7 For cases where private bodies have been found to be subject to judicial review, see: *R v Advertising Standards Authority, ex p Insurance Service plc* [1990] COD 42; *R v Advertising Standards Authority, ex p Insurance Service plc* [1990] 2 Admin LR 77; *R v British Pharmaceutical Industry Association Code of Practice Committee, ex p Professional Counselling Aids Ltd* [1991] COD 228, 10 BMLR 21; *R v Panel on Take-overs and Mergers, ex p Guinness plc* [1990] 1 QB 146; *R v Advertising Standards Authority Ltd, ex p Vernons Organisation Ltd* [1992] 1 WLR 1289; *R v Lloyd's of London, ex p Briggs* [1993] COD 66; *R v Life Assurance Unit Trust Regulatory Organisation Ltd, ex p Ross* [1993] QB 17.
8 [1983] 1 WLR 1302, CA. See further discussion of this case in chapter 9.

judicial review under Order 53 – in the power exercised.[9] But, as will be
shown in chapter 9, the fact that no remedy is obtainable in judicial
review in such a case does not mean that no remedy could be obtained in
private law proceedings. The existence of duties of fairness and rationality
in decision making need not depend upon the question whether the
body in question is public or private or performing public or
governmental functions.

R v Football Association Ltd, ex p Football League Ltd [10] differed from
Law, inter alia, because the league did not proceed by originating
summons in the Chancery Division, but was seeking judicial review of
the Football Association. It failed. Rose J observed that:

> 'Despite its virtually monopolistic powers and the importance of
> its decision to many members of the public who are not
> contractually bound to it, [the FA] is, in my judgment, a domestic
> body whose powers arise from and duties exist in private law only.
> … To apply to the governing body of football, on the basis that it is
> a public body, principles honed for the control of abuse of power
> by government and its creatures would involve what, in today's
> fashionable parlance would be called a quantum leap. It would
> also, in my view, for what it is worth, be a mis-application of
> increasingly scarce resources.'

Hence the reasoning was not only that the FA was not subject to judicial
review, but also that principles governing the abuse of power by
government – in shorthand the principles of legality, fairness and
rationality – did not apply to private bodies not exercising public or
governmental functions. (This would not have precluded the possibility
of contractual duties, or of liability for restraint of trade in appropriate
cases.[11]) The *Football Association* case assumed that the public-private
divide is substantive as well as procedural, in that duties of fairness and
rationality, if they were not consensual, could not have been imposed
outside restraint of trade situations.

In *R v Disciplinary Committee of the Jockey Club, ex p Massingberd-
Mundy* (1993)[12] the applicant sought to challenge the withdrawal by the

9   For discussion of the exclusion of powers derived from contract or a consensual
    submission to jurisdiction from judicial review see P Cane 'Self-regulation and
    judicial review' (1986) *Civil Justice Quarterly* 324; J Beatson 'The Courts and the
    Regulators' (1987) *Professional Negligence* 121; S Arrowsmith 'Judicial Review of
    the Contractual Powers of Public Authorities' (1990) 106 LQR 277; J Black
    'Constitutionalising Self-regulation' (1996) 59 MLR 24. See further discussion
    of *Law* in chapter 5.
10 [1993] 2 All ER 833.
11 See chapters 8 and 9.
12 [1993] 2 All ER 207, DC.

Jockey Club of approval of a steward chairman. Judicial review was refused on the grounds, first, per Neill LJ and Roch J, that the decision was not reviewable because it had no public element in it at all, and secondly, per Neill LJ, that no decision of the respondent was reviewable, that point having been decided in *Law*, which was binding on the Divisional Court. However, Roch J questioned whether *Law* precluded judicial review in the absence of a contract between the parties. He indicated that 'There may be cases where the authority of the stewards of the Jockey Club will not be derived from a contract between them and the person aggrieved by their act or decision or alternatively may not be derived wholly from a contract. It seems to me that, if such a case were to arise, then the question is such an act or decision of the Jockey Club susceptible to judicial review? may receive an answer different from that given by the court in *Law*'s case.'[13] A strong assumption here is that, if the court were to have jurisdiction over the Jockey Club, it would be via judicial review and not in private law.

In *R v Jockey Club, ex p RAM Racecourses*[14] the owners of a new race course sought to challenge the Jockey Club's race allocation. They claimed a declaration, an order of certiorari, an order of mandamus and an injunction. There was no contractual relationship between the parties. They claimed a legitimate expectation that they would be granted fixtures. Their application for judicial review was refused because the representation on which they relied was not unambiguous and had not been made directly to them. But Stuart-Smith LJ in the Divisional Court also based his decision on the fact that he felt bound by the decision in *Law* to hold that the decisions under challenge in this case were not amenable to judicial review, although he would have held them to be so were it not for the *Law* decision.[15] However, he did indicate that a remedy in private law might be available for an unreasonable restraint of trade. Simon Brown J agreed with Stuart-Smith LJ but he expressed disagreement with Neill LJ's view in *Massingberd-Mundy* that the Jockey Club could never be reviewable.[16] While agreeing that most decisions of the Club would be domestic and not reviewable he felt that '... just occasionally, as when exercising the quasi-licensing power here under challenge, I for my part would regard the Jockey Club as subject to review.'[17]

In *R v Disciplinary Committee of the Jockey Club, ex p Aga Khan*[18] judicial review was again refused; here the applicant had a contractual relationship

13 At 224.
14 [1993] 2 All ER 225, DC.
15 At 244.
16 At 245.
17 At 248.
18 [1993] 1 WLR 909, CA.

with the respondent and thus there was a possibility of a contractual remedy if there were express or implied terms in the membership contract regulating the procedures and processes of decision making in the sport.[19] The Master of the Rolls held that the club was not a public body, its powers were in no sense governmental and thus the decision was not subject to judicial review. Farquharson LJ found that there was no public element in the Jockey Club's position and powers, and that it was not performing a public or governmental role. Hoffmann LJ held that the Jockey Club operated entirely in the private sector and its activities were governed by private law. There was no public source for its powers, and they were not governmental in nature and it operated directly or indirectly by consent. Hoffmann LJ did however refer to the fact that there were a range of private law and other remedies outside judicial review which might be available where private power is alleged to be abused: the law of contract (which he felt would provide adequate remedies for the Aga Khan), the doctrine of restraint of trade, the Restrictive Trade Practices Act, articles 85 and 86 of the EC Treaty 'and all the other instruments available in law for curbing the excess of private power.'

In summary, since *Law* in 1983 the courts have consistently held that regulatory bodies in sport are not subject to judicial review, sometimes because their powers derive from contract,[20] sometimes because the contract of membership may provide an alternative channel for seeking redress for a grievance for other parties to the contract,[1] and sometimes because neither the functions at issue in these cases nor the bodies themselves were regarded as 'public' or 'governmental'.[2]

The often unarticulated assumption in these cases has been that it is not possible for the common law to impose duties of legality, fairness

---

19 Where a contract exists between a person and a regulatory body, a term is imposed that the body act fairly. In Scotland damages were awarded for breach of a contractual requirement of natural justice: *Tait v Central Radio Taxi (Tollcross) Ltd* 1989 SC 4, First Division (a taxi-driver raised an action in contract for damages for breach of natural justice when a disciplinary committee of the defenders, of which he was a member, required him to resign or be excluded from membership). However, no liability in damages arises for loss caused as a result of the careless exercise of a decision-making power: *Wright v Jockey Club* (1995) Times, 16 June, noted in *De Smith, Woolf and Jowell* at p 168.
20 See for instance *Law v National Greyhound Racing Club* [1983] 1 WLR 1302, CA; *R v Disciplinary Committee of the Jockey Club, ex p Aga Khan* [1993] 1 WLR 909, CA.
1   *Ex p Aga Khan* [1993] 1 WLR 909, CA.
2   For instance, *Law*, supra, *R v Football Association, ex p Football League Ltd* (1991) Times 22 August; *R v Disciplinary Committee of the Jockey Club, ex p Massingberd-Mundy* [1993] 2 All ER 207, DC; *Ex p Aga Khan* [1993] 1 WLR 909, CA. For the position of international sporting bodies see James A R Nafziger 'International sports law as a process for resolving disputes' 45 ICLQ (1994) 130.

and rationality outside judicial review or restraint of trade. Hence an element of the public law-private law divide is assumed to be that bodies not exercising public or governmental functions are not under these 'public law' duties. This is what the substantive divide is supposed to be all about. The point has already been made in this chapter that such duties are not essentially public law duties. In chapters 8 and 9 the argument will be developed that there are bases in common law and equity for the imposition of duties of legality, fairness and rationality in private law in some circumstances, which would include challenges to the decisions of regulatory bodies in sport. In other words, although these bodies may not generally be subject to judicial review because they are not engaged in public or governmental activity, they may be under similar duties to public bodies: there is no substantive public law/private law divide.[3]

CONCLUSIONS

In an article written before the decisions on *O'Reilly v Mackman* and *CCSU*, Harlow argued that 'the "public-private" distinction in the sense of an autonomous set of rules, is wholly incompatible with the English tradition and is unlikely to contribute in any meaningful way to the solution of the many problems which modern administrative law has to overcome.'[4] On the exclusivity rule she argued that 'An exclusive jurisdiction inevitably leads to sterile jurisdictional litigation which distracts attention from substantive issues ... the "public-private" classification is today irrelevant and devoid of intrinsic merit.'[5] It is suggested that the cases since the *O'Reilly* decision – and indeed developments in public administration including privatisation and contracting out of responsibility for services – bear out this view.

The decision in *O'Reilly v Mackman* has proved difficult to operate, and a number of exceptions to it have been recognised by the courts. But the existence of the decision has given rise to assumptions that the substantive law of judicial review is distinct from private law. The focus in the case on supposed differences between public and private law has diverted attention from the fact that before the decision in *O'Reilly v Mackman* there was no firm substantive divide between public law and private law as to the question whether duties of considerate decision making were owed to those affected by decision makers. That is not, of

---

3   See discussion in chapter 9.
4   C Harlow ' "Public" and "Private" law: Definition without distinction' 43 MLR (1980) 241 at p 242.
5   Harlow, op cit at p 251.

course, to say that all private bodies and all public bodies were subject to the same duties in this regard. But it is suggested that seeking out the similarities between public and private law rather than differences will enable us to resolve many of the difficulties caused by the decision in *O'Reilly v Mackman*. It is the purposes of the following chapters to identify and analyse these similarities and their implications for the divide.

Chapter Five

Public Law 2: Interests, Power and Democracy

In this chapter we focus on judicial review as a jurisdiction which protects the interests of individuals and public interests, and controls power. In chapter 2 we examined the theory that the ultra vires rule is the democratic basis for the jurisdiction and suggested that in reality ultra vires is not the rationale; the judicial review jurisdiction rests on common law foundations in favour of putting injustices right. In chapter 4 we explored the exclusivity rule laid down in *O'Reilly v Mackman*. In this chapter we focus on the grounds for judicial review, and for the developing European Community system of public law, and identify the ways in which interests are protected in these systems. We shall also identify the countervailing considerations which lead the courts to refuse to exercise the supervisory jurisdiction in order to establish the similarities in these respects between judicial review and private law.

PUBLIC LAW VALUES

In public law, as in private law, a range of values can be identified at different levels and in different sectors of the subject. Feldman, for instance, has focused on the values of democratic elitism in relation to Parliament, deference to authority in relation to central government, control of the abuse of power by local authorities, and deference to professionals and public administrators, as values implicit in House of Lords' decisions.[1] Galligan shows how values find expression in requirements of procedural fairness, including values of dignity and

---

1   D Feldman 'Public Law Values in the House of Lords' (1990) 106 LQR 246.

respect.[2] The Franks Report,[3] in its consideration of the principles that should govern tribunals and inquiries, identified values of openness, fairness and impartiality.

Some of these values are process orientated – the Franks principles for instance. Others are to do with substance – protection of individuals against the state, upholding the dignity of individuals, deference to Parliament, are examples. Harlow and Rawlings note that there are parallel, often inconsistent strands both in theories about public law and in the actual content of the decisions of the courts and the provisions of statutes. In some respects administrative law displays what they call 'red light' tendencies, restricting the state in the interests of individuals. In other respects administrative law adopts – or has adopted until recently – a 'green light' approach, in which the role of law is to facilitate state action, leaving to the political process the protection of the individual. Between these two poles is an amber light area in which administrative law both protects individuals and facilitates the process of government.[4] Given that our main focus is on the protection of individuals, the following survey is concerned with the ways in which the key values identified in chapter 3 operate in judicial review. It will be helpful to divide the cases into categories, starting with procedural fairness and legitimate expectations, and moving on to some of the ramifications of review for rationality.

Procedural fairness

We shall see in later chapters how procedural fairness is a requirement in some private decision making; for instance in a decision to dismiss an employee,[5] and expulsion from a professional association, trade union, and pension and insurance arrangements.[6] But procedural propriety is commonly regarded as preeminently a public law principle.[7] Perhaps this is because an analogy is often drawn with the expulsion of Adam and Eve from the Garden of Eden: God – naturally – gave them an opportunity to put their case before they were both expelled. Their interests in all of the 'key' or common underlying values were at stake.

2   D J Galligan *Due Process and Fair Procedures: A Study of Administrative Procedures* (1996).
3   Report of the Committee on Tribunals and Inquiries (Cmnd 218) (1957).
4   C Harlow and R Rawlings *Law and Administration* (2nd edn, 1998) chapter 3.
5   See chapter 6 on employment.
6   See chapters 8 and 9.
7   See G Richardson 'The legal regulation of process' in G Richardson and H Genn *Administrative Law and Government Action* (1994) for a discussion of the range of rationales for duties of fairness.

Adam blamed Eve. They both received the same, rather harsh (even disproportionate?), punishment.

In *Ridge v Baldwin*[8] the practice of the courts in the years running up to that case of holding that no duty of natural justice arose unless the decision maker was acting judicially (as opposed to administratively) was reversed by the House of Lords. The test, which denied a duty of natural justice in administrative decision making, had been concerned with the process of decision making rather than with the impact of a decision on the individual, had always been rather circular: there was a duty to act judicially ('like a judge') if you were acting as a judge. In other circumstances no such duty arose, implying a positivist-authoritarian conception of the position of a decision maker. In *Ridge* Lord Reid held that the duty to act in conformity with natural justice would prima facie arise wherever there was the exercise of a power to affect a person's rights or interests.[9] The decision thus introduced a broad participative-communitarian principle into decision making in such circumstances.

The question arises, what purpose is to be served by requiring decision makers to adopt fair procedures? Galligan rejects the notion that the purpose is simply to enable the 'victim' of a decision to participate and argues that the most convincing rationale for these duties is that 'participation is of instrumental value in leading to the right or best outcomes.'[10] Fair procedures may affect the substantive quality of the decision, in particular they may secure that the interests of the 'victim' are taken into account and may be afforded protection which they would not receive if the 'victim' were not able to influence the decision. This approach shows how a participative communitarian principle and considerate altruism may be entwined, the former promoting the latter approach to the relationships between those in positions of power and those affected by their decisions.

We shall note in chapters 8 and 9 that private law is mainly victim and impact oriented: the focus in public law cases about natural justice was shifted by *Ridge v Baldwin* from the respondent – the nature of the activity in which he or she was engaged – to the impact on the applicant and the nature of his or her interests that were affected by the decision, drawing public law closer to private law in this respect.

The interests of the applicant in *Ridge* (a Chief Constable who had been dismissed without notice of the charge against him or a proper opportunity for meeting it before the decision to dismiss was taken) were in his status as Chief Constable, his general standing in his

---

8 [1964] AC 40.
9 Lord Reid at 114; see also Lord Hodson at 130.
10 See D J Galligan *Due Process and Fair Procedures: A Study of Administrative Procedures* (1996) at 143. And see *Galligan* chapter 4, passim.

community – since his dismissal carried a slur on his reputation – and his security in the pension he stood to lose. His dignity was also affected by the fact that the decision was taken without his participation, implying that nothing he could say on the matter could be useful or relevant. And of course his autonomy was affected as the decision deprived him of the right to earn his living as he wanted. So the facts of this case provide strong illustrations of the values that will commonly underlie the requirement that fair procedures be followed when decisions are taken. It is, in practice, the fact that a decision will have an impact on these interests of the individual which, whether explicitly or not, will lead the court to require conformity with fair procedures.[11] For instance, in *Cooper v Wandsworth Board of Works*[12] the plaintiff's property rights – from which he derived both autonomy in the sense of freedom to use property as he wished, and security – were protected by the duty of natural justice; in *R v Barnsley Metropolitan Borough Council, ex p Hook*[13] the applicant's security in his livelihood was at stake.

In *R v Chief Constable of West Midlands Police, ex p Carroll*[14] it was held that it had been unfair to refuse a disciplinary hearing to a probationary constable who had been dismissed in circumstances where the impression was given that he had been suspected of an offence. His status in the sense of his reputation, together with the security he lost with his job, were the factors which led to the decision.[15] In each of these cases a hearing would have given additional protection to the applicants in securing that the decision makers were properly informed as to the facts and the applicant's position, and, where reasons are required, by ensuring that the decision was rational. In other words, procedural fairness was designed to secure that a person's interest in dignity, autonomy, respect, status or security will not be irrationally or disproportionately damaged by an ill-informed – or unreasoned – decision.

This is not to deny that values other than individuals' interests in these values might be at stake in some procedural propriety cases. For instance, fairness also leads to openness, and thus to accountability, and this protects not only individuals' interests, but also commercial interests

---

11   See for instance L Tribe *Constitutional Law* (1978) at p 503: protecting human dignity means that an individual is told why he is treated unfavourably and is consulted about what is to be done with him.
12   (1863) 14 CBNS 180.
13   [1976] 3 All ER 452.
14   (1995) 7 Admin LR 45.
15   See also *McInnes v Onslow Fane* [1978] 1 WLR 1520, Megarry V-C for discussion of the need for natural justice if a decision casts a slur on a person, and the absence of such a need in application cases if it does not do so.

and general public interests against irrational or ill-thought out decisions.[16]

Requirements to give reasons enable those affected by decisions both to know why – an indication of respect for them – and to challenge decisions if taken for unlawful or irrational reasons. There is not as yet a general requirement to give reasons for decisions[17] but the case law is building up to a point where reasons will be generally required unless there are strong public policy reasons to withhold them.[18] For instance, they will be required if the decision casts a slur on the applicant's reputation,[19] or if a person's liberty[20] or other highly regarded interest[1] is at stake, or the decision appears aberrant.[2]

The cases on procedural propriety discussed so far have been mainly concerned with the *audi alteram partem* aspect of natural justice. The other limb of the rule is that no one shall be judge in their own cause, in effect a principle of altruism or disinterestedness or, in judicial review, public service and consideration. This duty has parallels in private law, as in the rule that trustees shall not profit from the trust[3] and that membership bodies operating monopolies should not act 'arbitrarily or capriciously' in their own interests, or in restraint of trade;[4] the 'nemo iudex' limb of natural justice, like the 'audi alteram partem' rule, is not uniquely a public law principle.

Overall then the rationales for requirements for procedural fairness in judicial review (and also in private law[5]) include acceptance of the need to give protection to the individual's interests, sometimes requiring altruism or disinterestedness on the part of the decision maker. Allan has drawn a distinction between the rationales for natural justice

---

16 See for instance *Re Pergamon Press* [1971] Ch 388; *R v Independent Television Commission, ex p TSW Broadcasting Ltd* [1996] EMLR 291, HL; *R v Secretary of State for the Environment, ex p Norwich City Council* [1982] QB 808.

17 See eg *R v Gaming Board of Great Britain, ex p Benaim and Khaida* [1970] 2 QB 417; *R v Aylesbury Vale District Council, ex p Chaplin* [1998] JPL 49, CA. See *De Smith, Woolf and Jowell* para 9-039–9-041.

18 See *R v Ministry of Defence, ex p Murray* [1998] COD 134; *De Smith, Woolf and Jowell* chapter 9.

19 See for instance *R v Civil Service Appeal Board, ex p Cunningham* [1992] ICR 816; *McInnes v Onslow Fane* [1978] 1 WLR 1520.

20 *R v Secretary of State for the Home Department, ex p Doody* [1994] 1 AC 531 at 565, per Lord Mustill.

1   *R v Higher Education Funding Council, ex p Institute of Dental Surgery* [1994] 1 WLR 242, Sedley J.

2   See Sir Patrick Neill 'The duty to give reasons' in C Forsyth and I Hare (eds) *The Golden Metwand and the Crooked Cord* (1998).

3   See chapter 8.

4   See the case of *Ipswich Taylors' Case* (1614) 11 Co Rep 53a, 77 ER 1218 and chapter 9.

5   See chapters 6 to 9.

according to two contrasting theories of public law, the majoritarian, which is principally concerned to give effect to the presumed liberal intentions of Parliament; and the communitarian, which promotes a theory of equal citizenship and democracy.[6] These are rough equivalents of the liberal-majoritarian and participative-communitarian strands in democratic theory sketched in chapter 1. Given that rules of natural justice also arise in private law,[7] and that in that context the majoritarian view is of no application, what Allan regards as the communitarian view would best explain the commonalities between public and private law so far as natural justice and procedural fairness are concerned. 'A person's participation in a decision affecting his interests affirms his dignity as a citizen – one whose co-operation is sought with the public purposes in view, rather than someone treated essentially as an object of administration'.[8] In a private situation we could substitute for 'public purpose', 'private purpose' (of the employer, the trade union, or other private body bound by rules of natural justice) and the point about the dignity of the citizen with interests that should be respected in his or her freedom of action, status or security would be equally valid.

Legitimate expectations

As we shall see in chapters 6 to 9, legitimate expectations have parallels in other areas of law: in contract the parallel is with the protection of reliance interests; in equity there are parallels with the protection of the interests of those able to rely on equitable estoppel and interests under trusts.[9] In each of these private situations the law protects the security of individuals in their ability to trust and rely on others. Many of the legitimate expectation cases in judicial review are concerned with protecting these same interests of individuals. In the *Liverpool Taxi*[10] case, for instance, the security – the livelihoods – of existing taxi drivers were put at risk by a possible decision by the corporation to increase the number of licences in the area. And, to the extent that the case was about the fact that the taxi operators had been led to expect to be consulted and the corporation was held to its undertaking to consult, the case upholds

---

6 T R S Allan 'Fairness, equality, rationality: Constitutional theory and judicial review' in C Forsyth and I Hare (eds) *The Golden Metwand and the Crooked Cord* (1998).

7 See chapters 6 (employment), 8 (contract) and 9 (public policy).

8 Allan, supra, at p 30.

9 See in particular per Robert Walker J in *Scott v National Trust* [1998] 2 All ER 705 at 716, discussed in chapter 8.

10 *R v Liverpool Corpn, ex p Liverpool Taxi Fleet Operators' Association* [1972] 2 QB 299, CA.

the security of those who are promised consultation in their ability to trust or rely on public bodies, as well as the protection of their security in their livelihoods.

The *Ex p Khan*[11] case – which held the Home Office to the criteria it had distributed to would-be adopters of children from overseas – is an example of a case which upholds the autonomy in the sense of freedom of action of adopters, and their status[12] and security (children are considered to guarantee security in old age to their parents in some communities). The *Ruddock*[13] case gave people a degree of security against having their telephones tapped arbitrarily and outside published guidelines, and protected the dignity and autonomy that go with knowing that one's privacy will be respected.

These legitimate expectation cases illustrate, among other things, how the courts recognise that trust is an important source of security for individuals – and indeed for the public interest.[14] (In later chapters we shall see that private law too imposes duties of trust, confidence and reliability on those dealing with individuals, especially in matters which affect their security in other ways such as contract,[15] employment[16] and trusts.[17]) Thus, although there have been judicial and extra-judicial differences of opinion about the extent of legitimate expectations and in particular to what extent substantive expectations receive substantive as opposed to procedural protection,[18] it is suggested that the underlying reason why legitimate expectations are protected at all, when they are protected, is to protect the interests of individuals, especially in their security, and – an important aspect of security – trust. This is, in reality, what the principle of legal certainty, an aspect of the rule of law, is about. Looked at from this point of view there would be nothing strange about protecting substantive legitimate expectations by holding a public body to its undertakings, thus imposing a duty of considerate altruism.[19] Clearly allowance has to be made for the needs of government in the public interest to change policy, but this need not rule out holding public

---

11 *R v Secretary of State for the Home Department, ex p Asif Mahmood Khan* [1984] 1 WLR 1337.
12 In the Pakistani community having a child is probably of greater social importance than it is in ethnic English society.
13 *R v Secretary of State for the Home Department, ex p Ruddock* [1987] 1 WLR 1482.
14 See discussion of security and trust in chapter 3.
15 See chapter 8.
16 See chapter 6.
17 See discussion in chapter 8.
18 See for instance Sedley J in *R v Ministry of Agriculture, Fisheries and Food, ex p Hamble Fisheries* [1995] 2 All ER 714; *R v Secretary of State, ex p Hargreaves* [1997] 1 WLR 906, CA; Lord Irvine of Lairg QC in [1996] Public Law 59 at p 73.
19 On substantive legitimate expectations and theories of judicial review and democracy see Allan, op cit, pp 31-34.

bodies to the legitimate expectations they have encouraged in *specific individuals*.

Exceptions to the principles that legitimate expectations should be respected and that public bodies should be trustworthy and consistent may be justified, for instance, where a change of policy is considered by the decision maker to be in the public interest so that substantial public interests would be sacrificed if a change of policy were precluded by the fact that individuals had legitimate expectations that they would be treated in a certain way. However, the extent to which the public body can lawfully alter its policy in relation to a particular individual may depend upon how serious the change would be for the individual and how strong the public policy arguments for change are. In the *Ex p Khan* case, for instance, the detriment to the would-be adopters was very substantial, whereas any detriment to public interests from holding the government to its original published policy were minimal – there was no threatening army of children waiting to be adopted from outside the UK. On the other hand in *R v Secretary of State for the Home Department, ex p Hargreaves*[20] where a change in the policy of allowing prisoners home leave after a particular period disappointed the expectations of prisoners, it was held that the Secretary of State was within his rights to alter the policy, in the interests, as he saw it, of improving public safety and increasing public confidence in the administration of justice. The court took the view that it was entitled to decide whether the change of policy was *Wednesbury* unreasonable, but not to conduct a balancing exercise of fairness as against proportionality. In the earlier case of *Re Findlay* Lord Scarman had emphasised the importance in prison cases of 'the complexity of the matters the Secretary of State has to consider and the importance of the public interest in the administration of parole.'[1] The freedom of governments to change policy was regarded by Lord Diplock in *Hughes v Department of Health and Social Security*[2] as 'something that is inherent in our constitutional form of government.'

The importance of trust on *both* sides in legitimate expectation cases is illustrated by *Preston v IRC*:[3] a taxpayer had agreed to withdraw certain claims for capital loss and interest and was assessed to tax on the basis of information supplied by him. The Inland Revenue later sought to reopen the assessment. In principle the House of Lords accepted that judicial review might be available in such a case if the commissioners had been guilty of action equivalent to a breach of contract or breach of representations may by them. However, in this case the taxpayer did not disclose other information which was significant to the Inland Revenue's

20 [1997] 1 All ER 397.
1 [1985] AC 318 at 337-338.
2 [1985] AC 776 at 788.
3 [1985] AC 835.

decision – he had not made 'the full disclosure which the inspector had the right to expect and on which he plainly relied'. He had not in that sense been trustworthy, and he lost the case.

Out of these cases on legitimate expectations support can be drawn for an anti-authoritarian, anti-majoritarian, pro-participative and pro-considerate-altruism concept of democracy which accepts the importance of individuals' interests not only in their autonomy but in their security and their place in or access to civil society.

Rationality

We shall see in the following four chapters how private decisions may give rise to remedies if they are arbitrary or capricious. Under the unfair dismissal rules in employment employers must not act outside the 'band of reasonable responses to the employee's conduct'.[4] Trustees of private trusts must act reasonably when exercising discretion.[5] Pension trustees must not take into account irrelevant, improper or irrational factors, and their decision must not be one that no reasonable body of trustees properly directing themselves could have reached.[6] Directors are under fiduciary duties of good faith towards the company.[7] They must not in general fetter their future discretion, and they must exercise their own independent judgment.[8] The controlling groups of bodies such as trade unions are in a fiduciary position and are under a general obligation to act in good faith, not corruptly, or arbitrarily or capriciously.[9] Regulators of common callings and the governing bodies in sport and other occupations are under duties not to act arbitrarily or capriciously, which may include duties not to discriminate.[10]

The parallels with the duties in judicial review not to act 'Wednesbury unreasonably'[11] or, in terms of Council of Civil Service Unions v Minister for the Civil Service[12] 'irrationally' are clear. A decision will only be reviewed if it goes outside the four corners of the power granted to the

4   Per Browne-Wilkinson J in Iceland Frozen Foods Ltd v Jones [1983] ICR 17 at 24-25.
5   Re Turner [1897] 1 Ch 536. See chapter 8.
6   See Edge and others v Pensions Ombudsman [1998] 2 All ER 547, Sir Richard Scott VC.
7   P Davies Gower's Principles of Modern Company Law (6th edn, 1997) (henceforth Gower) pp 599-623. Percival v Wright [1902] 2 Ch 421.
8   Gower pp 608-610.
9   On trade unions see Maclean v Workers' Union [1929] 1 Ch 602; on clubs see Dawkins v Antrobus (1881) 17 Ch D 615.
10   See discussion in chapter 9.
11   See Associated Provincial Picture Houses v Wednesbury Corpn [1948] 1 KB 223.
12   [1985] AC 374, HL.

decision maker. The parallel with the bounds of reasonableness test for employers is plain.[13] In judicial review a decision will be reviewed if the decision maker took irrelevant considerations into account, failed to take account of relevant information, acted in bad faith, or if the decision was so unreasonable that no reasonable decision maker would have taken it. Again, the parallels with private law decision making are clear.[14]

In both public and private law, then, rules against irrationality – when they apply – are designed to protect individuals' interests. They require consideration, an aspect of the responsible altruism strand in democratic theory outlined in chapter 1. With the coming into effect of the Human Rights Act[15] in 2000 these interests will receive enhanced protection, introducing substantive standards of rationality into the system, and limiting the scope of discretion. This Act will move judicial review from what has been hitherto a predominantly formal conception of rationality which 'eschews the application of general principles of fair treatment and equal justice'[16] towards a 'considerate altruism' concept under which a decision maker 'cannot be at liberty to accord a high or low importance to a fundamental right … as he chooses.'[17] Given that principles of rationality very similar to those in judicial review are applied in private law, and that in private law there can be no pretence of giving effect to presumed legislative intent, the logic seems to be that the purpose of the rationality test in both public and private law is – or will increasingly become – to further this 'considerate altruism' purpose of the common law.

The *Wednesbury* test: relevance and irrelevance

In most public law cases in which issues of relevance arise the enabling statute expresses or implies relevant considerations. Much of the case law is on planning and compulsory purchase, and here the interests of individuals will be placed high in that it is recognised that refusing planning permission and compulsorily acquiring land inevitably interfere with the autonomy and security of individuals as owners. The system is constructed so as to provide safeguards for individuals, and yet

---

13 See chapter 6.
14 It was noted in chapter 1 that Lord Greene MR was a Chancery specialist, who drew explicitly on equitable principles for the control of discretion in formulating the *Wednesbury* test.
15 See chapter 10.
16 Allan (1998) at p 27. But compare J L Jowell and A Lester 'Beyond *Wednesbury*: towards substantive principles of administrative law' [1987] Public Law 386.
17 Allan (1998) at pp 27-28.

to weigh against them the interests of neighbours and general public interests.

In judicial review there are relatively few cases in which the range of relevant interests has had to be drawn from the common law rather than the statute. But *Wheeler v Leicester City Council*[18] provides an illuminating guide to the way in which the interests of individuals will be recognised as of importance under the head of relevance. A demand made by a local authority of the committee of a rugby club that the committee members express opposition to sporting links with South Africa under pain of loss of a licence to use sports facilities owned by the council was held to be unlawful on the grounds that it was a punishment of the club when they had done no wrong, and that it brought illegitimate pressure to bear on them. This first ground in effect required that the council should respect the club's members' liberty to form and express their own opinions, so both autonomy and respect were in issue; the second ground asserted autonomy, freedom from being subjected to exercises of power in a way that effectively limits freedom of action. The power of the council derived from its ownership of the land used by the club, in Galbraith's terms compensatory power,[19] though regulated by the Open Spaces Act 1906. In *Wheeler* the security of the club in its enjoyment of facilities provided by the council was at stake, and the decision in favour of the club protected its continued enjoyment of that facility.

Discrimination

Discriminatory decision making is an affront to the dignity of individuals.[20] As Allan puts it: 'The principle of equal citizenship requires the more demanding justification for the uneven imposition of burdens (or withholding of benefits) according to the significance for the human dignity of those affected.' Discrimination raises issues first, as to the relevance of the characteristics which found the discrimination (sex, sexual orientation, age and so on), and secondly, the weight that decision makers should give to the importance to an individual of their dignity in receiving equal treatment and not being subjected to inferior treatment. The common law has a mixed record on discrimination. In chapter 9 it will be noted that the common callings cases, and public policy cases such as *Nagle v Feilden* show the common law opposing discrimination. On the other hand the record of the courts in areas such as admission to membership of clubs shows them to favour the autonomy

18 [1985] AC 1054.
19 See discussion of Galbraith in chapter 2.
20 See discussion of dignity and discrimination in chapter 3.

of members to the dignity and freedom from discrimination of those seeking membership.

In judicial review, too, the courts have a mixed record when faced with discriminatory decisions.[1] Discrimination could be regarded as irrational within Lord Diplock's categorisation of grounds of review in the CCSU[2] case. In *Kruse v Johnson*[3] it was decided that byelaws could be held unreasonable and therefore ineffective because of 'partial and unequal treatment in their operation as between different classes'. In the case of *IRC v National Federation of Self Employed and Small Businesses*[4] the House of Lords indicated that the courts would intervene if satisfied that there was discrimination on the part of the IRC between different classes of taxpayer. In *Prescott v Birmingham Corpn*[5] it was held that the award of free bus passes for the elderly was unlawful because it was discriminatory, albeit it discriminated in favour of generally underprivileged persons.

However, in *Roberts v Hopwood* the court found a policy of equal pay for women to be eccentric and struck it down. And the courts have not been willing to hold discrimination on grounds of sexual orientation in the armed forces to be unlawful.[6] Hence in this area the courts have been inconsistent in dealing with discrimination and have not adopted a consistent policy of upholding the dignity of individuals in the face of discrimination.

Relevance and weight

In private law supervisory jurisdictions (for instance in relation to restraint of trade, employment, trusts and directors' duties) the courts generally leave it to the decision maker to decide how much weight to attach to relevant considerations. However, as will be suggested in chapter 9, *Nagle v Feilden* may be taken as an example of the courts condemning the lack of weight given to the importance of the plaintiff's opportunity to earn her living as she wished. But generally in private law cases questions of weight have not troubled the courts. This is not the case, however, in judicial review.[7]

---

1   See J L Jowell 'Is equality a constitutional principle?' (1994) 47 Current Legal Problems 1.
2   *Council of Civil Service Unions v Minister for the Civil Service*, supra.
3   [1898] 2 QB 291.
4   [1982] AC 617.
5   [1955] Ch 210.
6   *R v Ministry of Defence, ex p Smith* [1996] QB 517, CA.
7   See T R S Allen 'Pragmatism and theory in public law' (1988) 104 LQR 422.

The case law on the question how much weight should be given to a relevant consideration in judicial review is inconsistent. Forbes J in *Pickwell v London Borough of Camden* said that 'when exercising its supervisory jurisdiction the court is not concerned with whether due or proper weight is given to a material consideration: the weight to be given to such a matter is for the body exercising the discretion to determine; the court will no more substitute its own view of the importance of any relevant matter than it will do so for any other matter of statutory discretion.'[8]

However, later cases have taken a different view. *West Glamorgan County Council v Rafferty*[9] is a good illustration of the ways in which the interests of individuals in the key values are to be weighed up against other considerations; it also illustrates the fact that public bodies do not have their own interests in the values, including freedom to use their property as they wish – so their own interests cannot be weighed in the balance; public interests may, however, be given some weight.[10] *Rafferty* was a challenge to a decision by the council to evict gipsies from property owned by it and which it required for development. The gipsies were trespassers, but the council was and had been for many years in breach of its statutory duty to provide adequate accommodation for gipsies residing in or resorting to its area. The council were seeking eviction of the gipsies, who countered with an application for judicial review to quash the decision of the council to apply for a possession order. The council were not offering the gipsies alternative accommodation. Ralph Gibson LJ, with whom Slade LJ and Sir John Megaw agreed, said 'The court is not, as I understand the law, precluded from finding a decision to be void for unreasonableness merely because there are admissible factors on both sides of the question. If the weight of the factors against eviction must be recognised by a reasonable council, properly aware of its duties and its power, to be overwhelming, then a decision the other way cannot be upheld if challenged.'[11]

In the *Rafferty* case the security of the gipsies was at stake – if evicted without alternative accommodation being available they would have no lawful place to live, their children would have to change schools and so on. These considerations, taken with the fact that the council were in breach of their duties to provide sites for gipsies, had to be weighed against the property rights of the council. It was clear that those rights

8   [1983] QB 962 at 990.
9   [1987] 1 All ER 1005.
10 See discussion of state interests later in this chapter.
11 At 1021. See also *South Oxfordshire District Council v Secretary of State for the Environment* [1981] 1 WLR 1092 where the court quashed the decision of the Secretary of State in a planning matter, where he had attributed undue weight to a circumstance which was admittedly a relevant one. And see *British Oxygen Co v Ministry of Technology* [1971] AC 610 – too much weight should not be attached to a policy.

on their own could not outweigh the other considerations, including the interests of the gipsies, and the Court of Appeal therefore upheld the grant of certiorari to quash the decision of the council to apply for possession.

The case shows how the courts require not only that relevant considerations such as the impact on individuals of a decision must be taken into account, but also that the consideration be given due weight – and the courts are the judges of whether due weight was given. The same approach is found in the 'super-*Wednesbury*' case law, where, for instance, the right to life is at stake. Thus in *Bugdaycay v Secretary of State for the Home Department*[12] an applicant for asylum feared for his life should his application fail and he be returned to his home country. Lord Bridge stated that: 'The limitations on the scope of [the court's power of review] are well known … Within those limitations the court must, I think, be entitled to subject an administrative decision to the more rigorous examination, to ensure that it is in no way flawed, according to the gravity of the issue which the decision determines. The most fundamental of all human rights is the individual's right to life and when an administrative decision under challenge is said to be one which may put the applicant's life at risk, the basis of the decision must call for the most anxious scrutiny.'[13] By implication a decision maker should give great weight to the importance of the right to life when weighing up relevant considerations in such a case.

In *R v Secretary of State for the Home Department, ex p Brind*,[14] despite the fact that the court decided in favour of the Secretary of State, it was stressed by Lord Ackner that in a case involving a fundamental human right close scrutiny must be given to the reasons provided as justification for the interference with that right;[15] and Lord Bridge maintained that in a free speech case nothing less than an important competing public interest will be sufficient to justify limiting it.[16] Each of these cases required a decision maker to give particular weight to certain kinds of interests that will be affected by the decision.[17]

---

12 [1987] AC 514.
13 At 531. See also *R v Secretary of State for the Home Department, ex p Launder* [1997] 1 WLR 839, HL.
14 [1991] 1 AC 696.
15 Ibid at p 757.
16 Ibid at 748-749. See generally P Walker 'Unreasonableness and proportionality' in M Supperstone and J Goudie (eds) *Judicial Review* (2nd edn, 1997).
17 See also *R v Secretary of State for the Home Department, ex p Handscomb* (1988) 86 Cr App Rep 59 where the Home Secretary had decided not to release a prisoner because he had committed a minor misdemeanour while on temporary release some years earlier. The weight accorded to the relatively minor misdemeanour as against the importance to the prisoner of his liberty was taken to render the decision unreasonable. See J L Jowell 'Restraining the State. Politics, principle and judicial review' [1997] CLP 189 at 208.

Rationality – intensity of review

It is helpful to distinguish between the weight and the intensity of review. These words are sometimes used interchangeably, but here they are used to bring out a distinction which needs to be drawn between two aspects of review. Considerations of weight are concerned with the seriousness of the impact on individuals of decisions, and in particular the weight to be given to their interests by decision makers. There are other, related, issues to do with the *intensity* of review, which depends upon the nature of the body being subjected to review and the general decision making and appeal or review structure.[18] Our concern here is particularly with the intensity of review of decisions that affect individuals' interests. As Black and Muchlinski have put it: 'Simply determining that the body is or should be public and subject to judicial review does not end the debate. ... The question then arises as to the appropriate degree of intensity of review which should apply to the body's decisions. Should statutory and non-statutory bodies be subject to different intensities of judicial review?'[19] In practice, for instance, commercial regulators are subject to a less intense form of judicial review for irrationality than other respondents, for a range of reasons. In the normal case a body such as the Takeover Panel 'will retain a very wide discretion as to how it performs the task it sets itself and the Court will regard its role as being one of last resort reserved for plain and obvious cases.'[20] Walker suggests that 'In the context of review for unreasonableness I think one can say that the courts have recognised that the need for speedy and effective regulation of takeovers is such that very great caution should be exercised before concluding that an apparent departure from logic or accepted moral standards has gone beyond the limits of reasonableness.'[1] There also appears to be a lower standard of legitimate expectations in relation to self-regulatory bodies.[2]

Another reason for reduced intensity or even refusal of review might be that the decision maker has expertise which the courts lack and which, in effect, makes the issue less justiciable than in cases where no particular

---

18   See *De Smith, Woolf and Jowell*, supra paras 13-055 – 13-069.

19   J Black and P Muchlinski 'Introduction' in J Black, P Muchlinski and P Walker (eds) *Commercial Regulation and Judicial review* (1998) p 9.

20   Per Woolf L J in *R v Panel on Take-overs and Mergers, ex p Guinness Plc* [1990] 1 QB 146 at 193.

1   P Walker 'Irrationality and commercial regulators' in J Black, P Muchlinski and P Walker (eds) op cit at p 165.

2   See Colin Scott 'Regulatory relations in the UK utilities sector' in J Black, P Muchlinski and P Walker (eds) op cit pp 38-41; *R v British Advertising Clearance Centre, ex p Swiftcall District Council* (1995) LEXIS Enggen Library, cases file.

expertise is required on the part of the decision maker.[3] Further, there is a view that regulatory bodies often form a 'mini-legal system' which it would be wrong for the courts to interfere with, on grounds of constitutional pluralism.[4]

Questions of the appropriateness and intensity of review of 'mini-legal systems' are not, however, confined to judicial review. They also arise in private law supervisory jurisdictions. Intensity issues form part of the debate about review of regulatory bodies in sport.[5] A concern not to intervene in 'mini-legal systems' goes some way to explain the decision in *Page v Hull University Visitor*[6] that the decision of a university visitor was not subject to judicial review unless he acted outside his jurisdiction or abused his power in a manner wholly incompatible with his judicial role or acted in breach of the rules of natural justice. The same argument lies behind the view (which does not appear to command much support in the United Kingdom) that the employment relationship should not be subjected to legal regulation.[7]

On the other hand, and in favour of review – though possibly review of light intensity – of 'mini-legal systems' is the consideration that these bodies should be under legally imposed obligations to act in accordance with community norms and values, respecting each individual's freedoms, rights and ability to participate fully in the self-governing process of the body.[8] In effect, even if they are 'private' bodies, they should conform to participative-communitarian and responsible altruism models of governance. This seems to be the prevalent view in English law, being reflected both in the cases where the courts have accepted jurisdiction in judicial review of regulatory bodies, and outside judicial review in statutory provisions (as in employment rights, discussed in chapter 6) and in the common law relating to duties of considerate decision making in contract, restraint of trade and other situations discussed in chapters 8 and 9.

---

3   This consideration may explain the refusal of judicial review in *R v Higher Education Funding Council, ex p Institute of Dental Surgery* [1994] 1 WLR 242, DC.
4   See for instance H Arthurs 'Rethinking administrative law: A slightly Dicey business' (1979) 17 Osgoode Hall LR 1.
5   See discussion in chapter 8; James A R Nafziger 'International sports law as a process for resolving disputes' (1994) 45 ICLQ 130. See also Julia Black 'Constitutionalising Self-regulation' (1996) 59 MLR 24 for a discussion of the subjection of self-regulating bodies to judicial review.
6   [1993] AC 682.
7   Karl E Klare 'The public-private distinction in labor law' (1982) 130 U Pa LR 1358 at p 1417.
8   Black and Muchlinski, supra, at p 7.

Public law values – summary

In summary, then, in this consideration of the values in public law and in particular the extent to which the values we have identified as common to both public and private law are reflected in judicial review, there are strong threads supporting in general terms the need to protect the interests of individuals in their freedom of action, their dignity, respect, status and security from state intrusion unless that interference is clearly authorised by statute or by countervailing public interest considerations. In some of these cases the courts are developing participative-communitarian and responsible altruism models which recognise and weigh in the balance the interests of individuals when decisions are being made that affect them. These values have to be weighed against public interests in ways that do not arise in private law, which is less concerned than public law with weighing public interests against private interests, and more concerned with balancing conflicting private interests. This brings us to the next issue, does the state, like private bodies in positions of power, have interests of its own that it may lawfully promote against those of private individuals?

THE INTERESTS OF THE STATE

We shall see in the next four chapters that private decision makers are under varying duties of altruism in their decision making. Trustees must not profit from the trust, doctors must act in the patient's interests (though it is not clear whether these interests are defined by the patient or the doctor), professional bodies must not act solely in their own interests, employers have responsibilities for their employees and parents for their children. However, the general rule, subject to specific exceptions such as those outlined above, is that private individuals and commercial bodies are entitled to act in their own interests as they perceive them to be. Are state bodies any different in this respect? State bodies commonly claim to be entitled to the benefit of the five key values. In *Rafferty*, discussed above, the council claimed the right of a property owner to use its land as it wished. In *Wheeler v Leicester City Council* the council was seeking to use its land freely as a private landowner would.[9]

In the nature of things public bodies and individual officials or ministers will from time to time seek protection of their own freedom of action (autonomy), their dignity and the respect to which they consider themselves entitled. All too often public bodies will be concerned to

---

9   See also *R v Somerset County Council, ex p Fewings*[1995] 1 WLR 1037, CA. And note comments by Laws J at first instance: [1995] 1 All ER 513, discussed below.

protect their own status and security against pressures of public opinion and accountability – as we saw, for instance, in the account of *Bagg's case* in chapter 2, where the Mayor and commonalty of Plymouth expressed concern to protect their own authority, ostensibly in the interests of public order but, one suspects, for the sake of their own dignity, respect and status.

In the earlier case of *Rooke v Withers* Sir Edward Coke had been concerned with a case about the exercise of discretion by the Commissioners of Sewers. He stated: '... although the words of the commission give authority to the commissioners to act according to their discretion, their proceedings ought nevertheless to be limited and bound within the rule of reason and law, for discretion is a science ... and they are not to act according to their wills and private affections.'[10] (In that case the Commissioner of Sewers had imposed on one landowner charges for repairs to a river bank from which other riparian owners had also benefited. This decision was held to be contrary to the law and reason.)

Deference to authority

Such cases raise issues about the public interest in upholding the authority of those in positions of public power, and the deference which is owed to public bodies by individuals and by the courts when dealing with disputes between public bodies and others. They raise issues about the place of positivist authoritarianism in judicial review. In cases such as *Bagg's case* and *Rooke v Withers* the courts evinced a sceptical attitude to authority. But many cases have manifested judicial deference to public bodies, especially the Crown. The *Shipmoney* case, *R v Hampden*[11] and *Liversidge v Anderson*[12] are examples of this. The courts still defer to Parliament in not quashing statutory instruments that have been approved by Parliament on the basis that it would not be right to regard them as unreasonable. Thus in the case of *Nottinghamshire County Council v Secretary of State for the Environment* Lord Scarman said: 'If the action proposed complies with the terms of the statute ..., it is not for the judges to say that the action has such unreasonable consequences that the guidance upon which the action is based and upon which the House of

10   (1958) 5 Co Rep 99 at 100.
11   (1637) 3 State Tr 826.
12   [1942] AC 206. The majority decided that 'reasonable cause to believe' did not mean that there must be objectively reasonable cause to believe, but that the minister must have a belief which in his mind was reasonable. The upshot was that the applicant for habeas corpus could be detained on the say-so of the minister.

Commons had notice was perverse and must be set aside. For that is a question of policy for the Minister and the Commons, unless there has been bad faith or misconduct by the Minister.'[13]

Often, in claiming the benefit of the 'key' underlying values for themselves, state bodies' motives will be altruistic ones – efficient, effective public administration requires freedom of action, accountability is expensive and impedes administrative efficiency, state security benefits the whole community. The maintenance of the dignity of those in positions of authority can be of importance in the national interest, particularly in foreign policy.

In this area there are parallels with the employer's prerogatives in private law, where, as we shall see in chapter 6, the courts defer to employers' views of what is in the interests of the company. Tribunals aim for 'the striking of a balance between the need of the employer to control the business for which he is responsible, in the interests of the business itself – and after all it is upon its continued prosperity that everybody's interests depend – a balance between that need, on the one hand, and the reasonable freedom of the employee, on the other.'[14]

How much autonomy do public bodies enjoy?

There are two inconsistent strands in the developing case law in England about the area of state autonomy. Lord Woolf has expressed the view that public bodies, like private bodies, are entitled to a private life.[15] The *Malone* case of 1979 assumed that state bodies with legal personality that was not explicitly limited in its scope had the same freedom of action as individuals,[16] and thus that they did not have to justify their actions in terms of the public interest – or against any other criteria. That was a case about telephone tapping and the assumption was that, as there was nothing intrinsically unlawful – whether tortious or otherwise – about a telephone tap, a decision to do such a thing could not be subjected to judicial control. In 1993 in the *Hibbit and Saunders* case[17] the court decided that judicial review of the tendering process in contract

13 [1986] AC 240 at p 250. See also *R v Secretary of State for the Environment, ex p London Borough of Hammersmith and Fulham* [1991] 1 AC 521.
14 *Boychuk v H J Symons Holdings Ltd* [1977] IRLR 395 at 396.
15 'Public law – private law: Why the divide?' [1986] Public Law 220 at 223.
16 *Malone v Metropolitan Police Comr* [1979] Ch 344, Sir Robert Megarry V-C. See also John Allison's discussion of the law relating to 'the state' as being part of the law of persons in 'Theoretical and institutional underpinnings of a separate administrative law' in M Taggart (ed) *The Province of Administrative Law* (1997) at pp 74-75.
17 *R v Lord Chancellor, ex p Hibbit and Saunders (a firm)* [1993] COD 326, (1993) Times, 12 March.

was not available, even though the tenderer in that case had been treated unfairly by the government department, thus lending support to the principle that public bodies – or at least the Crown in the exercise of its common law contracting powers – have the same freedom of action and autonomy as private bodies in that area of activity.[18] The whole idea of jurisdiction – the ultra vires rule[19] – which has been said to lie at the heart of judicial review in England, rests on the view that, within the four corners[20] of its powers, a public body has freedom of action – autonomy – which the courts should not interfere with.

However, the law on the question of the autonomy of public bodies in England is changing. There is now authority for the view that public bodies must justify their actions against recognised criteria, and cannot simply rely on the same freedom of action as individuals enjoy. Laws J in *R v Somerset County Council, ex p Fewings* in 1995 maintained that:

'... for private persons, the rule is that you may do anything you choose which the law does not prohibit. It means that the freedoms of the private citizen are not conditional upon some distinct and affirmative justification for which he must burrow in the law books. Such a notion would be anathema to our English legal traditions. But for pubic bodies the rule is opposite, and of another character altogether. It is that any action must be justified by positive law. A public body has no heritage of legal rights which it enjoys for its own sake ... The rule is necessary in order to protect people from arbitrary interference by those set in power over them.'[1]

Sir John Laws repeated this position in his article on 'Public Law and Employment Law':[2] he suggests that the true difference between public and private law is 'whereas for the private individual everything is permitted that is not forbidden, for the public body, all its actions must be justified by positive law.' (Significantly he goes on to say that 'Yet

---

18 See also T C Daintith 'Regulation by contract: the new prerogative' [1979] *Current Legal Problems* 41 and 'The Executive Power Today' in J Jowell and D Oliver (eds) *The Changing Constitution* (3rd edn 1995); B V Harris 'The "third source" of authority for government action' (1992) 108 LQR 626.

19 See discussion in chapter 2. See De Smith, Woolf and Jowell *Judicial Review of Administrative Action* (5th edn paras 5-041 – 5-043; D Oliver 'Is the ultra vires rule the basis of judicial review?' [1987] Public Law 543; B V Harris 'The "third source" of authority for government action' (1992) 108 LQR 626.

20 *Associated Provincial Picture Houses v Wednesbury Corpn* [1948] 1 KB 223, per Lord Greene MR.

1   [1995] 1 All ER 513. See G Nardell 'The Quantock Hounds and the Trojan Horse' [1995] Public Law 27.

2   [1997] PL 455.

behind both the law's principle – that abuse of power is not to be tolerated – is the same'.)[3]

It will be noted that this broad statement is not consistent with the decisions in *Malone* and *Hibbit and Saunders* noted above, but it encapsulates a movement towards the position that public bodies do not have interests of their own or residual, unreviewable freedoms. They must justify their actions in terms of the public interest, not their own interests. They are under duties of altruism and public service, and they are not entitled to protection of their dignity, autonomy, respect, status or security in their own right: in effect they are subject to principles of considerate altruism.

Where public bodies are owners of property they do not have what Harris has called the 'crucial feature of legitimate self-seeking exploitation'.[4] The case of *Hazell v London Borough of Hammersmith and Fulham*[5] illustrates the point: it was held that local authorities do not have the freedom enjoyed by private owners to use the money in their possession as they wish, for instance to enter into risky loan-swap arrangement. Harris concludes that 'ownership' by public bodies is in reality only 'quasi-ownership' because of the restrictions on the freedom to exercise the normal rights of property owners.[6]

An earlier example of the courts making it plain that ministers are not entitled to act in their own interests, including their interests in escaping criticism in Parliament, is provided by *Padfield v Minister of Agriculture*[7] in which Lord Upjohn observed that a decision or policy must not be based on political considerations.[8] The Committee on Standards in Public Life's Seven Principles of Public Life include a duty of selflessness, which denies the right of public bodies to act in their own interests.[9] This duty of altruism and public service is, in effect, a pillar of British constitutional theory.

3   Ibid at p 466.
4   J W Harris 'Private and non-private property: what is the difference?' (1995) 111 LQR 421, at p 433.
5   [1992] 2 AC 1.
6   J W Harris, op cit.
7   [1968] AC 997.
8   Compare *R v London Borough of Waltham Forest, ex p Baxter* [1987] 3 All ER 671, CA: a local councillor had voted in accordance with the party line notwithstanding his view that the decision was unreasonable, because he believed that party unity was of great importance in the run up to the general election and he felt that his party's policies were very much in the public interest, even though in this particular respect he thought they were mistaken (at 676). Sir John Donaldson MR held that it could be proper for a local councillor to take the view that it was in the interests of a local government area that his own party should be returned to office and to vote with that outcome in mind.
9   Cm 2850 at p 14. The House of Commons has adopted a *Code of Conduct and Guide to the Rules Relating to the Conduct of Members*: 282 HC Official Report (6th

A further illustration of the position that public bodies do not have legally protected interests of their own is provided by the case law on confidence. Since public sector employers are not owed the same level of confidence by their employees as their private sector counterparts, disclosure of 'official' information may not involve a breach of confidence.[10] So, for instance, where the public interest is served by a disclosure it will involve no breach of confidence.[11] Where duties of confidence do arise in the public sector, they are only upheld to the extent that they do not conflict with the public interest.[12] On the other hand, public employees who 'whistleblow' have been vulnerable to dismissal or disciplinary proceedings,[13] an indication that in this area public bodies enjoy something akin to a right to privacy. (However, with the passing of the Public Interest Disclosure Act 1998 this public 'right to privacy' is greatly diminished.)

Wade and Forsyth note that 'The whole conception of unfettered discretion is inappropriate to a public authority, which possesses powers solely in order that it may use them for the public good. ... It is only where powers are given for the personal benefit of the person empowered that the discretion is absolute. Plainly this can have no application in public law.'[14]

A duty of selflessness and denial of residual freedom of action – autonomy – are consistently imposed on the activities of local authorities, which are normally statutory bodies with explicitly limited powers. The courts have been willing to limit the freedom of action of these authorities by restricting their powers to those expressly granted in enabling legislation, and imposing higher order standards of conduct than they would on ordinary private bodies[15] (though as we shall see in chapters 8

---

series) cols 392-407, 24 July 1996; Third Report from the Committee on Standards and Privileges HC (1995-96) no 604; the *Ministerial Code* (1997) also endorse this view of the restrictions on the freedom of action of government bodies.

10 See discussion of breach of confidence in chapter 9.

11 *Initial Services v Putterill* [1968] 1 QB 396.

12 See *A-G v Jonathan Cape* [1975] 3 All ER 484, QBD, and *A-G v Guardian Newspapers (No 2)* [1990] 1 AC 109, in both of which it was said that lack of a public interest in the disclosure of information is a prerequisite of any duty of confidence. And see L Vickers 'Whistleblowing in the public sector and the European Convention on Human Rights' [1998] Public Law 594.

13 See discussion in chapter 6.

14 Wade and Forsyth *Administrative Law* (7th edn, 1994) at p 393. And see Taggart *Corporatisation, Privatisation and Public Law* (1990).

15 See for instance *R v London Borough of Ealing, ex p Times Newspapers* (1987) 85 LGR 316 (boycotting of newspapers by local authority libraries for political reasons held unlawful); *R v London Borough of Lewisham, ex p Shell UK Ltd* [1988] 1 All ER 938 (boycotting of a company's products by a local authority for political reasons held unlawful); *R v London Borough of Brent, ex p Assegai* (1987) 151 LG Rev 891, DC (restriction of access to public areas of local authority

and 9 private bodies in positions of power are also increasingly subjected to higher order duties). In areas where contracting power is exercised under statutory as opposed to common law powers,[16] the tendering process may also be reviewable: in *R v Legal Aid Board, ex p Donn & Co (a firm)*,[17] Ognall J found that a decision not to award a contract to represent generic plaintiffs in a multi-party action might be challenged in judicial review. The board did not have the same contractual freedom of action as a private individual entitled to autonomy has.

A striking example of a court deciding that public bodies do not have the same interests, rights and freedoms in law as individuals is *Derbyshire County Council v Times Newspapers Ltd*[18] in which the House of Lords opined that 'a democratically elected body should be open to uninhibited criticism. The threat of a civil action for defamation must inevitably have an inhibiting effect on free speech'[19] and held that at common law a local authority did not have the right to maintain an action in defamation to protect its governing reputation, as it would be contrary to the public interest for the organs of government to have that right. Hence the authority in question could not bring an action in defamation[20] – a civil action whose purpose is to protect a person's dignity, respect, status and security in society.[1] The decision applies generally to public bodies – not only elected bodies – exercising governmental and administrative functions, and possibly where a public body is exercising broader functions.[2] It also applies to political parties.[3] It is not clear to what extent the principle may extend to private – or privatised – bodies exercising public functions.[4]

---

buildings held unlawful); *Wheeler v Leicester City Council* [1985] AC 1054 (withdrawal of licence to use local authority sports field for political reasons held unlawful); *West Glamorgan County Council v Rafferty* [1987] 1 All ER 1005, CA (local authority's claim for possession of its land defeated by the failure of the authority to fulfil its statutory duty to provide legitimate sites); *R v Wear Valley District Council, ex p Binks* [1985] 2 All ER 699 (local authority's withdrawal of an informal licence to a stall holder to set up on the authority's land was subject to review – see discussion of this case in chapter 4). And see S Arrowsmith 'Judicial review and the contractual powers of local authorities' (1990) 106 LQR, 277.

16 See *R v Lord Chancellor, ex p Hibbit and Saunders*, supra.
17 [1996] 3 All ER 1.
18 [1993] AC 534, HL.
19 Ibid per Lord Keith at 547.
20 Except malicious falsehood.
1   See chapters 3 and 8.
2   See Barendt 'Libel and freedom of speech in English law' [1993] Public Law 449. But on the question whether a Member of Parliament may sue for defamation in relation to his parliamentary functions, see *Hamilton v Al Fayed* [1999] 3 All ER 317, CA; Defamation Act 1996, section 13.
3   *Goldsmith v Bhoyrul* [1997] 4 All ER 268, Buckley J.
4   See *Reynolds v Times Newspapers* [1998] 3 WLR 862; I Loveland 'The constitutionalisation of political libels?' [1998] PL 633.

EUROPEAN INFLUENCES IN ENGLISH PUBLIC LAW

Within the European Community a new system of public law is developing, with sources in the Community treaties, directives (especially on public procurement), the jurisprudence of the European Court of Justice,[5] and what are seen to be general principles of law common to many member states. It is likely that the techniques developed by the European Court of Justice will influence the development of public law in the member states – and indeed that the public law systems of each state may influence others. A process of cross-fertilisation is already taking place.[6] As far as English public law is concerned the systems of France and Germany seem likely to be the most influential. Already the influence of civil law based doctrines of proportionality, legality and equality are being felt in English law.[7] And English law developments in the field of procedural propriety have influenced developments in Europe.

A public-private divide in European law

Let us consider the likely influence of European law on public-private divides in English law. In European Community law and in the law of the member states with civil law systems, public-private divides exist.[8] In many member states there are special administrative courts, and the substantive law that applies to public bodies is different from that which applies to private bodies.[9] A question that arises therefore is whether the position in the civil law systems in Europe will influence English law to retain or develop a firm public-private divide, or whether the internal logic of the common law as it develops in England, and the influences of common law systems elsewhere[10] will prevail on this question.

One way in which European Union law is already imposing on United Kingdom law a public-private divide is on the question of the vertical

5   See T Hartley *The Foundations of European Community Law* (4th edn, 1998); De Smith, Woolf and Jowell *Judicial Review of Administrative Action* (5th edn, 1995); J Schwarze *European Administrative Law* (1992).
6   J Bell 'Mechanisms for cross-fertilisation of administrative law in Europe' in J Beatson and T Tridimas (eds) *New Directions in European Public Law* (1998).
7   See De Smith, Woolf and Jowell *Judicial Review of Administrative Action* (1995) chapter 21.
8   For brief discussion of the civil law position, see chapter 1.
9   See generally J Schwarze *European Administrative Law* (1992).
10   See for instance M Taggart (ed) *The Province of Administrative Law* (1997) in which contributions drawing on administrative law developments in Australia, Canada, England, New Zealand, South Africa and the United States of America illustrate how similar problems to do with the public private divide are encountered in each of these countries and how flexible the common law can be, in the absence of statutory constraints, in finding solutions.

and horizontal effects of Community law, considered in the next section. Other areas in which European influences are being felt are the grounds for judicial review, and concepts of fundamental human rights. The influence in judicial review is considered briefly in this chapter, and the fundamental rights aspects are treated in chapter 10.

Vertical and horizontal direct effect

The core of a public-private divide in EU law is the set of rules about the horizontal and vertical direct effect of Treaty provisions and directives. By the Treaty of European Union member states are obliged to give effect to community measures such as Treaty provisions, directives, regulations and decisions. The question whether Treaty provisions have direct effect depends upon whether the article is clear and unambiguous, unconditional, and not dependent on further action being taken by Community or national authorities.[11] Regulations may give rise to rights that are enforceable by individuals in the courts of the member states – in that case they are directly applicable and directly effective.[12] In this sense they are often on a par with Acts of Parliament or statutory instruments in the United Kingdom. Directives, by contrast, are only binding 'as to the result to be achieved' and it is left to member states to choose the form and methods for achieving those results. Generally therefore the expectation is that member states will take legislative measures to implement directives and the directives themselves will not be directly effective or applicable. However, in certain circumstances directives may have direct effect without a member state taking implementing measures. This will be the case where the deadline for implementation has passed, the subject matter is unconditional and sufficiently precise and it gives rise to individual rights.[13] In such a case an individual can enforce those rights against state bodies, but not against private bodies – the directly effective directive has vertical but not horizontal effect.[14] This is where the public-private divide operates in European law.[15] The question whether a particular body is a state body is determined by reference to whether it is 'an emanation of the state', which includes area health authorities, as in *Marshall*, plus chief

11 See *Hartley* p 191; *Van Gend en Loos* [1963] ECR 1.
12 Treaty of European Union, Article 249, previously Article 189, renumbered by the Treaty of Amsterdam.
13 *Becker v Finanzamt Munster-Innenstadt* [1982] ECR 53; *Van Duyn v Home Office* [1974] ECR 1337.
14 *Marshall v Southampton and South West Hampshire Area Health Authority* [1986] ECR 723.
15 See *Hartley* pp 206-211.

constables of police acting in their official capacity[16] and local authorities.[17] It has also been held to include 'a body, whatever its legal form, which has been made responsible, pursuant to a measure adopted by the State, for providing a public service under the control of the State and has for that purpose special powers beyond those which result from the normal rules applicable in relations between individuals.'[18] It has been held by the House of Lords that this covered British Gas, before it was privatised,[19] and, by the High Court, that it includes a privatised water company.[20]

The fact that this vertical public-private divide operates in European law is, however, no reason why domestic public law in England should operate a substantive public-private divide which imposes special duties of fairness and rationality in decision making on public but not private bodies, and provides special procedural privileges for public bodies or those exercising public functions. One reason why directives may have vertical direct effect is that it would be wrong for member states to be able to benefit from their own wrong in failing to take implementing measures,[1] and this argument has no bearing at all on domestic public and private law and the exclusivity rule.

State liability for breach of European law

If a member state fails to implement EC law it may be liable in damages to those who suffer loss as a result: *Francovich v Italy*.[2] The conditions of liability are that the law in question was intended to create individual rights, there is a direct causal link between the loss and the failure to implement, and the breach by the member state was sufficiently serious. Liability arises whichever state organ is responsible for the failure to implement EC law.[3]

This position, and the fact that under the Human Rights Act there may be liability of the state in damages for breaches of Convention rights[4] may bring closer the possibility of a remedy in damages being

16 *Johnston v Chief Constable of the Royal Ulster Constabulary* [1986] ECR 1651.
17 *Fratelli Costanzo SpA v Comune di Milano* [1989] ECR 1839.
18 *Foster v British Gas* [1990] ECR I–3313.
19 *Foster v British Gas* [1991] 2 AC 306.
20 *Griffin v South West Water Services* [1995] IRLR 15.
1   See *Hartley*, pp 206-211.
2   [1991] I-ECR 5357.
3   *R v Secretary of State for Transport, ex p Factortame* (No 3) [1991] ECR I–3905; the Queens Bench Divisional Court found that the applicants were entitled to compensatory but not exemplary damages: *R v Secretary of State for Transport, ex p Factortame (No 5)* [1998] 1 All ER 736.
4   See chapter 10.

developed in domestic 'public' law as well as in European and Human Rights Act cases. This would narrow the public private divide by, in effect, introducing a form of tortious liability where otherwise, in English law, only non-pecuniary remedies would be available in judicial review.

The grounds for review in European law

Among the general principles of law that the European Court of Justice had expounded and adopted from the legal systems of member states are legal certainty, proportionality and equality.[5] For the most part the cases raising these principles have not been concerned with the interests of individuals but with commercial matters. However, they are influential sources which promote the rule of law and good administration, whether or not individuals are affected, and they do give some protection to the interests of private bodies against EC activity.

Legal certainty is principally concerned with retroactivity of law, and is thus close to what in Diceyan terms in England is the rule of law. It promotes the security of individuals – indeed the French term is 'sécurité juridique'. An aspect of legal certainty is the protection of legitimate expectations, a doctrine that protects the security of those who rely on others and, by imposing a duty of reliability, also promotes trust. The German term 'Vertrauensschutz' or 'protection of confidence' conveys the idea. One of the cases brings out the way in which this doctrine protects the security of individuals in the employment relationship: in *EC Commission v EC Council* (known as the first *Staff Salaries* case)[6] the Commission complained that the Council had not granted staff employed by the Community a sufficient increase in pay. A formula for calculating increases had been agreed between the Council, the Commission and staff associations, which was stated to be applicable for three years. It was held that this gave rise to a legitimate expectation that the terms of the agreement would be followed and new scales laid down by the Council were invalid in so far as they departed from it. Here it is notable that a substantive expectation was protected, whereas in English law in principle such expectations will not be protected.

Proportionality is regarded as being another general principle of law, which is not as yet directly recognised as such in England, though it may be an aspect of irrationality.[7] Where the doctrine is invoked the courts have to decide whether the challenged measure imposes disproportionate

5   See generally *Hartley* chapter 5.
6   [1973] ECR 575.
7   See *De Smith, Woolf and Jowell* (1995) paras 13-070 – 13-086; J L Jowell and A Lester 'Proportionality: neither novel nor dangerous' in Jowell and Oliver (eds) *New Directions in Judicial Review* (1988).

burdens on those concerned, and thus give an indeterminate but substantial weight to those interests. As Craig and de Burca put it: 'There must be some ascription of weight or value to those interests, since this is a necessary condition precedent to any balancing operation.'[8] The courts also have to determine what weight to give the public interest, since a balance cannot be achieved unless both sides have a weight. As it develops this doctrine is likely to provide guidelines that may be of utility in English law when the weighing up of interests of individuals against public interests has to take place.

The principle of equality is also part of European public law, which has set its face against irrational discrimination in a series of cases.[9]

Lastly, the right to a hearing has been held to be a general principle of European law: 'a person whose interests are perceptibly affected by a decision taken by a public authority must be give the opportunity to make his point of view known.'[10]

SUMMARY AND CONCLUSIONS

In this chapter it has been shown that judicial review is preeminently about the control of exercises of governmental or public power, particularly where acts or decisions are damaging to the interests of individuals. Its development reflects the constitutional theories that were sketched in chapter 1. In particular judicial review has moved away from principles of positivist authoritarianism towards more participative and altruistic approaches. In both judicial review and European law the courts impose duties of consideration on public decision makers, which protect individuals in their personal autonomy and in their status and involvement in civil society – their citizenship. The standards of fairness and rationality imposed in judicial review reflect a combination of participative-communitarian and considerate-altruism theories of democracy. The state itself, unlike individuals, has no interests.

Influences from Europe will no doubt continue to affect the ways in which the public-private divide, and public law, develop in England. In particular the fact that European law imposes liability in damages on

---

8 *EC Law* (1994) at p 341.
9 *Skimmed Milk Powder* case [1977] ECR 1211 (imposition of requirements on all livestock farmers which only benefitted dairy farmers held to be in breach of the equality principle); *Sabbatini v European Parliament* [1972] ECR 345 (requirement that allowances were paid only to male heads of the family save in exceptional circumstances held to be invalid).
10 *Trans Ocean Marine Paint Association v EC Commission* [1974] ECR 1063, at para 15 of the judgment.

states for certain breaches of European law – under the *Francovich*[11] and *Factortame*[12] decisions – may add impetus to the development of English public law in favour of damage awards – something which would undermine even further the English public-private divide.

11 [1991] I–ECR 5357.
12 [1991] ECR I–3905

The Law of Relationships 1: The Individual and the State, and the Employment Relationship

It was noted in chapter 1 that the early writers on English law, including Blackstone,[1] Hale[2] and Austin,[3] devoted sections of their works to 'The Law of Persons'. In this work they focused on the relationships of sovereign-subject, employment and marriage. In modern terms the relationship of sovereign-subject is conceptualised as the relationship between the individual and the state, or public or governmental bodies, and naturally falls within the scope of public law. Employment and marriage are generally regarded as private relationships, though regulated to a considerable extent by law.

Hale classified relations between the King and subject as 'political',[4] whereas the other relationships were 'oeconomical', meaning domestic.[5] Blackstone regarded employment, marriage and parent/child relationships as the 'great relationships' of private life.[6] While it has long been acknowledged that the sovereign-subject relationship differs in important ways from others, there were, as will be shown, strong similarities between them.

Our purposes in this chapter and the next one are, first, to note how these relationships of individual-state, employment, marriage and parent-child have developed over the last century or so, since they illustrate the

1   See Sir William Blackstone *Commentaries on the Laws of England* vol 1.
2   Sir Matthew Hale *An Analysis of the Civil Part of the Law* (4th edn, 1779).
3   J Austin *Lectures on Jurisprudence* (5th edn 1995) 404-405, 744-759.
4   Sir Matthew Hale *The Analysis of the Law* (1713) London, Walthoe, section XIV, p 45. According to Hale the category of persons or bodies politic covered Corps or bodies created by law (section XXII, p. 56). Relations of natural persons were politic and civil – the latter category including relations between ancestor and heir, lord and tenant, guardian and pupil.
5   *Hale*, supra, section XIV, p 45.
6   *Blackstone* vol 1, chapter 14, at p 423.

history of the infiltration into these areas of the law of the 'key' values identified in chapter 3. Later chapters will note how these values also operate in other areas of private law. The changes that have taken place in the legal aspects of these relationships illustrate well the point made in chapter 3 that the interests of individuals in their dignity, autonomy, respect, status and security have come to be recognised as common values in both public and private law. But they also highlight the tensions between these values as they affect the interests of parties to the relationships, particularly between values of autonomy, dignity and respect on the one hand and status and security on the other, and the tensions between these values and others, such as respect for authority.

Secondly, in this chapter and the next we shall note the legal techniques adopted for the protection of these interests. The baseline in each of these relationships at common law was the almost complete subjection of the inferior party in the relationship to the superior party. But over the last century or more a process of emancipation of the weaker parties to these relationships has taken place. Thus, for instance, the courts have assumed supervisory jurisdictions over decision making that may adversely affect an individual in the individual-state relationship and in employment, through judicial review and the jurisdiction of the Employment Tribunal in unfair dismissal cases respectively. There are also substantive legal protections in the criminal law and the law of tort, and in equity, for these interests in these relationships, many of which have developed only in the last century. For instance, the criminal law has only recently criminalised marital rape; the Crown's liability in tort dates back only to the Crown Proceedings Act 1947; equity has developed the law of trusts so as to grant beneficial interests to non-owning spouses, carrying with them rights of occupation of the matrimonial home; and statutory provisions have established the separate property regime in marriage, granted rights of occupation of the matrimonial home, and introduced the transfer of property jurisdiction of the court on divorce.

THE SOVEREIGN-SUBJECT RELATIONSHIP

The following account of the sovereign-subject or state-individual relationship is of necessity a sketch, designed to bring out the relevant contrasts and parallels with the other 'great' relationships.

The Crown's duty to the subject rested originally upon a semi-feudal bond: the King, as liege lord, was bound to maintain and defend his people in return for their service and obedience. Hale sets out the rights and liberties to be enjoyed by the people, in relation to both the King and all his subordinate magistrates, as: That they be protected by them and treated according to the laws of the Kingdom in relation to their lives, their liberties and their estates.[7] Yet until the passing of the Crown Proceedings Act 1947 no action could be taken in the courts to compel the Crown to fulfil any of its duties. The sovereign personally and the Crown were in effect immune from legal proceedings, even in respect of breaches of contract or torts. This was an aspect of the prerogative of 'perfection' or infallibility attributed to the monarch.[8] The theoretical and historical justification for this no doubt lay in the claim to the Divine Right of Kings, but the more probable pragmatic justification was that the authority of the sovereign needed to be maintained and protected against the chaos that would ensue if government collapsed – Hobbes' justification for the 'Leviathan'.[9] Similar concerns about the implications of undermining the authority of parties to relationships will emerge from discussion of other relationships later in this chapter and the next.[10]

Various devices were developed to mitigate the doctrine of the immunity of the Crown, including the Petition of Right, but it was not until the Crown Proceedings Act came into force that civil actions against the Crown became possible; and it was not until the decision in *M v Home Office*[11] that ministers of the Crown could be committed for contempt for breach of court orders. Hence it was only recently that the duties of the Crown in the sovereign subject relationship could be enforced at the suit of the subject.

At common law the sovereign had certain rights almost analogous to rights of property over his subjects. There was no element of democracy here. People were subjects, not citizens. The sovereign was expected to exercise his powers in the interests of his subjects, but those obligations were not legally enforceable. The sovereign's rights over his subjects included the right to their military or naval service: until the Restoration men could be compulsorily enlisted into the army under writs or Commissions of Array or Lieutenancy; they could be impressed into service in the navy,[12] injuring a man in such a way as to disable him from fighting in defence – military service – was mayhem, a felony and a tort. The duties of the subjects to their monarch which these royal rights implied – obedience and service – were known as allegiance, and were remnants of the feudal period.[13] They were based on trust and

---

7   *Hale*, section XIII, p 42.
8   See *Blackstone* vol 1, chapter 7 at p 246.
9   T Hobbes *Leviathan* (R Tuck, ed 1991).
10   See also discussion of power and authority and *Bagg's case* in chapter 2.
11   [1994] 1 AC 377, HL.
12   The practice of impressment was allowed at common law: *Ex p Fox* (1793) 5 Term Rep 276. From 1815 it began to be abandoned in favour of recruiting by voluntary enlistment.
13   Hale lists the rights and duties to be performed by the people to the King himself as perseverance and honour, fidelity and subjection, all which come under the name of allegiance; and payments of those rights and duties, customs,

confidence.[14] Allegiance was 'the tie, the *ligamen*, which binds the subject to the king, in return for that protection which the king affords the subject.'[15] (As we shall see, similar concepts of a duty of obedience and service on the part of the inferior party to a relationship arose in marriage and the relations of master and servant. Murder of a person to whom allegiance was owed was regarded as treason,[16] high treason if the victim were the monarch,[17] petit treason in other cases.[18])

Emancipation of the individual from the state

The present position as far as relations between the individual and the state are concerned is of course, very different. The Crown and other organs of the state such as the police and local authorities are in principle subject to the rule of law. The Crown still enjoys residual common law powers of a special kind under the prerogative, and certain public bodies benefit from immunities in tort.[19] The law relating to the position of the individual in relations with the state has evolved from the concept of subjecthood towards a concept of citizenship[20] – though a rather crude concept of citizenship – in which individuals have certain legally protected liberties and rights, including rights of participation in the political process and community activity through voting, standing for election, exercise of free speech and free association, and so on. The powers of the

---

subsidies which either by the common law or by Act of Parliament are settled on the King: *Hale*, section XIII, p 42.

14   See *Blackstone* vol 1 at p 366: 'Under the feodal system, every owner of lands held them in subjection to some superior or lord, from whom or whose ancestors the tenant or vasal had received them; and there was a mutual trust or confidence subsisting between the lord and vasal, that the lord should protect the vasal in the enjoyment of the territory he had granted him, and on the other hand, that the vasal should be faithful to the lord, and defend him against all his enemies.'

15   *Blackstone* vol 1, p 366.

16   See *Blackstone* vol. 4, chapter 14: '... the breach of civil or ecclesiastical connections, when coupled with murder, denominates it a new offence, no less than a species of treason, called *parva proditio*, or *petit treason*: which however is nothing else but an aggravated degree of murder; although on account of the violation of private allegiance, it is stigmatised as an inferior species of treason.... Petit treason... may happen three ways; by a servant killing his master, a wife her husband, or an ecclesiastical person his superior'

17   See *Blackstone* vol 4, at pp 74-76.

18   See *Blackstone* vol 4, at pp 203-204.

19   See discussion of immunities in chapter 8.

20   On the legal concepts of citizenship in the United Kingdom see D Oliver 'What is Happening to Relations between the Citizen and the State?' in J Jowell and D Oliver (eds) *The Changing Constitution* (3rd edn, 1994). See also D Heater *Citizenship: The Civic Ideal in World History, Politics and Education* (1990). See further the discussion in chapter 12.

Crown to conscript into military service are now regulated by statute and subject to formal procedures which remove the arbitrariness of the former practice.

The Crown is regarded as having responsibilities towards the citizenry rather than rights over them. The shift from power to responsibility has been gradual. Locke maintained that the Crown had a duty to protect property rights, for instance. (This evolution from the idea that power confers rights to the principle that power confers responsibilities – and duties of altruism – is mirrored in other relations, notably those of parent and child and employer to employees, discussed below.) Unlike many private individuals, the Crown does not have the right to pursue its own rights or interests in its activities.[1] This position was stated strongly by Mr Justice Laws at first instance in *R v Somerset County Council, ex p Fewings*: 'A public body has no heritage of legal rights which it enjoys for its own sake ...'[2] In principle state bodies are required to act in accordance with principles of legality, fairness and rationality[3] – in other words, they are under duties of considerate decision making – in their dealings with individuals. The scope for arbitrary action of former times is much reduced. Hence the position has been reached that, in sharp contrast to the picture as Blackstone painted it, individuals have a considerable degree of autonomy in their relations to the state and elements of participative-communitarian and considerate altruism theory have been introduced into the relationship. Individuals are treated, relatively at least, with respect, their dignity is respected and their security is not liable to be arbitrarily taken from them. All is not of course perfect or unproblematic in these respects – as discussion in other chapters will show – but the contrast with Blackstone's picture brings out the importance of a trend towards recognition of the importance to individuals of their interests in the key values in the development of public law, to which we shall return.

EMPLOYMENT

The employment relationship provides employees with their social status, and their jobs are the main source of financial security for most people.[4] This perspective was put well in the Canadian case *Reference re the Public Service Employee Relations Act*: 'Work is one of the most fundamental

1   See discussion in chapter 5.
2   [1995] 1 All ER 513. See G Nardell 'The Quantock Hounds and the Trojan Horse' [1995] Public Law 27.
3   See *Council of Civil Service Unions v Minister for the Civil Service* [1985] AC 374.
4   For an excellent full account of the law relating to the employment relationship see Simon Deakin and Gillian Morris *Labour Law* (2nd edn, 1998).

aspects of a person's life, providing the individual with means of financial support and, as importantly, a contributory role in society. A person's employment is an essential component of his or her sense of identity, self-worth and emotional well-being.[5] But given the imbalance of power between the employee and the employer, the former is vulnerable to interference with his or her dignity, autonomy and respect in the relationship. Deakin has suggested that 'What is missing is a unifying conception of the right of the individual to the protection of his or her personal dignity and autonomy in relation to employment.'[6] And, as we shall see, employers' prerogatives extend to powers to dismiss and thus to remove the security on which their employees commonly depend.

The discussion that follows will be concerned with how the law deals with these aspects of the relationship. In the space available it is not possible to cover all the ground, and the objective is to seek to identify the trends in the law in this respect. These trends are highlighted if we consider changes in the common law position, as well as statutory developments and European law[7] influences.

At common law the employment relationship was, from a legal point of view, historically a status relationship rather than a contractual arrangement between the parties.[8] The work obligations of the servant depended upon his status – the kind of worker that he was – and his rate of pay was laid down at various periods by the justices of the peace for the area or by statute.[9] Criminal sanctions were available for acts of indiscipline.[10] The relationship was also regarded, in essence, as a personal relationship – an individualist one.[11] But for present purposes the point of interest is that historically the employment relationship had strong parallels with the subject-sovereign relationship and relationships of marriage and parent-child, in each of which the incidents were laid down by law, were regarded as highly individualised and personal, and involved a strongly authoritarian, hierarchical relationship between the parties.

5   Per Dickson LJ in [1987] 1 SCR 313 at 368. These considerations led the court to decide that fair hearings were required before dismissal, by a term implied in the contract. The point illustrates how the recognition of key values can lie behind the imposition of procedures on decision makers.
6   S Deakin 'The utility of "rights talk": Employees' personal rights' in C Gearty and A Tomkins *Understanding Human Rights* (1996) at p 357.
7   See *Deakin and Morris* para 2.6.
8   See discussion of the concept of 'status' in chapter 3.
9   *Blackstone* vol 1, chapter 14.
10   For a history see *Deakin and Morris* chapter 1.
11   See Bob Hepple and Sandra Fredman *Labour Law and Industrial Relations in Great Britain* (2nd edn, 1992) paras 49-51; B Hepple chapter 18 in G S Bain (ed) *Industrial Relations in Britain* (1983).

The legal nature of the employment relationship altered to one of contract from the middle of the nineteenth century, as a result of a series of cases mainly concerned with the position of higher status employees.[12] This is still the way in which the relationship is conceived by the courts. However, there is a heavy overlay of legally imposed obligations on the relationship which gives it some of the characteristics of a status relationship. As Deakin and Morris have said 'The contract may be said to create a form of *status* which, as a source of the norms which govern the relationship of the parties, is separate from their express agreement.'[13]

Public law values in employment law

Under what is now the Employment Rights Act 1996, section 92 an employee who is dismissed is entitled to a written statement of the reasons for his dismissal. This is but one example of the importation of what are commonly – if mistakenly – regarded as public law values into a private relationship. But the courts too have developed a number of techniques for introducing into the contractual employment relationship some of the values normally associated with judicial review – fairness and rationality – through the device of implied contractual terms, or ultra vires.[14] For instance, it has been held that contractual terms may be implied that a hearing should be given before a person is dismissed if the rules of the employing body – such as a trade union – prescribe the conditions in which dismissal is permitted.[15] It has even been suggested that there should be implied duties of procedural propriety before dismissal in all employment contracts,[16] but this does not yet appear to be the law.

In *Clark v BET* the contract of employment provided for the salary to be reviewed annually and increased as the employer should in its absolute discretion decide. It was held that if the employer had capriciously or in bad faith exercised its discretion so as to determine the increase at nil, that would have been a breach of contract.[17] In relying on express terms in a contract which may be disadvantageous to the employee, there is authority for the view that an employer should act 'reasonably'. For instance, Browne-Wilkinson V-C held that the discretion given to an

---

12 See for instance *Emmens v Elderton* (1853) 13 CB 495; *Turner v Goldsmith* [1891] 1 QB 544; *Price v Mouat* (1861) 11 CBNS 508; and *Deakin and Morris* at para 1.2.
13 At p 132. See generally on this point *Deakin and Morris* para 3.2.
14 See *Deakin and Morris* para 5.3.
15 *Stevenson v United Road Transport Union* [1977] ICR 893.
16 *R v Derbyshire County Council, ex p Noble* [1990] IRLR 332 at p 337.
17 [1997] IRLR 348 at p 349.

employer, under the terms of an occupational pension scheme, to agree to increases in pensions, was not unqualified: the employer was not obliged to agree to an increase, but it was obliged to exercise its powers in good faith and avoid an arbitrary or capricious result – a set of tests very similar to *Wednesbury* unreasonableness in judicial review.[18] However, the case law is developing in this area and it cannot yet be confidently said that there are general duties of fairness and rationality on the part of an employer in the employment contract – or in tort.[19]

Remedies in private law for breach of employment contracts have developed so as to provide protection for employees facing disadvantageous changes in the terms of employment, or disciplinary measures or dismissal which are similar in many respects to the protection provided in judicial review for those whose interests have been adversely affected by decisions by public bodies.[20] For instance, injunctions may be available to restrain attempts by an employer to vary a contract unilaterally or to dismiss an employee in breach of contractual terms.[1] However, the cases where injunctions are awarded are exceptional, and many employees do not have job security clauses of the kinds the courts will enforce.

These developments represent a move away from the former position of the courts that contracts for services could not be specifically enforced, based, it is suggested, on the realisation that in fact many employment contracts are not truly 'personal'. Thus if in fact a relation of trust and confidence still exists between employer and employee, the courts will be more willing to grant relief by way of injunction, as happened, for instance, in a case where dismissal was contemplated by an employer in response to pressure from a trade union.[2]

The standards generally associated with public law have also found their way into *public* employment. This has been partly attributable to the position that used to be taken by the courts in relation to employment in the civil service to the effect that there was no contract of employment between the Crown and civil servants.[3] Hence there was no scope for the implication of contractual terms as to fair procedures to be followed

---

18 *Imperial Group Pension Trust Ltd v Imperial Tobacco Ltd.*[1991] IRLR 66; see also, on reasonableness on the part of an employer *United Bank Ltd v Akhtar* [1989] IRLR 507.
19 See discussion in *Deakin and Morris* para 4.2.2.
20 See chapters 4 and 5.
1   K Ewing 'Remedies for breach of the contract of employment' 52 Camb LJ 405, at p 406; see also *Deakin and Morris*, para 5.3.6.
2   *Hill v C A Parsons & Co Ltd* [1972] Ch 305. See also *Irani v Southampton and South West Hampshire Health Authority* [1985] IRLR 203.
3   See *Dunn v R* [1896] 1 QB 116.

before dismissal or a change of terms and conditions of employment could take place. The denial of a contractual character in civil service appointments was based in a fear that the exercise of discretion by the Crown would be fettered in the future, to the detriment of the public interest, if it were bound in contract.[4] This position enabled the courts to treat the public servant's relationship with the Crown – and with other public sector employers – as covered by public law and therefore susceptible to judicial review in certain, limited, circumstances, notably where there was a statutory underpinning in the relationship.[5] This was possible since generally the existence of a contract[6] will preclude judicial review: this argument against judicial review will clearly not apply if there is no contract.[7] So in *Malloch v Aberdeen Corpn*,[8] for instance, there was a duty to comply with the rules of natural justice before a school teacher could be dismissed, on the basis that there was a statutory status or protection in the appointment[9] – whereas no such duty is implied in private employment contracts[10] – or even on the basis that such duties arise where there is an element of public employment, or an office or status that is capable of protection.[11]

Another 'public law' aspect of public employment is that past practice may give rise to a legitimate expectation that trade unions will be consulted before decisions are made that affect the security or status of employees, and the courts will in principle protect this expectation by requiring consultation[12] unless, for instance, national security is at stake.[13]

---

4   See *Rederiaktiebolaget Amphitrite v R* [1921] 3 KB 500; *Ayr Harbour Trustees v Oswald* (1883) 8 App Cas 623.
5   See for example *Malloch v Aberdeen Corpn* [1971] 1 WLR 1578. See Sandra Fredman and Gillian Morris 'Public or private? State employees and judicial review' 107 LQR (1991) 298; *The State as Employer: Labour Law in the Public Services* (1989) chapter 3; *Deakin and Morris* paras 2.2.4.
6   See for instance *R v East Berkshire Health Authority, ex p Walsh* [1985] QB 152.
7   See generally *Deakin and Morris* para 3.6.
8   [1971] 1 WLR 1578, HL.
9   Per Lord Reid, at 1586 and Lord Wilberforce at pp 1595-1596.
10   *Ridge v Baldwin* [1964] AC 40 at 65.
11   Per Lord Wilberforce at 1595-1596. See Annex for an account of the Scottish position on the petition for judicial review and public employment.
12   For example, in *R v British Coal Corpn ex p Vardy* [1993] ICR 720 the failure by the employers to consult trade unions before reaching a decision to close a pit was held to be void as being in breach of a legitimate expectation of consultation.
13   In *Council of Civil Service Unions v Minister for the Civil Service* [1985] AC 374, there would have been a duty to consult trade unions if 'national security' had not trumped that duty.

More recently it has come to be accepted that public servants may have contracts of employment[14]. Generally in such cases judicial review is not possible unless there is a statutory underpinning in the contract.[15] But in such contracts requirements for fair procedures before dismissal are likely to be implied.[16] There may also be parallel jurisdiction in judicial review where a decision is of general application.[17] However, the case law on the question whether and when public servants may apply for judicial review of decisions affecting them – most frequently decisions to dismiss them – and when they may sue in contract, is difficult to reconcile.[18]

Sir Stephen Sedley has observed, extra-judicially, that in the late 1960s 'the developing doctrines of public law, largely based on the concept of power, began to converge with the doctrines of employment law.'[19] He suggests that the courts have circumvented the doctrine in *The Moorcock*,[20] to the effect that terms may only be implied in contracts for the purpose of the efficacy of the contract, by importing principles from public law and imposing them – especially in public employment contracts.[1]

However, contractual rights and remedies in public employment may be narrower and less effective than judicial review. Few contracts of employment will contain express duties of natural justice; such duties are not generally implied.[2] Nor do contracts of employment contain express duties of rationality in decision making on the part of the employer that could be equivalent to duties imposed in judicial review. Reinstatement is seldom ordered in unfair dismissal cases. The courts are reluctant to award injunctions regulating disciplinary or dismissal

---

14 See *R v Civil Service Appeal Board, ex p Bruce* [1988] 3 All ER 686; *McClaren v Home Office* [1990] ICR 824 where the Court of Appeal found that there was arguably a contract of employment. In *R v Lord Chancellor's Department, ex p Nangle* [1991] ICR 743 it was held that civil servants do have contracts of employment. And see S Fredman and G Morris 'Judicial Review and Civil Servants: Contract of Employment Declared to Exist' [1991] PL 485.

15 See for instance *R v East Berkshire Health Authority, ex p Walsh* [1985] QB 152; *R v BBC, ex p Lavelle* [1983] ICR 99.

16 See *R v East Berkshire Health Authority, ex p Walsh* [1984] 3 All ER 425; and see discussion of unfair dismissals infra.

17 See *De Smith, Woolf and Jowell* para 3-066. This is the position in Scotland: see *Watt v Strathclyde Regional Council* 1992 SLT 324 and discussion in Annex, below.

18 See Fredman and Morris, 'Public or private? State employees and judicial review' 107 LQR 298.

19 (1994) 23 ILJ 302 at 204. See also Sedley J in *Aspden v Webbs Poultry & Meat Group (Holdings) Ltd* [1996] IRLR 521.

20 (1889) 14 PD 64.

1   S Sedley 'Public law and contractual employment' (1993) 23 Ind LJ 201.

2   *Ridge v Baldwin* [1964] AC 40, at p 65; cf *R v Derbyshire County Council, ex p Noble* [1990] IRLR 332 at 337, per Lord Woolf.

procedures. An order for certiorari, by contrast, may be effective to quash a dismissal, producing in practice reinstatement.[3]

Unfair dismissals

One result of the move from a status to a contractual basis for the employment relationship in the nineteenth century was that it opened up possibilities for the servant to sue for wrongful dismissal. In practice however, this was not an effective protection against arbitrary dismissal; damages were likely to be small, generally being limited to the notice period; and it was not until recently, as we have seen, that the courts were willing – exceptionally – to grant injunctions requiring adherence to contractual terms as to procedures before dismissal. As Sir Stephen Sedley has observed, 'It was the failure of the common law which was partly responsible for the introduction of the statutory jurisdiction ...'.[4]

The Industrial Relations Act 1971 introduced a right not to be unfairly dismissed.[5] Under the unfair dismissal provisions (now found in the Employment Rights Act 1996) employees may apply to an Employment Tribunal for reinstatement, re-engagement or compensation[6] if they allege that they have been unfairly dismissed. The application must be made within three months of the dismissal, unless the tribunal extends the time[7] (the same limitation period, incidentally, as that for applications for judicial review). There is an upper limit on the compensation that may be awarded for unfair dismissal, save in discrimination cases.

There is also a two-year qualifying period for unfair dismissal claims.[8] This is likely to be reduced to one year under new legislation. So the protection for the employee's security in employment is hedged about with various exceptions or preconditions.

---

3   For comparison of contractual and public law remedies see S Fredman and G Morris 'Public or private? State employees and judicial review' 107 LQR 298.

4   Sir Stephen Sedley, op cit.

5   See now Employment Rights Act 1996, sections 94(1), 114, 115.

6   Employment Rights Act 1996, section 118. In practice reengagement and reinstatement are rarely ordered, because the relationship has usually completely broken down by the time the case reaches the tribunal: see *O'Laoire v Jackel International Ltd* [1990] ICR 197 at 201 (Lord Donaldson MR). These remedies provide interesting examples of a jurisdiction to order specific restoration of a person's status and security by a court, redolent of the former right of a spouse to an order for restitution of conjugal rights – see P Bromley *Family Law* (2nd edn, 1962) pp 156-161. However, in divorce law irretrievable breakdown is now regarded as a reason for termination of the relationship: there are parallels between the employment and divorce position in this respect.

7   Employment Rights Act 1996, section 111.

8   Employment Rights Act 1998, section 108(1).

The unfair dismissal provisions are of particular relevance for the purpose of the thesis being put forward here not only because they provide some protection for the employee's security and indeed his interests in the other key values, but also because they involve a supervisory jurisdiction which bears interesting similarities to the judicial review jurisdiction, and imply the introduction into the employment relationship of elements of democratic theory, particularly requirements of participation and considerate altruism – in effect of a degree of 'civil democracy'.

First, a brief summary of the meaning of 'fairness' in dismissal decisions. Certain reasons are automatically unfair – for instance, trade union membership, pregnancy or maternity.[9] Only certain other 'potentially fair reasons' are acceptable. These include reasons relating to the capability or qualifications of the employee, his or her conduct, redundancy, or that the employee could not continue in the position without contravention of a statutory duty. In addition a dismissal will be potentially fair if it is for 'some other substantial reason of a kind such as to justify the dismissal'.

In deciding whether an employer has acted fairly in dismissing an employee for a potentially fair reason, the Employment Tribunals are exercising a kind of supervisory jurisdiction. The answer to the question whether the dismissal is fair depends on whether the employer acted reasonably or unreasonably in treating the reason for dismissal as a sufficient reason.[10] It also has to be determined in accordance with equity and the substantial merits of the case.[11] As in judicial review, the focus is on the employer's conduct rather than on the impact of a decision on the employee,[12] although, unlike the position in judicial review, the remedies are designed to provide substantive relief or protection for the employee.

In deciding on the reasonableness of the employer's conduct in relation to the dismissal the Employment Tribunal must not 'substitute its own decision as to what was the right course to adopt for that of the employer – in many, though not all, cases there is a band of reasonable responses to the employee's conduct within which one employer might reasonably take one view, another may quite reasonably take another.'[13] Thus the function of the tribunal is to determine whether the employer's decision fell within the band of reasonable responses which a reasonable employer

---

9   See *Deakin and Morris* para 5.5.3.
10   Employment Rights Act 1996, section 98(4).
11   Section 98(4)(b).
12   *W Devis & Sons v Atkins* [1977] IRLR 314 at 317; and see S Deakin 'The utility of "rights talk": Employees' personal rights' in C Gearty and A Tomkins *Understanding Human Rights* (1996) at p 364.
13   Per Browne-Wilkinson J in *Iceland Frozen Foods Ltd v Jones* [1983] ICR 17 at 24-25.

might have adopted. This is a similar exercise to the 'four corners' (intra/ultra vires) exercise in judicial review, in which the courts decide whether the decision maker was within the four corners of the power or discretion granted or outside them.[14]

The supervisory jurisdiction of the tribunal in unfair dismissal cases is concerned with the fairness of procedures and the rationality of decision making, in ways which are similar to, though not identical with, approaches in judicial review – and other supervisory jurisdictions.[15] Thus in principle employers should adopt fair procedures before dismissing an employee on disciplinary grounds, including warnings and hearings.[16] This set of requirements finds no explicit expression in the legislation, but it is set out in the ACAS Code, which must be taken into account when relevant by tribunals, and has been adopted by the courts.[17] However, a procedural lapse does not mean that a dismissal is automatically to be treated as unfair, as the tribunal may find that a reasonable employer would have dispensed with the procedure: 'there may be cases where the offence is so heinous and the facts so manifestly clear that a reasonable employer could take the view that whatever the explanation the employee advanced it would make no difference'.[18] There are parallels here with some of the case law in judicial review, though it is not clear in those cases whether the courts are deciding that there was no duty of natural justice, or that there was such a duty but a remedy should be refused.[19]

There is not the equivalent in unfair dismissal cases of the public law requirement on employers not to be influenced by irrelevant considerations, and to take into account all relevant considerations.[20] There is in other words no general principle of considerate decision making on the part of the employer in relation to employees, although there are statutory provisions which protect the employee from certain

14 *Associated Provincial Picture Houses v Wednesbury Corpn* [1948] 1 KB 223.
15 For instance, in medical negligence cases a 'range of legitimate responses' approach is also applied: *Bolam v Friern Hospital Management Committee* [1957] 1 WLR 582.
16 See ACAS Code of Practice on Disciplinary Practice and Procedures in Employment; this code should be consulted in cases of disciplinary dismissal: *West Midland Co-operative Society Ltd v Tipton* [1986] AC 536. And see *Deakin and Morris* paras 5.5.6.
17 Trade Union and Labour Relations (Consolidation) Act 1992 section 207; *Deakin and Morris* paras 2.2.3 and 5.5.6.
18 *Sillifant v Powell Duffryn Timber Ltd.* [1983] IRLR 91 at 97; *Polkey v A E Dayton Services Ltd* [1988] AC 344.
19 See De Smith, Woolf and Jowell *Judicial Review of Administrative Action* (5th edn) paras 10-031 – 10-036. See for instance *Cinnamond v British Airports Authority* [1980] 1 WLR 582; *Glynn v Keele University* [1971] 1 WLR 487 (no duty); *R v Aston University Senate, ex p Roffey* [1969] 2 QB 538 (no remedy).
20 *Associated Provincial Picture Houses v Wednesbury Corpn* [1948] 1 KB 223.

irrational decisions by the employer, and, as we saw earlier, there may be express or implied contractual duties.[1] Thus, as we shall see in the next section, the employer retains extensive prerogatives in relations with employees. In effect on this approach only in extreme cases will a tribunal find the employer's decision to have been outside the band of reasonableness. Tribunals aim for 'the striking of a balance between the need of the employer to control the business for which he is responsible, in the interests of the business itself – and after all it is upon its continued prosperity that everybody's interests depend – a balance between that need, on the one hand, and the reasonable freedom of the employee, on the other.'[2]

The remedy of reinstatement is the rough equivalent of an order quashing a decision in judicial review. It is intended to put the employee in the same position as if he or she had never been dismissed. It will not be awarded if the relationship of trust and confidence that should exist between employer and employee[3] has broken down. We have here parallels both with the refusal of a remedy in judicial review if the interests of good administration so indicate,[4] and with the law of divorce in which a marriage is dissolved by the grant of a decree if the relationship has irretrievably broken down.

A contrast between judicial review and the unfair dismissal jurisdiction is that compensation is awarded for unfair dismissals whereas compensation is not available – or is assumed not to be available – for unfair decisions in judicial review.[5] In principle a successful complainant of unfair dismissal is entitled to a remedy, although the tribunal may reduce compensation for contributory fault.[6] Indeed the compensation may be reduced to nil if the tribunal finds that would be 'just and equitable.'[7] By contrast in judicial review remedies are discretionary and it is open to the court to refuse a remedy, even where the grounds for the exercise of a supervisory jurisdiction are made out.

1   See for instance *Clark v BET* [1997] IRLR 348 at 349.
2   *Boychuk v H J Symons Holdings Ltd* [1977] IRLR 395 at 396.
3   On this aspect of the relationship see D Brodie 'Beyond exchange: The new contract of employment' (1998) 27 ILJ 79. A distinction needs to be made between the question whether, in fact, there was a relationship of trust and confidence in employment, and whether a contractual duty of trust and confidence exists. A relationship of trust and confidence is not presumed to exist in fact in the employment relationship but arises if one party can establish that he or she was accustomed to repose confidence in the other: per Millett LJ in *Credit Lyonnais v Burch* [1997] 1 All ER 144 at 154. But there is in any event an implied contractual duty of trust and confidence in employment relationships.
4   See Supreme Court Act 1981, section 31(6); De Smith, Woolf and Jowell *Judicial Review of Administrative Action* (5th edn) paras 20-002, 20-010 – 20-011.
5   See discussion in chapter 11.
6   Employment Rights Act 1996, section 123(6).
7   *W Devis & Sons Ltd v Atkins* [1977] IRLR 314.

Discrimination

Claims for discrimination in employment on grounds of sex, race and disability are brought under specific statutes. There is no qualifying period for these claims. The burden of proof is on the applicant to show discrimination, whereas in unfair dismissal cases the burden is on the employer to show a fair reason. There is no limit to the awards for sex,[8] race[9] and disability[10] discrimination. The former upper limit was removed in sex cases as a result of the European Court of Justice decision to the effect that it precluded real equality of opportunity through adequate reparation for loss and damage sustained as a result of discrimination.[11] Compensation may include an award for injury to feelings, an example of the recognition of the value of a person's dignity and respect in this relationship.

The employer's prerogatives

In individual employment law in the private sector the common law took, until recently, a very pro-employer position.[12] Although, as we shall see in the next section, the authority of the employer has been weakened by developments in the common law, statute and European law, the employer remains entitled to impose managerial – or bureaucratic[13] – decisions about the needs of the enterprise on employees.[14] Hence, for instance, it may not be unfair dismissal to dismiss an employee for managerial, economic, or 'sound, good business'[15] reasons, such as a need to reorganise the business or working arrangements.[16] These examples of the power of management illustrate the aptness of Galbraith's analysis of power as including organisation or bureaucracy.[17]

---

8   SI 1993/2798.
9   Race Relations (Remedies) Act 1994.
10 Disability Discrimination Act 1995.
11 *Marshall v Southampton and South West Hampshire Area Health Authority (No 2)* [1993] IRLR 445.
12 See *Deakin and Morris* para 1.2.3.
13 See J G Galbraith *The Anatomy of Power* (1983). See also H Collins 'Market power, bureaucratic power, and the contract of employment' (1986) 15 Industrial Law Journal 1; E Jaques *A General Theory of Bureaucracy* (1976).
14 See *Deakin and Morris*, para 4.2.1-4.2.2.
15 *Hollister v National Farmers' Union* [1979] ICR 542 at 551 (per Lord Denning).
16 See *Ellis v Brighton Co-operative Society* [1976] IRLR 419, EAT.
17 See chapter 2; see also H Collins 'Against abstentionism in labour law' in J Eekelaar and J Bell *Oxford Essays in Jurisprudence* (Third Series) (1987) p 79.

The employer's prerogatives as far as the hiring of employees is concerned include, for instance, a right to discriminate (save on specific statutorily defined grounds such as race, sex or disability, trade union membership or non-membership or a 'spent conviction'[18]) in deciding who to employ,[19] – this is regarded as part of an employer's freedom of contract. Employers have the prerogative to employ people on short term contracts which may not attract the protections from redundancy that are otherwise available. On the matter of hiring then, there are both similarities and contrasts with application cases in judicial review: a public decisionmaker dealing with an application is not under full scale duties of fairness and rationality. However, he or she is not entirely free of constraints in dealing with applications and must reach an honest conclusion without bias and not in pursuance of any capricious policy.[20]

Once in employment, the employee has few rights as against the employer. Collins has described the subordinate position of the employee during the relationship in vivid terms: 'Once inside the factory gates or on the elevator to the officedom, the typical employee is classified as a subordinate under a hierarchy of ranks. In exchange for wages, an employee relinquishes his right to self-determination, to equal dignity, and to freedom from arbitrary power'.[1]

Pending the coming into effect of the Human Rights Act 1998, nowhere are the civil and political rights of employees, particularly to freedom of speech, association (though freedom to join a trade union is protected[2]), privacy[3] or religion (save in Northern Ireland[4]) codified or spelled out. Indeed, there are statutory provisions relating to public employment which specifically limit the freedom of action of some

---

18   On racial discrimination see the Race Relations Act 1976; on sex discrimination see the Sex Discrimination Act 1975, the Equal Treatment Directive 76/207; on disability discrimination see the Disability Discrimination Act 1995; on union membership discrimination see Trade Union and Labour Relations (Consolidation) Act 1992; on spent convictions see Rehabilitation of Offenders Act 1974. See generally *Deakin and Morris* para 3.3.1.

19   See *Deakin and Morris* para 3.3.2.

20   *McInnes v Onslow Fane* [1978] 1 WLR 1520 at 1530; see also *British Oxygen Co Ltd v Minister of Technology* [1971] AC 610. For a criticism of this position see De Smith, Woolf and Jowell *Judicial Review of Administrative Action* (5th edn) paras 8-006 – 8-010.

1   H Collins 'Against abstentionism in labour law' op cit at p 81.

2   Trade Union and Labour Relations (Consolidation) Act 1992, sections 152(1), 153.

3   But in *Halford v United Kingdom* [1997] IRLR 471 the tapping of an employee's telephone at work was held to be in breach of Article 8 of the European Convention on Human Rights. The Data Protection Act 1998 regulates the use of information. See M Ford *Surveillance and Privacy at Work* (1998).

4   See Fair Employment (Northern Ireland) Act 1976, as amended.

employees, for instance by restricting their political activity and freedom of expression.[5] For all employees there is only a patchwork of common law and statutory provisions which provide some protections for their civil and political rights in employment: again, the freedom to restrict the activity of employees is regarded as part of the employer's freedom of contract.[6] And under the 'range of reasonable responses' test in unfair dismissal cases respect for the civil liberties of employees 'rarely surfaces in the reasoning of courts or tribunals. Even when they do they seem to be easily swamped by considerations reflecting respect for the breadth of managerial prerogatives.'[7] It is notable how little bearing the automatically unfair reasons have in relation to civil and political rights.

Employers also retain considerable freedom in decisions to dismiss employees.[8] The provisions on unfair dismissal have been noted above, and this statutory overlay on the common law position substantially restricts the employer's freedom. There is no qualifying period in relation to automatically unfair reasons for dismissal, or for discrimination. But apart from such reasons, in the first two years of employment employers are free to dismiss employees for any or no reason.[9] As Lord Reid put it in 1964, '… the master can terminate the contract with his servant at any time and for any reason or for none.'[10] The common law, in dealing with the master-servant relationship, thus gave priority to the autonomy – and the authority – of the employer and attached relatively little weight to the status and security of the employee.

Collins has suggested that a purely contractual image of the employment relationship is no longer viable, given the recognition of the extent of the bureaucratic power of the employer. 'Within this bureaucratic framework the ideals of autonomy and individual dignity take on a new resonance … a new concern arises for the protection of

---

5   On political free speech see G Morris 'Political activities of public servants and freedom of expression' in I Loveland (ed) (*Importing the First Amendment*) (1998) pp 101-104; on political activity by local government employees see Local Government and Housing Act 1989, section 1, 2; G Morris 'Local government workers and rights of political participation: time for a change' [1998] Public Law 25; *Ahmed and others v United Kingdom* (Case no 65/1997/849/1056, 2 September 1998, unreported), ECHR, upheld the restrictions of political activity in local government: (1998) Times, 2 October); and G Morris 'The political activities of local government workers and the European Convention on Human Rights' [1999] Public Law 211.

6   *Allen v Flood* [1898] AC 1 at 173, per Lord Davey.

7   H Collins *Justice in Dismissal* (1992) p 185.

8   See J Bowers and A Clarke 'Unfair dismissal and managerial prerogative: A study of "some other substantial reason"' (1981) 10 ILJ 34.

9   Employment Rights Act 1996, section 108(1). The government plans to reduce the period to one year.

10   *Ridge v Baldwin* [1964] AC 40 at 65.

autonomy and dignity and the potential abuse of bureaucratic power.'[11] This, in effect is what the law of unfair dismissal seeks to regulate.

There are a number of similarities between the employer's prerogatives and the notion of justiciability in judicial review. Until the CCSU[12] case the prerogative powers of the Crown, directly exercised,[13] were not regarded as being subject to judicial review save to the extent of deciding whether a claimed power existed. For this deference was substituted a justiciability test in CCSU, which permits review of prerogative powers save where decisions are in essence not justiciable, or 'polycentric,'[14] so that the courts accept that they are not equipped to evaluate sensitive issues or questions involving the allocation of scarce social and economic resources.[15] These are the kinds of issue with which employers may also be concerned, and recognition of this factor goes some way to explain the courts' refusal to interfere in management prerogatives. Other considerations appear to be a perceived need to uphold the employer's authority and autonomy.

From employer prerogatives to responsibility?

Despite the continuing extensive prerogatives of employers, their responsibilities towards their employees have been increased, through European and United Kingdom legislation and common law developments, over recent years. Lord Slynn of Hadley in *Spring v Guardian Assurance plc* noted:[16] '... the changes which have taken place in the employer/employee relationship, with far greater duties imposed on the employer than in the past, whether by statute or by judicial decision, to care for the physical, financial and even psychological welfare of the employee.' The point may be illustrated by examples. In *Spring* the House of Lords decided that employers owe duties of care to their employees or former employees in providing references: the future status and security of employees are often dependant upon references. As noted earlier the Equal Pay Act 1970, and the sex and race discrimination legislation have set some controls over employers' former freedom to

---

11 H Collins *Justice in Dismissal* (1992) pp 271-272.
12 *Council of Civil Service Unions v Minister for the Civil Service* [1985] AC 374; see chapters 4 and 5.
13 Indirectly exercised prerogative powers were held reviewable in *R v Criminal Injuries Compensation Board, ex p Lain* [1967] 2 QB 864.
14 See discussion of this concept by L Fuller 'The forms and limits of adjudication' (1978-79) 92 Harv LR 395.
15 See De Smith, Woolf and Jowell *Judicial Review of Administrative Action* (5th edn, 1995) paras 6-030 – 6-035, 6-047, 13-056–13-058.
16 [1995] 2 AC 296 at 335.

discriminate. It was noted in chapter 3 that discrimination is an offence against the dignity of the individual. Anti-discrimination legislation seeks, among other things, to protect the dignity of those who might suffer discrimination.[17] In this context European law has been influential, for instance in requiring equal treatment of men and women in employment,[18] and in particular in requiring removal of the upper limit on compensation in discrimination cases.[19] However, discrimination on grounds of religion, age, political or religious beliefs or sexual orientation[20] are not regarded as unlawful in employment in Great Britain[1] (unless they can be brought within the concepts of indirect discrimination[2]). In Northern Ireland, by contrast, there is greater protection, especially against discrimination on grounds of religion.[3]

The Public Interest Disclosure Act 1998 gives some protection to freedom of speech in employment by introducing protection for whistleblowers:[4] employees (and certain other 'workers') are not in breach of contract in making 'protected disclosures' within the Act, and are not to be victimised by employers for making such disclosures.[5] Some restrictions on freedom of expression would of course be legitimate under any system, for instance disclosures of confidential commercial information, but apart from the protection for whistleblowing the freedom of expression of employees is not protected.

However, the Human Rights Act 1998[6] incorporating articles containing substantive rights in the European Convention on Human Rights into UK law will increase the protection for freedom of action of employees, notably freedom of speech – including whistleblowing[7] –

---

17 And see *Deakin and Morris* chapter 6, esp para 6.2.2.

18 See for instance, Equal Pay Directive 75/117, Article 119, Equal Treatment Directive 76/207; see generally *Deakin and Morris* chapter 6.

19 *R v Secretary of State for Employment, ex p Equal Opportunities Commission* [1994] IRLR 176; *Deakin and Morris* paras. 6.3.2 and 6.5.5.

20 See *Deakin and Morris* pp 596-597.

1 See *Deakin and Morris* para 6.4.

2 For instance, discrimination on grounds of religion may amount to indirect discrimination on grounds of race.

3 Fair Employment (Northern Ireland) Act 1976.

4 On whistleblowing by employees see L Vickers *Protecting Whistleblowers at Work* (1995) and 'Whistleblowing in the public sector' [1997] Public Law 594; D Lewis 'Whistleblowers and job security' (1995) 58 MLR 208; *Ticehurst v British Telecommunications plc* [1992] IRLR 219.

5 See the Public Interest Disclosure Act 1998, section 1, inserting a new Part IVA (sections 43A to 43K) in the Employment Rights Act 1996, and making other amendments to the unfair dismissal and victimisation provisions of that Act.

6 See chapter 10 below.

7 For discussion of this see L Vickers 'Whistleblowing in the public sector', op cit; J Bowers and J Lewis 'Whistleblowing: freedom of expression in the workplace' [1996] EHRLR 637.

and association.[8] There is not the space to explore the implications of the Act for employment in any detail here, but it is notable that under the Act it will be unlawful for public authorities to act in ways that are incompatible with Convention rights, and hence public employers will be bound to comply with the Act in their employment practices. The Act also binds persons certain of whose functions are public, but not if the nature of a particular act is private. This opens up possibilities for some 'private' employers to be bound by the Act in at least some of their employment practices.[9]

By section 6 of the Human Rights Act courts and tribunals are required not to act incompatibly with Convention rights, and by section 3 primary and subordinate legislation is to be read and given effect in a way which is compatible with the Convention. Although it was not anticipated by the Lord Chancellor when the Human Rights Bill was introduced in Parliament that new causes of action will be developed under this provision,[10] it will be open to the judges to develop the implied terms in employment contracts to protect Convention rights. This would mark a further step away from the doctrine in *The Moorcock*, noted above, to the effect that terms may only be implied in contracts for the purpose of the efficacy of the contract.[11] The section 3 requirement to interpret legislation compatibly with Convention rights opens the way for the concept of constructive dismissal to embrace interferences with freedoms of speech, association, religion and so on. If a dismissal were found to infringe a Convention right the employer may have difficulty satisfying the court that it was fair. But here we are in the realms of speculation and must wait for the case law to develop.

There are further ways in which employers have responsibilities for their employees. They are required to insure against accidents at work,[12] and to comply with health and safety requirements[13] – the Health and Safety at Work Act 1974 aims at 'securing the health, safety and welfare of persons at work'.[14] Under article 118a of the EC Treaty and directives

8   The effect of the Human Rights Act 1998 on autonomy in the employment relationship is discussed by Bob Hepple in 'The impact on labour law' in B S Markesinis (ed) *The Impact of the Human Rights Bill on English Law* (1998) p 63.
9   See G Morris 'The Human Rights Act and the public-private divide in employment law' 27 ILJ 293 (1998).
10 See chapter 10.
11 S Sedley 'Public law and contractual employment' (1993) 23 Ind LJ 201.
12 Employers' Liability (Compulsory Insurance) Act 1969, section 1.
13 Health and Safety at Work Act 1974, as amended, Part I.
14 Section 1(1).

made under it employers are responsible in various ways for the working environment, including the regulation of working time.[15]

At common law employers owe a duty of care for the safety of employees and must provide a safe system of work.[16] A term may be implied into the employment contract that employers must 'provide and monitor for ... employees, so far as is reasonably practicable, a working environment which is reasonably suitable for the performance by them of their contractual duties.'[17] This may include protection from passive smoking. The duty of care has been held to include ensuring that the employee is not placed under undue mental stress, leading to physical or psychiatric injury, even if the stress results from the working hours and duties contracted for.[18]

There is an implied term in the contract of employment that an employer will not, without reasonable and proper cause, conduct himself in a manner likely to destroy or seriously damage the relationship of confidence and trust between the employer and the employee.[19] This has been expressed as an overriding obligation of trust and respect.[20]

The emergence of this duty in the employment relationship harks back to earlier periods, and has parallels with the duty of trust and confidence in the sovereign/subject relationship noted earlier. Brodie suggests that this development 'serves to challenge abuse of power and promotes the dignity of the employee.'[1] This trend in the common law is illustrated by the case of *Malik v Bank of Credit and Commerce International SA* (BCCI), and *Mahmud v BCCI* in which employees of a corrupt employer claimed compensation for the effect on employability of their having been employed in a corrupt organisation.[2] It was held

---

15 See Working Time Regulations, SI 1998 1833. See also Working Time Directive 93/104; *United Kingdom v EU Council (Working Time)* [1996] ECR I-5755; Framework Directive 89/391. And see *Deakin and Morris* para 4.7.3.

16 *Wilsons and Clyde Coal Co v English* [1938] AC 57.

17 *Waltons & Morse v Dorrington* [1997] IRLR 488, EAT.

18 *Johnstone v Bloomsbury Health Authority* [1992] QB 333; *Frost v Chief Constable of South Yorkshire Police* [1997] IRLR 173; *Walker v Northumberland County Council* [1995] IRLR 35.

19 *Woods v WM Car Services (Peterborough) Ltd.* [1981] ICR 666, EAT, affirmed [1982] ICR 693, CA. For a recent example see *French v Barclays Bank plc* [1998] IRLR 646, CA: where an employer changed the policy on providing bridging loans to employees who were required to relocate, where the policy had applied to other employees over many years and appeared in the manual at the time the loan was made, this represented a breach by the employer of the duty of trust and confidence.

20 *United Bank Ltd v Akhtar* [1989] IRLR 507, T 512, EAT.

1 D Brodie 'Beyond exchange: The new contract of employment' (1998) 27 ILJ 79 at 101.

2 [1997] 3 All ER 1, HL. See also D Brodie 'Beyond exchange: The new contract of employment' 27 ILJ (1998) 79.

that an employer should not conduct its business in a manner likely to destroy or seriously damage the relationship of confidence and trust between employer and employee which was implied at common law. The appellants were held to be entitled to damages if they proved that they were handicapped in the labour market in consequence of the bank's corruption.

Lord Nicholls, giving one of the main judgments in the House of Lords, emphasised that:

> 'Employment, and job prospects, are matters of vital concern to most people. Jobs of all descriptions are less secure than formerly, people change jobs more frequently, and the job market is not always buoyant. Everyone knows this. An employment contract creates a close personal relationship, where there is often a disparity of power between the parties. Frequently the employee is vulnerable. ... Employers must take care not to damage their employees' future employment prospects, by harsh and oppressive behaviour or by any other form of conduct which is unacceptable today as falling below the standards set by the implied trust and confidence term.'[3]

We have here an unusually explicit recognition of the importance of trust to security, of security itself, and of the responsibilities that attach to the more powerful party in a relationship of unequal power.

In practice employees rely to a considerable extent for their security on insurance and pension arrangements. On this a question arises as to the employer's responsibilities in relation, for instance, to the terms on which employees may take early retirement. Here the courts have wavered between expecting the employer to take reasonable steps to bring to an employee's attention the existence of pension rights of which he was not aware at all and which he could not have been expected to know about,[4] and holding that it is not the duty of an employer to do any more than pension fund holders need do to give advice to beneficiaries, which did not include an obligation to advise that the way in which an employee proposed to exercise his pension rights might not be to his financial advantage.[5]

Overall, imposition of responsibilities for their employees has considerably eroded the prerogatives of employers. In this respect the starting point, that employers are entitled to act in their own interests, has to find a place alongside duties of altruistic decision making.

---

3   Ibid at 8.
4   *Scally v Southern Health and Social Services Board* [1992] 1 AC 294.
5   *University of Nottingham v Eyett and anor* (1998) Times, 3 December, Hart J.

Employment is not the only aspect of company activity in which obligations of altruism are imposed. Directors are obliged to act, if not totally altruistically, in the interests of companies and not primarily in their own interests.[6] These are paralleled in other relationships that were once regarded as spheres for self-seeking activity, such as the parent/child relationship[7] and judicial review.[8]

COMMENTS AND COMPARISONS

Overall the trend in the last thirty-odd years has been to increase the security of employees as compared with the original common law position, and this has been achieved via a combination of statutory provisions, implied contractual terms and – in public employment – judicial review, and a cross-fertilisation between the two. This is not to say that security is as great as it could be. The possibility of employers going into liquidation, for instance because of lack of competitiveness, and threats of redundancy and unemployment, hang over the heads of many employees. They may have to rely on other sources for security, such as state benefits, insurance, pensions, their families and voluntary agencies – a point which goes some way to explain the increased acknowledgement in other areas of law such as insurance and pensions of the importance of security to those with whom providers of these benefits deal.[9]

Developments since the late-1960s (the Race Relations Act 1968 first introduced some protection against discrimination in employment) have aimed to provide some protection for the employee's dignity[10] and autonomy in the relationship, to provide a degree of protection for security in employment, and to increase the responsibilities of the employer. These values have thus influenced the development of the common law of contract, and the content of legislation.

There are parallels in employment law with the way in which judicial review (considered above and in chapters 4 and 5) and the law of parent and child (which will be considered in chapter 7) have developed. In the parent/child relation the common law position was that the parent's rights were exercisable for the parent's benefit; this has now developed to a position where they are part of the responsibility of the parent, to be exercised for the child's benefit.[11] In judicial review what were regarded

6   See discussion of directors' duties in chapter 8.
7   See chapter 7.
8   See chapter 5.
9   See discussion in chapters 8 and 9.
10   See the discussion of dignity and discrimination in chapter 3.
11   Children Act 1989, sections 2, 3 and 4.

as the prerogatives of state bodies are now regarded as their responsibilities, not to be exercised for self-interested reasons, but only in the public interest.[12] Of course the parallel is not exact as employers are regarded as entitled to advance their own self-interests in their employment relationships whereas public bodies and parents are not entitled to do so in relations, respectively, with individuals and children. However, even here the prerogatives of employers in pursuing their own interests have been eroded by provisions requiring directors to have regard to the interests of employees, though these duties do not appear to be enforceable by employees.[13]

The employment relationship is also characterised by supervisory jurisdictions. Terms may be implied in the employment contract that require the employer to act fairly and reasonably; the statutory provisions on unfair dismissal have been interpreted by the courts to require procedural fairness and reasonableness on the part of the employer in making dismissal decisions. It is significant that the courts have adopted phrases such as 'arbitrary and capricious', and 'reasonableness'[14] in their decisions, bringing out the similarities with the grounds for judicial review. These phrases set limits to the circumstances in which the courts can intervene, but they also open up possibilities for the courts to supervise decision making which would not have existed at all if such formulae had not been developed.

A parallel with concepts of justiciability and the interests of good administration, which are features of the judicial review jurisdiction, is the notion of employer's prerogatives. There are further important similarities between judicial review and employment law, including the three-month time limit for complaints to an employment tribunal, and the availability of the remedy of reinstatement having parallels with certiorari, injunctions and declarations in judicial review.

Overall, the trend in both the sovereign-subject and employment relationships has been towards increased autonomy and respect for the 'subject' or employee, and the imposition of increased responsibilities on the state and the employer. This may be interpreted as the development – by no means complete – in both public law and employment of concepts of participative-communitarian democracy and considerate altruism, in which the responsibilities of the powerful towards those over whom they have authority increase and come gradually to replace their earlier 'rights' to the self-interested exercise of power and authority.

12 See chapter 5, and discussion of public service in chapter 11.
13 See discussion in chapter 8.
14 See Employment Rights Act 1996, section 98 (4): whether a dismissal is fair depends on whether 'the employer acted reasonably or unreasonably in treating [the reason relied on] as a sufficient reason.'

Chapter Seven

The Law of Relationships 2: Family Relationships

In this chapter we continue our consideration of the law of relationships, focusing on marriage and the parent-child relationship. The ways in which the law governing these relationships has changed over the last century or more brings out the trend towards the emancipation of the weaker parties, the policy in favour of the control of the power of the dominant party, and ways in which interests in, on the one hand, dignity, autonomy and respect and on the other hand security and status have had to be balanced. Comparisons will be made with the relationships considered in the previous chapter, those of the individual and the state, and employment.

MARRIAGE

Traditionally marriage, until recently, has been designed to secure the orderly descent of the husband's family's status, property and power. Nowadays, marriage is supposed to provide a loving, supportive and protective environment for the couple and their children.[1] The law has reflected each of these purposes. As Hale has observed, however, the stability which traditional marriage was supposed to promote was bought at the cost of 'two great inequalities: between husbands and wives and between the children of married and unmarried parents.'[2] In this section we focus on the development of the relationship between husband and wife, as it illustrates the way in which the five values have evolved in this

---

1   See Mrs Justice Hale *Private Lives and Public Duties* (1997) ESRC p 2.
2   Op cit at p 3.

relationship (and the ways in which they can conflict). In the following section we consider children.

At common law husband and wife were one: 'By marriage, the husband and wife are one person in law: that is, the very being or legal existence of the woman is suspended during the marriage, or at least is incorporated and consolidated into that of the husband: under whose wing, protection, and *cover*, she performs every thing'.[3] We can see that this position paid little regard to the values of autonomy, dignity or respect for the wife, but they did purport to protect her status and security – and those of the husband. As with employment, status and security were legally recognised values before the more individualistic values of autonomy, dignity and respect.

Among the implications of the doctrine of unity were the following. The husband was entitled to all his wife's property, including property acquired by her before and after the marriage, and her earnings. He was also entitled to her sexual and other services – consortium – and had causes of action for damages against those who deprived him of those services. He was entitled 'by the old law' (as Blackstone put it) to chastise his wife 'in the same moderation that a man is allowed to correct his apprentices or children.'[4] At common law the husband also had sole parental rights over the children of the marriage. In effect the law upheld the authority of the husband over his wife, which was seen as forming part of the stable social fabric both of family and of society.

Legal status has of course until this century been closely linked with social status, founded often on birth, on breeding and, in the case of women, on marriage. This factor goes some way to explain the law's disapproval of adultery on the part of a wife,[5] who might foist an illegitimate child on the husband, and of illegitimacy, which threatened the status of other members of the family of the parents. Wives derived their social status from their husbands, but the reverse was not the case. (Remnants of this position remain: women use titles that reflect their husbands' status, whereas men married to women with titles do not acquire status from their wives.)

The marriage relationship bore some resemblances to earlier feudal relationships. A woman who murdered her husband was guilty of the common law offence of petit treason, like the vassal who slew his lord or

---

3   Sir William Blackstone *Commentaries on the Laws of England*, vol 1, p 442. For a history of the law of marriage see Bromley *Family Law* (1st edn 1957).

4   *Blackstone* vol 1, chapter 15, at p 444.

5   Under the Matrimonial Causes Act 1857 adultery by a wife provided grounds for divorce by the husband, but adultery by a husband was only grounds for divorce if it was 'aggravated'. A wife who committed adultery forfeited her right to maintenance.

the servant who slew his master.[6] A husband who murdered his wife did not attract such special condemnation. The distinction between petit treason and murder was abolished in 1828.[7] Treason involved breach of duties of allegiance, which were owed by the 'subject' in relationships to the 'superior'. At common law, then, the marriage relationship was essentially positivist-authoritarian in nature.

As the sovereign owed duties of protection to his subjects,[8] so the husband owed duties of protection – in practice maintenance and a right to live in the matrimonial home – to his wife. However, as was the case in relations between the subject and the sovereign, these duties were difficult to enforce. The wife was entitled under the doctrine of the wife's agency of necessity to pledge her husband's credit to purchase necessaries. (But traders were commonly reluctant to provide goods on credit in case the husband should refuse to pay.) A concession to the idea that a wife owed her status to her husband and that that was the status which deserved protection was the rule that under the doctrine of the agency of necessity a husband's credit could be pledged to provide the wife with necessaries appropriate to the standard of living granted to her by the husband. (But if the husband chose a lower standard of living than he could have afforded the wife's agency was restricted to the standard adopted by the husband for her.) The doctrines of agency designed to secure protection for the wife were clearly ineffective and in due course statutes were passed which entitled wives to apply to the courts for alimony. The magistrates' courts and eventually the high court and divorce county courts were granted jurisdiction to make awards of maintenance, later periodical payments in favour of women who were not being maintained by their husbands.

Towards the emancipation of married women

The common law came to be mitigated in favour of the wife in various ways in the nineteenth and early twentieth centuries.[9] The equitable doctrines of the wife's equity to a settlement, her separate estate and the restraint on anticipation, all developed in the nineteenth century to mitigate the common law position, by protecting her against the husband taking her property for himself, thus improving her security. The various Married Women's Property Acts of the nineteenth and early twentieth

6   See *Blackstone* vol 4, at pp 75, 203-204.
7   9 Geo 4, c. 31, s 2. Murder of the sovereign remains treason – high treason – to this day.
8   See chapter 6.
9   For an account of the development of family law, including the law of marriage, in the twentieth century see M. Freeman 'Family Values and Family Justice' in M Freeman (ed) *Law and Opinion at the End of the Twentieth Century* (1997).

century and the Law Reform (Married Women and Tortfeasors) Act 1935 eventually placed a married woman in the same position as a single woman as far as property was concerned, securing to the wife entitlements to her own property. Thus her autonomy, dignity and respect were formally enhanced; but, given that in practice most of the property of spouses was likely to be owned by the husband, separate property did not add anything to the security of a propertyless wife. It is worth noting the contrast with community property regimes in civil law systems here, which treated spouses as equal owners of property within the community property regime.

The pattern until the 1960s was for the husband to be the legal owner or tenant of the matrimonial home. It was not until the Matrimonial Homes Act 1967 that the non-owner acquired statutory rights to live in the home, and that those rights became enforceable against third parties. Thus the security of the non-owner was strengthened. But a non-owner could only acquire a beneficial interest in the home under an implied, resulting or constructive trust; unless she actually made a direct contribution to the purchase price it would not be easy to prove such a trust. If a wife chose to pay for food and household expenses and the husband made the mortgage payments then she would normally not be able to acquire an interest.[10]

By the Trusts of Land and Appointments of Trustees Act 1996 property which is held on trust, notably for our purposes the matrimonial home, is no longer automatically held on trust for sale and it is for the settlor and beneficiaries to decide whether trust property is to be treated as an investment or somewhere to live. Beneficiaries will have a right to occupy the land it if is available for occupation, and the purposes of the trust include making the land available for occupation.[11] Thus the security of beneficiaries in the occupation of the matrimonial home is explicitly recognised as worthy of legal protection, rather than the interest in realising the capital value of the asset by sale.

Property relations

The Married Women's Property Act 1885 transformed the previous regime of unity which meant that all of a wife's property vested in her husband, to a regime of separate property in which each party to a marriage in principle retained their own property. However, until

---

10 *Lloyds Bank v Rosset* [1991] 1 AC 107.
11 Trustees Act 1996 ss 12, 13. See A Clarke 'Property Law: Reestablishing Diversity' in M Freeman (ed) *Law and Opinion at the End of the Twentieth Century* at pp 137-147.

relatively recently the reality has been that the husband owns the principal asset of the marriage, the matrimonial home; this is an important source of security for both parties in that normally ownership carries with it a right of occupation. While a marriage relationship is amicable there will generally be few problems if one spouse – normally the husband – is the legal owner of the home, for the other will in practice be secure in occupying the home with the other spouse. However, if the sole owner mortgages the home to a third party, or if the owner dies, or if the marriage breaks down, the fact that only one spouse is legal owner may have serious consequences for the security of the other. At common law a husband is under an obligation to provide his wife with a roof,[12] but this right is not enforceable against third parties and is of limited utility. These problems have been 'solved' or dealt with by a combination of equitable and statutory developments.[13]

Equity has developed a number of unorthodox rights of occupation of land, especially the matrimonial (or other) home, and rights to a share of the equity and doctrines of proprietary estoppel.[14] This is not the place for a lengthy exposition of the position, but examples will illustrate the point. A person who is not the legal owner of the home, but who has contributed to its acquisition, may acquire equitable interests in it which may be protected by orders that he or she be permitted to continue to occupy it, or is entitled to a share of the equity, thus limiting what were believed to be the strict legal (as opposed to equitable) property rights of the owner. This has been done via resulting, constructive and implied trusts: if it was the intention of the parties at the time of acquisition of the home that the non-owner should have a share of the property,[15] and if on the strength of that common intention the non-owner acted to his or her detriment[16] (for instance, by contributing to the payments towards the purchase) then the non-owner will acquire a share in the equity. This equitable interest will confer not only a share in the equity but also a right to occupy the property.[17]

The use of implied, resulting and constructive trusts is of limited usefulness in many cases. If there was no common intention at the time of purchase of the property that the parties would share the equity – perhaps because the relationship started after the owner had acquired

---

12 *National Provincial Bank v Ainsworth* [1965] AC 1175, per Lord Wilberforce at 1244.
13 See generally S Cretney and J Masson *Principles of Family Law* (6th edn 1997) chapters 5 and 6.
14 See generally *Cretney and Masson* pp 127-157.
15 *Lloyds Bank v Rosset* [1991] 1 AC 107.
16 *Midland Bank plc v Dobson and Dobson* [1986] 1 FLR 171; *Grant v Edwards* [1986] Ch 638.
17 Trusts of Land and Appointment of Trustees Act 1996.

the property – it will be hard to establish that the non-owner has an interest.[18] The need to establish a common intention protects the dispositive rights of the legal owner in many cases, since it will not always be easy to establish the required common intention. Detrimental reliance will not always be easy to establish.[19]

Whether or not a person's security in the occupation of a home is protected by an equitable interest acquired as above, some statutory provisions provide protection. For instance, by the Family Law Act 1996, Part IV[20] a non-owning spouse has a statutory right to occupy the matrimonial home, which is registrable so as to bind third parties,[1] and may be regulated by the courts. On divorce, however these remedies normally cease to be available and the court may instead make a property transfer order.[2]

In summary, then, both statute and equity have sought to provide some security for the spouse who is not a legal owner of the matrimonial home, both as against the other, owning, spouse, and as against third parties such as purchasers or mortgagees. In these developments we see examples of the search for a balance between the interests of the property owner in their own autonomy and security as it derives from their property, and the non-owner's need for security. The approach has been to mitigate the hardship caused by the separate property regime, which was introduced in order to enhance the autonomy of wives. In reality the separate property regime did not take account of the economic realities of marriages at that time: this involved the subjection of the wife to the husband because of her dependence upon him; this was due to the limited opportunities for employment of women and their vulnerability to pregnancy, coupled with assumptions about the roles of mothers and fathers in relation to domestic duties and responsibilities for the day-to-day care of their children.

18 See for instance *Thomas v Fuller-Brown* [1988] 1 FLR 237, CA; *Grant v Edwards* [1986] Ch 638, CA.
19 On the development of the doctrine of detrimental reliance see *Lloyds Bank plc v Rosset* [1991] 1 AC 107; and see A Lawson 'Detrimental reliance in the family home' (1996) 16 *Legal Studies* 218; *Cretney and Masson* chapter 5; S Cretney *Elements of Family Law* (2nd edn 1992), paras 7.14-7.22.
20 See section 30. This provision re-enacts the Matrimonial Homes Acts 1967 and 1983.
1 By the Family Law Act 1996, section 31, the right is registrable under the Land Registration Act 1925 or as a Class F land charge under the Land Charges Act 1972.
2 See *Cretney and Masson* chapter 10.

Marriage and parenthood

As far as the parental rights of wives were concerned, equity first mitigated the severity of the common law rule that only the father had parental rights in respect of legitimate children by developing its wardship jurisdiction to award the care of young children to their mother. Parliament gave the court the power to award custody to the mother in the Custody of Children Act 1839; the Guardianship of Infants Act 1925 enacted the principle that the welfare of the child was paramount in any dispute relating to a child, and provided that neither the father nor the mother should be regarded as having a claim superior to the other. But it was not until 1973 that mother and father were treated as having equal parental rights. (Now, by the Children Act 1989 sections 2, 3 and 4, they are regarded as having equal parental responsibilities – another example of the move from rights to responsibilities for the more powerful parties in relationships, which was noted in relation to the sovereign-subject and employment relationships in the previous chapter.)

Marriage law, power relations and the five values

In sum, in the marriage relationship at common law the husband had a dominant position under which his wife owed him allegiance and obedience and his duty to her was a (legally virtually unenforceable) one only of protection. He was entitled to her property, her services (both sexual and others – marital rape was criminalised by the House of Lords only in 1992[3]) and her 'products' – their children – and to control her. The parallels with the common law on the sovereign subject and employment relationships are obvious. But from these beginnings, as a result of developments in the law of equity, common law and, most crucially, statute, the position has now been reached where, as far as private law is concerned, wives have obtained autonomy in relations with their husbands through the rejection of the doctrine of unity, the criminalisation of marital rape, the end of the husband's right to chastise his wife, the introduction of separate property, the right to maintenance where needed, and equal rights – now responsibilities – for children. These reforms have recognised the wife's interest in her own dignity, autonomy and respect.

Divorce law has also developed in line with changing concepts of the relations between the sexes and acceptance of the possibility for women to live autonomous lives outside – and after – marriage. Whereas under the Matrimonial Causes Act 1857 judicial divorce was available to the

3   *R v R* [1992] 1 AC 599, HL

husband on the ground of his wife's adultery, a wife could only petition for divorce on the grounds of adultery coupled with cruelty, desertion or other aggravating factors. The Matrimonial Causes Act 1923 put both spouses on the same footing by permitting each to petition for divorce on the ground of adultery simpliciter.

What was in principle a lifelong right to maintenance, even after divorce, for wives has been replaced by a presumption in favour of transitional support provisions enabling the wife usually to become self-supporting. This indicates that the reliance of spouses on each other after the relationship has broken down is no longer regarded as appropriate and each should strive for independence of the other – a matter of individual responsibility for one's own autonomy.

But what of status and security, which *were* protected for both spouses under the old law? Divorce law still has built into it a number of protections for the status and security of the parties, particularly the wife, who was normally in the weaker position economically and relied on the marriage for her status and security. For instance, under the Matrimonial Causes Act 1969 neither party could complain of a 'matrimonial offence' (in effect, adultery and cruelty or unreasonable behaviour) if the parties had lived together for more than six months after the offence became known to the 'innocent' party; the rationales for this included the perceived need to encourage parties to forgive one another and not to rely on past offences and to increase the security of the 'guilty' spouse by not exposing him or her in the long term to loss of the benefits of marriage with the status and security that it carried with it (and a desire to spare the courts the need to investigate domestic differences many years after the event when the evidence might be stale). Under the Matrimonial Causes Act 1969 an 'innocent' spouse cannot be divorced against his or her will unless the parties have lived apart for five years and proper financial provision is made for the 'innocent' party in the divorce. This is supposed to protect the security and status of these parties.

The development of the law relating to marriage and divorce over the last century and a half 'adds up to a considerable shift in the balance of legal power within marriage'.[4] This of course reflects changing economic and social realities. Industrialisation and scientific advance, especially the development of reliable contraception, change the position of women in society, making it possible for them to be self-supporting and autonomous in relations with their partners. This in turn affects the roles of the parties within a marriage, reducing the need for the husband to support his wife and enabling him, too, to be autonomous.

---

4   See *Hale*, n 1, supra, p 11.

In reality, marriage is no longer regarded as a prime source of status and security for the parties. The real trend is for parties, even during a marriage, to be self-sufficient and not entitled to look for protection against financial insecurity and loss of status from the other.

Marriage and employment compared

Glendon has traced how the importance and role of the family, based on marriage, has changed. Whereas in, say, the eighteenth century, marriage was determinative of social status, distinguishing those persons entitled to derive rank and property through the family, nowadays rank and status, wealth and power are decreasingly determined by family relationships.[5] Increasingly status – and security – in society are dependent on a person's job, pension, qualifications, insurance arrangements, access to state benefits and so on rather than family or marriage.

Glendon has observed how the fact that marriage has become less important to the status of a woman (or a man) while employment has become more important to the status of all individuals is reflected in the similarities between the development of the law relating to divorce until the mid-twentieth century, which protected the wife's status and the security she derived from it, and the development of the law relating to employment, where employees are protected from dismissal by provisions bearing very close relationships with the earlier grounds for divorce.

The grounds for dismissal from employment and the procedures for dismissal reflect in many ways the old law of divorce. The grounds for divorce under the 1969 Act are irretrievable breakdown, but until 1969 they were adultery, cruelty and desertion. From 1969 irretrievable breakdown could be proved by evidence of adultery, unreasonable behaviour, desertion or living apart from two years if the respondent consented to the divorce or five years if they did not consent. Adultery's parallel in employment law would be unfaithfulness of various kinds, including disclosure of confidential information belonging to the employer to a rival, and other breaches of the duties of trust and confidence in the relationship;[6] the parallels between desertion and quitting a job are obvious; and the former matrimonial offences of cruelty, later 'unreasonable behaviour' have parallels in the grounds for actual and constructive dismissal in employment. In practice of course many

---

5   M A Glendon *State, Law and Family* (1977) pp 320-323.
6   On which see discussion in section on employment in chapter 6, supra, and *Malik v BCCI* [1997] 3 All ER 1, HL.

divorces were and still are due to the effective 'redundancy' of at least one of the parties. The parallel is that a dismissal of an employee will be potentially fair if the employee is redundant.[7]

Both family law and employment law give dependent parties – normally the wife in the marriage relationship and the employee in the employment relationship – financial security for a transitional period after the termination of a marriage or employment to enable the dependent party to become self-supporting. In marriage this is done by property transfer orders or orders for periodical payments related inter alia to need. In employment transitional security is provided through redundancy payments or awards for unfair dismissal.

The common factor between employment and marriage is that a dependent party – employee or spouse – relies on the relationship for their security and status in society. Honoré noted in his Hamlyn lectures that: 'In our pursuit of security for the weak we have overlooked the paradoxical fact that the interests of the weakest often depend upon the security of the strong'.[8] Implicit in the law relating to dismissal and redundancy on the one hand and dissolution of marriage on the other is a recognition that the less dependent party should make some provision for the weaker party once the relationship ends. The analogy cannot be pushed too far however: the statutory redundancy payment is relatively little and is unrelated to actual need; it is paid regardless of financial commitments, or whether the employee gets another job immediately or never.[9] Financial provision on divorce normally assists the more dependent spouse during the time that it is likely to take him or her to become self-supporting and thus to establish their own status and make new provision for their security.

---

7   Under the Employment Rights Act 1996, section 139(1), a dismissal of an employee is taken to be by reason of redundancy if it is attributable wholly or mainly to one of two circumstances:
    (a) the fact that the employer has ceased, or intends to cease -
        (i)   to carry on the business for the purposes of which the employee was employed, or
        (ii) to carry on that business in the place where the employee was so employed; or
    (b) the fact that the requirements of that business –
        (i)   for employees to carry out work of a particular kind, or
        (ii) for employees to carry out work of a particular kind in the place where the employee was employed by the employer, have ceased or diminished or are expected to cease or diminish.
8   T Honoré *The Quest for Security: Employees, Tenants, Wives* (1982) p 117.
9   See Deakin and Morris *Labour Law* (1998) para 5.6.2.

From the security of marriage to emancipation and self-reliance

The changed importance of marriage to its parties reflects a move in the boundary between the public and private. Philippe Aries has described how until the eighteenth century family law – at least for the wealthy property owners – was a matter of state and public concern; from the eighteenth century, as Glendon has put it, 'the family began to hold society at a distance, and to push it back beyond a steadily expanding zone of private life. The evolution of private life spread from nobles to the middle class to other social strata until it has come finally to embrace nearly the whole of society. But at the same time, the family was losing many of its functions to a series of impersonal institutions.'[10]

Individual family members were also kept out of public life – in other words certain people were essentially family members and only that. Memorably in *Beresford-Hope v Lady Sandhurst*[11] Lord Esher MR said 'I take it that by neither the common law nor the constitution of this country from the beginning of the common law until now can a woman be entitled to exercise any public function'.[12]

Writing in 1977 Glendon was able to suggest that 'The care which the State and its laws once lavished on the protection of private property has now been extended to maintaining the machinery of the social welfare state.' The Western democracies had, to a greater or lesser extent, taken over the economic and educational tasks which were once primarily the responsibility of the family. These countries had systems for distributing the risks of unemployment, sickness, death of a provider, and providing security in old age. State concern was then shifting, Glendon suggested, from providing protection against the worst aspects of insecurity to attempting to provide each individual in society with the minimum wherewithal for a decent level of existence.[13]

It was not possible to anticipate, at that time, what has turned out to be a strong trend in the last two decades, to transfer the risks of unemployment, sickness, death of a provider and old age to individuals themselves or their employers, encouraged by tax breaks for insurance and the like, and for the state no longer to seek to provide the minimum wherewithal for a decent existence. This reduction of the role of the state has largely been due to the rejection by electors across much of Western Europe and in the USA of the high tax rates that were needed to finance such provision. So currently, more than ever, the status and security of

---

10   *Glendon* p 324.
11   (1889) 23 QBD 79.
12   Ibid at 95. The Sex Disqualification (Removal) Act 1919 removed most of these legal disabilities.
13   *Glendon* p 325.

individuals, inside marriage and out, depends on their own efforts, their insurance arrangements, their membership of social organisations, and their ability to obtain skills and qualifications and find and retain employment. Recognition of the importance of these matters is evident in private law, as will be shown in chapters 8 and 9. The importance of these matters to the security and status of individuals is increasingly recognised by the courts in the development of duties of fairness and rationality, including non-discrimination, on the part of those private bodies on whom individuals increasingly have to rely for their status and security.[14]

PARENTS AND CHILDREN

In this section we note the way in which the position of children in relation to their parents has moved from one in which at common law they were virtually the property of their father if born in wedlock, to one in which they have a considerable degree of autonomy. That is not to suggest that their position in these respects is ideal. Children whose parents' relationships are unstable or have broken down may suffer from considerable insecurity, both financially and emotionally; status as derived from parents is of less importance in a more mobile society than the status that children can achieve through education or their own efforts at work; their dignity, autonomy and respect will depend in large part on how children are treated in their families and at large, rather than on their legal position. Nevertheless, the legal trend has been strongly in favour of recognising and giving weight to children's interests in the last century or so.

Illegitimacy

At common law a child born outside wedlock was 'filius nullius', and was not even recognised as the child of its mother.[15] It was thus denied all social status, and neither of its parents strictly owed it any duties.[16] Such a child would not inherit from either side of its family unless express provision were made to that effect. In the late nineteenth century this position was relaxed and mothers were recognised as having rights – subject to the welfare of the children – to custody of their illegitimate

---

14 See discussion in chapters 8 and 9; and D Oliver 'Common Values of Public and Private Law and the Public Private Divide' [1997] PL 630.

15 See *Cretney and Masson* chapter 18.

16 *Blackstone* vol 1, pp 458-459.

children.[17] Equity, in the exercise of its wardship jurisdiction, came to recognise the mother as a parent entitled to custody of the child, thus giving the child a degree of security and protection and status – though single women, especially single parents, had very little recognisable status to pass on to their children, either in society generally or in law until the period of reform that started at the end of the nineteenth century. With the passage of, first, the Legitimacy Act 1926 and most recently the Family Law Reform Act 1987 the position has now been reached that children are treated equally in law, regardless of whether their parents or other ancestors were married, save in respect of the recognition of the father (which is not automatic if the child is born out of wedlock) and the child's citizenship.

Legitimacy – the father's prerogatives

Until the passage of the Guardianship of Infants Act 1925 the father alone of a child born in wedlock had parental rights in law, though the wardship jurisdiction had developed to allow the courts to award care and control to the mother. Such children derived their social status from their fathers. But at common law they had little or no autonomy, dignity, respect or security in their relationships with their parents. Fathers were entitled at common law to the services of their (legitimate) children, and had a cause of action for damages if they were deprived of them.[18] Fathers, along with others who had the care of children, such as schoolmasters, had the right at common law to chastise their charges. The cause of action for loss of a child's services was substantially abolished by the Law Reform (Miscellaneous Provisions) Act 1970, and the parental right to chastise has been controlled by criminal law and under the European Convention on Human Rights.[19] In effect the relationship paralleled in private the positivist-authoritarian model of democracy sketched in chapter 1.

From paternal prerogatives towards equal parental rights

The Guardianship of Minors Act 1925 was passed in response first to the increasing emancipation of women, especially as a result of the Married Women's Property Act 1885 and the extension of the franchise

---

17 *Barnardo v McHugh* [1891] AC 388.
18 See J Eekelaar 'The emergence of children's rights' 6 Oxford Jo LS (1986) 161.
19 See *A v United Kingdom* Case no 100/1997/884/1096, European Court of Human Rights (1998) Times, 1 October. See generally *Cretney and Masson* chapter 18.

to women, and also in response to public concern about abuses of power by husbands in relation to their wives in disputes about the upbringing of children. In requiring that in determining disputes about the upbringing of children the first and paramount consideration should be the welfare of the child the Act echoed the position of the Chancery court in wardship. The Act was designed to protect the interests both of children and of mothers.

Cretney[20] has shown how the case for equality of parental rights was based in part on the argument that women were entitled to equal citizenship before the law; and partly on the basis that giving mothers equal parental rights would raise the *status* (my emphasis) of motherhood. The arguments against extending equal parental rights to mothers were, first, that family life required there to be a single head of the family and since the beginning of civilization the burden of taking decisions had been given to the father as the stronger and the better able to protect his children.[1] This reflected positivist-authoritarian political theory at that time which considered that it was essential that there should be a sovereign, and that the people should be tied to the sovereign in effect by ties of allegiance and obedience to the sovereign's law.[2] Another argument against joint parental rights was that divided authority was bad for children. Concern about the consequences of removing authority, similar in many respects to concerns in political theory, constitutional law, judicial review and employment law, permeated family law reform at the turn of the nineteenth century.

One implication of the extension of parental rights to mothers then is acceptance of the desirability both for parents and for children of participation by both parents in decisions about their children's upbringing, a micro-example of a political phenomenon of retreat from an authoritarian assumption that a 'sovereign' was required in any social organisation or unit including the state,[3] towards a more participative-communitarian set of assumptions about the possibilities of joint decision making and its desirability.

A bureaucratic objection to equal parental rights was put forward by Sir Claude Schuster, Permanent Secretary to the Lord Chancellor and therefore involved in the law reform questions, that it was 'essential from an administrative point of view' that a household should be treated as a single unit and that there should be 'some person within it taking decisions'.[4]

20 S M Cretney ' "What will the women want next?" The struggle for power within the family 1925-1975' (1996) 112 LQR 110.
1 *Cretney* p 116.
2 See for instance J Austin *Lectures in Jurisprudence* (5th edn, 1885).
3 See T Hobbes *Leviathan* (R Tuck, (ed) 1991).
4 Cretney 'What will the women want next?', op cit, p 119.

Towards parental responsibilities and children's rights

Eventually – but not until the Children Act 1989 – full legal equality between the parents of children born in and out of wedlock was achieved. Under that Act parents are no longer regarded as having rights arising out of their relationship with their children, but responsibilities.[5] Although the Act provides that responsibility means 'all the rights, duties, powers, responsibilities and authority which by law a parent of a child has in relation to the child and his property', the various rights, duties and so on of parents are, since the *Gillick*[6] decision, exercisable in the child's and not the parent's interests; it is this factor which converts what were the rights of parenthood into responsibilities. Fathers of children born out of wedlock may apply to a court for parental authority. In *Re C (Minors)(Parental Rights)*[7] Waite J said that entitlement to parental authority has 'real and tangible value, not only as something [the parent] can cherish for the sake of his own peace of mind, but also as a *status* carrying with it rights in waiting' (my italics), and that to give a father parental authority gives him an appropriate legal status. We have here an interesting illustration of the court acknowledging the importance of a person's status in society, in the sense of public acknowledgement (for instance, by the law) of the importance of a significant element of his life.

As far as children's rights and autonomy are concerned, these have only gradually developed, filling in the voids left by the erosion of parental authority.[8] It is of course accepted that children cannot make all decisions for themselves, because they need to be protected against their own mistakes. But the trend has been strongly in favour of increasing the autonomy of children, and a process of gradual emancipation as they mature. For instance, where disputes about children and their upbringing arise, children are now in principle entitled to make their own decisions once they have achieved a sufficient degree of maturity and intelligence to do so.[9] If such decisions are taken to the courts, children have rights to have their wishes and feelings taken into account.[10] A child who

---

5   Children Act 1989, section 3. See S Cretney and J Masson, op cit, chapter 19.
6   *Gillick v West Norfolk and Wisbech Area Health Authority and the Department of Social Security* [1986] AC 112; see S Cretney and J Masson *Principles of Family Law* (6th edn, 1997) pp 587-595.
7   [1992] 1 FLR 1 at 3.
8   See *Cretney and Masson* chapter 18; J Eekelaar 'The emergence of children's rights' (1986) 6 OJLS 161; MDAF Freeman *The Rights and Wrongs of Children* (1983).
9   *Gillick v West Norfolk and Wisbech Area Health Authority and the Department of Social Security* [1986] AC 112; see *Cretney and Masson* pp 587-595.
10   Children Act 1989, section 22.

wishes to live separately from parents may apply to the court.[11] Overall, if we consider the developments of the parent-child relationship over the last century or more we can detect a move away from a private law version of the positivist-authoritarian model towards a relationship containing elements of what in public law are participative-communitarian and responsible altruism relationships.

PARALLELS IN THE PUBLIC AND PRIVATE LAW OF RELATIONSHIPS

It may be helpful at this stage to summarise the position we have reached in this and the previous chapter in consideration of the law relating to relationships where there is an imbalance of power between the parties. In each of the relationships considered there has been a process of emancipation of the weaker parties. Private law has developed particular protective devices over the last century or more where these private relationships involve imbalances of power which expose the weaker party to interference with their dignity, autonomy, respect, status or security. This is particularly the case in the relationship of marriage. The weaker parties – wives – relied on these relationships for their status and security. But within those relationships they were entitled to very little dignity, autonomy or respect. Their emancipation has come about partly because of legal developments in the law of marriage and parenthood outlined above, and partly because of increased opportunities for women to be educated, to find employment, and to avoid pregnancy.

In employment law the additional protections for employees in the form of unfair dismissal and redundancy legislation, health and safety rules and implied terms in contract have to be counterbalanced against other developments which have reduced employee security, such as the weakening of trade unions, competition from countries where lower wages are paid, technology and changes in the labour market which mean that jobs in, for instance, manual work are fewer than they were.

The evolution in these relationships, once carrying duties of allegiance (in the case of husbands and wives and employers and employees) and obedience on one side and rights of control, almost ownership on the other, has been taking place through concepts such as the right not to be subjected to physical violence (including marital rape and chastisement), the right to be treated reasonably, the right to assert autonomy within the relationship, the control of the exercise of power by the more powerful party to a hierarchical relationship and, for wives, the right of exit from the relationship, and for children the possibility of separation from one

11 Children Act 1989, section 10(3).

or both parents. (For employees the position is different since most people need employment and a 'right of exit' is not what most employees seek.)

It has been noted that both the sovereign subject and employment relationships were based on duties of trust and confidence. These duties still exist, though disguised in various ways. In employment law they are explicit. In judicial review they can be detected in the doctrine of legitimate expectations which binds state bodies to keep faith with those in whom they have encouraged expectations, and, on the other side, in the duties imposed on individuals relying on legitimate expectations against the state to put their cards face up on the table.[12] The importance of trust in society generally is also recognised in other legal doctrines, such as fiduciary relationships, and duties of good faith.[13]

In each of the relationships considered in this and the previous chapter – and others – there is increased consciousness of the existence of power imbalances which put at risk the individual's interest in his or her dignity, autonomy, respect, status or security. And a more relaxed attitude to removing authority from the party who was the most powerful in the relationship has developed.

There are strong similarities between the development of judicial review and the law of relationships. These relationships have in common de facto and, to a much reduced extent nowadays, de jure imbalances of power. In the relationship between the subject and the sovereign and in the three relations of marriage, employment and parenthood, there were imbalances of power that were underpinned by the common law and statute. In both sets of relationships the weaker party owed duties of obedience and loyalty, and was liable to have their labour appropriated by the superior. They were subject to varying degrees of physical coercion. In both sets there were duties of protection on the part of the superior but these were virtually legally unenforceable.

In both sets of relationships the trend has been towards enhancing the autonomy, dignity, respect, status and security of the weaker party within the relationship. The move from parental rights to parental responsibility – altruism – is mirrored in public law: as with the relationship between parents and children so in relations between the state and the individual; it is now a matter of responsibility for the state to take the interests of individuals into account when making decisions, where once decisions were a matter of right deriving from sovereignty and authority.

The individual is no longer solely dependent for his or her status and security on the personal relationship with employer, spouse, parent, even, on this set of analogies, with the state, but on the legal and social

---

12 See for instance *Preston v IRC* [1985] AC 835, and discussion in chapter 5.
13 See discussion in chapter 8.

recognition of their worth as individuals, both within and outside the relationship. The state provides a safety net in terms of health care and income. As we shall see in chapters 8 and 9, there are also requirements in private law that are designed to protect the security and status of individuals outside these great relationships, for instance in their relationships with professional associations, suppliers of necessities, and of security-protecting services such as insurance, pension funds and the like.

These developments in individual-state relations and in employment, marriage and parenthood have led, I suggest, not just to increased, if not absolute, emancipation in relationships, but to a process of democratisation of relationships and of decision making and dispute resolution. Parties are increasingly entitled to considerate decision making, to have the impact on them of a decision, for instance on the determination of employment or marriage, or in decisions affecting them by public authorities taken into account and weighed in the balance against other considerations.

COMMENTS

The discussion in this and the previous chapter has focused on the ways in which the values of dignity, autonomy, respect, status and security are recognised and protected by a combination of statutory provisions and common law developments in four relationships. These concepts are not often explicitly articulated or defined and refined by the courts – the *Malik* case was exceptional in this respect – and so the exact meanings and extents of the concepts are not precise. There is of course a large literature on these values,[14] but the courts do not for the most part resort to it, partly because the values are unarticulated. These values are therefore rather simply formed but, it is suggested, they have been and will continue to be nevertheless a strong driving force in the development of both public and private law, especially where relationships of unequal power are involved.

Cotterrell has identified two opposite approaches to public law as being evident in current developments and the history of public law – a dichotomy between community and *imperium*, or, as he puts it 'between reasons, values and negotiated consensus, on the one hand, and authority, power and hierarchical control on the other'.[15] These parallel the

---

14 See for instance R Dworkin *Taking Rights Seriously* (1978); J Raz *The Morality of Freedom* (1986); J Finnis *Natural Law and Natural Rights* (1980); D Held *Models of Democracy* (1987).
15 Roger Cotterrell 'Judicial review and legal theory' in Genevra Richardson and Hazel Genn *Administrative Law and Government Action* (1994) at p 34.

participative-communitarian and positivist-authoritarian models sketched in the first chapter. We can clearly see the development from *imperium* to community in the sovereign/subject relationship and Blackstone's 'great relations' in private life since his time.

In other relationships too, when undue influence exists between a stronger and a weaker party, the trend is for the law to impose a duty on the superior to take 'reasonable steps' to ensure that the potentially improperly pressured party is properly advised.[16] Hence the examination in this and the previous chapter of the evolution of the law relating to these four relationships is not intended to suggest that the evolution of the law to a principle of respect for the key values is limited to these relationships. They illustrate sharply a set of developments in the control of the potential abuse of power which can also be traced in other aspects of the law and which reflect the development in both public and private law of principles of participative communitarianism and considerate altruism.

The history of the legal development of these relationships suggests that public law, if it is a separate category from private law, is not so old and not so very different, even today, from what we now regard as private law. The law relating to subject sovereign relations has its roots in the law of persons, part of private law. A public-private divide is of very recent pedigree. Legal developments have been very similar across the relationships considered here – the move from rights to responsibilities and altruism on the part of the more powerful parties, from exploitation to emancipation, from authority to democracy, from imperium to community. These relationships all illustrate the interweaving of strands in democratic and citizenship theory noted in chapter 1 and a move over time from the positivist-authoritarian theory towards a combination of participative-communitarian and considerate altruism theories.

One thing that is common in the relationships considered in this and the previous chapter is the decreasing ability of citizens, employees, spouses or children to rely for their security or status on the superior parties to these relationships. Hence the exercise of power by institutions of civil society on whom individuals have to rely becomes the more important to them as a source of security and status. These institutions include those with whom they are in property or contractual relationships, professional and sporting associations, other membership associations (trade unions, pensions, insurance societies and the like), providers of necessities (the utilities, those in positions of monopoly). In the next two chapters we consider these – and other – private law relationships, and

---

16 *Barclays Bank v O'Brien* [1994] 1 AC 180, AC; *Lloyds Bank v Bundy* [1974] 3 All ER 757.

ways in which private law protects the dignity, autonomy and respect of individuals against the exercise of private power and introduces elements of civil democracy into those relationships.

Chapter Eight

Private Law 1: Tort, Contract and Equity

We now move to note some of the ways in which private law protects the interests of individuals, controls exercises of power and is influenced by the models of democracy and citizenship sketched in chapter 1. The topics covered in this and the next chapter are only a sample of this function of private law. There is not the space for an exhaustive analysis of the subject, but it should be borne in mind that restitution, property law and specific aspects of contract and tort that are not covered in what follows also perform these functions.

   The emphasis will be on the similarities between private and public law. Our concern will also be with the public-private divide and in ways in which public law is integrated into private law in some areas, notably in tort.

TORT

The arguments against imposing civil obligations on private bodies were analysed in chapter 1. It was suggested that in practice the courts do impose duties and obligations of consideration towards others in private law and that public and private law are not distinguishable by the question whether duties are consensual or imposed. The law of tort provides strong examples of the willingness on the part of the courts to impose duties of considerate altruism – to adopt one of the models of democracy discussed in chapter 1 – on private bodies. In the case of *Donoghue v Stevenson*[1] the House of Lords imposed on producers a regime of product liability, and indeed very wide duties of consideration for

---

1   [1932] AC 562.

'neighbours' outside contract. In the light of the debates about the basis for judicial review, it is worth noting at this point that there is not the same degree of controversy about the legitimacy of the courts developing the law in radical ways in tort, imposing obligations on private bodies, as there is about the courts imposing obligations in public law. This raises the question why so much controversy surrounds the suggestion, discussed in chapter 2, that the courts in the exercise of their ancient functions in the development of the common law – and equity – are not simply giving effect to the intentions of Parliament, and may legitimately *impose* obligations on state bodies. What the decision in *Donoghue v Stevenson* has in common with judicial review is that the courts are developing duties of considerate and responsible altruism where activity may have detrimental effects on individuals. In imposing duties of care – of considerate action – on manufacturers and others the House of Lords in *Donoghue v Stevenson* and in the subsequent development of the law of negligence have in effect been democratising the private sector, and this forms part of the system of 'civil democracy' which it is suggested is being constructed as the common law and statute, in both public and private law, evolve.

The integration of public and private law in tort

Tort law provides a good example of an integrated approach to public and private law, in that where points of substantive public law arise in a tort action the courts will deal with them alongside the private law points. Normally no question arises of short time limits, permission to apply, or other procedural privileges for 'public' defendants in tort actions. It was noted in chapter 4 that short time limits in civil actions against public bodies were removed by the Limitation Act 1936, and such bodies are subject to the same limitation periods as private bodies in tort litigation. In other words there is no procedural or remedial public-private divide in tort, though there are differences in substantive tort law – but no divide – between purely private torts and tort actions where there are elements of public law. For instance, *Anns v London Borough of Merton*[2] establishes that a duty of care may be owed by a public body for the negligent exercise or non-exercise of statutory powers which result in injury to a person or physical damage to property. This inevitably involves the court in determining the extent of the statutory power, and it may require the court to decide whether there had been a failure to exercise the power or whether it has been exercised unreasonably or ultra vires. *Anns* introduced a distinction between 'policy' and 'operational' decisions.

---

2   [1978] AC 728, HL. See also *Barrett v London Borough of Enfield* [1999] 3 WLR 79, HL.

Liability in negligence may not be imposed in respect of 'policy' decisions, but may be imposed in respect of 'operational' decisions – even though those decisions may have been discretionary. Questions as to the extent to which discretionary decision making is controlled by the courts are matters which, in other contexts, could also be raised in judicial review – essentially public law issues. But if such a point arises in a tort action the court has jurisdiction to deal with it. *Anns*, therefore, provides a good example of an integrated approach to public and private law.

Justiciability issues in tort: implications for the public-private divide

Although the basic position on the tortious liability of public authorities, as established by *Entick v Carrington*[3] is that they are in the same position as private tortfeasors and must show statutory authority for what would otherwise be tortious actions, recently the courts have developed a number of limitations to the tortious liability of public bodies in situations in which there would appear to be prima facie liability, on public policy grounds. Thus public bodies may be in a privileged position as compared with private defendants in some tort actions. For instance, in *Hill v Chief Constable of West Yorkshire*[4] an action against the Chief Constable of the area police force for negligence in failing to apprehend a murderer before the plaintiff's daughter was killed was struck out on the basis, first, that in the absence of any special ingredient over and above reasonable foreseeability of likely harm which would establish proximity of relationship between the victim of a crime and the police, the police did not owe a general duty of care to individual members of the public to identify and apprehend an unknown criminal, even though it was reasonably foreseeable that harm was likely to be caused to a member of the public if the criminal was not detected and apprehended; and, secondly, even if such a duty did exist, public policy required that the police should not be liable in such circumstances.[5] In the later case of *Osman v Ferguson*[6] there was much stronger evidence of the direct threat to a murder victim by the murderer, whose identity and threatening activity were known to the police in advance, and yet the Court of Appeal upheld the immunity of the police on public policy grounds. Thus there are special common law immunities in some torts for public bodies.

---

3   (1765) 19 State Tr 1029.
4   [1989] AC 53, HL.
5   On immunities, see J Beatson '"Public" and "private" in English administrative law' (1987) 103 LQR 34.
6   [1993] 4 All ER 344, CA.

However, *Osman* was taken to the European Court of Human Rights in Strasbourg, where it was held that such an immunity would be contrary to the European Convention on Human Rights, although it would be appropriate for a domestic court to make a considered assessment on the basis of arguments before it as to whether a particular case was or was not suitable for the application of a rule that liability in negligence should not be imposed on the ground that it was fair, just and reasonable to apply an exclusionary rule.[7] In the light of the Convention jurisprudence it seems likely that, when the Human Rights Act 1998 comes into force in 2000, remaining common law immunities will go, and instead the parties will have to argue the case for or against denying liability in each particular case where previously there has been immunity.[8]

The significant points about the *Osman* case and other cases where public bodies enjoy immunity for present purposes are, first, that issues of public policy and public law arise and are dealt with by the courts in 'private law' actions: there is no substantive, procedural or remedial 'divide' here, though there are differences between the tort liability of public and private bodies or those exercising private as opposed to governmental or public functions. Secondly, the five values may yield to public interests, illustrating how they are values and not rights. And thirdly, the European Convention on Human Rights affects the substance of private law in radical ways.

In tort actions against public bodies there will commonly be implications for the allocation of scarce resources if liability is imposed – that was one of the issues in *Osman v Ferguson*. In *Stovin v Wise*[9] the plaintiff had been injured at a road junction where visibility was impaired because of a bank on private land. The local authority had not taken steps that were open to it to alter the bank to improve visibility. It was held that the authority was not liable for a failure to exercise a mere statutory power to remove a danger not created by it, despite the fact that the injury was foreseeable. This was because the local authority had the right to decided how to allocate resources between this and other calls on it. In effect decisions about allocation of resources were not justiciable.

7   *Osman v United Kingdom* Case No 87/1997/871/1083, Human Rights Law Report, (1998) Times, 5 November.
8   Note that statutory provisions providing immunity from personal liability for individuals who are members of local authorities, National Health Service bodies and others, but preserving the liability in tort of the body itself, as in the Public Health Act 1875, section 265, as amended, may not be objectionable: see S Bailey 'Personal liability in local government law' [1999] Public Law 461.
9   [1996] AC 923.

Claimants' interests in tort

Harlow has commented that 'modern tort law is increasingly "victim orientated"' noting that academic lawyers classify cases according to the nature of the plaintiff's injury: personal injuries, injuries to property, to reputation, to economic interests, etc.[10] This is not to deny that tort law is concerned at all with the defendant's conduct – negligence clearly is. But tort remedies are concerned to put things right for the plaintiff. In this respect tort law provides a contrast with judicial review which is primarily concerned with controlling the respondent's actions and decision-making processes in the public interest rather than with providing a 'victim' with an adequate remedy. This is partly at least because one purpose of judicial review is to promote the rule of law and uphold legality in government and good administration – respondent-oriented purposes. However, with the coming into force of the Human Rights Act it is to be expected that judicial review will have to focus to a greater extent on providing complainants with an effective remedy than hitherto.[11]

By contrast with judicial review, the law of tort is commonly concerned with protecting[12] the plaintiff's interests, and restoring the status quo ante so far as possible, normally by payment of compensation, if damage has been suffered as a result of tortious actions. Defamation, which protects a person's reputation by providing a remedy for allegations which tend to lower him in the estimation of right-thinking members of society generally,[13] is an obvious example of the law of tort seeking to protect the status, in the sense of social standing, of individuals. But a person's interest in their standing in society is also recognised as forming part of the rationale for other torts – for instance, in false imprisonment: the point was made in *Meering v Grahame-White Aviation Co Ltd*[14] that knowledge on the part of the 'prisoner' of his imprisonment is not necessary, since the 'imprisoner' may be boasting to others that the plaintiff is imprisoned. If this is indeed an explanation, or part of the

---

10 C Harlow ' "Public" and "Private" Law: Definition without Distinction' (1980) 43 *Modern Law Review* 241 at p 254. There are of course other possible classifications of tort law, for instance in terms of the state of mind of the defendant, as with strict liability, negligence, intentional torts.

11 See chapter 10.

12 Weir has commented that '... tort law is protective' (comparing tort with contract, which is 'productive'): T Weir 'Complex Liabilities' *Int Encl Comp L* (1976), 5.

13 *Sim v Stretch* [1936] 2 All ER 1237, 1240, per Lord Atkin. See also *Lewis v Daily Telegraph* [1964] AC 234, *Byrne v Deane* [1937] 1 KB 818 and *R v Bishop* [1975] QB 274 for the difficulties in deciding what a right-thinking member of society is and what he or she would think.

14 (1920) 122 LT 44, 53-54.

explanation, of the decision, the implication is that the tort does not only protect the plaintiff's interest in autonomy – freedom of movement – but also his or her status as a free person in society. The tort of negligence has recently been extended to include a duty of care in the preparation of references, for instance by employers or ex-employers,[15] and others who have assumed responsibility for the subject of the reference and are relied on – for instance, universities providing references for their students: references are of vital importance to the status – and future security – of those in respect of whom they are provided (and their opportunities to pursue the occupation of their choice).

The law of tort also provides some protection for individual security, both physical and financial. Watching and besetting is a tort. The tort of harassment protects a person's 'legitimate interest' in being free from being pestered and having his or her peace of mind disturbed, as well as being free from torts of assault and battery.[16] The torts of interference with contract and negligence resulting in financial loss are examples of torts protecting financial – security – interests. But there is no tort of mere damaging commercial competition[17] – as noted in the discussion of the concept of values in chapter 3, security is not a right, only a value.

Autonomy and dignity in privacy are protected by the torts of nuisance and trespass to land. Autonomy and dignity are also protected by the torts of false imprisonment, assault and battery, and negligence resulting in personal injury. It is particularly notable that liability for false imprisonment arises regardless of fault, thus emphasising the primacy of the interest of the individual in freedom of movement.[18]

Value clashes in the law of tort: medical cases

The point was made in chapter 3 that values, not being rights, will often give way to other considerations. This is well illustrated in the law of tort by a number of cases in the area of medical treatment, where problems arise if a patient is unable or unwilling to consent to treatment which doctors consider to be advisable, either because it is in the interests of the patient as perceived by doctors, or because other interests or considerations prevail. Professional 'prerogatives' of determining what

15 *Spring v Guardian Assurance* [1995] 2 AC 296.
16 See *Khorasandjian v Bush* [1993] 3 All ER 669; *Burris v Azadani* [1995] 4 All ER 802, CA and cases there cited. See also Protection from Harassment Act 1997.
17 Restrictive Trade Practices Act 1976.
18 See *R v Governor of Brockhill Prison, ex p Evans (No 2)* [1999] 2 WLR 103, CA (a prison governor, without fault, miscalculated the term for which the applicant was imprisoned. Held, that the applicant was entitled to be compensated for the whole period of unlawful detention).

is for the best have frequently clashed in this area with patient autonomy. For instance, courts have ordered that a sixteen year old anorexic girl be subjected to treatment she did not wish to have,[19] that a pregnant woman in labour should have her baby delivered by Caesarian section against her will to save her and the child,[20] that a patient should receive a blood transfusion despite her (religious) objections,[1] that a mentally disabled young woman should be sterilised – such examples could be multiplied.

However, in each of these cases the courts have accepted that in principle individuals who are capable of giving or refusing consent to treatment are entitled to have their wishes respected. In some of these areas the law has developed from an initial willingness to override the refusal or lack of consent by the individual patient on the ground that the medical profession's views of the patient's interests should prevail over those of the patient, in favour of upholding the patient's autonomy in various way. Thus in the anorexia case referred to above there was a finding of fact that the patient, when well, had a sufficient degree of maturity and understanding to meet the *Gillick* test[2] for autonomous decision making, but that she was at the time of the case severely ill, so that her ability to make a judgment about treatment was removed. The court therefore felt justified in ordering that treatment should be administered as it would, in the view of the court, be in her best interests even though she did not agree. But the court decided generally judges should not override the decisions of minors who were well enough and of sufficient maturity to make the decisions for themselves. But it is significant that in that case the court did not apply the test 'what would the patient have wished if she had been fit?'

In *St George's Healthcare NHS Trust v S; R v Collins, ex p S*[3] the court decided that a woman in labour was entitled to refuse a caesarian section, even though that would put the life of her unborn baby at risk. The court rested its decision squarely on respect for her autonomy. 'Even when his or her own life depends on receiving medical treatment, an adult of sound mind is entitled to refuse it. This reflects the autonomy of each individual and the right of self-determination'.[4] This decision followed a number of others in which the courts had sanctioned such operations, on the ground that the woman was unable to consent and the doctors in

---

19 *Re W (A minor) (Medical treatment: court's jurisdiction)* [1992] 3 WLR 758. See also *B v Croydon Health Authority* [1995] 2 WLR 294.

20 *Re S (Adult: refusal of treatment)* [1992] 3 WLR 806.

1 *Re T (Adult: refusal of treatment)* [1992] 3 WLR 782.

2 *Gillick v West Norfolk and Wisbech Area Health Authority and the Department of Social Security* [1986] AC 112. See discussion in chapter 7.

3 [1998] 3 All ER 673, CA; see R Bailey-Harris 'Pregnancy, autonomy and refusal of medical treatment' (1998) 114 LQR 550.

4 Per Judge LJ at p 685.

attendance were therefore entitled to operate in their view of her interests,[5] rather than on the basis of what, on the evidence, she would have wanted had she been capable of deciding. (In such cases a decision in favour of the autonomy of the mother as against the life and therefore the autonomy of the unborn child is not at all easy to make, especially when the case is brought before the judge as an emergency.)

In *Re F (Mental Patient: Sterilisation)*[6] the question was whether a mentally handicapped, sexually active woman should be sterilised. She was not able to understand the consequences of sexual intercourse and would not be able to care adequately for any children she might bear. The House of Lords was willing to authorise sterilisation if the doctors having care of the patient were satisfied that this would be in her best interests. This decision replaced the autonomy of the patient with judicial – and medical – paternalism. If the test had been, would the patient have agreed to this treatment if she had had the necessary capacity, then the decision would have synthesised, or replicated as far as possible, the patient's own autonomy.[7]

Ex p L[8] concerned an autistic adult who was so disabled as not to be able to consent to medical treatment. He was living with carers, attending a day centre. One day he became agitated at the day centre, his carers were not contactable, the day centre could not cope with him and he was taken into hospital, sedated, and remained in hospital thereafter. The House of Lords held that, as he could neither consent nor refuse consent to treatment, the hospital was entitled at common law, under the doctrine of necessity, to give him such treatment as might be prescribed in (what the medical practitioners regarded as) his best interests. However, Lord Steyn expressed great concern that this position left such patients without statutory protection for their 'moral right to be treated with dignity'.[9]

As the case law develops in these medical cases, the courts are feeling their way towards a balance in favour of autonomy, dignity and respect for patients on a case by case basis, often having difficulties resolving very hard choices between paternalism and autonomy on the way. It is significant for our thesis, however, that even where hospitals are entitled to treat a patient without his or her consent, this must always be done altruistically and in what are regarded as the patient's interests, not in the

5   *Re S (Adult: Refusal of Medical Treatment)* [1992] 4 All ER 671, Sir Stephen Brown P.

6   [1990] 2 AC 1.

7   See M D A Freeman 'Sterilising the mentally handicapped' in Freeman (ed) *Medicine, Ethics and the Law* (1988); J Shaw 'Sterilisation of mentally handicapped people: Judge rules OK?' (1990) 53 MLR 91; Feldman *Civil Liberties and Human Rights in England and Wales* (1993) p 149.

8   *R v Bournewood Community and Mental Health NHS Trust, ex p L (Secretary of State for Health and others intervening)* [1998] 3 All ER 289, HL.

9   Ibid at 309.

general public interest or the interests of others, for instance, a patient's parents or carers.[10] Where a patient has given an advance directive, before becoming incapable, treatment and care should normally be subject to the advance directive, but if there is reason to doubt the reliability of the advance directive, then an application to the court for a declaration may be made. What is lacking is a principle that the court should make such order as it believes the patient would wish, if he or she were capable of making an autonomous decision. Instead, the court will sanction either the decision that the medical practitioners would consider to be in the interests of the patient, or what the court considers to be in those interests. This leaves little scope for a patient who, if he or she were capable of giving or refusing consent to treatment, would prefer to refuse medical treatment – for instance, surgery or a blood transfusion – to have those preferences respected where a practitioner or a judge considers that surgery or a blood transfusion would be in his or her interests.

Given the case law in medical cases it would be impossible to argue that there is a wholesale commitment in tort to acknowledging the importance of the five values or elevating them to 'rights'. But these values are important background considerations for the courts when deciding cases about interference with the individual's enjoyment of these values. Kennedy argues, persuasively, that 'medical law [should be] seen as part of human rights law, and that an approach based on parties' rights offers the most fruitful basis for legal development. ... I regard the right to inviolability and the right privacy as the two central pillars.'[11] In effect in this area the tension is between a paternalistic approach to the doctor-patient relationship – a benevolent but essentially positivist-authoritarian approach – and a democratic, participative-communitarian approach, to adopt the democratic models outlined in chapter 1.

Tortious abuse of power by public bodies

We are used to thinking of tort law as preeminently private law. However, as Samuel has commented, the law of tort, while on the one hand performing functions analogous to those of delictual liability in civil law, has, on the other hand, a fundamental public law dimension.[12]

10 This was established in the *Gillick* case, discussed in chapter 7.
11 I Kennedy 'The fiduciary relationship between doctors and patients' in P Birks (ed) *Wrongs and Remedies in the Twenty-first Century* (1996) 111 at pp 117-118.
12 G Samuel 'The impact of European integration on private law – a comment' 18 *Legal Studies* (1998) 167 at 171. And see G Samuel and J Rinkes *Law of Obligations and Legal Remedies* (1996) pp 352-356.

Historically tort law has performed important political functions in protecting the political rights of individuals and promoting good administration and the rule of law – for instance through the torts of misfeasance in a public office,[13] usurpation of a public office, and interference with the right to vote.[14] Many of the central features of the British constitution are laid down in tort – *Entick v Carrington*[15] – which upheld the rights of individuals not to have their property removed or to be imprisoned on the sayso of a public official – is a prime example.[16] Liability under the *Francovich*[17] case in European law, as long as the vertical effect doctrine continues[18] is a further example of the role of tort law in upholding individuals' interests against the state and the principle of legality. This is an area in which public and private law cannot be separated.

The action for misfeasance in a public office illustrates how tort law performs a function of protecting individuals – and public interests – against abuses of power. In *Three Rivers District Council v Bank of England (No 3)*[19] some six thousand depositors had lost their money when the Bank of Credit and Commerce International went into liquidation. Their security in their savings had been lost. They sued the Bank of England, which had the statutory function of regulating banks, for failing to supervise BCCI in accordance with its statutory responsibilities. The action was for misfeasance in a public office rather than negligence because the common law does not recognises a duty of care on the part of banking supervisors to the depositing public.[20] On the point of law relating to liability for misfeasance Clarke J held that a holder of a public office will be liable if it has deliberately taken action which it knows to be unlawful, if it knew or should have known that the action would probably injure the plaintiff. The office holder will also be liable if it acts recklessly.[1] The Court of Appeal in due course struck out the claim, and held that there should not be a rigid distinction between the

---

13   See *Three Rivers District Council v Governor of the Bank of England (No 3)* [1996] 3 All ER 558, Clarke J; and (1998) Times, 10 December, CA.

14   *Ashby v White* (1703) 2 Ld Raym 938.

15   (1765) 19 State Tr 1030.

16   See also discussion of the tortious liability of medical practitioners for non-consensual treatment of patients earlier in this chapter, and the discussion in chapter 1 of instances where public and private law mingle.

17   *Francovich v Italy* [1991] ECR 1-5357.

18   See discussion in chapter 5.

19   [1996] 3 All ER 558, Clarke J; (1998) Times, 10 December, CA.

20   See *Davis v Radcliffe* [1990] 1 WLR 821, PC.

1   See *Three Rivers District Council v Bank of England (No 3)* [1996] 3 All ER 558, Clarke J; *Bourgoin SA v Minister of Agriculture* [1986] QB 716; and see C. Hadjiemmanuil 'Civil liability of regulatory authorities after the Three Rivers case' [1997] Public Law 32.

two limbs of the tort, but the need to prove a guilty state of mind on the part of an official body was not out of date or unjustifiable. The law relating to misfeasance was not set in stone and was susceptible of judicial development.[2]

It seems likely that under the Human Rights Act 1998 the courts will develop a tort of breach of privacy under article 8, maintainable only against public authorities within the meaning of the Act (it does not seem to be intended that there will be a new tort of breach of privacy as such maintainable in respect of private acts or activity under the Human Rights Act).[3] Yet these public authority tort actions will be brought in the ordinary courts according to the normal procedure, without being subjected to short limitation periods or permission requirements.

Privacy is but one example of what may develop into a 'family' of constitutional torts or sui generis wrongs under the Human Rights Act. The assumption seems to be that remedies in these cases will be discretionary, including the award of damages, which, in normal common law tort actions are awarded as of right. Here, then, the borderline between public and private law rules of liability will be breaking down – as indeed are the borderlines between contract and tort, and equity and the common law, as later discussion will show.

No doubt in due course the liability of private bodies for invasions of privacy will develop in tune with the liability of public bodies. There is no procedural or remedial divide in such cases, and the substantive public and private law of tort operate alongside one another in an integrated fashion, cross-fertilising in the process.

CONTRACT

In considering the ways in which the law of contract protects the interests of individuals, and the parallels between contract and judicial review we need to bear in mind the orthodox theoretical position that in judicial review the courts are *imposing* duties of considerate decision making which protect the enjoyment of these values by those affected by public activity, whereas in contract obligations are *consensual or self-imposed*, deriving either from promises by the parties, or from detrimental reliance by the plaintiff on the defendant, or from the fact that the defendant has (voluntarily) received a benefit.[4]

2   *Three Rivers District Council v Bank of England (No 4)*, (1998) Times, 10 December, CA.
3   See chapter 10.
4   For the debates about the rationales of contract, which we do not seek to resolve here, see the following: on contract as promise: C Fried *Contract as Promise* (1981); on reliance and benefit theories: P S Atiyah *Essays on Contract* (reprinted

Classically contract theory upholds individual autonomy by granting freedom to contract on such terms as are agreed between the parties, and then holding both parties to the contract.[5] In practice, however, contractual agreements limit the autonomy of one or more of the parties for the duration of the contract, and commonly they create unequal power relations between the parties. We can make sense of much of the legislation in the field of contract (for instance, the Unfair Contract Terms Act 1977 provisions against exclusions or limitations of liability, the Consumer Credit Act 1974 protection against exploitation, and provisions in the Employment Rights Act 1996 protecting employees against unfair dismissal) if we see such measures as redressing power imbalances and protecting the weaker contracting party's interests in the five values – their real autonomy in relation to particularly important matters during the relationship, their respect and their security.

It is not only statutory provisions, however, which seek to protect the interests of contracting parties and to prevent exploitation from imbalances of power. As Smith has argued, common law doctrines against self-enslavement contracts, restrictive covenants (ie in restraint of trade), equitable relief clauses and stipulated damages clauses are best understood as 'expressing the principle that the state should not help individuals to limit their freedom unduly'; in reality 'the value of freedom itself, in particular the value of future freedom, provides one reason for limiting freedom of contract.'[6]

The orientations of contract law: interests and the control of power

The point has already been made that tort law is 'victim orientated', focusing on the impact of action on the plaintiff.[7] Is this true of contract too? Collins advances the theory that the principles underlying contract have altered since the nineteenth century, when the dominant principles were the morality of promise-keeping and individual autonomy in the form of freedom of contract, so that it now rests on principles of fairness,

---

1990); Fuller and Perdue 'The reliance Interest in Contract Damages' (1936) 46 *Yale Law Jo* 52 and 373; on justice theory: H Collins *The Law of Contract* (1997). See also J Wightman *Contract. A Critical Commentary* 1996, chapter 3.

5   See D Levine *Needs, Rights and the Market* (1988); D H Parry *The Sanctity of Contract* (1959); H Collins 'The sanctimony of contract' in R Rawlings (ed) *Law, Society and Economy* (1997) 63 at pp 65-67.

6   See S Smith 'Future freedom and freedom of contract' (1996) 59 MLR 167 at p 187.

7   See C Harlow ' "Public" and "Private" Law: Definition without distinction' (1980) 43 *Modern Law Review* 241 at p 254.

reliance and cooperation – concepts of the social market[8] which focus on the vulnerability of parties rather than the assumed autonomy of both sides. This 'victim oriented' perspective is borne out by examples. The equitable jurisdiction in contract, for instance in setting aside transactions entered into under duress or undue influence, or where the defendant's conduct was unconscionable, illustrate how there can be two focuses when analysing contractual relationships, especially where there are imbalances of power: defendant-sided focuses and plaintiff-sided focuses. This is not the place to enter into the debates about what the relationships are between undue influence and unconscionable dealings in contract.[9] Relief given for duress or undue influence clearly protects the autonomy of individuals by releasing them from obligations which were not freely entered into. They may, secondarily, also serve to protect other values such as security, respect, dignity. They are plaintiff-sided or impact-oriented. Relief granted on the ground of unconscionable conduct by the other party to a contract manifests a defendant-sided approach. But such relief nevertheless protects the dignity and respect of the weaker party, by penalising the exploiter who did not treat the weaker party with consideration and respect. The implication of giving relief for duress or undue influence is that the more powerful contracting party is under a certain duty of altruism which requires him or her to give some weight to the other party's interests in the relationship[10] – one of a number of examples we shall encounter in which private law expects altruism of private parties.[11]

In some of these cases the relief against unconscionable conduct will protect the security of the weaker party, as where, for instance (as in *Barclays Bank v O'Brien*[12]), the ownership or occupation of the family home is at stake. In other words, whether the approach is defendant-sided or plaintiff-sided, the ultimate rationale for granting relief to the plaintiff in these cases is recognition of the importance of his or her

8   See H Collins *The Law of Contract* (1986); and 'The sanctimony of contract' in R Rawlings (ed) *Law, Society and Economy* (1997) 63 at p 68; see also R Brownsword 'From co-operative contracting to a contract of co-operation' in D Campbell and P Vincent-Jones (eds) *Contract and Economic Organisation* (1996); J Wightman in *Contract, A Critical Commentary* (1996), chapters 7 and 8.
9   On this see P Birks and Chin Nyuk Yin 'On the nature of undue influence' in J Beatson and D Friedmann (eds) *Good Faith and Fault in Contract Law* (1995) pp 57-97 and literature cited there; and D Capper 'Undue influence and unconscionability: a rationalisation' (1998) 114 LQR 479.
10 See *Wightman*, at pp 104-109.
11 In contract the idea of cooperative contracting involves acceptance that there may be a contractual community of interest between the parties which sets the limits to self-regarding conduct and imposes degrees of altruism: see R Brownsword, 'From co-operative contracting to a contract of co-operation' in D Campbell and P Vincent-Jones (eds) op cit at pp 37-38.
12 [1994] 1 AC 180.

dignity, autonomy, respect, status or security. Both defendant-sided and plaintiff-sided approaches are in practice victim and impact-oriented approaches. A further point about undue influence is that where what has occurred is 'presumed undue influence'[13] it is behaviour which breaches the duties of trust and confidence which the law *imposes* in certain relationships.[14] But it can also be exploitative behaviour by a more powerful party which breaches the trust and confidence which is found *to exist in fact* in a relationship.[15]

Collins focuses on the importance of trust in contractual relationships, noting that in reality legal sanctions present no credible threat to parties to the contract, and contractual transactions are effective in practice because they often rest on mutual trust between the parties which it would not be worthwhile for the parties to break.[16] From this perspective it is possible to see that the mitigation of the rigours of strict contract law on the nineteenth century model through rules which protect individuals from exploitation, taken with the reality of the need for trust in contract on the part of the more powerful as well as the weaker parties, can serve to promote the real, effective security of both sides in contractual relations.[17]

Contract and the control of discretion

There are strong parallels between aspects of contract law and judicial review. The ways in which the courts have developed principles for the construction of the express terms of some contracts and the implication of terms have incorporated acknowledgement of the importance of the five values into the values of contract law. In practice the courts are exercising a supervisory jurisdiction in some contract cases, thus controlling exercises of power that might interfere with the interests of weaker individuals.

We are concerned here primarily with purely 'private' contracts between parties who would not on any interpretation of the current case law be regarded as 'public' or discharging public or governmental functions. But Beatson has noted that ' ... the issues raised by ... good

---

13   See per Lord Browne-Wilkinson in *Barclays Bank plc v O'Brien* [1994] 1 AC 180; see also per Millett LJ in *Credit Lyonnais v Burch* [1997] 1 All ER 144.
14   See D Capper 'Undue influence and unconscionability' (1998) 114 LQR 479 at 482-484. See discussion of trust and confidence in employment in chapter 6.
15   *Credit Lyonnais v Burch* [1997] 1 All ER 144, per Millett LJ at 154.
16   Collins in Rawlings (ed) supra, at pp 70-73.
17   The importance of trust and confidence in the relationships between sovereign and subject, and in employment, was also noted in chapter 6.

faith and fairness, pre-contractual duties, and long term or "relational" contracts can usefully be illuminated by public law principles.'[18]

A problem that Beatson identifies, which separates contract law from judicial review, is that 'contract law has difficulty in dealing with discretion ...'[19] The starting point, historically at least, has been until recently that a discretion granted by contract is unfettered. This point is well illustrated by the case of *Weinberger v Inglis (No 2)*[20] in which the House of Lords was not willing to interfere with a refusal by the Committee of the London Stock Exchange to re-elect the plaintiff to the Exchange, because he was of German birth. The rules of the exchange empowered the Committee to admit such persons as it 'shall think proper'. However, following the analysis by Collins mentioned earlier, this case may be characteristic of a period where the justice of exchange dominated contract law – which was also the period in which in public law a positivist-authoritarian theory about the exercise of state power was dominant. Other cases demonstrate a preference for justice ideals of the social market, namely fairness of exchange, individual autonomy and cooperation in the treatment of discretionary power enjoyed under contracts, especially but not only where the effect of a discretionary decision upon an individual will be to damage their interests in the five key values.[1] For instance, in the shipping case of *Tillmanns & Co v SS Knutsford Ltd* (1908) the master of a ship had a contractual power to land a cargo at a port other than the port of discharge where that port was unsafe or inaccessible. It was held that he must 'exercise that discretion fairly as between both parties, and not merely to do his best for the shipowners, his masters, disregarding the interests of the charterers.'[2] Beatson gives further examples of how tests similar to those which are currently applied in applications for judicial review have been employed in contract cases to control the possible abuse of discretion or power for many years. The themes that emerge from these cases are very similar to those that were identified in relation to judicial review in chapter 5, namely the lack of the right to act partially, or entirely selfishly.[3] They impose a private law equivalent of the considerate altruism model of democracy on contracting parties.

---

18 J Beatson 'Judicial review in contract' in J Beatson and D Friedmann (eds) op cit at p 263.
19 *Beatson and Friedmann* at p 267.
20 [1919] AC 606.
1   This is also the case in contracts of a more commercial nature where the five key values for individuals are not at stake, such as shipping contract of various kinds: see Beatson, op cit at p. 268.
2   [1908] 2 KB 385 at 406.
3   See *Beatson and Friedmann* at pp 268-269.

One point here is that the common law seeks often to uphold a high degree of trust in civil society and the limitation of rights to act partially and selfishly will engender trust. Trust is particularly important in mutual undertakings such as mutual insurance, and bodies exercising self-regulatory powers over business, profession or sport. Here, Beatson suggests 'contractual discretions have been held not to be unfettered but to be subject to common law principles of procedural propriety (ie fairness or natural justice), "*Wednesbury*" reasonableness (or rationality), bona fides, propriety of purpose, and relevancy.'[4] This requirement of trustworthy behaviour in turn fosters a culture of participation, democracy and citizenship – and incidentally, a culture against corruption – even in civil society, topics that will be explored in chapter 12.

However, Beatson's conclusion is that contract law *generally* has not been influenced either by public law principles or by the rules of statutory regulatory regimes, and that it is only in a number of particular situations that a limited concept of 'abuse of rights' has been recognised in a contractual context. These include formal precontractual tendering processes or where one contracting party has power which he is supposed to use to hold the balance between a number of competing interests, so that the power is in some sense administrative, or where the liability is a cooperative one, or one that depends upon the party being satisfied upon a point which involves investigating a matter which the other ought fairly to be heard on.[5]

Daintith sees things differently.[6] In his consideration of the ways in which the exercise of contracting power by government is controlled by the court he seeks comparisons in the way in which the courts have treated disputes about the exercise of discretionary powers in private contracts. In a constitutive contract where the contract is a way of regulating the continuing relationship of a group with a common purpose such as a club, a trade union or a company, he argues, if the common purpose is clear then the courts will use it as a criterion against which to measure the exercise of discretion;[7] in the absence of such guidance, the courts have relied on the fiduciary position of the controlling group, and have founded on this a general obligation to act

---

4   Beatson in *Beatson and Friedmann* at p 269.
5   *Beatson and Friedmann* at p 288.
6   See T C Daintith 'Regulation by contract: The New Prerogative' in [1979] CLP 41.
7   Op cit at p 55-56. Cases on this include *Punt v Symons & Co Ltd* [1903] 2 Ch 506; *Hogg v Cramphorn Ltd* [1967] Ch 254. See also *Stevenson v United Road Transport Union* [1977] ICR 893, discussed in chapter 6. However, in the case of trade unions the courts have not shown sympathy with the collective objectives of the organisation: see S Deakin and G Morris *Labour Law* (1998) chapter 10.

in good faith, not corruptly, or arbitrarily or capriciously.[8] In commercial contracts too, Daintith shows, power – for instance power to approve of goods or of improvements by a lessee – must be exercised in good faith, not capriciously, in accordance with the presumed intentions of the parties.[9] Daintith observes that, as far as substantive requirements of, broadly, reasonableness, are concerned, leaving special cases aside, '... one is struck by the similarity of the results obtained by applying, on the one hand, administrative law tests to the exercise of discretionary statutory power, and on the other, common law tests to discretionary contractual power.'[10]

The parallels between aspects of contract law and judicial review were recently made explicit in *Shearson Lehman Hutton Inc v Maclaine Watson & Co Ltd* in which Webster J questioned the assumption that public law rules cannot be applied in private law.[11] His view was that the differences between private and public law rights were to do with the procedures by which they might be protected rather than their substance. This is borne out by the supervisory jurisdiction in employment law,[12] trusts and directors' duties,[13] and in restraint of trade and other public policy situations which will be discussed in chapter 9. Beatson makes the important point that, on this approach, 'English law is not as distant from Scottish law as some have suggested, since it is clear that in Scottish law the court's supervisory jurisdiction extends to all "administrative" functions, whether based on statutory or governmental powers or on contract.'[14] On this approach elements of a considerate altruism theory for the control of power are influential in contract.

In *Wood v Woad*[15] a duty of procedural fairness was extended to a mutual insurance society, and in *Lapointe v L'Association de Bienfaisance et de Retraite de la Police de Montréal*[16] they were extended to the board of a pension fund trust. The common thread in such decisions, it is suggested, is that there is an inequality of power between the association and its

---

8   See Daintith, 'Regulation by contract' op cit at p 56. On directors see P Davies, *Gower's Principles of Modern Company Law* (6th edn, 1997) chapter 23; on trade unions see *Maclean v Workers' Union* [1929] 1 Ch 602; on clubs see *Dawkins v Antrobus* (1881) 17 Ch D 615.
9   Daintith, at p 57. Cases on this point include *Dallman v King* (1837) 4 Bing (NC) 105; *Braunstein v Accidental Death Insurance Co* (1861) 1 B and S 782; *Andrews v Belfield* (1857) 2 CB NS 779.
10   Daintith, op cit at 58.
11   [1989] 2 Lloyd's Rep 570 at 625.
12   See chapter 6.
13   See discussion later in this chapter.
14   Beatson 'Judicial review in contract' in Beatson and Friedmann (eds) supra, at p 270. See Annex on the Scottish position.
15   (1874) LR 9 Exch 190.
16   [1906] AC 535 at 538-540, PC.

members, the membership of the association is important to the status and security of the member and those interests should not be disregarded in decision making. In effect these requirements democratise the relationship between the parties, introducing a participative element.

Membership bodies

The rules of membership bodies are often considered to create a contract between the members, which can provide the basis for obligations of considerate decision making by committees and officials of the body. Examples can be found in the line of cases starting with *Lee v Showmen's Guild of Great Britain*.[17] An unincorporated association was held bound by the implied contractual terms of the membership contract to comply with the rules of natural justice in disciplining a member. This was one of the cases which marked the transition from property theory as providing the 'peg' on which to hang a supervisory jurisdiction over private associations to contract theory.[18] Under contract theory it is not so much the fact that technically the property of an association is divisible between its members on dissolution which provides the basis for the jurisdiction of the court to supervise its decision making (the point being that the court was only protecting property rights in doing so) as the fact that a contract of membership is said to exist between the members. Wightman observes that these contracts of membership are far from the normal contract in which parties seek commercial gain, but 'are characterised by a merging of private interests in a collective interest in a shared project' and that to the extent that the contract also regulates how the rules of the association are to be changed or implemented it is a vehicle for democracy.[19] This is a good example of a 'mini-legal system' in which the courts seek a balance between respecting pluralism by not intervening,[20] while at the same time protecting individuals' interests by requiring a participative-communitarian approach to the exercise of power under the contract.

The court is technically giving effect to the express or implied agreement of members in imposing duties of considerate decision making in such situations. Damages may be available as a remedy for

17 [1952] 2 QB 329. See further discussion in chapter 9.
18 J Alder 'Obsolescence and renewal: judicial review in the private sector' in P Leyland and T Woods (eds) *Administrative Law Facing the Future: Old Constraints and New Horizons* (1997) at p 174. Alder gives as illustrations of this point the following cases: *Baird v Wells* (1890) 44 Ch D 661; *Rigby v Connol* (1880) 14 Ch D 482
19 J Wightman *Contract, A Critical Commentary* (1996) at p 108.
20 See discussion in chapter 1.

breach of contractual duties of natural justice,[1] as well as injunctions or declarations.

The protection of security and status in contract

The point was made in chapter 3 that the five 'key' values are not the only ones that operate in the law; contract also has its own particular values. But in contract these five key values, especially status and security, operate particularly explicitly, and the parallels with judicial review are most striking. In contract, as in trusts, the concern is often to fulfil legitimate expectations or reliance interests created in the plaintiff by the defendant:[2] in different ways both of these protect the security of individuals, in the sense of their being able to trust or rely on those with whom one deals, and not having unwelcome change thrust upon one. This is particularly clear in the field of promissory and proprietary estoppel, for instance. Here there is a strong parallel with the development of legitimate expectations as a ground for judicial review. Wightman suggests that in personal as opposed to commercial contracts 'the expectation of enjoyment created by a promise can provoke anticipation and longing which, when defeated, results in a much sharper sense of loss than can be experienced by the firm whose bare economic expectation is defeated.'[3] Here we have an echo of the justification put forward by Bentham for the 'disappointment principle', noted in chapter 3.

In contractual situations where the status and security of a party are at stake, the use of contract as a means of protection has developed considerably. The development of employment law has been considered in chapter 6. There are parallel developments in other contractual relationships which extend the underlying principles of statutory provisions such as employment protection legislation into contractual relationships that are not strictly covered by statute. So for instance, as noted in chapter 6, in *Stevenson v United Road Transport Union*[4] the dismissal of a trade union member from the office of regional officer in the union without a proper hearing was held to be void in private law proceedings based on the contractual relationship of the plaintiff to the

---

1   See for instance the Scottish case of *Tait v Central Radio Taxi (Tollcross) Ltd* 1989 SC 4, First Division, discussed in Annex, infra.
2   See Fuller and Perdue 'The Reliance Interest in Contract Damages' (1936) 46 *Yale Law Jo* 52 and 373; H Collins 'Contract and legal theory' in W L Twining (ed) *Legal Theory and Common Law* (1986); B S Markesinis and S F Deakin *Tort Law* (3rd edn, 1994) at p 10; R Brownsword 'Static and dynamic market individualism' in R Halson (ed) *Exploring the Boundaries of Contract* (1996).
3   J Wightman *Contract, A Critical Commentary* (1996) at p 103.
4   [1977] ICR 893.

union through the union rules, into which the court implied a duty of natural justice. Here we have an example of the same underlying values that produced the employment protection legislation being influential in the development of the common law of contract. Sedley has also observed that in this case public law concepts of power and nullity were deployed in a strictly contractual context of union membership and employment.[5] The reason for extending protection into these areas, I suggest, is that the dignity, respect, status and security of the plaintiff were at stake in the exercise of power (here compensatory power, a form of property or dominium[6]) over the plaintiff by the union – the five key values are often protected in similar ways – and were protected by democratising the relationship on the participative-communitarian model: democracy often crosses the public-private divide.

Some comparisons

Considering what is happening in contract in Australia, Judge Paul Finn argues that there is a strong trend in modern contract law to develop duties of fairness – 'decency in human dealings' – which is evidenced in the implied duty to act reasonably, to use best endeavours,[7] to give reasonable notice,[8] opportunity,[9] etc.[10] Finn relates this to a policy adopted by the Australian courts to control exercises of power, to uphold standards of conduct, notably fairness, fidelity and moral responsibility, and to uphold basic human values including dignity, integrity, security of one's property, and reputation, and the rights of parents in relation to their children. The trend is not limited to contract.

In some civil law jurisdictions the general function of the law to control power and abuses of power is acknowledged. For instance, Samuel and Rinkes discuss the concept of 'abuse of rights'[11] in civil law systems and in Roman law. In French law an unreasonable exercise of a right can give rise to an action in tort on the basis that any damage caused by the unreasonable exercise is damage flowing from the fault of another. (And

5   Sir Stephen Sedley 'Public law and contractual employment' (1994) 23 ILJ 201 at p 204.
6   See earlier discussion of Galbraith and Daintith in chapter 3.
7   His example is *Perri v Coolangatta Investments Pty Ltd* (1982) 149 CLR 537 at 654.
8   His example is *Laurinda Pty Ltd v Capalaba Park Shipping Centre Pty Ltd* (1989) 166 CLR 623 at 654.
9   His example is *Presmist Pty Ltd v Turner Corpn Pty Ltd* (1992) 30 NSWLR 478.
10   See *Renard Constructions (ME) Pty Ltd v Minister for Public Works* (1992) 26 NSWLR 234.
11   G Samuel and J Rinkes *Law of Obligations and Legal Remedies* (1996) at pp 306-308.

in French public law 'detournement de pouvoir' is a ground for intervention by the Conseil d'Etat.) In the general part of the Netherlands Civil Code (Book 3, Patrimonial Law in General) article 13 lays down that nobody is allowed to exercise any power abusively, so that abuse of power transcends the law of obligations as such in Dutch law.[12]

Looked at in this light we can interpret the intervention of equity to give remedies to prevent abuses of power as the English version of a continental doctrine, and as an example of how different legal systems find different, but often equivalent, ways of dealing with commonly recognised problems. *Samuel and Rinkes* give the case of *Hollywood Silver Fox Farm v Emmett*[13] as an example: conduct that would otherwise not have been regarded as a nuisance was rendered unlawful by the fact that it was malicious and thus amounted to an abuse of power for which an equitable remedy – an injunction – was awarded.

FIDUCIARY RELATIONSHIPS: TRUSTS

We turn now to some of the ways in which equity protects individuals' interests, and controls what it considers to be abuses of power, either by imposing limitations on the freedom of activity of one party to a relationship – the fiduciary, or by controlling his or her decision-making processes. It will be remembered that it was suggested in chapter 2 that the jurisdiction of the courts to control exercises of public or state power in judicial review, and the grounds for judicial review, derive from the common law and equity: hence the topic has bearing on our argument that there is no firm public-private divide.

Finn suggests that 'First, but by no means uniquely, fiduciary law's concern is to impose standards of acceptable conduct on one party to a relationship for the benefit of the other where the one has responsibility for the preservation of the other's interests. Secondly, again in common with other bodies of law, it does this by proscribing one party's possible use of the power and of the opportunities his position gives, or has given, him to act inconsistently with that responsibility.'[14] Thus 'A fiduciary relationship, ultimately, is an imposed not an accepted one. If one needs an analogy here, one is closer to tort law than to contract; one is concerned with an imposed standard of behaviour.'[15] The relationships which give rise to fiduciary duties are very diverse, and include contractual relationships, relationships of trustee and beneficiary and other

12 *Samuel and Rinkes* at pp 306-308.
13 [1936] 2 KB 468.
14 P D Finn 'The fiduciary principle; in T G Youdan (ed) *Equity, Fiduciaries and Trusts* (1989) at p 2.
15 Op cit at p 54.

relationships not necessarily based in contract, as where information is received in confidence. The fiduciary duty originates in public policy, a view of desired social behaviour.[16] In effect it represents a considerate altruism approach to the exercise of power.

The trust is just one example of a range of fiduciary relationships. It illustrates well the ways in which equity imposes obligations on those in positions of power, and controls certain decision making in ways that are very similar to those adopted in judicial review. The original rationale behind the law of trusts was 'defendant-oriented', namely a concern that it would be immoral or unconscionable for the legal owner of land conveyed for the benefit of another to hold it for his own benefit. The origin of the trust is to be found in the power of the Lord Chancellor to intervene and control the execution of a use, or later, trust: the court must be in a position to execute the trust if the trustee fails to do so.[17] Looked at from the point of view of a modern public lawyer the rationale that would more immediately spring to mind in relation to a trust from which a person had already benefitted would be that the beneficiary might have a legitimate expectation that the benefit would continue to be received, so that a decision to stop payments might be capricious. This view is reflected in the comments of Robert Walker J in *Scott v National Trust*:[18]

'... if (for instance) trustees (whether of a charity, or a pension fund or a private family trust) have for the last ten years paid £1,000 per quarter to an elderly, impoverished beneficiary of the trust it seems at least arguable that no reasonable body of trustees would discontinue the payment, without any warning, and without giving the benficiary the opportunity of trying to persuade the trustees to continue the payment, at least temporarily. The beneficiary has no legal or equitable right to continued payment, but she or he has an expectation. So I am inclined to think that legitimate expectation may have some part to play in trust law as well as in judicial review cases ...'[19]

---

16   Op cit at p 27. See also P D Finn 'Fiduciary law and the modern commercial world' in E McKendrick (ed) *Commercial Aspects of Trusts and Fiduciary Obligations* (1992).

17   *Re Baden's Deed Trusts (McPhail v Doulton)* [1971] AC 424.

18   [1998] 2 All ER 705.

19   At 718.

General principles

The principles for the exercise of duties and discretions by trustees are well settled, but they will be summarised here to bring out the similarities and contrasts with principles of decision making in other supervisory jurisdictions, particularly judicial review.[20] Generally trustees must not profit from the trust, they must distribute to beneficiaries in accordance with the terms of the trust, exercising any discretion for the benefit of the beneficiaries (which generally means the financial benefits of the beneficiaries[1]) and not in accordance with a whim. They must administer the trust equitably as between the beneficiaries.[2] Trustees are under a duty not to delegate powers unless they have authority to do so.[3] In making decisions as to investment of the trust property trustees must act prudently, and have regard to the suitability of and the need for diversification of all investments in the fund.[4]

Supervisory jurisdiction in trusts: legality and rationality

A similarity between judicial review and the law of private trusts is that the courts have a supervisory jurisdiction over discretionary decision making, for instance by trustees of discretionary trusts. As in judicial review, as Nobles has observed, there is no single standard for the exercise of the jurisdiction: 'Instead, there is a range of standards which the courts can bring to bear, which depend on the rules of the trust and the circumstances in which those rules are interpreted. These duties range from duties to act in the beneficiaries' best interests down to a duty to act in good faith. In between there are duties not to exercise a power contrary to its purpose, to exercise discretions impartially as between different groups of beneficiary, and not to act capriciously or wholly unreasonably.'[5] The grounds on which the two jurisdictions are exercised are clearly similar, and impose duties of considerate altruism on the person exercising power.

Powers must be used to effectuate the purpose for which they were conferred and not to secure indirectly some other purpose (the doctrine of 'fraud on the power'). Trustees may be entitled to have regard to the

---

20 For summaries of the duties of trustees see Robert Walker J in *Scott and anor v National Trust* [1998] 2 All ER 705.
1   *Cowan v Scargill* [1984] 3 WLR 501, Sir Robert Megarry VC.
2   See, for instance, *Cowan v Scargill*, supra, at 513.
3   *Re Hay's Settlement Trusts* [1981] 3 All ER 786. Note that the Trustees Delegation Bill 1998 proposes to permit further delegation.
4   Trustee Investments Act 1961, section 6(1).
5   R Nobles *Pensions, Employment and the Law* (1993) at p 65.

wishes of the beneficiaries, and hence if the beneficiaries desired an ethical investment policy, avoiding for instance investment in tobacco companies, compliance with that wish by the trustees might be in the best interests of the beneficiaries.[6] But it would not always be so, and the paramount duty is to promote financial interests. Trustees may themselves adopt an ethical investment policy, but this would only be regarded as proper if it did not jeopardise financial benefits.[7]

Trustees of discretionary trusts, exercising trust powers, are entitled to distribute to some but not all of the class or to make an unequal distribution: they have discretion in these matters. In exercising discretions, trustees as fiduciaries must not act capriciously or outside the field permitted by the trust, they must act fairly as between the beneficiaries and they must take all relevant considerations into account.[8] If a trustee of a discretionary trust fails to give his or her mind to the matter of exercising discretion, or acts without a proper understanding of what is involved, or at the direction of some other person – for instance the settlor or his solicitor – then the exercise of discretion is void.[9]

On the circumstances in which the court will itself exercise powers or discretions, the position as far as powers are concerned is that, although a trustee may, and normally will, be under a fiduciary duty to consider whether or in what way to exercise a power, the court will not normally compel its exercise. But the court will intervene if the trustees exceed their power, and possibly if they are proved to have exercised a power capriciously.[10]

In the case of a trust power the position is different: if the trustees do not exercise such a power, the court will do so in the manner best calculated to give effect to the settlor's or testator's intentions. It may do so by appointing new trustees, for instance, or by itself directing the trustees to distribute.[11]

Sir Richard Scott summed up the supervisory jurisdiction over trustees in *Edge v Pensions Ombudsman*[12] as follows: a judge may only interfere if the trustees had 'taken into account irrelevant, improper or irrational factors, or their decision was one that no reasonable body of trustees

---

6   *Cowan v Scargill*, supra, at 514.
7   *Harries v Church Comrs for England* [1993] 2 All ER 300.
8   *Re Baden's Deed Trusts (McPhail v Doulton)* [1971] AC 424, per Lord Wilberforce.
9   *Turner v Turner* [1984] Ch 100.
10 *Re Baden's Deed Trusts (McPhail v Doulton)* [1971] AC 424, per Lord Wilberforce.
11 *Re Baden's Deed Trusts (McPhail v Doulton)* [1971] AC 424, per Lord Wilberforce.
12 [1998] 2 All ER 547, Sir Richard Scott V-C.

properly directing themselves could have reached.'[13] The reference to *Wednesbury* here must be deliberate.

Procedural propriety in trusts

As far as duties of procedural fairness in trusts are concerned, in principle there is no duty to consult on the part of trustees before exercising a discretion that may adversely affect, for instance, a beneficiary. However, Robert Walker J in *Scott v National Trust*[14] indicated that, although trustees are not under any general duty to give a hearing before making decisions, a beneficiary may have a legitimate expectation that a discretionary benefit will continue to be paid, and if the trustees are considering terminating the payments the beneficiary might be entitled in equity to a warning and an opportunity to try to persuade the trustees to continue the payment, at least temporarily. Failure to do this might amount to 'capricious' behaviour on the part of the trustees. We have here an embryonic duty of natural justice and rationality in equity. A rare example of a duty to consult before a decision is made that may adversely affect others in trust law is provided by section 11 of the Trusts of Land Act 1996, under which there is a limited duty to consult beneficiaries with an interest in possession under a trust of land.

There are additional duties which are analogous to requirements of procedural propriety in judicial review. Beneficiaries are entitled to be provided with information which will enable them to determine whether the trust is being administered correctly; they have a right to see the trust accounts, to know how trust money is invested, to inspect documents

13 Pension law is a mix of trusts and contract law, and statutory regulation, and some of the basic principles of equity have been modified in relation to pensions: by way of example, the Pensions Act 1995 reverses the rule that a trustee cannot act in a matter in which his personal interest may conflict with his duty to others, thus enabling, for instance, employee representatives to be among the trustees. Nevertheless, the case law brings out some of the similarities with judicial review. In *Edge and Ors v Pensions Ombudsman and another* [1998] 2 All ER 547 trustees of a pension fund appealed against the finding by the Pensions Ombudsman that they had acted in breach of trust in making amendments to the pension scheme. The Vice Chancellor decided that the ombudsman had had no power to make an order setting aside the amending deed. While the courts do have a supervisory jurisdiction over this sort of decision making, neither a judge nor the Pensions Ombudsman could interfere with the way in which trustees exercised their discretion simply because he or she thinks it was not fair: ibid at 568. In *Cowan v Scargill* [1984] 2 All ER 750, where a question arose as to the investment policy of a pension fund, the court held that it was the 'duty of trustees to exercise their powers in the best interests of the present and future beneficiaries of the trust ...' at 760.

14 [1998] 2 All ER 705 at 718.

and so on (though documents about discussions between trustees about the exercise of discretion are privileged). The court may order that a beneficiary be informed of the identity of trustees to enable them to exercise these rights.[15] But beneficiaries are not entitled to be given reasons or explanations for trustees' decisions, although if a decision of trustees in challenged in legal proceedings they may well have to disclose the substance of their reasons.[16]

Enforcement of the duties of trustees

A difference between judicial review and trusts is that the court may itself execute a trust, thus substituting its own view of what should be done for that of the trustees. Thus if, for instance, the trustees fail in their duty to consider whether and if so how to exercise their discretions, the beneficiaries may seek the aid of the court, and the court will take whatever course seems appropriate: it may appoint fresh trustees, or apply the maxim equality is equity and order that the property should be divided equally (though this will often not be appropriate or in line with the settlor's intentions), or the court may itself direct how a trust power is to be exercised or how property is to be distributed.[17]

Remedies for a breach of trust may include an order for an account, an injunction, equitable damages[18] and tracing. As we have already noted a beneficiary may apply to the court if he or she anticipates a breach of trust. Trustees too may apply to the court for directions.

Comparisons with judicial review

The requirements in relation to discretionary decisions in trusts are, it is obvious, very close to the duties of legality, and *Wednesbury* reasonableness duties imposed by Lord Greene MR in that case in public law.[19] This is not surprising since Lord Greene was a distinguished trust and equity lawyer and may well have been drawing deliberately on equitable principles in formulating the grounds for review in the *Wednesbury* case.[20]

15 *Murphy v Murphy* [1999] 1 WLR 282.
16 See per Robert Walker J in *Scott v National Trust*, supra at 718-719, referring to *Dundee Hospitals* case [1952] 1 All ER 896 at 900, per Lord Normand.
17 *Re Baden's Deed Trusts (McPhail v Doulton)* [1971] AC 424.
18 An award of damages at common law, as for breach of contract, is a separate and distinct remedy and not available for breach of trust. Equitable damages are available under the Supreme Court Act 1981, section 50: see chapter 9 for discussion of remedies.
19 See chapter 5.
20 [1948] 1 KB 223, CA.

Thus in judicial review too there is a duty of selflessness – altruism – on the part of public decision makers;[1] public decision makers must act in accordance with the intention of the body from whom their power derives – Parliament normally – as signified in enabling legislation;[2] they must not act capriciously or '*Wednesbury* unreasonably', nor must they act for ulterior or improper purposes;[3] they must take account of relevant considerations, and not be influenced by irrelevant considerations; they may take into account ethical considerations, as long as they do not allow these to run counter to the overall purpose of their functions;[4] they must exercise discretions with an open mind;[5] they may not delegate their discretions to others,[6] or fetter their discretion.[7]

The absence of rights on the part of beneficiaries to be consulted in trust law presents a contrast with the position in judicial review, where those prospectively adversely affected by decisions are commonly entitled to fair procedures that will offer them some protection.[8] However, the rule that a trustee must not benefit from the trust provides a parallel with the rule against bias in judicial review.[9] And, as has already been noted, entitlements to see documents and know the identity of trustees may be viewed as, in practice, requirements of procedural propriety or natural justice, though far less developed than duties in judicial review.

As far as enforcement and remedies are concerned, in judicial review, by contrast with the position in trusts, for a court to substitute its own decision for that of the decision maker would be regarded as an undemocratic usurpation of power. Judicial review is based on assumptions that public bodies will comply with orders of the court quashing decisions or requiring them to be retaken, and that if they do not the contempt[10] jurisdiction of the court will be an adequate remedy. Here there is a clear difference between trusts and judicial review.

The particular significance of the parallels between rules for the exercise of discretion in trusts and in judicial review is sixfold. First, they

---

1   See for instance *Padfield v Minister of Agriculture* [1968] AC 997.
2   See discussion in chapter 2.
3   See *De Smith, Woolf and Jowell* chapter 6, esp paras 6-059 – 6-083.
4   *R v Somerset County Council, ex p Fewings* [1995] 3 All ER 20, at pp 28, 31, 34, CA; cf *Roberts v Hopwood* [1925] AC 578.
5   *British Oxygen Co v Ministry of Technology* [1971] AC 610.
6   *Lavender (H) & Son Ltd v Minister of Housing and Local Government* [1970] 1 WLR 1231. On the exercises of discretion in judicial review see generally De Smith, Woolf and Jowell (*Judicial Review of Administrative Action*) (5th edn, 1995) chapter 6.
7   See De Smith, Woolf and Jowell *Judicial Review of Administrative Action* (1995) chapter 11.
8   See generally *De Smith, Woolf and Jowell*, chapters 7-12.
9   See *De Smith, Woolf and Jowell* chapter 12.
10 See *M v Home Office* [1994] 1 AC 377.

indicate that the rules governing decision making in judicial review are not uniquely 'public', so that these rights are not accurately described as 'public law rights' as Lord Diplock seems to have described them in *O'Reilly v Mackman*. Secondly, they show that duties of fair and rational – considerate – decision making have roots both in equity and in the common law.[11] This is all part of a legal framework for the control of power which is not by any means confined to public law. Thirdly, the duties in decision making in trusts are *imposed* by equity, and are not – or not solely – derived from the intentions of the settlor, the terms of the trust or the agreement of the parties: in other words, equity provides examples of duties arising in decision making which cannot be rationalised in terms of the equivalent of legislative intent or consent of the parties.[12] They are imposed as a matter of justice, and thus provide support for the position that it is not contrary to principle or tradition for the courts to impose obligations on those in positions of power. Fourthly, these duties in decision making are suitable for the protection of individuals whose security or other interests are threatened by decision making, as well as for the general purpose of controlling the exercise of power on public policy grounds, including the need to prevent abuse of power and frustration of the wishes of the settlor or donor of a power. Fifthly, in private law (as in public law) there are duties of altruism. And finally, in equity as well as in public law there are democratic – in equity 'civil democratic' – requirements of responsible altruism and, in some degree, participative communitarian standards.

COMPANY LAW

Duties analogous to those imposed in judicial review arise in relation to company directors. The power relationships here depend upon who is affected by the directors' decisions. In effect, by virtue of the contract contained in the articles of association of the company and their contracts of employment directors have control over the property of the company and over its general conduct. The members of the company – the shareholders – are dependent for their security derived from their shareholding on the directors. Directors' decisions also affect employees of the company in their security and status.

---

11 On the common law roots of duties of legality, fairness and rationality see discussion in this chapter, and in chapters 5 and 10.
12 See chapter 2 for discussion of the doctrines of legislative intent and ultra vires in judicial review.

There is not the space here to explore the duties of directors in detail.[13] It will suffice for present purposes to focus on the most obvious parallels with judicial review and other supervisory jurisdictions. But first a word about the salient differences: there is no legal, as opposed to political,[14] parallel with the shareholders' meeting in judicial review; generally duties of procedural propriety are not imposed on directors;[15] and directors are not under strict duties of altruism or selflessness in the way that public decision makers – and trustees – are.

General principles

The sources of the duties of directors are varied – equity, statute and the common law. In equity, directors are not strictly trustees of the company property,[16] but they resemble trustees in that they owe fiduciary duties towards the company (but not towards its individual members).[17] This entails that they must each and all act bona fide in the interests of the company and, subject to their interests as shareholders and the articles of the company, not in their own interests (the self-dealing rule)[18] or those of third parties.

If a question arises as to whether the directors have breached their duty to the company, the court exercises a supervisory jurisdiction: the court holds that it is for the directors and not the court to consider what is in the interests of the company. Directors must direct their minds to the question whether a transaction was in fact in the interests of the company. (A transaction may be held not to be binding on a company if a director fails in this respect.[19]) Certain matters are prescribed as relevant in decision making: directors must take into account the interests of shareholders, and this entails that they may have some regard to their own interests if they happen to be shareholders. Thus they are 'not required by the law to live in an unreal region of detached altruism and to act in a vague mood of ideal abstraction from the obvious fact which must be present to the mind of any honest and intelligent man when he

---

13 For a full account see P Davies *Gower's Principles of Modern Company Law* (6th edn, 1997) (henceforth *Gower*) chapter 22. See also Mrs Justice Arden 'Codifying directors' duties' in R Rawlings (ed) (*Law, Society and Economy*) (1997) pp 91-108.

14 Ministers and local authorities are regarded as being politically accountable to Parliament and the electorate: is this the political equivalent of a shareholders' meeting?

15 See *Andrews v Mitchell* [1905] AC 78; *Weinberger v Inglis (No 2)* [1919] AC 606.

16 *Gower* at p 598.

17 *Gower* pp 599-623. *Percival v Wright* [1902] 2 Ch 421.

18 See *Movitex Ltd v Bulfield* (1988) 2 BCC 99, 403, Vinelott J.

19 *Gower* pp 601-605; *Re W & M Roith Ltd* [1967] 1 WLR 432.

exercises his powers as a director.'[20] Directors are also, by section 309 of the Companies Act 1980, under a duty to have regard to the interests of the company's employees in general, as well as the interests of its members. This duty is enforceable as a fiduciary duty owed to the company (section 309(2)) and may not therefore be enforceable by the employees.

Directors must exercise their powers for the purpose for which they were conferred, and not for improper purposes. An improper purpose would include the advancement of the directors' own interests if this is contrary to the interests of the company as a whole.[1] The criteria for determining a proper purpose are objective, drawn from the articles of association and in this respect are comparable to the 'legality' ground in judicial review.

Directors must not in general fetter their future discretion, and they must exercise their own independent judgment.[2] However, this does not prevent them from entering into a contract under which they agree to take further action in future in order to carry out the contract. Outside the realm of contract, however, the rule against fettering of discretion still applies; for instance directors may not fetter their discretion as to the advice they will give shareholders on a matter on which the shareholders have the right to decide in the future.[3]

Lastly, as far as duties in equity are concerned, in principle and unless the Articles of Association provide otherwise (which they usually do), directors must not place themselves in a position where their personal interests or duties to others are liable to conflict with their duties to the company, unless the company gives its informed consent.[4]

So much for duties in equity. At common law directors are under, broadly, objective duties of care towards the company, which are enforceable in tort.[5]

The formal position of directors then has considerable similarities with those of decision makers in public law, and these similarities will be explored in the next section. However, the reality of the matter is to some degree different, since the majority of shareholders determine whether the company should pursue complaints against directors and frequently the majority will not wish to do so.[6] However, under section

---

20 *Mills v Mills* (1938) 60 CLR 150, Australian HC, quoted by Gower op cit at p 602.
1   *Gower* pp 605-608.
2   *Gower* pp 608-610.
3   *John Crowther Group plc v Carpets International* [1990] BCLC 460; *Gower* at p 609.
4   *Gower* pp 610-623.
5   *Gower* pp 640-644.
6   See *Foss v Harbottle* (1843) 2 Hare 461, 67 ER 189; *Smith v Croft (No 2)* [1987] 3 All ER 909, Knox J.

459 of the Companies Act 1985 a petition may be brought alleging that the company has been conducted in a manner which is 'unfairly prejudicial' to the petitioner, usually a minority shareholder.

The remedies for breach of directors' duties where, exceptionally, actions are taken, include injunction or declaration where a breach is anticipated, damages or compensation, restoration of the company's property, rescission of a contract, an account for profits, and summary dismissal by the shareholders.[7] Given the complexities of the law relating to remedies for breaches of duties imposed by common law or equity, discussed in the next chapter, it is to be noted that Gower observes that 'Damages are the appropriate remedy for breach of the common law duty of care; compensation is the equivalent equitable remedy granted against a trustee or other fiduciary to compel restitution for the loss suffered by his breach of fiduciary duty. In practice, the distinction between the two has become blurred, and probably no useful purpose is served by seeking to keep them distinct.'[8]

Comparisons with judicial review

Each of these points has interesting parallels, at least formally, in judicial review, which will be briefly pointed up here. In some cases, as in local government, public decision makers, like company directors and trustees, may be regarded as being in a fiduciary relationship with their public, the council tax payers.[9] Another close parallel is with the idea that 'public' decision makers must not act in their own interests,[10] and must be altruistic. The parallel in company law with the public law requirement that decision makers are impartial and must act in the public interest and within the purpose of the enabling statute[11] is the requirement that they must act in the interests of the company and according to its articles of association.

Like directors, public decision makers must act in good faith in the area with which their powers are concerned, and for a proper purpose. In judicial review the duty of altruism is strict, and may involve the rule against bias. It also entails that a minister should not be influenced by

---

7   *Gower* pp 649-654.
8   *Gower* at p 649.
9   See for instance *Bromley London Borough Council v Greater London Council* [1983] 1 AC 768. See *De Smith, Woolf and Jowell* para 6-096.
10 On the rule against bias (nemo iudex in causa sua) see *De Smith, Woolf and Jowell* chapter 12. On acting for an improper purpose, see op cit paras 6-059–6-083; on fettering discretion, see op cit, chapter 11.
11 See *De Smith, Woolf and Jowell* paras 6-059–6-084.

the political flak that an unpopular decision may attract.[12] This is not the case with directors. However, just as there are exceptions to a director's duty of impartiality (ie where he is a shareholder), so in public law a minister may decide in favour of a policy to which he is committed[13] (ie about which he or she is not impartial) and may even take the view that it is in the public interest for his or her own party to remain in power.[14]

In public law statutory provisions may make clear that particular sectional interests are relevant in certain decisions (for instance the interests of property owners in compulsory purchase, and of neighbours in planning cases), just as the Companies Act 1985 provides for employees' interests to be taken into account in directors' decisions. Statute will also be a guide to what is a proper purpose in public law.[15]

As in company law, discretion must not be fettered in public decision making,[16] though the position in public law in relation to contracts which may reduce the area of free decision making in the future is complex. (Contracts entered into by the Crown are not to be construed as being subject to implied terms that would exclude the exercise of general discretionary power for the public good, and are to be construed as incorporating an implied term that such power remain exercisable.[17] But 'How and where the line is to be drawn is not clear.'[18]) Overall it will be seen that the rules relating to directors in company law embody elements of majoritarian and considerate altruism theories of governance having parallels in public law.

As far as remedies are concerned, at least formally there are clear parallels with remedies for breach of directors' duties, in the availability of injunctions and declarations in judicial review. In practice orders of certiorari, prohibition and mandamus in judicial review fulfil many of the same functions as declarations and injunctions. However, as with trusts, there is no parallel in judicial review with the award of compensation (subject to points to be made about remedies in chapter 11). In reality, however, a majority of shareholders are in a position to block actions against directors, and the availability of remedies is formal or theoretical only.

As indicated above employees are not in a position to enforce the duty of directors to take their interests into account under the Companies Act 1980, section 309, and this provides a contrast with the locus standi

---

12 *Padfield v Minister of Agriculture* [1968] AC 997, HL.
13 *Franklin v Minister of Town and Country Planning* [1948] AC 87, HL.
14 *R v Waltham Forest London Borough Council, ex p Baxter* [1988] QB 419.
15 *Padfield v Minister of Agriculture*, and *De Smith, Woolf and Jowell*, supra.
16 See *De Smith, Woolf and Jowell* chapter 11.
17 *De Smith, Woolf and Jowell* p 518.
18 *De Smith, Woolf and Jowell* para 11-014; *Ayr Harbour Trustees v Oswald* (1883) 8 App Cas 623; *Rederiaktiebolaget Amphitrite v R* [1921] 3 KB 500.

position in judicial review which entitles those with a 'sufficient interest' to apply for judicial review, which would normally include those adversely affected by a breach of a duty to take their interests into account.[19]

The significance of the parallels between the law relating to directors' duties and judicial review is similar to the significance of the parallels in trusts. They show that duties in decision making may be *imposed* by equity, that such duties need not rest on an ultra vires doctrine or legislative intent, that duties such as those laid down in the *Wednesbury* case are not uniquely public law in nature but have their roots in equity and thus in private law, and that they are apt for the protection, inter alia, of the interests of individuals such as shareholders and employees. The rules also indicate, however, how important rules of standing can be for the protection of interests, in the facts that employees cannot enforce the duties of consideration owed to them by directors, and in practice only companies, controlled by the majority of the shareholders (who may not wish to sue the directors) can enforce directors' duties.

CONCLUSIONS

Our analysis of the underlying rationales or justifications for many liabilities in private law has sought to show how the law acknowledges the importance of the common values we have identified to individuals in their relations with other private parties or bodies, particularly, though not only, where imbalances of power exist, and seeks to democratise them. In this important respect public and private law are engaged on a common enterprise.

Often there will be conflicts between the common values which underlie public and private law which were identified in chapter 3, and considerations of managerial necessity or administrative convenience in private law. For instance, when the duties of company directors are at issue the courts will respect the judgment of directors in matters of management;[20] similarly in employment law the courts concede

---

19 *De Smith, Woolf and Jowell* chapter 2.
20 See *Howard Smith Ltd v Ampol Petroleum Ltd* [1974] AC 821 at 835: 'Having ascertained … the nature of [the power of directors to allot shares], and having defined as best as can be done in the light of modern conditions, the, or some, limits within which it may be exercised, it is then necessary for the court, if a particular exercise of it is challenged, to examine the substantial purpose for which it was exercised and to reach a conclusion as to whether that purpose was proper or not. In doing so it will necessarily give credit to the *bona fide* opinion of the directors, if such is found to exist, and will respect their judgment as to matters of management; having done this, the ultimate conclusion has to be as to the side of a fairly broad line on which the case falls.'

managerial prerogatives to employers.[1] In such cases there are strong parallels with the privileges granted to the interests of good administration in judicial review, where the courts may withhold remedies if those interests so indicate, and with questions of justiciability, which may lead the courts to decline to intervene.

The point was made in chapter 2 that the courts have long claimed and exercised a broad jurisdiction to right wrongs and give remedies for injuries: underlying many of the situations in which the courts find wrongs and injuries that require a remedy is the fact that the plaintiff's interests in the five values have been damaged by an exercise of power. Increasingly the common law and equity, and statutory provisions, are imposing responsibilities on those in positions of power over individuals to take into consideration their interests when exercising discretions, and are subjecting exercises of power to control by the court.

In this way a theory of civil democracy is developing in the private sphere, in which private bodies and associations owe duties of consideration to their fellow citizens, whether involving considerate action, as in negligence and other torts, or considerate decision making as in some contractual relationships, trusts and company law. These duties reflect in varying degrees participative-communitarian and responsible altruism democratic models, and support the view being advanced here that it is unrealistic to operate on the basis that public and private law can be divided from one another.

---

1   See chapter 6.

Chapter Nine

Private Law 2: Public Policy and the Public-Private Divide

The point was made in chapter 4 that, before the decision in *O'Reilly v Mackman*, there was no sharp public-private divide, and the common law and equity had been developing principles and remedies in a number of kinds of cases to protect individuals against procedurally unfair or irrational decision making. In the previous chapter we saw how tort and other parts of private law have imposed duties of considerate action and decision making on private bodies. In this chapter we extend our consideration into further ways in which, outside judicial review, higher order duties of, for instance, legality, fairness and rationality are imposed on decision makers, and duties of consideration – reasonableness and altruism – in their actions, are imposed on those in positions of power whose activity affects the interests of individuals or public interests. The scope for extension of these duties on grounds of public policy will be explored, and remedies for their breach, and the implications of the position in private law for democratic theory will be considered.

MONOPOLIES AND PUBLIC SERVICES

The position at common law of bodies exercising monopoly power or providing services of importance to members of the public illustrates the point that duties of consideration may be imposed outside of judicial review on private bodies. The common law has for a long time recognised that special duties should be imposed, as a matter of public policy, on those 'in common calling' such as innkeepers, common carriers and ferrymen. The basis of the duties was that certain services were necessaries supplied to members of the public. Persons or corporations engaging in these callings were obliged to serve all comers and to charge only

reasonable prices for their services.[1] In effect the individual providers of
these services were under duties of non-discrimination and rationality
towards potential customers, and breach of these duties gave rise,
originally, to common law causes of action.[2] This is an important point,
because it would be easy to assume that it would be most appropriate for
actions against the modern day equivalent of common callings, privatised
utilities, to be brought in judicial review on the basis that they were in
some way 'public' and that private law actions were inappropriate or not
available. However, under the common callings doctrine the courts
permitted civil actions to be brought by actions on the case or trespass.
Thus, for instance, *Directors of the London and North Western Rly Co v
Evershed*[3] was an action for money had and received where the defendant
railway company had been charging the plaintiff discriminatory prices
for carriage of his goods in breach of statutory provisions. Lord
Blackburn indicated that he could recover in exactly the same way as if
the money had been extorted by unreasonable charges for which a
common law action was available. In a rare relatively recent case,
Constantine v Imperial Hotels,[4] the plaintiff, a famous West Indian cricketer,
successfully sued in tort for the discriminatory refusal of accommodation
in a hotel, a breach of the duties of those in common callings.

Those engaged in common callings were often subject to control by
what we would now regard as incorporated self-regulatory professional
bodies. The legality of the ways in which these bodies regulated the
calling could be raised in the courts, for instance by way of defence to a
claim by the body to enforce their rules or ordinances. In the *Ipswich
Taylors* case,[5] the Corporation of the Tailors of Ipswich had found one
William Sheninge in breach of a rule and purported to fine him. They
brought an action of debt to recover the fine. The court decided that the
ordinances made by the tailors were not authorised by statute, and they
were contrary to common law because they purported to restrain the
defendant in the exercise of his trade. Ordinances for the good order and
government of men of trades and mysteries were good, but ordinances
to restrain any one in his lawful trade were not good: '… at the common

---

1   See B Wyman 'The Law of the Public Callings as a Solution of the Trust
    Problems' XVII Harvard Law Review (1903-1904) 156; N Arterburn 'The
    Origin and First Test of Public Callings' 75 U Penn LR (1926-27) 411; A W B
    Simpson *A History of the Common Law of Contract: The Rise and Rise of the Action of
    Assumpsit* (1975) at p 230; for an example see *Harris v Packwood* (1810) 3 Taunt
    264. See also the discussion of this topic in M Taggart *Corporatisation, Privatisation
    and Public Law* (Legal Research Foundation, 1990) at p 29; P P Craig [1991]
    Public Law 538.
2   See B Wyman, op cit at p 158.
3   (1877-78) 3 App Cas 1029.
4   [1944] 1 KB 693, Birkett J.
5   (1614) 11 Co Rep 53a, 77 ER 1218.

law, no man could be prohibited from working in any lawful trade ... the common law abhors all monopolies, which prohibit any from working in any lawful trade.'[6] So the action – a private law action for debt – by the tailors failed. In effect, they were not entitled to act arbitrarily and purely selfishly to promote the corporation's members' own interests. They were under duties of consideration – a degree of altruism – towards individual tradesmen, and the common law would protect tradesmen from oppressive abuse of the regulatory power.

In *Allnutt v Inglis*,[7] a tort action, the issue was whether the London Dock Company, which by licence from Parliament possessed a monopoly to receive certain wines, could lawfully refuse to allow cargo owners who objected to paying their schedule of charges to use the docks. The company's case rested on their rights as owners of the dock land to decide who should have access to it. But it was held that in such a case 'private property [is] clothed with a public right.'[8] The statutory monopoly was not granted for the sole benefit of the company, but for the public benefit. Thus the company was not free to impose whatever charges it wished, but must act reasonably. The plaintiffs were entitled to be compensated for the losses they had suffered by not being able to have the goods warehoused and consequently having to pay the duties and thereby losing the interests and profits they would otherwise have made on the sum, and the fact that their goods remained unhoused for a long time and were injured. Here the protection of the common law went beyond that offered in the *Ipswich Taylors* case, where the abuse of power was a defence against a claim in debt, to give the 'victim' of the abuse of power a cause of action for damages.

The prerogative writs were available in actions to which self-regulatory bodies were parties, as the decision in the *Case of the Company of Horners in London*[9] shows. In this case the Court of King's Bench issued a writ of certiorari to 'call for the file' with a view to amending the record if conscience should so require. (It is worth pausing to note the contrast with the current position in judicial review, where self-regulatory bodies such as the Jockey Club are not regarded as being subject to the prerogative orders, which are now only available in applications for judicial review.[10] The *Company of Horners* case is significant both because the company was regarded as subject to the prerogative writs and because that fact carried with it a power on the part of a court of common law to control its activities.[11])

6   Ibid at 54a.
7   (1810) 12 East 527.
8   Ibid at 542.
9   (1642) 2 Roll Rep 481.
10 See discussion in chapters 4 and 5, and below.
11 In the United States of America the writ of mandamus was, and still is, available against those in common calling.

At about the same time as the law of common callings was being developed the common law extended a similar control over persons or corporations enjoying a legal or de facto monopoly in the provisions of services to the general public.[12] (The common callings were not, of course, monopolies, though they were important public services.) The court viewed certain monopolies – notably ports, harbours and wharfage services[13] – as 'businesses affected with a public interest' and regulated them in the public interest, requiring them to serve the public at reasonable prices and without discrimination.[14] This regulatory regime fell into disuse in Britain,[15] being largely replaced by statutory regulation or public ownership.

Sir Matthew Hale stressed that a wharf is 'public' where it is either licensed by the monarch or is the only wharf in a port, and in such cases 'duties must be reasonable and moderate' because the wharf is 'affected with a public interest' and so ceases to be 'juris privati' only.[16] It is significant that the two different considerations – licence by government or de facto monopolistic power – both produced the result that the owner's entitlement to act solely in his or her own interests was restricted, even though the owner might in other respects be a purely private body exercising private self-interested functions.

Thirdly, the common law developed the 'prime necessity' doctrine which holds the suppliers of 'prime necessities' who have a practical monopoly to be under implied duties to supply those necessities to all who need them and are willing to pay a fair and reasonable price.[17] This jurisdiction has been supplanted, in the case of modern, privately-owned utilities – gas, water, electricity, telecommunications, rail services – and their provision of services to the public, by statutory regulation by bodies such as Oftel, Ofgas and so on, which control the terms on which they supply their services to the public and the prices they may charge. There is often an explicit public law or public policy element in the legal

---

12 M Taggart *Corporatisation, Privatisation and Public Law* (1990) at p 29. See also Taggart *The Province of Administrative Law* (1997) at pp 6-8.

13 See P Craig 'Constitutions, property and regulation' [1991] Public Law, 538; M Taggart *Corporatisation, Privatisation and Public Law* (1990); *De Smith, Woolf and Jowell* at paras 3-11, 3-1; A W B Simpson *A History of the Common Law of Contract: The Rise of the Action of Assumpsit* (1975) *Harris v Packwood* (1810) 2 Taunt 264; McAllister 'Lord Hale and Business Affected with a Public Interest' (1929-30) 43 Harvard LR 759.

14 See McAllister, 'Lord Hale and Business Affected with a Public Interest' (1929-30) 43 Harv LR 759.

15 Cf in the USA: see *Munn v Illinois* 94 US 77 (1876).

16 Hale *Tracts* pp 77-78.

17 See *Minister for Justice for the Dominion of Canada v City of Levis* [1919] AC 505, PC; and see Taggart *The Province of Administrative Law* at p 7.

regime to which they are now subject.[18] Potential abuse of monopoly is in part reduced by the existence of competition and alternative sources of supply – for instance, gas and electricity for heating. But it remains a possibility that the common law jurisdiction might still be invoked against both regulators and suppliers of utilities if regulation should fail.[19]

In summary, the common law assumed jurisdiction on public policy grounds to regulate the activities of bodies exercising private functions which had serious implications for particular individuals, and a serious impact on the public generally. These regulated activities were not themselves regarded as public or governmental, though some of them were 'affected with a public interest'. They were subjected to both tortious liability and a supervisory jurisdiction of the court which required these service providers to act reasonably and in a non-discriminatory manner.[20] These common law jurisdictions still exist, for instance in relation to common callings, and they could be revived in relation to public utilities and other monopolies.

Importantly, the duties of non-discrimination and reasonableness imposed on common callings at common law did not rest on contract. If they had done so a similar result might have been achieved by implying terms in the contract. Nor did the jurisdiction rest on statute. It was, essentially, a public interest jurisdiction developed by the common law courts. The courts considered themselves entitled to impose duties of altruism and public service on the service providers – duties of consideration for individuals and restraint in their activities in the market so as to further what the courts considered to be public interests. This jurisdiction may be regarded as an example of the power of the common law courts, enunciated by Sir Edward Coke in *Bagg's case*[1] 'to correct ... errors and misdemeanours extra-judicial, tending to the ... oppression of the subjects, or to ... any manner of misgovernment; so that no wrong or injury, either public or private, can be done but that it shall be (here) reformed or punished by due course of law.'[2] The public policies the courts were promoting in these jurisdictions included, as well as the protection of individuals' interests in their autonomy, security and status, policies in favour of securing access on a non-discriminatory basis to

18 See Sir Gordon Borrie 'The regulation of public and private power' [1989] Public Law 552.

19 See M Taggart, op cit, (1990) at p 30: 'It is conceivable that with the privatisation of "public utilities" exercising dominant market power, these older common law doctrines might be revived.'

20 Compare the American case law on employment contracts affected by a public interest: Karl E Klare 'The Public-private Distinction in Labor Law' (1982) 130 U Pa LR 1358 at p 136, noted in chapter 6.

1   (1615) 11 Co Rep 93b, 77 ER 1273. See discussion of this case in chapter 2.

2   (1615) 11 Co Rep 93b, 98a.

necessaries, both services and goods, promotion of trade and competition as a method of securing non-exploitative, non-discriminatory pricing, and avoiding abuses of monopoly power.

OTHER CONTROLS ON PRIVATE POWER

Despite the fact that the courts nowadays do not consider regulatory bodies in sport and many other 'private' bodies exercising regulatory or legislative power as being subject to judicial review,[3] nevertheless private law duties of non-discrimination, reasonableness (and procedural fairness) which closely resemble the higher order duties imposed in public law are imposed by the common law on private bodies in a range of non-contractual situations besides those considered in the previous section.

The point is illustrated by *Law v National Greyhound Racing Club*,[4] in which the plaintiff member of the NGRC had issued an originating summons to challenge the decision of the club in relation to him in the Chancery Division. The respondents were arguing that proceedings should have been commenced in the Queen's Bench Division under Order 53 of the Rules of the Supreme Court (RSC). The Court of Appeal held that he was entitled to start proceedings in the Chancery Division, and that a remedy by way of declaration would be available.[5] The pegs on which this jurisdiction hung were, first, contract, in that a court could imply a duty of fairness or rationality in the membership contract of the club;[6] and secondly, public policy, including policy against restraint of trade, to which we now turn.

Restraint of trade, *Nagle v Feilden* and *McInnes v Onslow Fane*

The prime example of the imposition of duties of fairness and rationality outside judicial review is that of restraints of trade. An unreasonable restraint of trade is a 'wrong' in the sense that it gives rise to a range of possible remedies, both at common law and in equity. For instance, a

---

3   See chapter 4.
4   [1983] 1 WLR 1302.
5   The declaration sought was that the decision was void and ultra vires, in that (i) it was a breach of an implied term of the agreement between the parties that all actions taken by the stewards which could deprive the plaintiff of his licence would be reasonable and fair and made on reasonable grounds, and (ii) it was in restraint of trade and contrary to public policy. It is not known what the outcome of the case was.
6   See discussion of membership contracts in chapter 8.

contractual term that is in unreasonable restraint of trade will be invalid, unenforceable. Decisions taken or rules adopted by a sporting or similar association in restraint of trade are unlawful and the court may grant declarations and injunctions restraining the body from implementing decisions that are in unreasonable restraint of trade.[7] So, for instance, in *Nagle v Feilden*[8] the Court of Appeal indicated that it would have jurisdiction to grant a declaration that an arbitrary and capricious decision by the Jockey Club to refuse to allow a woman a trainer's licence was unlawful and an injunction requiring the defendants to rectify the error.[9]

There are two particular kinds of restraint of trade which the courts will control, those where the restraint is unreasonable in the interests of the parties, and those where it is unreasonable in the interests of the public.[10] The onus in restraint of trade cases depends on whether the case is based on a privately or publicly unreasonable restraint.[11] 'The onus of establishing that an agreement is reasonable as between the parties is upon the person who puts forward the agreement, while the onus of establishing that it is contrary to the public interest, being reasonable between the parties is on the person so alleging.'[12]

7   See *Nagle v Feilden* [1966] 1 All ER 689; *McInnes v Onslow Fane* and other cases referred to above. And see *Pharmaceutical Society of Great Britain v Dickson* [1970] AC 403.

8   [1966] 1 All ER 689, CA.

9   See later for discussion of remedies.

10 'The public have an interest in every person carrying on his trade freely: so has the individual. All interference with the individual liberty of action in trading, and all restraint of trade of themselves, if there is nothing more, are contrary to public policy, and therefore void. That is the general rule but there are exceptions: restraints of trade and interference with individual liberty of action may be justified by the special circumstances of a particular case. It is a sufficient justification, and indeed it is the only justification, if the restriction is reasonable – reasonable, that is, in reference to the interests of the parties concerned and reasonable in reference to the interests of the public, so framed and so guarded as to afford adequate protection to the party in whose favour it is imposed, while at the same time it is in no way injurious to the public.' Per Lord Macnaghten in *Nordenfelt v Maxim Nordenfelt Guns and Ammunition Co Ltd* [1894] AC 535, 565.

11 *A-G of Commonwealth of Australia v Adelaide Steamship Co* [1913] AC 781, 795-6; *Herbert Morris Ltd v Saxelby* [1916] 1 AC 688.

12 *Esso Petroleum Co Ltd v Harper's Garage Ltd* [1968] AC 269, 319. And see *Herbert Morris Ltd v Saxelby* [1916] 1 AC 688. *Greig v Insole* [1978] 1 WLR 302 was a restraint of trade case. The rules of the bodies governing cricket were in issue. These were designed to prevent cricketers contracted to Mr Kerry Packer from playing test and county cricket. Slade J held that the governing bodies had failed to discharge the onus of showing that the bans, which were prima facie void as being contrary to public policy and in restraint of trade, were reasonable. In *Newport Association Football Club Ltd v Football Association of Wales* (1995) the rules of the Football Association of Wales were challenged as being unreasonable

Nagle v Feilden[13] and *McInnes v Onslow Fane*[14] provide interesting examples of the operation of restraint of trade doctrine, and of possible other public policy bases for the award of remedies for breach of duties of fairness and rationality, notably discrimination, in the common law. The reasons for the court's jurisdiction to intervene in *Nagle v Feilden* were, per Lord Denning, that the Jockey Club exercised a 'virtual monopoly in an important field of human activity' and that the common law of England recognises that a man (sic) has a right to work at his trade or profession without being unjustly excluded from it.[15] The case may thus be viewed either as authority on restraint of trade, or as authority on more general duties of non-discrimination on public policy grounds, where the right or liberty to work is at stake. It is significant that, although the case was pleaded in restraint of trade and on public policy grounds, Lord Denning did not base his judgment on restraint of trade.

Under the Treaty of European Union, article 119, the sex discrimination legislation and other measures, the particular facts in *Nagle v Feilden* might be dealt with nowadays without recourse to the common law. But the case still stands as authority for the duty of private regulatory bodies not to discriminate. However, the record of the common law in recognising the wrong of discrimination has been mixed: '... not all sex discrimination is unlawful .... Discrimination is only unlawful if it occurs in one of the fields in which it is prohibited in the [Sex Discrimination Act 1975].'[16] The same could be said of other forms of discrimination. Thus, for instance, refusal to admit a member from an ethnic minority to a members' club has been held not to be unlawful.[17] The common law does not prohibit discrimination on grounds of sex,[18] sexual orientation,[19] religion,[20] or disability.

restraints of trade. They were designed to promote a Welsh Football League by restricting the right of clubs who were members of the English Leagues to play their games from grounds within Wales. Blackburn J held that the defendant had not discharged the onus of showing that the restraint was no more than was reasonably necessary to protect the FAW's legitimate interest, an illustration of the operation of the burden of proof in this area.

13 [1966] 2 QB 633.
14 [1978] 1 WLR 1520.
15 [1966] 2 QB 633 at 645.
16 Per Lord Fraser in *R v Entry Clearance Officer, ex p Amin* [1983] 2 All ER 864 at 871.
17 *Charter v Race Relations Board* [1973] AC 868 and *Dockers' Labour Club v Race Relations Board* [1976] AC 285.
18 See S Fredman *Women and the Law* (1997).
19 See *R v Ministry of Defence, ex p Smith* [1996] QB 517; *Grant v South-West Trains* [1998] 1 RLR 165, ECJ; *P v S and Cornwall County Council* [1996] IRLR 347; *Chessington World of Adventures v Reed* [1997] IRLR 556; R Wintemute *Sexual Orientation and Human Rights* (1995).
20 See for instance *Ahmad v Inner London Education Authority* [1978] QB 36, CA.

There are, then, two opposite trends in authorities on discrimination, those which permit it, and the common callings cases and *Nagle v Feilden*, which regard it as irrational and unlawful. But on the strength of *Nagle*, if a person were refused a trainer's licence for discriminatory reasons not covered by European law or British legislation, such as their religion, sexual orientation, the colour of their hair, their political affiliations or personal animosity on the part of a member of the licensing body, the court could again find that this was unlawful, expressing it either as an unlawful restraint of trade or as contrary to a wider public policy, in effect imposing duties of reasonableness (as in the common callings cases) or of rational decision making on the regulatory body.

The case of *McInnes v Onslow Fane*[1] provides an interesting contrast with *Nagle v Feilden* as it was not based on restraint of trade at all, but on other public policy considerations. In *McInnes v Onslow Fane* the plaintiff's application for a boxing manager's licence was refused and he was complaining of the lack of a hearing. There was no contractual relationship in which to base duties towards the plaintiff. The plaintiff failed because this was an application case, not a case of forfeiture or legitimate expectation, and there had been no breach of the relevant duties in dealing with the application. But Megarry VC laid down requirements of decision-making procedures in application, forfeiture or legitimate expectation cases affecting a 'liberty to work' which, developed by subsequent case law, now also form part of the requirements in judicial review. In effect these principles require the interests of the plaintiff to be considered fairly and rationally when decisions affecting him are made. They include a duty, in application cases, 'to reach an honest conclusion without bias and not in pursuance of any capricious policy'[2] – a formulation, like that in *Nagle*, that is reminiscent of *Wednesbury* reasonableness. In renewal and forfeiture cases additional duties are imposed, because these affect the existing interests of licensees – their security and status in particular – in ways in which applications do not.

Megarry VC's requirements in *McInnes* did not depend on the existence of a contractual relationship, and nor did he base his decision in restraint of trade. He was drawing analogies from a wide range of cases on immigration, reputations, privacy and status as well as livelihood. The foundation of the jurisdiction to control the decision-making processes of private regulators with various degrees of intensity, and outside contract, appears to have been public policy, in this case policy in favour of enabling people to earn their living in their own way – in favour of their autonomy. But, given Megarry VC's reference to other

1   [1978] 1 WLR 1520.
2   [1978] 1 WLR 1520 at 1530.

areas of the law in which rationality is imposed, public policy may also require degrees of rationality where other subject matter than livelihoods and other interests than autonomy are at stake – dignity, status and security in particular.

It is worth noting at this point the similarities between Megarry VC's formulations of decision-making requirements in *McInnes v Onslow Fane* and those adopted by Lord Greene MR in *Wednesbury Corp*: both were distinguished Chancery lawyers, and from the phrases they used it is obvious that both were drawing on equitable principles in formulating common law requirements in decision making.

Given the decision in *Law v National Greyhound Racing Club*,[3] discussed earlier, the British Board of Boxing Control, the defendants in *McInnes*, would not be judicially reviewable nowadays. So if *McInnes* still stands for anything it must be that as a matter of public policy the common law and equity impose on a regulatory body of this kind, and even on other bodies whose decisions and actions may be damaging to the vital interests of individuals, duties of fairness and rationality that are enforceable in private law and are not based in restraint of trade. Some of the public policy considerations which the courts apply have been noted in the discussion of common callings and associated causes of action above.

A question that arises is whether the jurisdiction in private law with which these cases have been concerned does in fact survive in the light of recent judicial comments about the public-private divide and the exclusivity rule. In *RAM Racecourses* Simon Brown J commented that cases such as *Nagle*, if they had arisen then, 'would have found a natural home in judicial review proceedings'. But this approach cannot stand with the decisions in *Law*, *Aga Khan*[4] and other cases to the effect that such decisions by such bodies are not subject to judicial review.

Hoffmann LJ in *Aga Khan* disagreed with Simon Brown J. He felt that the decision in *Nagle* had an 'improvisatory air' and that the possibility of obtaining an injunction to protect the plaintiff in *Nagle* had not survived the *Siskina* case, which requires a cause of action to exist before an injunction or declaration may be granted.[5] But Hoffmann LJ did refer to the fact that remedies might be available in contract, restraint of trade or 'all the other instruments available in law for curbing the excesses of private power,'[6] though he did not elaborate on what those were. It might be, Hoffmann LJ felt, that the remedies available in private law

3   [1983] 1 WLR 1302, CA. See also chapter 4.
4   *R v Disciplinary Committee of the Jockey Club, ex p Aga Khan* [1993] 1 WLR 909, CA.
5   *Siskina (cargo owners) v Distos Cia Naviera SA, The Siskina* [1979] AC 210. See discussion of remedies, infra.
6   Ibid at 873.

were inadequate, but he did not think that one should try to 'patch up the remedies available against domestic bodies by pretending that they are organs of Government.'[7] However, in the light of other case law on duties of fair and rational decision making in private law discussed in the previous chapter and earlier in this chapter, it is suggested that there are in fact available to the courts causes of action and effective remedies to deal with such cases outside judicial review.

The point may be illustrated by the case of *Stevenage Borough Football Club Ltd v Football League Ltd*.[8] Stevenage Football Club sought, in the Chancery Division, to challenge the validity of the criteria applied by the Football League in refusing Stevenage promotion to the third division. Stevenage alleged that the criteria were in restraint of trade and unreasonable. Carnwath J at first instance observed that there appeared to be three lines of cases in private law in which the courts had exercised a supervisory jurisdiction, awarding declarations or injunctions as remedies. First, those in which the court focused on the control of power exercised by regulatory bodies, treating their rules as legislative in nature.[9] Second, those which like *Nagle v Feilden*,[10] approached this kind of matter as raising issues of restraint of trade. And third, those, including *Nagle* in places, which have held that it was unlawful to deprive a person of the right or liberty to work.[11]

Carnwath J refused a remedy in *Stevenage* on the basis of delay and prejudice to third parties, but he saw no reason why the tests applied to the exercise of discretion by regulatory bodies should be materially different from those applied to bodies subject to judicial review, given that the former was part of the elaborate structure established for the control of professional football in the interests of the participants and the public generally. Those dealing with these bodies have a legitimate expectation that the relevant criteria will be applied to them fairly and justly, not arbitrarily or capriciously. The league's criteria did not amount to an unreasonable restraint of trade as between the parties, but they might nevertheless be controllable as being contrary to public policy. Whether the matter was approached as a restraint of trade or as contrary to public policy was less important than the substance of the principles applied. But the onus was on those who make the challenge to establish their case and the court would give due weight to the judgment of the

7   At 933. Remedies will be considered below.
8   (1996) Times, 1 August (Carnwath J).
9   Transcript of *Stevenage*, p 28. Carnwath J particularly mentioned Lord Denning's judgments in *Enderby Town Football Club v Football Association* [1971] Ch 591 and *Breen v Amalgamated Engineering Union* [1971] 2 QB 175.
10 [1966] 1 All ER 689, CA.
11 Transcript of *Stevenage*, p 28. See also *McInnes v Onslow Fane* [1978] 1 WLR 1520, supra.

responsible bodies. He approved the approach taken in 1995 in an arbitration award by Sir Michael Kerr and two senior Queen's Counsel in which Enfield Town Football Club were complaining about their unsuccessful application to join the Vauxhall Conference, that '... Enfield are entitled to contend ... that they had a legitimate expectation that the relevant criteria, including the financial criteria, would be applied to it fairly and in accordance with the rules of justice, to which we have compendiously referred as the duty of fairness and that we have a jurisdiction to determine whether or not there has been a breach of that duty.' Carnwath J felt that *Nagle* established that if admission criteria are shown to be arbitrary or capricious in effect, whether because of the way in which they are formulated or in the way in which they are applied, they are open to challenge.

The Court of Appeal upheld Carnwath J's refusal of a remedy in *Stevenage*.[12] On the substance of the claim the court was ambivalent. Millett LJ noted that the case was pleaded as a claim based on restraint of trade but also observed that the authorities relied on, such as *McInnes v Onslow Fane*, were not restraint of trade cases. Given Stevenage's delay and the prejudice to third parties he concluded that no remedy should be granted and that it was not necessary to consider whether Carnwath J was right in concluding that the rules in question were objectionable on the ground of restraint of trade, nor what test was appropriate. He dismissed the appeal. Hobhouse LJ agreed that the court was not concerned with the question whether or not there was a restraint and whether or not it was unreasonable and decided the case, as Millett LJ did, on the ground that no remedy should be granted. Thus Carnwath J's reasoning still stands as an indication that there is a jurisdiction in private law proceedings to control decision making and in particular to secure fair and rational procedures and processes.

These rights and causes of action are still developing, but they are potentially very wide: Lord Upjohn in *Pharmaceutical Society v Dickson*[13] in which involuntary restraints of trade and professional rules were at issue, suggested that 'A person whose freedom of action is challenged can always come to the court to have his rights and position clarified.'

To return to the particular subject of self-regulatory bodies, in *McInnes v Onslow Fane* and other cases[14] doubts have been expressed about the wisdom of the courts interfering with the decisions of self-regulatory bodies through a supervisory jurisdiction, whether in judicial review or in private law. This is indeed an issue. It has been argued that such

---

12   (1997) 9 Admin LR 109.
13   [1970] AC 403 at 433.
14   Eg *Cowley v Heatley* (1986) Times, 24 July, Browne-Wilkinson VC; *Gasser v Stinson* (15 June 1998, unreported) Scott J, unreported but noted in M Beloff 'Pitch, Pool, Rink ... Court? Judicial Review in the Sporting World' [1989] Public Law 109.

bodies are well qualified to make these decisions themselves and they provide a workable 'alternative dispute resolution' system.[15] This is certainly a legitimate consideration to take into account when the courts are considering the granting of remedies; but it should not of itself be taken to justify findings that the bodies are public or private, or their functions are public, governmental or private, or that they are not subject to duties of fairness and rationality in their actions.

Public policy: general considerations

On one view – probably the prevailing view – *Nagle v Feilden* and the restraint of trade rules are simply manifestations of a laisser faire liberal policy of free trade and economic activity, and this is the only public policy with which the courts have been concerned. But it is suggested that this would be too narrow an explanation of the common law's objections to restraints on trade and similar limits on the freedom of individuals to earn their living as they wish. There are also justifications in terms of social policy against unemployment and idleness, against exploitation and against interferences with the liberty of the subject. In the Ipswich Taylors' case,[16] the King's Bench resolved that 'at the common law, no man could be prohibited from working in any lawful trade, for the law abhors idleness, the mother of all evil, ... and especially in young men, who ought in their youth ... to learn lawful sciences and trade, which are profitable to the commonwealth, and whereof they might reap the fruit in their old age, for idle in youth, poor in age.' Restrictive ordinances sought to be enforced by the tailors were unlawful as they were 'against the liberty and freedom of the subject, and are a means of extortion in drawing money from them, either by delay, or some other subtle device, or of oppression of young tradesmen, by the old and rich of the same trade, not permitting them to work in their trade freely; and all this is against the common law, and the commonwealth.'[17] The public policies elaborated here are far wider than those associated with laisser faire liberalism.

The impact of such a decision as that of the Jockey Club that was challenged in *Nagle v Feilden* was to deny the applicant for the licence access to the status and security that nowadays is normally only achievable

---

15 See James A R Nafziger 'International sports law as a process for resolving disputes' (1994) 45 ICLQ 130. See also Julia Black 'Constitutionalising Self-regulation' (1996) 59 MLR 24 for a discussion of the subjection of self-regulating bodies to judicial review. See also discussion of 'mini-legal systems' in chapters 1 and 11.

16 (1614) 11 Co Rep 53a, 77 ER 1218.

17 At 1220.

through work (though even work does not give total security, as the discussion in chapter 6 shows), and the respect and dignity that each individual is morally entitled to in a liberal system. The decision prevented the plaintiff's involvement in what, for her, was an important institution of civil society, from which she would have gained status and security. Such a decision may also deny an individual their autonomy, in that they will not be permitted at all to do the job they wish, and so it interferes with their basic freedom of action – for no good reason. The issue in *Nagle v Feilden*, in other words, was not simply that refusal of the licence was an irrational exercise of monopoly power against the public interest, and a denial of the right to work, but the more fundamental consideration that the decision did not give due weight to the importance of the interests of the individual which underlie much of the law.

In fact there is further case law, beyond that on common callings, restraints of trade and *McInnes v Onslow Fane*, imposing duties of non-discrimination, fairness and rationality in decision making on private bodies exercising power that adversely affects individuals in significant ways outside doctrines of contract or restraint of trade – and even outside monopoly situations. In *Wood v Woad*,[18] a case on expulsion of the plaintiff from a mutual insurance society, Kelly CB founded his decision in favour of the plaintiff not on implied contractual terms, but on the basis that the audi alteram partem rule 'is applicable to every tribunal or body of persons invested with authority to adjudicate upon matters involving civil consequences to individuals.' This proposition was approved by Lord Macnaghten in *Lapointe v L'Association de Bienfaisance et de Retraite de la Police de Montreal*[19] (a Privy Council case). That case concerned the decision of the board of a pension fund trust to deprive the plaintiff of his pension. Lord Macnaghten based his decision that the rules of natural justice applied on both 'the rules of the society' and, significantly for our purposes, 'the elementary principles of justice'. It is worth observing at this point that, as has been noted in previous chapters, insurance companies, banks, building societies, pension schemes and personal investment organisations often have in their hands the security of individuals – in fact arrangements with these bodies are often far more likely to provide individuals with security than, for example, employment or traditional property rights, or even the welfare state. These financial institutions are in positions of power in relation to their clients or members in the sense that their negligence or arbitrary action or wrongdoing can cause serious damage to the security of those dependent upon them. It is suggested that it is this factor that has led the courts, through the development of the common law and equity, and Parliament,

18 (1874) LR 9 Exch 190.
19 [1906] AC 535 at 538-540, PC.

to impose duties of consideration and natural justice upon them, and thus to democratise their relationships with their clients or members.

Public policy and the control of power

In 1911 Lord Loreburn – in a public law case – asserted that the duty of natural justice rests upon 'anyone who decides anything'.[20] These sentiments were echoed by Lord Denning in *Breen v Amalgamated Engineering Union*,[1] and extended: 'Call it prejudice, bias, or what you will. It is enough to vitiate the discretion [of] any body, statutory, domestic or other'.[2] Lord Reid in *Ridge v Baldwin*[3] also endorsed the proposition of Kelly CB in *Wood v Woad*. (Indeed in *Ridge v Baldwin* the majority argued by reference to the law relating to expulsions from various kinds of private bodies – clubs and trade unions among others.) Each of these authorities represents a trend towards the democratisation of relationships, recognising the need to protect the interests of individuals, and imposing duties of fair and rational decision making, and thus of a degree of altruism, on the exercise of private power which do not depend on contract.[4]

There is also a line of cases on the duties of universities to comply with rules of fairness and natural justice in their dealings with their students. It is not clear whether this obligation stems from a contract between the student and the university or whether it is imposed only (or in addition) as a matter of public law.[5] In some cases duties of fairness have been found to exist as implied terms in the contract between the student and the university;[6] in other cases the duty is imposed in public law[7] because the university was a 'public institution discharging public functions' (per Sedley J); and in others where there is a visitatorial jurisdiction the visitor has exclusive jurisdiction, but the visitor is subject to judicial review.[8] In these cases students, who are generally in vulnerable positions with no established status in society and no qualifications, receive some protection against the university authorities'

20 *Board of Education v Rice* [1911] AC 179.
1   [1971] 2 QB 175 [1971] 1 All ER 1148.
2   [1971] 1 All ER 1148 at 1155.
3   [1964] AC 40, 70.
4   See also *Uston v Resorts International Hotel Ltd* (1982) 445 A 2d 370; *Forbes v New South Wales Trotting Club* (1978-9) 143 CLR 242; M Taggart 'The province of administrative law determined?' in M Taggart (ed) *The Province of Administrative Law* (1997) op cit.
5   See J Wightman *Contract, A Critical Commentary* (1996) at pp 132-133.
6   Eg *Herring v Templeman* [1973] 3 All ER 569.
7   Eg *R v Manchester Metropolitan University, ex p Nolan* [1994] ELR 380, DC.
8   *R v Hull University Visitor, ex p Page* [1993] AC 682.

exercise of their power, in particular in Galbraith's terms[9] their compensatory power, in that they can control student access to university property, and their condign power, in that they can punish students by withdrawing cooperation.

A policy in favour of the exercise of a private law supervisory jurisdiction to control power was made explicit in *Jones v Welsh Rugby Football Union*.[10] J had been sent off for fighting during a match and appeared before a disciplinary committee to make representations about the referee's report. The committee imposed a suspension. It was held that as sport was now big business it could not be conducted free from restraint as it had been; it was arguable that the failure by a disciplinary committee either to allow a player to challenge by question or evidence the factual basis of the allegation against him or to vary its procedure for viewing video evidence without good reason was unfair; it was held that it was appropriate to grant a mandatory injunction lifting the suspension pending resolution of the dispute. Recognition of the need, as a matter of public policy, to control accumulations of 'big business' power being used to affect the player adversely, was clear in this case.

DUTIES OF CONSIDERATION IN PRIVATE LAW

In this and the previous three chapters we have noted how duties of consideration in actions and in decision making have developed in various areas of the law. These may be summarised briefly. In chapter 6 it was shown that in employment, under the Employment Rights Act 1996, where an employer is considering the dismissal of an employee duties of, broadly, procedural fairness and rationality are imposed; employers also owe duties of consideration for the health and safety of employees. In chapter 7 it was shown how spouses and parents owe duties of consideration to each other and to their children. In chapter 8, in considering tort, it was noted that *Donoghue v Stevenson* imposed duties of care and consideration on producers and more generally towards 'neighbours.' The position in equity was also considered: in discretionary decision making by trustees and company directors where fiduciary relationships exist, what would, in a judicial review context, be referred to as duties of legality and rationality are imposed. In addition, although full-blown duties of natural justice are not imposed in such relationships, some duties involving procedural propriety, including duties of altruism and rules against bias or partiality, arise.

9   See chapter 2.
10 (1997) Times, 6 March.

It has also been shown, in chapter 8 and in this chapter, that in many contractual relationships, especially in membership associations, or where there are explicit discretionary decision-making powers, duties of fairness and rationality may be imposed or implied by the courts. In this chapter it has been noted that duties of rationality may arise in a range of non-contractual relationships: in the law of common callings, or where a relationship of monopoly exists, or where a vital public service is refused; where a person's 'liberty' or right to work is at stake; where restraint of trade is involved; or on a number of other public policy grounds.

These relationships in which it is established that duties of fairness or rationality in decision making are imposed have a number of features in common. In many of them the vital interests of individuals are at stake, notably their interests in their autonomy, dignity, respect, status or security, which were identified as common to public and private law in chapter 2. They are also relationships in which a private decision maker is in a position of power over other parties, in one or more of the senses considered in chapter 2, particularly Galbraith's 'compensatory' power or Daintith's notion of 'dominium'; or where the decision, though it may not impact very seriously on particular individuals (as with many of the decisions taken by company directors and trustees) is one in which the decision maker would be in a position to abuse the power either by acting illegally in various ways, as by overstepping the limits set to the power by the donor; or by acting selfishly where altruism is required by law; or by acting against a recognised public interest, such as the interest in the general availability of public services including the utilities, and interests against exploitation or monopoly.

Towards general principles of decision making

It is suggested that, in the light of these developments, the courts can be seen to be developing general principles of consideration, including considerate decision making: this latter set of principles manifests itself in a right, in circumstances not confined to particular heads such as restraint of trade, on the part of individuals to be considered and to have the effect of a decision on their interests (and certain public interests) taken into account and balanced against other considerations before a decision is made. In principle, it is suggested, this duty of consideration arises where a decision maker is in a position of power in relation to the possible plaintiff, and where plaintiffs' vital interests – particularly in their own autonomy, dignity, respect, status or security – may be affected by the decision; and where certain public interests are at stake.[11] This jurisdiction to control exercises of power by imposing requirements on decision making is an aspect of the jurisdiction to right wrongs and injustices[12] that was asserted in *Bagg's case*[13] and *R v Barker*,[14] and of 'the justice of the common law' referred to by Byles J in *Cooper v Wandsworth Board of Works*.[15] This jurisdiction is not confined to public law. In effect the common law, equity and statutes, in imposing duties on private bodies, are imposing what might be termed duties of 'civil citizenship' which resemble in many ways the civic duties imposed on public bodies in public law. These developments have in common that they democratise, rationalise and equalise private relationships.

REMEDIES IN PRIVATE LAW

In many cases of breach of duties of considerate decision making in private law, as in public law, the decision will be quashed or declared to have been unlawful: the decision should never have been taken. The plaintiff or claimant should be put in the position he or she would have been in had the decision not been made. Generally declarations or injunctions may be awarded in such cases, making plain that the original decision was wrongly taken, and possibly requiring the decision maker to reconsider the matter, fulfilling requirements of rationality and procedural propriety.

Damages

In many such cases it would be unrealistic to take the position that the decision was void and the claimant should have disregarded it: this option is not normally available in practical terms to the victim of an irrational

11 In chapter 11 the parallels between this right to considerate decision making, and the rights protected in judicial review will be considered, and the countervailing considerations which may negative a prima facie right to consideration will be explored. These include: the need in some situations to uphold the authority of a decision maker, the desirability of protecting the freedom of action of private regulatory bodies in the interests of pluralism, the decision maker's own interests, the needs of the market, and justiciability issues.
12 See P Craig 'Ultra Vires and the foundations of judicial review' 57 Camb LJ (1998), 63, at pp 77-78; M Beloff, 'Pitch, Pool, Rink – Judicial review in the sporting world' [1989] Public Law 95; and M Beloff in M Supperstone and J Goudie (eds) *Judicial Review* pp 8.21-8.22.
13 (1615) 11 Co Rep 93b 77 ER 1273. See discussion in chapter 2.
14 (1762) 3 Burr 1265. See discussion of this case in chapter 2.
15 (1863) 14 CB NS 180. See discussion in chapters 3 and 5.

or procedurally unfair decision. So the question arises whether damages are available in such cases. One objection to the award of damages for breach of duties of fairness and rationality when discretions are exercised is that the award is usurping the power of the decision maker by substituting the court's view of what decision should have been taken. As we shall see this is not necessarily the case.

The cases may be divided into two categories: those where the claimant has been deprived of a benefit or office or position which he or she already enjoyed; and those in which the claimant has been denied the chance of a favourable decision which would have resulted in him or her receiving such a benefit.

Where a person has been wrongly deprived of an existing benefit, for instance by breach of a duty of natural justice before a decision was taken, damages are sometimes available at common law or, in some cases, under statutory provisions. In the law of unfair dismissal, as we have seen, damages are available under the Employment Rights Act 1996. So too – since damages are the proper remedy in common law actions – in cases based on breach of contract. By way of example, in the Scottish case of *Tait v Central Radio Taxis (Tollcross) Ltd*[16] damages were awarded in a private law action based on contract for breach of the duties of natural justice.

There may also be jurisdiction to award damages where the right to natural justice is not implied in a contract, but is imposed at common law: in the Scottish case of *McMillan v Free Church of Scotland*[17] damages were awarded in a private law action based on breach of the (non-contractual) rules of the Church.[18] In cases such as these, there should be no problems of usurpation of decision-making powers by the courts in awarding damages for findings of breach of the duties of considerate decision making.

A question that arises is whether there is jurisdiction to award damages where a decision has not deprived someone of a benefit to which they were entitled, but has unfairly or irrationally denied them the opportunity of receiving a benefit which they sought. Lord Denning was willing to award damages in *Breen*[19] for breach of duties of natural justice in private decision making. The plaintiff had been elected shop steward of his union by his fellow workers, but the district committee's approval was required and they refused it, in breach of the duties of natural justice. The damages would have compensated the plaintiff for the damage to his dignity and status caused by the denial of the office – damage which,

16 1989 SC 4, First Division. See discussion of Scots law in Annex.
17 1861 SC 1314, Court of Session.
18 See discussion of these cases and the Scottish position in relation to the public-private divide in Annex.
19 [1971] 2 QB 175, [1971] 1 All ER 1148.

of course, could not have been remedied retrospectively by holding the decision to be void. (The other members of the Court of Appeal disagreed with Lord Denning on the result as they felt themselves to be bound by the findings of fact of the trial judge, whereas Lord Denning was prepared to review them.)

In cases where damages are claimed for denial of the opportunity of a favourable decision as opposed to withdrawal of an existing benefit, the question arises, on what basis could damages be assessed? It could not be on the basis that the plaintiff was entitled to the benefit itself: for instance, a right to be granted a trainer's licence could not have been enforced against the Jockey Club in *Nagle*, so damages could not place the plaintiff in the position she would have been in if she had been awarded a licence.[20]

In *Nagle* Lord Denning assumed that damages for capricious refusal of membership could not be awarded. It is suggested that this assumption was not warranted. Damages could be awarded for *the loss of the chance* of a favourable decision that would have existed if the application for a licence had been properly considered. An analogy may be drawn here with the position in contract: in *Chaplin v Hicks*[1] the plaintiff had lost the chance to enter and win a beauty competition, and was compensated on the basis that there would have been a twenty-five per cent chance of winning and so twenty-five per cent of the prize money was awarded. The award of damages on the basis of valuing a lost chance would not assume that, for instance, membership of an association or the licence applied for would or should have been granted, and would not usurp the decision-maker's functions. But it would compensate for the breach of the duty of considerate decision making.

Injunctions and declarations

We have already noted a number of situations in which injunctions or declarations may be awarded in private law proceedings in respect of decisions taken in breach of duties of considerate decision making – for instance in trusts and company law where directors' decisions are challenged, where the decisions of membership bodies are in issue, and in relation to regulatory bodies in sport.

A question arises, what is the basis of this jurisdiction, and how far could it be developed in respect of general duties of considerate decision

---

20 See also per Denning LJ in *Lee v The Showmen's Guild of Great Britain* [1952] 2 QB 329 at 341-342; *Faramus v Film Artistes' Association* [1964] AC 925 at 942.

1   [1911] 2 KB 786; see also H Reece 'Losses of chances in law' 59 MLR (1996) 188; and N Jansen 'The idea of the lost chance' 19 Oxford Jo LS (1999) 271.

making? By section 37(1) of the Supreme Court Act the High Court may by order (whether interlocutory or final) grant an injunction 'in all cases in which it appears to the court to be just and convenient to do so'. It is clear that this jurisdiction is not unfettered. It was decided in *The Siskina*[2] that the power to grant an injunction in what is now section 37 of the Supreme Court Act 'presupposes the existence of an action, actual or potential, claiming substantive relief which the High Court has jurisdiction to grant and to which the interlocutory orders referred to are ancillary'. In *Southern Carolina Insurance Co v Assurantie Maatschappij de Zeven Provincien NV*[3] Lord Brandon said that the power conferred by section 37 was confined to two situations, namely where one party can show that the other party has invaded or threatened to invade a legal or equitable right, or where one party has behaved or threatens to behave in a manner which is unconscionable.

On this basis there would be jurisdiction to award interlocutory injunctions in claims based on tort (as in the common callings cases) or breach of contract (as in the trade union or membership association cases), and in claims based on equitable wrongs – breach of fiduciary duties by trustees or directors, breach of confidentiality, breach of a duty of trust and confidence, and duties, including duties of considerate decision making, that are grounded in public policy (as in *McInnes v Onslow Fane* and *Nagle v Feilden*).

Reservations have been expressed in the House of Lords as to whether the law as laid down by *The Siskina* (as subsequently modified) is correct in restricting the power to grant injunctions to certain exclusive categories.[4] On the case law it seems that there is also jurisdiction to grant an interlocutory injunction where no wrong is alleged but a remedy by way of declaration might be available. In the *Stevenage* case, discussed above, Carnwath J refused a remedy on the basis of delay and prejudice to third parties, but he was of the view that he would have had jurisdiction to grant a declaration if the complaints had been made out, and he would have had jurisdiction to grant an interlocutory injunction in support of a right to a declaration. In the *Welsh Football* case[5] Jacob J granted ancillary injunctive relief under section 37 of the Supreme Court Act 1981 on the basis that, although there was no contractual relationship between the parties, there was a well-established right to seek a declaration – in this case a declaration that an arrangement was in restraint of trade – and this

2   [1979] AC 210 at 245, per Lord Diplock.
3   [1987] AC 24.
4   See for instance per Lord Browne-Wilkinson, with whom Lord Keith and Lord Goff agreed in *Channel Tunnel Group v Balfour Beatty Ltd* [1993] AC 334.
5   *Newport Association Football Club v Football Association of Wales* [1995] 2 All ER 87, Jacob J.

was a sufficient 'cause of action' under the Supreme Court Act 1981 to give him jurisdiction. A subtle point taken in *Welsh Football* was that the arrangement in restraint of trade in this case was null and void and therefore created no wrong – and yet the court accepted that a remedy was necessary to clarify the position and protect the plaintiff. This decision pushes the jurisdiction of the courts further than hitherto, by assuming jurisdiction to grant a remedy – an injunction – in the absence of a substantive right or equitable wrong.

Jacob J drew support for his decision from the High Court of Australia in *Buckley v Tutty*:[6] a Rugby League player was affected by unreasonably restrictive rules of a football association. Barwick CJ observed that 'It would indeed be a strange weakness in the law if it afforded no protection to a person who was against his will subjected in fact to an unreasonable restraint of trade.' He granted an interlocutory injunction pending determination of the question whether the plaintiff was entitled to a declaration. Thus the Australian High Court recognised the jurisdiction to grant declaratory or injunctive relief, notwithstanding the lack of any contractual underpinning to the plaintiff's claim.

Jacob J in the *Welsh Football* case approved of the decision in *Nagle v Feilden* as illustrating the existence of jurisdiction to award a declaration and injunction despite the absence of a contractual relationship. He took the view that the right to obtain a declaration was a sufficient cause of action to ground the power to award an interlocutory injunction.

The same approach to the jurisdiction to grant remedies in the absence of a substantive cause of action was adopted by Lightman J in *Greenwich Healthcare National Health Service Trust v London and Quadrant Housing Trust and ors*;[7] this case concerned whether a declaration could be awarded as to entitlement to an injunction:

'I am quite satisfied that I have jurisdiction to grant the declarations sought [that the Defendants are not entitled to claim an injunction or damages if and when the Plaintiff realigns rights of way to which they are entitled] and that I should do so. One special feature of this case is that the declarations sought extend to the entitlement of the Defendants, not to proprietary rights eg to easements or the benefit of restrictive covenants, but to their entitlement to the equitable remedy of injunction. The jurisdiction of the Court to grant declarations must extend to entitlement both to proprietary rights and to particular remedies.'[8]

6   (1971) 125 CLR 353 at 380-352.
7   [1998] 1 WLR 1749.
8   See also *A-G v Blake* [1998] 1 All ER 833, per Lord Woolf MR: 'The power to grant [injunctions under section 37(1) and (2) of the Supreme Court Act 1981] is limited to cases where the plaintiff has a legal or equitable right. For reasons

An injunction, being a discretionary remedy, would not be awarded requiring that a person be admitted to an association. In *Lee v Showmen's Guild of Great Britain*[9] (an action for a declaration that the expulsion of the plaintiff from the Guild was ultra vires and void) Lord Denning emphasised, obiter, that the court would not grant an injunction to give a member the right to enter a social club, 'because it is too personal to be specifically enforced ...'.[10] However, the court may grant other remedies in such cases, including a declaration and, on the argument advanced in the previous section, damages. Lord Denning was willing to grant a declaration in *Breen* and it seems that the other members of the Court of Appeal would have done so had they felt able to review the findings of fact of the trial judge.

CONCLUSION

This chapter and the previous one have considered a range of situations in which duties of consideration, including considerate action and decision making, lie on private bodies. In many situations these duties are imposed and are not consensual or contractual. This raises a question mark over any assumption that it is not the role of private law to impose obligations, and that a distinguishing feature of public law is the imposition of obligations – a point which was discussed in chapter 1. The topics considered in these two chapters show how the trend is towards extending duties of consideration into the private sphere, thus increasing the protection offered by the law for individuals' interests, and promoting the public interest in the control of power. In effect, what is developing, alongside public law theories of government, democracy and citizenship, are parallel theories of civil governance, democracy and citizenship. Duties of care and consideration in action lie on many private bodies; and duties of fairness and rationality in decision making lie on private decision makers where the jurisdiction in judicial review is not available.

In the next chapter we consider the effect of the Human Rights Act on the public-private divide, and in the penultimate chapter it will be suggested that, given the strong parallels between public and private law identified in previous chapters, an alternative to the exclusivity rule laid down in *O'Reilly v Mackman* would more accurately reflect the

---

already explained the Attorney General has a legal right in public law to apply to the court for an injunction in a case [where a criminal offence has been committed].'

9   [1952] 2 QB 329.
10   341-342.

development of the law relating to public and private power and the protection of individual and public interests and would facilitate the development of civic and civil models of democracy and citizenship.

Chapter Ten

The Human Rights Act, Europe and the Public-Private Divide

The Human Rights Act 1998 is expected to come into effect in 2000. Our focus here will be on the ways in which the Act treats the 'key' values and the control of power, and democratises both civic and civil society. In sum, it is suggested, this Act will give added impetus to the trend towards upholding certain central or 'key' interests of individuals – in both public and private law – by adding to the weight to be given to them when choices have to be made between these interests and countervailing considerations. This point is illustrated by the decision of the European Court of Human Rights in the case of *Osman v United Kingdom*, which was noted in chapter 1:[1] there the court decided that blanket immunities of public bodies in the law of tort were not compatible with the Convention, and the case for relieving a public body of civil liability had to be considered on its merits in each particular case.

Let us start this chapter with a summary of the main provisions of the Act which are relevant to this argument.

THE HUMAN RIGHTS ACT 1998 – THE PROVISIONS SUMMARISED

Section 1 of the Act provides that certain articles of the European Convention on Human Rights and its Protocols 'are to have effect'[2] subject to certain derogations and reservations.

The 'Convention rights' protected are, broadly, the rights to life (article 2), not to be subjected to torture or inhuman and degrading treatment (article 3), freedom from slavery or servitude (article 4), liberty

---

1   Case No 87/1997/871/1083, ECtHR, (1998) Times, 5 November.
2   Human Rights Act 1998, section 1(2).

and security of the person (article 5), respect for private and family life (article 8), freedom of thought, conscience and religion (article 9), expression (article 10), peaceful assembly and association (article 11), to marry and found a family (article 12) and not to be discriminated against in the enjoyment of the rights and freedoms in the Convention (article 14). In addition there are rights to a fair trial in the determination of a person's civil rights and obligations or criminal charges (article 6).

The Act also provides for certain provisions in the First and Sixth Protocols to the Convention to have effect, namely the right to the peaceful enjoyment of possessions, the right to education and the right to free elections (articles 1, 2 and 3 of the First Protocol), and the abolition of the death penalty save in time of war (articles 1 and 2 of the Sixth Protocol).

Article 13 of the Convention is not included in the Human Rights Act. That article provides for an effective remedy for violation of the rights and freedoms in the Convention. The assumption behind this is that the courts are capable of remedying breach of Convention rights through the exercise of their existing powers to award remedies.

British courts will have to take into account (though they will not be bound by) the jurisprudence of the European Court and Commission on Human Rights and decisions of the Committee of Ministers where these are relevant. British primary and subordinate legislation is to be read and given effect 'so far as it is possible to do so'[3] in a way that is compatible with the Convention rights; but the courts will not have the power to disapply incompatible primary legislation,[4] whether passed before or after the Act. However, the higher courts will have the power to make a declaration of incompatibility if they are satisfied that a provision of British primary legislation is incompatible with a Convention right.[5] Thereupon a minister may – but the power is discretionary – initiate remedial action by making an order amending the primary legislation.[6] Provision is also made for dealing with incompatibilities in subordinate legislation.

Subject to the precedence of Acts of Parliament, which is preserved by the provisions mentioned above, under the Human Rights Act 'it is unlawful for a public authority to act in a way which is incompatible with a Convention right.'[7] In other words, the Act has direct[8] 'vertical' effect. Public authority includes 'pure public authorities' such as the government, local authorities, the police, and courts or tribunals; it also includes 'any person certain of whose functions are functions of a public

---

3   Section 3(1).
4   Section 3(2)(b).
5   Section 4(2).
6   Section 10 and Schedule 2.
7   Section 6(1).
8   See discussion of 'direct effect' in European law in chapter 5.

nature'.[9] This definition follows that for judicial review in the *Datafin* case;[10] however, the definition used by the courts in judicial review may have moved on since that case, requiring that a person subject to judicial review should be exercising 'governmental' functions.[11] A person other than a 'pure' public authority is not to be treated as a public authority if the nature of the act in question is private.[12] It follows that public authorities will be bound by the Act whether their acts are public or private in nature, whereas only the public acts of private bodies will have to conform to the Act.

A person who is or would be 'a victim of an unlawful act'[13] by a public authority may bring proceedings against the authority, and may rely on Convention rights in litigation to which he or she may be a party. The normal limitation period within which a 'victim' may bring proceedings is one year from the date of the act complained of, though in applications for judicial review the limitation period will continue to be three months. Those who are not victims within the Act – for instance, pressure groups – who apply for judicial review may not therefore rely on the convention rights, and the court will presumably decline to hear any argument on the Convention.

As far as remedies are concerned,[14] a court 'may grant such relief or remedy, or make such order, within its powers as it considers just and appropriate'. However, damages for an unlawful act of a public authority may be awarded only by a court which has power to award damages in civil proceedings.[15] Damages may be awarded for 'judicial acts' and will be payable by the Crown.[16] Thus if a judge acts in breach of the requirement of section 6(1) the 'victim' has a remedy against the state.

It was feared that the right to privacy under article 8 of the Convention would interfere unduly with press freedom under article 10; so 'The court must have particular regard to the importance of the Convention right to freedom of expression and, where the proceedings relate to material which the respondent claims, or which appears to the court, to be journalistic, literary or artistic material ...., to – (a) the extent to which – (i) the material has, or is about to, become available to the public; or (ii) it is, or would be, in the public interest for the material to be published; (b) any relevant privacy code'.[17]

---

9   Section 3(a) and (b).
10 [1987] 2 WLR 699, CA.
11 *R v Disciplinary Committee of the Jockey Club, ex p Aga Khan* [1993] 1 WLR 909, CA.
12 Section 3(5).
13 Section 7(1).
14 On remedies see D Feldman 'Remedies for violations of Convention rights under the Human Rights Act' [1998] EHRLR 691.
15 Section 8.
16 Section 9(3), (4).
17 Section 12(4).

Religious bodies were concerned that their freedom of action might be limited under the Act. Thus, as far as freedom of thought, conscience and religion are concerned, section 13(1) provides that 'If a court's determination of any question arising under this Act might affect the exercise by a religious organisation (itself or its members collectively) of the Convention right to freedom of thought, conscience and religion, it must have particular regard to the importance of that right.' It is difficult to see what this adds to the terms of the Convention rights.

THE RATIONALES FOR CIVIL AND POLITICAL RIGHTS: THE VALUES THEY EXPRESS

The Human Rights Act thus introduces into the law of the United Kingdom a concept of civil and political rights as deserving special legal protection – although the protection is not as strong as in countries where the courts have power to strike down primary legislation which is incompatible with a Bill or Charter of Rights, such as the United States of America or Canada. The Act broadly follows the New Zealand model and the method adopted in Canada for protecting rights without limiting the legislative sovereignty of Parliament. Previously in English law individuals' interests have had the status of 'liberties' in the sense that they were only weakly protected by law and yielded to incompatible provisions of Acts of Parliament and subordinate legislation. The common law does not embody a specific and consistent preference for civil and political rights or liberties over other values in the law such as autonomy of public bodies, the needs of public administration or the importance of upholding authority[18] – including the sovereign authority of Parliament.[19]

It is relevant at this point, then, to consider what the rationales might be for giving the special protection in the Human Rights Act to civil and political rights or liberties.

The rationales or justifications – or 'tele'[20] – for treating certain civil and political rights as 'fundamental' are varied,[1] and depend in part on

18   See on this J A G Griffith *The Politics of the Judiciary* (3rd edn, 1985); *(Judicial Politics since 1920)* (1993); K Ewing and C Gearty *Freedom under Thatcher* (1990).

19   On this and its relation to different theories of democracy see T R S Allan, 'Fairness, Equality, Rationality: Constitutional Theory and Judicial Review' in C Forsyth and I Hare (eds) *The Golden Metwand and the Crooked Cord* (1998).

20   See S I Benn 'Human Rights – for whom and for what?' in Kamenka and Tay (eds) *Human Rights* (1978).

1   See for instance A Clapham *Human Rights in the Private Sphere* (1993) chapter 5; R Dworkin *Taking Rights Seriously* (1977); A Gewirth *Human Rights: Essays on Justification and Applications* (1982); J Rawls *A Theory of Justice* (1971); J Raz *The Morality of Freedom* (1986).

the level of abstraction at which they are considered. Some rationales are predominantly deontological, asserting that freedom generally, or a particular right or liberty, is good in itself and is not advanced for any ulterior purpose. Other rationales are teleological, looking to the advantages which flow from the right or liberty. Thus freedom from torture might be viewed as deontological, reflecting our respect for the individual's dignity and autonomy; freedom of speech might be teleological, since it enables democratic processes to operate effectively.[2] Dworkin in *Taking Rights Seriously*[3] argues that justice as fairness rests on the assumption of a natural right of all men and women to equality of concern and respect, a right they possess not by virtue of birth or characteristic or merit or excellence but simply as human beings with the capacity to make plans and give justice.[4] This then, is a deontological rationale for the right or value of justice as fairness.

In practice deontological values lie behind most teleological arguments for rights.[5] For instance, if one rationale for the protection of free speech is that it will promote democracy, and if we ask ourselves why democracy is supposed to be a good thing, we are likely ultimately to claim, among other possible justifications for democracy, that true democracy enables individuals to live their lives autonomously and with dignity, according to their own wishes and in a self-fulfilling way – a deontological belief.

Rationales for the right to privacy

There may be a range of possible justifications for each of the rights which are regarded as fundamental in a human rights instrument. The right to privacy, expressed in article 8 of the ECHR as a person's 'right to respect for his private and family life, his home and his correspondence' provides a useful example.[6] Among the justifications that could be advanced for a right to privacy are: the desirability of protecting the moral personality of individuals,[7] their autonomy and dignity, from unwelcome interference; the interest of an individual in freedom from being subjected to abuse of power by others who gather information which could be used, for instance, to criticise or harass the individual. These are justifications that give explicit expression to the key values identified in chapter 3. Other possible justifications for privacy are less

---

2   See J Hart Ely *Democracy and Distrust* (1980).
3   (1977).
4   Chapter 6.
5   D Feldman *Civil Liberties and Human Rights in England and Wales* (1993) p 7.
6   See generally on the justifications for a right to privacy, *Feldman* chapter 8.
7   Benn, op cit, at p 63. See also *Feldman* chapter 8.

concerned with these values – for instance the protection and furthering of an individual's commercial or proprietorial interests, such as the interest a professional sportsman or film actor may have in controlling advertisers' use of his likeness or reputation.

It can be seen that different results will be achieved in cases raising human rights issues according to the rationale for the right that is adopted by the court. If a court were to accept that a rationale for the right to privacy is to protect the commercial interests of individuals, then protection would be given to the professional sportsman seeking to limit commercial exploitation of himself. As Feldman argues, 'It is important to work out where one stands on the question of the fundamental justification for privacy rights, because it is likely to dictate the use to which one can put them.'[8] The same is true of most civil and political rights.

The right to freedom of expression

The right to freedom of expression provides a further example of the range of rationales for rights. Barendt has identified two groups of rationales for this right.[9] First, arguments for democracy: political and social discussion should be immune from government suppression because it enables people to participate fully and knowledgeably in public affairs and to deal with government with a level of equality. Second, arguments for self-fulfilment and self-development. In his view the argument for democracy is the stronger. Raz argues that the right to free expression can be justified in four ways: as meeting the fundamental need for public validation of one's way of life; as a prerequisite of a democratic government; as vital for the prosperity of a pluralistic culture; and as a crucial element in controlling possible abuses and corruption of power. 'All four arguments point to the need to make freedom of expression a foundational part of the political and civic culture of pluralistic democracies.'[10]

The courts, rationales for rights, and the Human Rights Act

Feldman considers that, in the context of civil liberties, arguments for self-fulfilment and freedom of conscience are the strongest, since he

---

8　*Feldman* at 399.
9　E Barendt *Freedom of Speech* (1985).
10　J Raz 'Free Expression and Personal Identification' in (1991) 11 OJLS, 305, at p 324.

grounds the rationales for civil liberties in personal autonomy.[11] Allan's view is that fundamental rights 'are themselves a reflection of underlying ideas of human dignity and equality'[12] and he suggests that freedom of conscience and religion are of fundamental importance to the values of human dignity and individual autonomy which lie at the heart of our political culture.[13] Clapham considers that the twin rationales for rights in the European Convention are human dignity and democracy.[14] Inevitably British courts will be faced with determining which rationales for rights prevail when deciding under the Human Rights Act whether limitations on a prima facie right in the name of public interests set out in the Convention are incompatible with the Convention rights in cases brought before them.[15]

Hart Ely[16] considers that it is not the role of the courts but of elected representatives to determine what values if any are *fundamental* in the law; but he concludes that the judges have a proper constitutional role (which will often involve applying and interpreting a Bill of Rights or Constitution) in policing the process of representation, clearing the channels of political change and facilitating the representation of minorities. It is worth noting at this point that the European Court of Human Rights has held that one function of the Convention is to protect democratic processes. Article 17 of the Convention provides that 'Nothing in this Convention may be interpreted as implying for any state, group or person any right to engage in any activity or perform any act aimed at the destruction of any of the rights and freedoms set forth herein or at their limitation to a greater extent than is provided for in the convention.' In the case of *KPD v Federal Republic of Germany*[17] the court held that the function of this provision was 'to protect the rights enshrined in the convention by safeguarding the free functioning of democratic institutions.'

Many of the American cases which Hart Ely uses to develop his thesis have concerned due process and freedom of speech and association: these rights perform important functions in the political process. But that is not to say that he denies the importance of other rationales for rights or of the underlying values, only that their identification is not a matter for judges.

11 *Feldman* chapter 12.
12 T R S Allan 'Fairness, Equality, Rationality: Constitutional Theory and Judicial Review' in C Forsyth and I Hare (eds) op cit at p 34.
13 Allan, supra; at p 24.
14 *Clapham* pp 143-145; see also A Gewirth 'Are there any Absolute Rights?' in J Waldron (ed) *Theories of Rights* (1984) p 108.
15 See C McCrudden 'The impact on freedom of speech' in B Markesinis (ed) *The Impact of the Human Rights Bill on English Law* (1998) 85.
16 Hart Ely, op cit.
17 Application 250/57, 1 YB 222 E Com HR at 223 (1957).

In English law the common underlying values in public and private law can be deduced both from the way in which the judges have developed the common law, and from statutory provisions introduced by Parliament. So the judges this side of the Atlantic have had a role in identifying underlying legal values. Until the Human Rights Act, however, they have not had a role in identifying or protecting 'fundamental' values in the American sense of values which have specially protected legal status – the doctrine of parliamentary sovereignty has denied British judges that role. They have on occasions, as we have seen, given special weight to rights considered fundamental in human rights instruments.[18]

Although the Human Rights Act preserves Parliament's right to enact legislation that is incompatible with the Convention, the overall effect of the Act, it is suggested, will be to elevate the 'key values' to a more fundamental status – both in public and private law. This flows from the facts that these values are implicit in the text of the Convention, and, as we shall see, that they have been made explicit by the European Court and Commission on Human Rights in a number of cases. (It will be remembered that the Act requires British courts to 'take into account' the jurisprudence of the court and Commission.) It will be suggested later in this chapter that the identification of the values in the Convention will be particularly important when the courts are developing the common law, especially private law, in line with the Convention.

THE EUROPEAN CONVENTION ON HUMAN RIGHTS AND THE KEY VALUES

In each of the substantive articles of the Convention except article 3 (prohibition of torture) statements of the substance of the right are followed by exceptions – typically such as are prescribed by law and are necessary in a democratic society in the interests of national security or public safety, for the prevention of disorder or crime, for the protection of health or morals or for the protection of the rights and freedoms of others (as in article 11, for instance). Hence the Court (and the Commission until recently[19]) has to find a fair balance between the rights of the individual claimant and various public interests.

The European Commission and Court of Human Rights have given explicit consideration from time to time to what the rationales for particular rights might be. These points shed light on the values implicit

18 See for instance the discussion of *Bugdaycay v Secretary of State for the Home Department* [1987] AC 514 in chapter 5.
19 The Commission has been replaced by a new unified Court. See A Mowbray [1999] Public Law 219.

in the Convention and on the balance that has to be achieved between the prima facie right and the exceptions provided for in all but article 3. It will be seen that the values of dignity, autonomy, respect, status and security are strongly present in most of the articles. Examples in the operation of articles 3 (freedom from torture) and 8 (privacy) and article 2 of the First Protocol (right to education) will illustrate the point.

Article 3: Torture and inhuman and degrading treatment

Protection from torture and inhuman and degrading treatment or punishment protect the autonomy, dignity and respect – sometimes even the status – of victims. One aspect of suffering in cases of torture and inhuman and degrading treatment is the sense of powerlessness of the victim. Psychological evidence suggests that stress is most often caused by powerlessness and it is no doubt this which exacerbates the suffering in cases of ill-treatment short of physical violence such as the 'five techniques' for interrogation used by British soldiers in the case of *Ireland v United Kingdom*.[20] The wall-standing, hooding, subjection to noise, deprivation of sleep and deprivation of food and drink 'caused, if not actual bodily injury, at least intense physical and mental suffering to the persons subjected thereto and also led to acute psychiatric disturbances during interrogation.'[1] The European Court of Human Rights therefore found that they amounted to inhuman treatment contrary to article 3.

In that case it was also found that the UK was guilty of degrading treatment. This occurs if it arouses in the victim feelings of fear, anguish and inferiority capable of humiliating and debasing him and possibly breaking his physical and moral resistance.[2] In the *East African Asians* case the Commission found that an action which lowers a person in rank, position, reputation or character may be degrading, provided the treatment reaches a certain level of severity, as may be an action which grossly humiliates a victim before others or drives him to act against his will or conscience: on this approach article 3 protects the individual's interests in their status and security as well as their dignity, autonomy and respect – all of the key values.[3]

Article 3 was also considered in the case of *Tyrer v United Kingdom*,[4] in which a judicial sentence of three strokes of the birch imposed by an Isle of Man juvenile court on a fifteen year old boy for assault, and

---

20   (1978) 2 EHRR 25.
1   At 167.
2   (1978) 2 EHRR 25 at para 167.
3   *East African Asians v United Kingdom* (1973) 3 EHRR 76 at 80, European Commission on Human Rights.
4   (1978) 2 EHRR 1.

executed by a police constable at a police station, was found to be a degrading punishment contrary to article 3. With regard to the 'manner and method of its execution' the birching had occurred in private, but the court said that it did not consider that the 'absence of publicity will necessarily prevent a given punishment from falling into the category of "degrading punishment": it may well suffice that the victim is humiliated in his own eyes, even if not in the eyes of others.[5] Also the 'indignity of having the punishment administered over the bare posterior aggravated to some extent the degrading character of the applicant's punishment' although it was not the only or determining factor.[6] The court emphasised that such punishment was 'institutionalised violence' imposed in the name of the state, the individual being 'treated as an object in the power of the authorities'; it was 'an assault on precisely that which it is one of the main purposes of article three to protect, namely a person's dignity and physical integrity'.[7]

The Commission has also expressed the opinion that racial discrimination – a denial of equal respect and subjection to indignity – may in certain circumstances amount to degrading treatment.[8] The UK legislation terminating the right of entry of UK citizens lacking ancestral or 'place of birth' connections with the UK was considered by the Commission to be racially discriminatory, and the applicants' subjection to it, with the accompanying publicity and in the special circumstances of their cases, was an affront to their dignity to the point of being 'degrading' treatment.[9]

Article 8: Respect for private and family life, home and correspondence

Article 8 has provided the occasion for the Court and Commission to bring out explicitly the rationales and values of this set of rights on a number of occasions, particularly in relation to prisoners. For instance, in *S v United Kingdom*[10] the Commission expressed the view that the practice of 'ghosting' by transferring prisoners to another prison at short notice without informing family members can interfere with the right to private and family life because it make family visits difficult. The Commission has also stated that 'in exceptional circumstances' a refusal

---

5   At 32.
6   Ibid at 35.
7   Ibid at 33.
8   *East African Asians v United Kingdom* (1973) 3 EHRR 76.
9   Ibid.
10 Case Application 9466/81, 36 DR 41.

to transfer a prisoner to a prison near his home may interfere with this right.[11] The significant point for the common underlying values is that individuals commonly rely for their security and status on their families and contact with them, and the maintenance or provision of contact protects these interests. Thus in *Niemietz v Germany*[12] the court said of the right to family life that it must also 'comprise to a certain degree the right to establish and develop relationships with other human beings', something which produces security and status in a social group. In *McFeeley v UK*[13] the Commission underlined the importance of relationships with others, so that it required a degree of association for persons imprisoned – again facilitating the development of senses of security and status in a group. This illustrates the point made in chapter 3 that status and security are essentially social as well as individualistic values.

Article 2 of the First Protocol: A right to education

The right to education is provided for by article 2 of the First Protocol. This provides that 'No person shall be denied the right to education. In the exercise of any functions which it assumes in relation to education and teaching, the state shall respect the right of parents to ensure such education and teaching in conformity with their own religious and philosophical convictions.' The European Court of Human Rights has held that '... the education of children is the whole process whereby, in any society, adults endeavour to transmit their beliefs, culture and other values to the young, whereas teaching or instruction refers in particular to the transmission of knowledge and to intellectual development.'[14] The significance of this for our purposes is that education enables children to take their place in society and to acquire security and status there; teaching or instruction enable a child to obtain skills and knowledge that should enable them to establish themselves in employment. The fact that the right implies a right to be educated in the national language or in one of the national languages,[15] also facilitates the acquisition of status and security within the nation.

As far as the need for education to respect the religions and philosophical convictions of parents is concerned, the philosophical

---

11 See *Hacisuleymanoglu v Italy* 79 DR 125 and *Ouinas v France* 65 DR 265, 277. Note that the Commission was categorical in stating that there was no right to be detained in a particular prison under the Convention in *X v Federal Republic of Germany* 20 CD 28 and ditto 32 CD 23.
12 A 251-B (1992) 16 EHRR 97.
13 (1981) 3 EHRR 161, 20 DR 44.
14 *Campbell and Cosans v United Kingdom* A 48 (1982) 4 EHRR 239.
15 *Belgian Linguistics* Case (No 2) A 6 (1968) 1 EHRR 252.

convictions to be respected are '… such convictions as are worthy of respect in a "democratic society" … and are not incompatible with human dignity; in addition, they must not conflict with the fundamental right of the child to education.'[16] Thus a balance is sought between parental convictions and the child's own dignity and access to security and status in society.

Teleological values in the European Convention

These examples have illustrated the point that the common values of public and private law underlie the European Convention on Human Rights in a selection of areas. The exercise could be extended into the other articles. In each the value has been expressed as deontological. The point was made earlier that there are also teleological rationales for rights, and these can be found reflected too in the case law. The European Court of Human Rights has identified values such as the importance of protecting plural centres of power and influence in democratic society such as trade unions and professional bodies[17] and the desirability of participation by citizens in the political process and of holding governments to account for their actions. For instance, in *Castells v Spain*[18] the court said: 'in a democratic system the actions or omissions of the government must be subject to close scrutiny not only of the legislative and judicial authorities but also of the press and public opinion.' Thus there will be a heavy burden on a state to show it is necessary in a democratic society to restrict freedom of expression under article 10. Freedom of assembly and association also have important political implications and significance.[19]

THE WEIGHT TO BE ATTACHED TO THE KEY VALUES

It is clear that the key values do not have the status of rights under the Convention, and nor will they under the Human Rights Act. As was suggested in chapter 2, values are too vague and general to constitute legally enforceable rights. However, because Convention rights embody values, the Human Rights Act will have the effect of increasing the weight to be given to the key values when a court is seeking the 'fair

16 *Campbell and Cosans v United Kingdom* A 48 (1982) 4 EHRR 239.
17 *Le Compte, Van Leuven and De Meyere v Belgium* (1981) 4 EHRR 1 65.
18 (1992) 14 EHRR 445.
19 *Rassamblement Jurassien Unité Jurassienne v Switzerland* Application 8191/78 (1979) 17 DR 93 at 119 (1979), E Com HR; *Christians against Racism and Fascism v United Kingdom* Application 8840/78 21 DR 148 (1980), E Com HR.

balance' between rights protected by the Convention and countervailing considerations. The jurisprudence of the European Court of Human Rights has made explicit that the rationales of Convention rights are the need to uphold these values, and this will enable British courts to focus on them and give them weight which, when they remained unarticulated, the courts could not do.[20]

THE VERTICAL AND HORIZONTAL EFFECTS OF THE HUMAN RIGHTS ACT

It was noted above that section 6 of the Human Rights Act uses the concepts of 'public authority', 'any person certain of whose functions are functions of a public nature', and 'the nature of the act ... [as] private', in order to define the scope of the Act in terms of a public-private divide. Thus the Act will have direct 'vertical' effect where an action (whether public or private) by a purely public body such as government or local government is under challenge, or where action of a public nature by a hybrid body ('a body certain of whose functions are functions of a public nature') is at issue.

The fact that the Act binds public authorities in respect of all of their actions, whether of a public or private nature[1] opens up the possibility of actions being brought against public bodies in respect of, for instance, employment relationships,[2] contracting by central government, and exercises of other non-statutory common law powers or capacities which the courts have hitherto regarded as beyond the reach of judicial review and as being governed purely by private law.[3] As far as pure public bodies acting in ways that affect Convention rights are concerned, then, the Act precludes any substantive public-private divide, so that even purely private activity by pure public bodies is subject to the Act. This implication of the Human Rights Act underscores the point made in chapter 5 that public bodies do not have self-regarding interests but must always act altruistically, by adding a duty to respect the human rights of those with whom they deal. Hybrid bodies, on the other hand, will only be bound by the Act where the nature of the act was not private.

20 See discussion of weight in chapter 5.
1   Official Report HL, vol 583, col 811, 24 November, 1997, (the Lord Chancellor).
2   See European Court of Human Rights decisions in *Swedish Engine Drivers' Union v Sweden* (1976) 1 EHRR 617, and *Schmidt and Dahlstrom v Sweden* (1976) 1 EHRR 632; G Morris 'The Human Rights Act and the public-private divide in employment law' (1998) 27 ILJ 293; and see discussion of public employment in chapter 6.
3   See for instance the discussion of *R v Lord Chancellor, ex p Hibbit and Saunders* [1993] COD 326, and *Malone v Metropolitan Police Comr* [1979] Ch 344 in chapter 3.

Many of the Convention rights are already protected in general terms in the law of tort, but some of them are not. For instance, there is no tort of breach of privacy or interference with family life. If a case should arise where a public authority is found to have interfered with a person's rights under article 8 in a way that is not protected by the law of tort – where existing causes of action, for instance for breach of confidence, trespass or nuisance cannot be developed in a way that provides a remedy – then the courts will have to develop a new head of tortious or quasi-tortious liability for breach of the article. In effect the Act may create a new category of 'constitutional torts'. One aspect of such causes of action that would be new is the assumption that the award of remedies is discretionary,[4] which is not the case in ordinary tort actions. But it does not follow that the same head of liability would be available against private bodies engaged in private activity – indeed it was widely anticipated during the passage of the Bill that the courts would not develop new private torts, but would rather develop existing causes of action to meet the requirements of the Convention. Thus a new category of public torts is likely to develop, alongside the actions under the *Francovich* decision, and for misfeasance in a public office, to give effect to Convention rights against public authorities.[5] That being the case it is likely that, in time, the inhibition against developing new causes of action in private law will weaken, and new public torts may well spread their tentacles into private law.

THE HUMAN RIGHTS ACT AND THE PUBLIC-PRIVATE DIVIDE

Such possibilities will inevitably raise issues as to the justifications for the public-private divide, some of which were briefly discussed in chapter 1. One justification for the divide that is sometimes put forward is that it is not appropriate to subject private bodies to the kinds of regulation that are appropriately applied to public bodies – duties of fairness and rationality in decision making, concern for public interests, willingness to allow those affected by decisions to participate in decision making.[6] However, if we focus on the fact that both public law and private law are concerned to protect the interests of individuals in the very values with which the European Convention and the Human Rights Act are concerned, and to control exercises of power that damage those interests, we can see that this justification for a substantive public-private divide

4　See discussion of section 8, below.
5　See discussion in chapter 1.
6　See for instance K E Klare 'The public-private distinction in labour law' (1982) U Penn LR 1358.

and therefore for denying any kind of horizontal effect to Convention rights would run counter to the way in which both public and private law have been developing. Clapham makes this point in suggesting that 'The challenge will be to ensure that human rights are enforced in order to protect the values of dignity and democracy, and that no flexible public-private distinction is introduced in order to carve out privileges and immunities for anyone.'[7]

During the passage of the Human Rights Bill through Parliament the view taken by the government was that the Human Rights Act would bind bodies such as 'companies responsible for areas of activity which were previously within the public sector, such as the privatised utilities'[8] unless the action or decision in question was private in nature. Although no explanation was given for this view, the assumption seems to be that the function of providing utility services is public – or perhaps more accurately 'not private'. Here an ambiguity in the word 'public' may cause difficulty. In the case law on the availability of the application for judicial review the test is whether the action or decision being challenged was public or governmental in character.[9] Drawing on this position, an implication of this provision of the Act might be that action in breach of Convention rights taken by bodies such as utilities in the course of providing utility services is 'public' and challengeable. The question then arises whether such an act would be challengeable only by an application for judicial review, where remedies by way of damages are not normally available, or whether it could also be challenged outside judicial review in broadly private law or 'constitutional tort' actions, where damages might be available and where normal limitation periods apply.

We have seen in chapter 9 how the law on common callings developed. The obligations of those engaged in common callings have not been enforced in England through the prerogative writs or orders, but by actions in the Chancery or Queen's Bench Division for damages or injunctions. On one view these callings are 'affected with a public interest', but this consideration does not operate to preclude the bringing of private law actions; rather it serves to justify the imposition of private law liability. It may be therefore that privatised utilities and other hybrid bodies will find themselves subject to liability in tort under the Human Rights Act rather than in judicial review, thus opening up the possibility of damages awards under the Act.

---

7   *Clapham* at p 356.
8   Home Office White Paper (*Rights Brought Home: The Human Rights Bill*) Cm 3782 para 2.2.
9   See chapters 4 and 5.

Horizontal effects

In other cases, where a potential defendant is a purely private body, or where the actions of a hybrid body are private in nature, the Act will not have 'direct effect', as the Act in terms applies only to public authorities, as defined. In terms the Act has direct vertical effect but not direct horizontal effect.[10] This is not to say, however, that the (private) law of contract, tort, property and so on will not be affected by the Act, since the Act's provision that it is unlawful for public authorities to act in a way that is incompatible with Convention rights binds courts and tribunals. Thus there will be an 'indirect horizontal effect' in the Act. This will take the form of the development of the common law in line with the values of the Convention and the requirement for the courts to act compatibly with it, rather than direct application of the Convention in private law disputes.[11]

Lessons from Canada

In cases in Canada whose Charter of Rights has indirect horizontal effect rather similar to that envisaged for the Human Rights Act, the Supreme Court has described the obligation to interpret the common law consistently with Charter principles as 'simply a manifestation of the inherent jurisdiction of the courts to modify or extend the common law in order to comply with prevailing social conditions and values'.[12] This is in line with observations in the English legal literature before the Human Rights Act about the status or relevance of the Convention and other international human rights instruments, to the effect that it is no less acceptable to take account of human rights instruments than it is to take into account the case law of other jurisdictions, especially common law jurisdictions, in developing the common law in accordance with contemporary needs.[13] In *Manning v Hill*[14] the Canadian Supreme Court noted that private litigants challenging the common law could not allege that it violates a Charter right, because Charter rights do not exist in the

10   On direct horizontal effect of the European Convention on Human Rights generally see *Clapham*.
11   For discussion of the range of possibilities of horizontal effect in other jurisdictions see M Hunt 'The "horizontal effect" of the Human Rights Act' [1998] Public Law 423. See also discussion of the implications of the Human Rights Act in employment law in chapter 6.
12   *Manning v Hill* (1995) 126 DLR (4th) 129 at 156. See *Hunt* at pp 429-432.
13   Sir John Laws 'Is the High Court the guardian of fundamental constitutional rights?' [1993] Public Law 59.
14   (1995) 126 DLR (4th) 129.

absence of state action. The most that the private litigant could do was to argue that the common law was inconsistent with Charter *values*. If the British courts were to adopt the same approach then the exercise of identifying the values in the Convention will be particularly significant and the case law on the underlying or fundamental values from the European Court and Commission on Human Rights, some of which was noted earlier in this chapter (and to which the courts in the United Kingdom are required to have regard by section 2(1)), will form a central part of the argument.

DEVELOPING THE COMMON LAW: HOW FAR CAN YOU GO?

It is clear that under the Convention governments are responsible to the Council of Europe for ensuring that their law, including private law, is compatible with the Convention, and indeed some of the cases have raised issues to do with breaches of Convention rights by private bodies – the closed shop case of *Young, James and Webster v United Kingdom*[15] was an example. So in private law cases between private parties the courts will not only be required by the Human Rights Act to interpret legislation 'so far as it is possible to do so' in a way which is compatible with Convention rights, but they will also be required by section 6 (1) and (3)(a) to develop the common law so as to be compatible with the Convention.[16] The question is bound to arise, how far can the courts go in developing the common law in line with the values of the Convention? In *Manning v Hill* the Supreme Court of Canada took the view that far-reaching changes to the common law should be left to the legislature. On this approach the case could be put that it will be open to the British courts under the Human Rights Act to develop the common law incrementally, but not to create, for instance, new causes of action. This is the approach anticipated by the Lord Chancellor, Lord Irvine as the Human Rights Bill was passing through Parliament. He stated that:

> 'In my opinion, the court is not obliged to remedy the failure by legislating via the common law either wherever a Convention right is infringed by incompatible legislation or wherever, because of the absence of legislation – say, privacy legislation – a Convention right is left unprotected. ... In my view, the courts may not act as legislators and grant new remedies for infringement of Convention rights unless the common law itself enables them

15 (1981) 4 EHRR 38.
16 See M Hunt, 'The "horizontal effect" of the Human Rights Act' [1998] Public Law 423.

to develop new rights or remedies. I believe that the true view is that the courts will be able to adapt and develop the common law by relying on existing domestic principles in the laws of trespass, nuisance, copyright, confidence, and the like, to fashion a common law right to privacy.'[17]

REMEDIES

The Canadian system may be distinguished from the British on a number of counts. A difference between the Canadian Charter and the Human Rights Act is that the Convention rights also form part of the international law obligations of the United Kingdom, and under the Convention, article 50, the government is under a duty to make just satisfaction to a person whose rights have been breached. Neither this article nor article 13 are expressly incorporated under the Human Rights Act, but this consideration may serve to give added justification, if it were needed, to a court seeking to develop the common law radically in the direction of compliance with Convention requirements. Further, by section 8 of the Act the court has a wide discretion to grant 'such relief or remedy, or make such order within its powers as it considers just and appropriate' (though the power to award damages is limited to 'a court which has power to award damages … in civil proceedings' so that tribunals, for instance, will not be able to award damages). It seems very likely, therefore, that the courts will effectively develop new causes of action under the Human Rights Act – or perhaps more accurately that they will award damages or other remedies for interference with Convention rights which effectively create or imply new causes of action. This may presage a move away from a tort law that is still, in practice, based on causes of action towards one based more on general principles of liability such as exist in civilian jurisdictions in Europe.

Given that the Human Rights Act preserves the legislative supremacy of the United Kingdom Parliament, it remains open to a government to seek parliamentary approval for legislation reversing a decision by a British court which might be regarded as too radical in its development of the common law (an option not open to the Canadian government and legislature under their constitution and Charter). It is suggested that the inhibitions felt in Canada about radical development of the common law need not prevent a British court from developing the common law under the Human Rights Act in quite radical ways.

---

17   Lord Irvine 'Opening address' in B Markesinis (ed) *The Impact of the Human Rights Bill on English Law* (1998) at p 13.

State liability and the Human Rights Act

The question arises whether the state, ie the British government, might be liable for breaches of Convention rights by state organisations. A point to note at the outset is that there may be cases where a Convention right has been infringed in a European law context. In this event, state liability will exist. Where a European law right is at stake and the courts or any other institution of a state have failed to uphold the right, the state is obliged to provide a remedy, which may include compensation.[18]

Apart from cases where there is a European law element, the question of liability for judicial acts needs to be separated from state liability for non-judicial acts. There is very little scope for the development of state liability for judicial acts. The starting point is that the Crown Proceedings Act 1947, section 2(5) provides that 'no proceedings shall lie against the Crown ... in respect of anything done or omitted to be done by any person while discharging ... any responsibility of a judicial nature ...'[19] The question arises whether the Human Rights Acts changes that position.

The Human Rights Act requires avenues of appeal to be exhausted in the case of actions in respect of judicial acts before any question of compensation can arise.[20] Subject to that, section 9(3) provides that 'In proceedings under this Act in respect of a judicial act done in good faith, damages may not be awarded otherwise than to compensate a person to the extent required by Article 5(5) of the Convention.' Section 9(5) defines 'judicial act' as 'a judicial act of a court and includes an act done on the instructions, or on behalf, of a judge.' Article 5(5) provides that 'everyone who has been the victim of arrest or detention in contravention of the provisions of this Article shall have an enforceable right to compensation'. The net result is that there could be no damages award for judicial acts done in good faith except under Article 5.[1] There could however, be damage awards in respect of judicial acts done in bad faith.

Were it not for the Crown Proceedings Act there is considerable scope for the development of state liability for judicial acts. Authority both in the Privy Council and in Canada points the way. The Privy

---

18 This is the result of a combination of the decision in *Francovich v Italy* [1993] 2 CMLR 66; *Brasserie du Pêcheur v Germany* [1996] 2 WLR 506; see discussion by Olowofoyeku, 'State liability for the exercise of judicial power' [1998] Public Law 444 at pp 458-459.

19 See Olowofoyeku, supra.

20 Section 9(1)(a).

1   In Canada state liability has been held to extend under the Charter to a decision by a judge to imprison a party for contempt which was arbitrary and contrary to the Charter and in breach of the principles of fundamental justice as required by section 7 of the Charter: *R v Germain* (1984) 53 AR (2d) 264, QBD. See Olowofoyeku, supra at p 455 for discussion.

Council decided, in a case from Trinidad and Tobago, *Maharaj v A-G of Trinidad and Tobago (No 2)*[2] that there was state liability for breach of constitutionally entrenched rights. The case concerned the committal of a barrister to prison by a judge for contempt without giving him a hearing. The constitution protected the rights of individuals not to be deprived of their liberty save by due process of law. But the reach of state liability under *Maharaj* is narrow. Olowofoyeku argues that the case imposes state liability only where a case has involved a fundamental failure of justice amounting to a denial of due process, which then results in irreparable damage.[3]

On the question of state liability for non-judicial acts, the experience of New Zealand is instructive. The Human Rights Act 1998 is modelled to some extent on the New Zealand Act, in that neither enables the courts to strike down inconsistent prior or subsequent primary legislation. In *Simpson v A-G [Baigent's case]*[4] the police had conducted an unlawful search under a valid warrant (the problem was that they had gone to the wrong address and after they found out that they had the wrong place they nevertheless continued with the search). The occupier of the premises sued the Crown (not the police) for damages under the New Zealand Bill of Rights Act and succeeded. The New Zealand Bill of Rights Act contains no general enforcement or remedies provisions, whereas the British Human Rights Act contains the general provisions in section 8 referred to earlier, which places the courts in a stronger position to develop remedies than the New Zealand Act did. Like the Human Rights Act, however, the New Zealand Act is not entrenched. The New Zealand Court of Appeal, finding in favour of the plaintiffs, held that it was relevant that the New Zealand Act seeks to fulfil the obligations of New Zealand under the International Covenant of Civil and Political Rights, article 2(3) of which requires the provision of effective remedies for breach of its provisions. The obvious parallel under the Human Rights Act is that the Convention requires that effective remedies be provided under article 13 – though this article is not incorporated under the Act. The New Zealand Court of Appeal in *Simpson* also relied on the decision in *Maharaj v A-G of Trinidad and Tobago (No 2)*[5] (noted above), and found support there for its finding of state liability for breach of the Bill of Rights Act by a state body.[6]

2   [1979] AC 385, PC.
3   Olowofoyeku, op cit.
4   [1994] 3 NZLR 667, New Zealand Court of Appeal.
5   [1979] AC 385. For extended consideration of this case see A Olowofoyeku *Suing Judges* (1994).
6   For comment on the *Simpson* case see J A Smillie 'Fundamental rights, parliamentary supremacy and the New Zealand Court of Appeal' (1995) 111 LQR 209; A. Hunt 'Fundamental rights and the New Zealand Bill of Rights Act' (1995) 111 LQR 567.

Would United Kingdom courts adopt the same approach as the New Zealand court, drawing on *Maharaj* as an authority in favour of state liability for non-judicial acts? It is suggested that it would certainly be open to our courts to develop the common law in this direction, invoking the New Zealand case and the Privy Council's decision in *Maharaj*, and drawing on the case law on state liability for breach of European law.

EUROPEAN LAW AND THE KEY VALUES

We have seen how the common values of dignity, autonomy, respect, status and security find expression in the European Convention on Human Rights and will do so also under the Human Rights Act 1998. These values are also reflected in European Union law and thus, through the doctrine of direct effect[7] they find their way into aspects of United Kingdom law. The European Court of Justice has supervisory jurisdictions both in relation to challenges brought directly by, for instance, member states or its own officials, and in references from the courts of member states under article 177 of the Treaty of European Union (article 234 of the Treaty of Amsterdam). The ECJ has decided in a series of cases that fundamental rights form an integral part of the general principles of law which they are obliged to give effect to, and that in identifying these principles the court is bound to draw inspiration from the constitutional traditions common to many member states, and from international treaties.[8] As Craig and de Burca have commented, these international declarations can be seen as 'an important expression of common values shared by the member states, which in turn made them a valuable indicator of the Community's general principles of law and of human rights'.[9] In practice, however, most of the case law on this in the ECJ has raised issues to do with commercial activity and have not been directly concerned with the interests of individuals in their own dignity and other key values. The ECJ has indicated that 'mere commercial interests or opportunities' will not receive the same protection as the personal interests of individuals.[10] For our purposes, however, the important point is that the same values as have been

---

7   See brief discussion of direct effect in chapter 5.
8   See T Hartley *The Foundations of European Community Law* (4th edn, 1998) pp 132-142; *Stauder v City of Ulm* [1969] ECR 419; *Internationale Handelsgesellschaft* case [1970] ECR 1125; *Hauer v Land Rheinland-Pfaltz* [1979] ECR 3727.
9   P P Craig and G de Burca *EC Law* (1995) at p 294.
10 *Nold v EC Commission* [1974] ECR 491; see also A Clapham 'A human rights policy for the European Community' (1990) 10 YBEL 331; J Coppel and A O'Neill 'The European Court of Justice: Taking rights seriously' (1992) Legal Studies 227.

developed across the public-private divide in English law are also pervasive in European Community law.

CONCLUSION

Let us return to the starting point of this discussion – the relevance of the European Convention and the Human Rights Act to the key values and the control of power, and the effect of the Act on the public-private divide. Under the Human Rights Act 1998 the policy of the law in favour of the key values will become much more explicit than hitherto. The courts will have to engage in a process of balancing these values against others, such as public interests in national security, public safety, public order and the like. The Act gives added weight to these values, thus going some way to deal with the problems in determining the relative weights to be attached to the key values and other considerations which have been encountered in the development of judicial review[11] – and indeed in protecting key values in private law.

This set of considerations opens up the possibility that many of the areas of the law in which the key values have hitherto been weakly protected, such as in the employment relationship, in discrimination cases and in privacy law, will be developed by the courts so as to increase the protection of these interests of individuals and to impose responsibilities on those in positions of power.

Although at first sight the Human Rights Act appears to reinforce an institutional and functional public-private divide by limiting its direct effect vertically, in practice the divide is likely to be weakened as the courts develop the common law by imposing duties of respect for rights and thus for the key values on private bodies in their dealings with others, thus bringing the obligations of public authorities and private bodies closer to one another.

In practice the private law disputes in which Convention rights questions arise are likely to be between vulnerable individuals on the one hand, and companies and other bodies in positions of power on the other. As the common law develops in line with the Human Rights Act in imposing duties of respect for individuals on those in power, it will be furthering the trend in the law towards imposing responsibilities in the exercise of power, and protecting individuals' interests in the key values, which has been described in previous chapters. In effect the Human

---

11 See discussion in chapter 5 of the cases of *Pickwell v London Borough of Camden* [1983] QB 962, *West Glamorgan v Rafferty* [1987] 1 All ER 1005; *Bugdaycay v Secretary of State for the Home Department* [1987] AC 514 and *R v Secretary of State for the Home Department, ex p Brind* [1991] 1 AC 696.

Rights Act seeks to preserve liberal majoritarianism, though shifting the emphasis on the liberal aspect of the model. It will act as a stimulus to the development of considerate altruism in both the public and the private sphere. And it will further marginalise the positivist-authoritarian model of governance.

Chapter Eleven

'There is no Public-Private Divide'

Klare suggests that '… it is seriously mistaken to imagine that legal discourse or liberal political theory contains a core conception of the public-private distinction capable of being filled with determinate content or applied in a determinate manner to concrete cases. *There is no "public-private distinction."*[1] In this chapter it will be argued that an integrated approach to substance, remedies and procedures should be adopted in place of the public-private divide. This would enable the common law and equity to develop, with statutory provisions and European and human rights law, so as to promote the protection of individuals and public interests against abuses of all kinds of power.

THE CASE FOR SUBSTANTIVE INTEGRATION SUMMARISED

Since the decision in *O'Reilly* it has come to be assumed that duties of considerate decision making can only be imposed in public law. Discussion of areas of private law in previous chapters has shown that this is not the case. Legality, procedural propriety and rationality are not peculiarly public law duties. In judicial review these may be phrased as duties not to behave outside the four corners of a power, or in breach of the terms of an enabling statute; in private law legality requires a decision maker not to act in breach of the terms of a trust deed, contract, articles of association or other enabling instrument. Private and public law also both impose duties to adopt fair decision-making procedures involving, often, an absence of bias or interest, and varying versions of the 'audi

---

1   K E Klare 'The public-private distinction in labour law' (1982) U Penn LR 1358, at p 1361. Klare's italics.

alteram partem' rule, where public policy so requires. This is the case, for instance, in relation to decision making by employers, trustees, company directors, committees of trade unions and other membership organisations, pension fund trusts and mutual insurance organisations, those in positions to act in restraint of trade, and in judicial review.

In judicial review rationality is expressed as a duty not to make decisions irrationally, or *Wednesbury* unreasonably. In private law similar duties arise, for instance in trusts, company law and other fiduciary relationships, contractual membership association relationships, employment, and in restraint of trade and other relationships where public policy so requires. The phrases used in these private situations include duties not to decide arbitrarily or capriciously, in bad faith, outside the band of reasonableness.

The conditions giving rise to these duties are similar whether they operate in public or private law: broadly a supervisory jurisdiction will be exercisable if a decision will seriously affect the vital interests of an individual, notably their interests in their dignity, autonomy, respect, status or security, or if other public policy interests are at stake, many of which are related to monopolies and restraints of trade. It is suggested that, out of this material, general principles of considerate decision making in both private and public law are being formed which are designed to protect individuals and public interests against abuses of power. These duties do not depend upon whether a decision is made in the exercise of a public or governmental function. There is no public-private divide.

Sir Stephen Sedley and Sir John Laws among the judiciary have had particularly important things to say on this point.[2] After surveying the development of the law relating to public employment, private employment and judicial review in public employment cases, Sir John Laws put his views of the matter thus:

'The common law will not permit abuse of power. This is the basis of judicial review, and it reflects also the basis of all those private law doctrines where public policy has been held to restrain one man's hold over another. I think that indirectly it infuses the law of tort as well, and is reflected in the difficult conjunction of Lord Atkin's neighbour principle and the limits placed upon it by the modern, sometimes problematic, jurisprudence in this field. [The distinction between public law and private law] casts no or little light on the essential basis upon which the common law proceeds,

2 Sir Stephen Sedley 'Public law and contractual employment' (1994) 23 ILJ 201 and Sir John Laws 'Public law and employment law: Abuse of power' [1997] Public Law 455, both noted in chapter 6; Sir John Laws 'The constitution – morals and rights' [1996] Public Law 622, noted in chapter 9.

whether in public or private law, when it must confront abuse of power … The cases unfold a moral principle for which only the common law can provide a sure protection.' (By this he means 'the principle against abuse of power'.)[3]

Sir Stephen Sedley, in the second 1998 Hamlyn lecture, reached the following conclusion:

'… the law's chief concern about the use of power is not who is exercising it but what the power is and whom it affects; and that the control of abuses of power, whether in private or in public hands, is probably the most important of all the tasks which will be facing the courts in a twenty-first century democracy.'[4]

COUNTERVAILING CONSIDERATIONS

It is not the case either in public or private law that a duty of considerate decision making will always be imposed whenever a decision would affect an individual's interests or public interests adversely. Nor will remedies always be granted, even if such duties have been breached. There are similar countervailing considerations in both public and private law which will either negative duties of consideration, or justify the exercise of discretion by the courts to refuse remedies. These considerations may be divided into four categories: cases where the 'key' interests of an individual decision maker are also at stake; those where the decision in question is regarded as not being justiciable; cases where the court recognises that the authority of the defendant would be unduly undermined if there were restrictions on freedom in decision making; and cases where considerations of democratic pluralism require the courts to refrain from intervening.

Weighing up the defendant's interests

Given the importance of the five 'key' values of individual dignity, autonomy, respect, status and security which pervade the law in ways outlined throughout this work, it is natural that the interests of defendants (including respondents) in these values need to be weighed in the balance

---

3   Sir John Laws, 'Public law and employment law: Abuse of power' [1997] Public Law 455 at pp 464-465.
4   Sir Stephen Sedley 'Public power and private power' in *Freedom, Law and Justice* (50th series of Hamlyn lectures) (1999) at p 54.

when deciding whether duties of considerate decision making – or considerate action – arise, what their content is, and whether or how they should be enforced. A defendant may have other interests, for instance commercial interests, which it will seek to weigh in the balance against those of the claimant. The relevance of these interests will depend upon the nature of the defendant and what interests the defendant has.

Applying the principles developed in the previous chapter, where the defendant is a public or governmental body, it will not be regarded as entitled to place its own interests in the balance as against the interests of private bodies: public bodies do not have interests.[5] Unless there are justiciability problems, for instance (see below) the courts will increasingly readily impose duties of considerate decision making on public bodies. It is not clear what the position in relation to interests is if a private body exercising public or governmental functions is the defendant: presumably if a function is truly public or governmental the body should be acting altruistically and its own interests would be irrelevant.

If the defendant in a case is a private body which is under special duties of altruism (a charity, a pension trust, for instance) and the challenge is to its private decision making, then its own interests will not be weighed against those of the claimant, and the courts are more likely to impose duties of consideration. If the defendant is a private commercial body then no interests in the 'key' values, which are essentially individuals' interests, will be in the balance. But other interests, for instance in commercial profit, may have to be considered. The claimant's interests in the key values, however, are likely to carry more weight in principle, unless the threat to them is de minimis. But this is not to imply that commercial bodies will always be under duties of considerate decision making, since these may be negatived by other countervailing considerations such as justiciability.

Justiciability

In public law we are accustomed to the idea that certain decisions are not justiciable, often, though by no means invariably, because they are 'polycentric'.[6] The judgment of Lord Diplock in the CCSU[7] case explains this concept and gives examples, largely drawn from the fields of defence, foreign relations and national security. The CCSU case itself

---

5   See chapter 5.
6   See L Fuller 'The forms and limits of adjudication' (1978) 92 Harv LR 353.
7   *Council of Civil Service Unions v Minister for the Civil Service* [1985] AC 374. See discussion in chapter 5.

provides a good example of a non-justiciable issue – national security – prevailing over security and other individual interests. It has already been noted that those cases in which judicial review is not available on grounds of justiciability and other grounds represent perpetuations of a positivist authoritarian approach to power. *R v Higher Education Funding Council for England, ex p Institute of Dental Surgery*[8] indicates that matters of subjective or professional judgment – if a situation is one in which a subjective judgment can legitimately be made – are in principle regarded by the courts as not justiciable, in the sense of not being suitable for the exercise of supervisory jurisdictions on grounds of irrationality. Hence reasons were not required to be given in that case for an academic judgment about the quality of the institute's research. This does not of course imply that professional judgments can never be challenged in the courts. Actions may be brought in tort for negligence on the part of professionals, and their judgments will then be subjected to scrutiny against, for instance, the practice accepted as proper by a responsible body of practitioners skilled in that particular art.[9] It is not unthinkable that a board of university examiners, though probably not subject to judicial review of their academic judgments, might nevertheless be liable in negligence in the discharge of their examining duties.

Parallels may be found in private law with non-justiciability in judicial review. Justiciability is not an essentially public law problem. The parallels include cases where the courts refuse to interfere in managerial decisions in employment cases.[10] It is possible to envisage other situations in private law where decisions as to whether or what duties of consideration, especially in decision making, should be imposed would depend – as in judicial review – on matters of judgment. For instance, commercial judgments as to whom to contract with and on what terms might be regarded as non-justiciable, as might the needs of the market, which cannot operate if there are repeated delays caused by review of decisions. Judgments about risk and the state of the market are highly subjective and often not amenable to rational analysis. On the other hand, it is not self-evident that requiring a commercial body whose decisions might adversely affect the vital interests of an individual or other public interests not to act 'arbitrarily or capriciously' or to listen to what affected parties wish to say would in fact interfere unduly with the operation of the market.

There are many other examples of non-justiciable issues in private law. For instance, in the law of divorce the concept of fault was finally abandoned largely because fault in marriage situations – and in other

8   [1994] 1 WLR 242, DC.
9   This was the test laid down in medical negligence cases in *Bolam v Friern Hospital Management Committee* [1957] 2 All ER 118.
10 See discussion in chapter 6.

personal relationships no doubt – came to be regarded as a non-justiciable issue (or else to be regarded as too time-consuming, costly and boring for the courts to wish to engage in). Some of the immunities of public bodies in tort are another example of justiciability excluding a remedy in private law actions. (This is a border which is being rapidly dismantled by the European Court of Human Rights' decision in *Osman v United Kingdom*,[11] and in its place is a duty on the court to hear the case and arguments against imposing state liability on their merits.)

But the range of non-justiciable decisions is shrinking. Non-justiciability is not a popular ground for refusing judicial control. With the introduction of the Human Rights Act 1998 the weight problem when the interests of individuals have to be balanced against public interests – a large factor in justiciability – will be eased, though not solved. The presumption will be in favour of the Convention rights, which it has been shown serve to advance the interests of individuals in the key values, and the countervailing 'non justiciable' considerations such as national security and other interests are narrowly defined and are only to prevail over these values if such a result is 'necessary in a democratic society'.[12]

Deference to authority

In both public and private law issues arise to do with the alleged need to protect the authority of the defendant against undesirable challenges. The Sunday Times Thalidomide case[13] was an example of the policy of English law to uphold the authority of the court in contempt proceedings prevailing over other interests, in that case freedom of the press and access to information. It is most significant, however, that the *Sunday Times* decision by the House of Lords was held to be contrary to the provisions of article 10 of the European Convention on Human Rights by the Strasbourg court.[14] The *Nottinghamshire*[15] case, noted in chapter

11 Case No 87/1997/871/1083, Human Rights Law Report, (1998) Times, 5 November. See discussion of this case in chapter 8.
12 See chapter 10.
13 *A-G v Times Newspapers Ltd* [1974] AC 273 (later overruled by the European Court of Human Rights in *Sunday Times v United Kingdom* (1979) 2 EHRR 245).
14 This case provides an example of the ways in which the incorporation of that Convention into domestic law under the Human Rights Act is likely to increase the weight to be attached to individual rights in relation to the authority of those in positions of power and public interests. The courts will have to engage in an exercise of weighing the value of human rights against public interests and may only allow other interests to outweigh those of individuals if, for instance, it is necessary in a democratic society to do so, on specific public interest grounds: see chapter 10.
15 [1986] AC 240.

5, is another example, in this case of deference on the part of the courts both to Parliament and to a minister in public law.

By contrast, *Bagg's* case 1615, discussed in chapter 2, is an excellent, early example of the argument for upholding the dignity of those in authority finding no support from a court: the Court of King's Bench was not persuaded by the argument that, as Plymouth was a port frequented by 'many ill-minded men …, contemners of good government, and disturbers of the peace' it was necessary for the authority of the mayor and other burgesses to be upheld and protected from 'the contempt of the vulgar'.[16] The decision in *Anisminic Ltd v Foreign Compensation Commission*,[17] in which the House of Lords found a way round an ouster clause which purported to protect the Commission from judicial review is a modern illustration of reluctance on the part of the courts to defer to Parliament in the exclusion of a body from judicial review. Overall the trend in recent years has been to give less weight to considerations of a need to defer to authority or to accept claims of national security as precluding judicial review than, for instance, during the second world war when the notorious case of *Liversidge v Anderson*[18] was a low water mark in the courts' respect for national security and the authority of the state over the individual.

In private law cases, in the past more than currently, the courts have sought to uphold the dignity of those in authority over the interests of subordinate individuals. Blackstone's accounts of the relationships of employment[19], marriage and parenthood[20] provide strong examples, as does Cretney's work on the reforms to family law in the early years of the twentieth century.[1] This is still the case to an extent in the employment relationship where managerial prerogatives are upheld, though as in the parent child relationship, these prerogative also attract responsibilities. In family relationships far less importance than hitherto is now attached to the upholding of authority in the family, and far more weight is attached to the autonomy and other interests of weaker or vulnerable family members and the responsibilities of the more powerful towards the weaker.

Respect for pluralism

At various points in previous chapters it has been noted that subjecting private bodies to a supervisory jurisdiction may run counter to principles

16 (1615) 11 Co Rep 93b at 94, 77 ER at 1273.
17 [1969] 2 AC 147.
18 [1942] AC 206.
19 See chapter 6.
20 See chapter 7.
1   S M Cretney ' "What will the women want next?" The struggle for power within the family 1925-1975' (1996) 112 LQR 110, discussed in chapter 7.

of democratic pluralism. This is an aspect of the case against imposing legal obligations on parties outside public law, noted in chapter 1. In particular in relation to private bodies, including regulatory bodies in the commercial sector, self-regulatory bodies in sport or in the professions, and private associations such as churches, the case could be put that, for a range of reasons, they ought not to be subjected to legal regulation in their decision making. For instance, there are legal and conceptual arguments that the coherence of principles of judicial review will be damaged if they have to apply in 'private' situations,[2] controlling 'mini-legal systems' imposes uniformity and undermines pluralism,[3] it is an unjustified interference with the autonomy of private bodies to impose legal constraints on their activities;[4] it will interfere with their effective operations if they have the prospect of litigation hanging over them; the courts do not have the expertise to adjudicate on their activities.[5] These considerations may each be weighed in the balance and taken into account when particular cases invoking a supervisory jurisdiction imposing duties of considerate decision making arise. Each of these considerations may affect the precise content of the duties of fairness and rationality in a given case and the exercise of discretion as to the award of equitable remedies. However, it is suggested that none of these considerations is sufficiently persuasive to rule out entirely the possibility of the imposition of duties of considerate decision making and the availability of a supervisory jurisdiction where the body in question has power over an individual's status, security or other vital interests.

INTEGRATING THE PUBLIC AND PRIVATE LAW OF REMEDIES

The remedies in public and private law are in many respects the same or similar.[6] But damages are considered not to be available for failures of considerate decision making in judicial review, and the prerogative orders are only available in respect of the supervisory jurisdiction exercised under RSC Order 53, and section 31 of the Supreme Court Act 1981. To

---

2   See for instance Rose J in *R v Football Association, ex p Football League* [1993] 2 All ER 833 at 849.

3   See discussion in chapter 1. And see comment of Megarry V-C in *McInnes v Onslow Fane* noted in chapter 9.

4   This is essentially a neo-liberal argument: see F Hayek *Law, Legislation and Liberty*, vol 3 (1982).

5   See the excellent treatment of these issues by J Black and P Muchlinski in J Black, P Muchlinski and P Walker, (eds) *Commercial Regulation and Judicial Review* (1998) at p 9, and the essays in that collection.

6   Note however that injunctions may not be awarded against the Crown in civil actions except on the Crown side of the Queen's Bench Division: Crown Proceedings Act 1947, s 38(2).

this extent there is a remedial public-private divide. Let us consider these aspects of the divide in more detail.

Damages

In chapter 9 it was suggested that remedies for breach of duties of considerate decision making in private law may include damages, and that awards of damages need not mean that the court substitutes its own views on the merits for those of the decision maker. In judicial review damages and compensation may not, it is generally assumed, be awarded for breach of duties of fairness and rationality in decision making.[7] This has been said to be a 'fundamental tenet' of the common law.[8]

In *Dunlop v Woollahra Municipal Council* it was decided that a failure to give a person a hearing when one was required by the rules of natural justice did not of itself give rise to a cause of action for damages.[9] In that case the decision in question (imposing a building line restriction on a land owner) was held to be void, and the Privy Council took the view that the plaintiff could have ignored it. In effect no loss need have been suffered.

A number of points arise from this decision. First, it will not always be the case that no damage is suffered as a result of a decision taken in breach of duties of consultation or rationality in decision making or otherwise unlawfully. The decisions to dismiss in *Ridge v Baldwin*, and to withdraw a licence in *Ex p Hook*, could not have been ignored by the parties; losses will be suffered in such cases as a result of the applicants' inability to continue working pending the retaking of the decision or other settlement of the case. *Dunlop* is not authority for the proposition that no damages may be awarded in such cases. Secondly, in *Dunlop* the claim was pleaded as a common law action in trespass on the case,[10] in

---

7   For discussion of the instances in which private law claims for damages against public authorities are available see *X (minors) v Bedfordshire County Council* [1995] 2 AC 633, HL.

8   See De Smith, Woolf and Jowell *Judicial Review of Administrative Action* (5th edn, 1995) para 19-003.

9   [1982] AC 158, PC, 171-172.

10 Under the doctrine in *Beaudesert District Shire Council v Smith* (1966) 120 CLR 145, to the effect that 'a person who suffers harm or loss as the inevitable consequence of the unlawful, intentional and positive acts of another, is entitled to recover damages from that other.' This case was disapproved in *Lonrho Ltd v Shell Petroleum (No 2)* [1982] AC 173, doubted in *Dunlop* on the ground that the conditions for liability were too uncertain, and overruled by the High Court of Australia in *Northern Territory of Australia v Mengel* (14 April) (1995) 129 ALR 1. See *De Smith, Woolf and Jowell* para 19-066.

negligence[11] and in misfeasance in a public office.[12] The claim failed on each basis. The case is not authority for the proposition that a claim will never lie for damages for failure of considerate decision making at common law – or for an equitable wrong.

Discussing the unavailability of compensation in judicial review, Cane comments that:

'It is by no means clear why monetary compensation is not, in theory, available, as a common-law remedy at least for loss inflicted by governmental action which is unlawful. It cannot be on account of the constitutional principle against governmental expenditure not approved by parliament, because this would equally rule out judgments in contract, tort and so on. It may be because damages are, in private law, available as of right whereas all public law remedies are discretionary. There is no apparent reason why damages ought not to be made available as a discretionary public law remedy.'[13]

The position that damages are not available for breach of duties in public or governmental decision making needs to be challenged. It has been argued above that there are general principles of considerate decision making which arise where the interests of an individual or other public policy considerations are at stake. These duties do not depend for their existence on the question whether a decision is taken in the exercise of a public or governmental function. In private law breach of these duties may give rise to a claim in damages.[14] The sources of these duties of considerate decision making in private and public law are the same – common law and equity – and sometimes statute; the rationales for imposing these duties are the same, namely the existence of imbalances of power, the fact that individuals' interests are seriously affected by a decision or public interests are affected, and public policy

---

11 It was alleged that the council had failed in a duty to take care that their decisions were lawful. It was held that there had been no breach of such a duty, if it existed, as the council had taken legal advice, and in any event the question of legality was evenly balanced. It was also alleged that there was a duty of care sounding in negligence to give the plaintiff a hearing before making a decision that was damaging to him. On this it was held that as the resulting decision was void as being outside the provisions in the statute the plaintiff could have ignored it and so did not suffer damage from it.

12 This claim failed because there was no evidence of malice on the part of the council.

13 P Cane 'Public law and private law: A study of the analysis and use of a legal concept' in J Eekelaar and J Bell *Oxford Essays in Jurisprudence*, Third series (1987) at p 72.

14 See discussion of remedies in private law in chapter 9.

in favour of controlling exercises of power to protect individuals or in the general interest. Looked at in this way the unavailability of damages for breach of duties in decision making by public bodies looks like an immunity for which there is no principled justification. There is no reason in logic – in principle – why the remedies available in private law cases for failures of considerate decision making, where such duties arise, should not also be available in cases brought against public bodies, whether by way of application for judicial review or otherwise.

On this line of argument, damages could be awarded against a public decision maker for loss caused by a decision taken in breach of duties of considerate decision making, for instance, a decision taken in breach of natural justice, as in *Ex p Hook*[15] (compare *Tait*,[16] a private law case); and for loss of a chance of a favourable decision, or a failure to consider an application (compare *Chaplin v Hicks*,[17] a private law case).

An objection in principle to the proposition that damages should be – or are – available for failure of considerate decision making by public bodies would be that this would impose large costs on the state.[18] However, not all failures of considerate decision making result in damage to the interests of individuals. Other remedies such as injunction and declaration may be adequate in many cases. It is to be expected that administrative practice will improve if the prospect of liability to compensate victims of faulty decision making hangs over decision makers. And lastly, it should be noted that what is being suggested is that *private law* is moving in the direction of developing general duties of considerate decision making where private interests or other public policy considerations arise, and providing remedies by way of damages, and that these duties of considerate decision making would extend logically to public bodies: *the liability would be essentially a tortious or quasi-tortious law one* and there is no reason why public bodies should be immune, though their particular circumstances would be taken into account, as set out above, in determining whether duties arise and what their content is in a particular case.

Such a development would also be in line with the way public law is developing. The situations in which compensation may be paid to those who have suffered from decisions by public bodies have expanded

15 [1976] 1 WLR 1052.
16 1989 SC 4.
17 [1911] 2 KB 786; see also H Reece 'Losses of chances in law' 59 MLR (1996) 188; and N Jansen 'The idea of a lost chance' 19 Oxford Jo LS (1999) 271.
18 See discussion by P Cane 'Damages in public law' (1999) 9 Otago Law Review 489; P P Craig in *Administrative Law* (3rd edn, 1994) pp 646-650; 'Compensation in public law' (1980) 96 LQR 413; C Harlow *Compensation and Government Torts* (1982).

considerably in recent years.[19] Damages are available under the
Francovich[20] and *Factortame (No 4)*[1] decisions for non-implementation
of European law in what are in effect quasi-tort actions.[2] The
Parliamentary Commissioner for Administration may recommend ex
gratia payments, including in cases where decisions have not been
properly taken;[3] the Revenue Adjudicator may also recommend such
payments; the tort of misfeasance in a public office is undergoing
something of a revival.[4] Looking to the future, under the Human Rights
Act it will be possible for the courts to develop the law so as to award
compensation for breaches of Convention rights by public authorities,
creating a further form of tortious or quasi-tortious liability. It already
appears from the European Court of Human Rights decision in the
Osman case (considered in chapter 8) that the immunities of public
authorities in tort law are unlikely to survive the under Human Rights
Act. It may be that an effect of that Act will be the development by the
English courts of general rights to remedies in damages in judicial review
cases even where Convention rights are not at issue.[5] In other words the
trend in various quarters related to decision making by public bodies is
in favour of the availability of damage awards, and the extension of
awards of damages for failures in public decision making would be in
line with this trend.

Under a system in which compensation is available for unlawful
decision making in the exercise of a public or governmental function,
many of the justifications for the short limitation periods and requirement
for permission to apply for judicial review in public law cases disappear.
Compensation can be a substitute for injunctions or the quashing of
decisions where necessary – as in private law[6] – and the disadvantages to
the public interest and interests of third parties flowing from late
quashing of decisions – the only available remedy if compensation is not
possible – would be avoided.

19 For discussion see C Harlow *Compensation and Government Torts* (1982) Part 3; P Birkinshaw *Grievances, Remedies and the State* (2nd edn, 1994).
20 [1995] ICR 722, ECJ.
1   See *Brasserie du Pecheur SA v Federal Republic of Germany* [1996] QB 404, ECJ.
2   See chapter 5.
3   For an example see Parliamentary Commissioner for Administration, Case No 3/87: a taxi driver's PSV licence had been revoked in breach of natural justice and he succeeded in an application for judicial review. The PCA awarded him compensation, though for less than the full loss he had suffered because he was partly to blame.
4   See chapter 8.
5   See chapter 10 discussion of the Human Rights Act. See also the discussion of remedies for private law decision making in chapter 9.
6   See *Jaggard v Sawyer* and *Wrotham Park Estate Co v Parkside Homes* [1974] 2 All ER 321.

Cane, having considered the debates about the unavailability of damages outside existing causes of action, concludes that there are no sound reasons of legal or political policy for excluding remedies by way of damages in public law when the amenability of government to other remedies is not so limited, and that there is nothing in the nature of damages as a remedy which justifies the adoption of the 'fundamental tenet' in relation to it.[7] It must surely be right that issues of governmental damages liability should be addressed on their merits, and not ruled out by reference to what is, in reality an unsound tenet. In particular, to the extent that liability in damages is imposed in private law, as has been suggested above, there would need to be strong arguments in favour of immunity against such liability for bodies exercising public or governmental functions, given the process of dismantling state immunity that is currently taking place in European human rights law.

The prerogative orders

Once it is accepted that there is no substantive public-private divide and that there are generally applicable duties of considerate decision making in areas of both public and private law, a question remains over the place of the prerogative orders in supervisory jurisdictions.[8] Given that in the current state of the law these remedies are only available in respect of public or governmental decision making, there is clearly a 'remedial divide' between public and private law.[9]

A remedial divide is not inevitable. The prerogative remedies are not essential to an effective system of public law. In Scotland there are no direct equivalents to the prerogative orders, and yet the system provides effective supervisory jurisdiction to control public or governmental decision making, using the equivalents of declaration (declarator) and injunction (interdict), and cancellation of documents (reduction).[10] In England the prerogative writs originated in the Court of King's Bench, a common law court, at a time when damages were the only remedy available at common law. Their importance was largely due to the fact that they introduced a non-pecuniary remedy where otherwise no remedy would have been available for a common law wrong. Since then, remedies of injunction, cancellation of documents and declaration have been

7   P Cane 'Damages in public law' (1999) 9 Otago Law Review, 489.
8   See discussion in chapter 1.
9   But note that this has not always been the case. See discussion of *R v Barker* (1762) 3 Burr 1265 in chapter 2, in which mandamus was awarded against the trustees of a non-conformist meeting-house requiring them to admit the elected minister.
10   See discussion of the Scottish system in Annex.

developed, which are available in respect of both equitable and common law, legal and statutory wrongs, and some statutory quashing orders have been introduced in specialist areas such as planning and compulsory purchase. The prerogative orders are no longer as important as when they were first developed.

It is also worth noting that a relaxed approach to the grant of prerogative writs or orders, under which entitlement to the remedy was not dependent upon a public or governmental function or the existence of a public-private divide was exported to the United States. There mandamus is available in respect of activities that are not public or governmental,[11] so that the remedial public-private divide as it operates in England is not known in the USA.

A particular feature of certiorari is that it 'quashes' or cancels instruments which may have effects on third parties besides the applicant for judicial review and on general public interests. It is understandable that there should be special safeguards for third parties and public interests in the use of such a remedy. But no equivalent exists in Scotland in relation to the remedy of reduction, to the English requirements for permission to apply for judicial review and short time limits. Issues to do with third party and public interests, for example where formal orders are challenged, are dealt with there by the courts in decisions on the exercise of discretion to award remedies.[12] In England, in private law too issues arise about third party and public interests if transactions are to be set aside, and these are dealt with by the exercise of discretion in the grant of equitable remedies of injunction and declaration, as we shall see in the next section.

Lastly, the courts will take into account the interests of good administration, implications for third parties and the conduct, including delay, of the applicant in deciding whether to award the prerogative orders – their award is discretionary. But very similar considerations are entertained by the courts in deciding whether to grant equitable remedies, notably injunctions, and declarations in judicial review and in private law actions.

---

11 See for instance *Nash v Page* 80 Ky 539 (1882) – tobacco warehousemen regarded as in common calling and therefore subject to mandamus to prevent them from refusing to deal with certain tobacco traders; *Salisbury and S Ry Co v Southern Power Co* 105 SE 28 (1920) (South Carolina) – writ of mandamus will lie against electricity supplier, and discovery will be ordered to establish what was the lowest price charged to other customers; *Portland Gas Co v State* 135 Ind 54: 'A gas company is bound to supply gas to premises with which its pipes are connected. It has often been held that mandamus is the proper proceeding by which to compel a gas company to furnish gas to those entitled to receive it.' See generally B Wyman 'The law of public callings as a solution to the trust problem' XVII Harvard LR (1903-1904) 156.

12 See Annex.

In sum, on this point, differences between the remedies available, and the ways in which discretions to award remedies are exercised, between judicial review and private supervisory jurisdictions are not fundamental. In an integrated system the old common law position in which certiorari and mandamus were available against private bodies not exercising governmental functions[13] could be revived. Or these remedies could be maintained as being available only in respect of public or governmental functions, but made available outside the application for judicial review, in ordinary High Court actions. The differences that matter, it is suggested, lie not in the remedies themselves, but in the procedural law that surrounds them. To this we now turn.

THE APPLICATION FOR JUDICIAL REVIEW

The third limb of the public-private divide is procedural: the requirement that challenges to decisions taken in the exercise of public or governmental functions must be brought by way of application for judicial review. Respondents to applications for judicial review enjoy considerable procedural protections in the form of the requirement for permission to apply, the requirement that an application be made promptly and in any event within three months, and the absence of the automatic giving of oral evidence or discovery.[14] This set of differences between judicial review and private law actions, it is suggested, is neither essential nor fundamental. First, no such protections exist in Scotland:[15] the British government enjoys greater procedural privileges in litigation south of the border than north. Yet the absence of such protections seems not to be an issue in Scotland. Second, these procedural privileges in applications for the prerogative orders are of recent origin. It was not essential to the development and exercise of supervisory jurisdictions through the prerogative writs that such protections should be accorded to public bodies. This point is not intended to deny that there may be sound public policy reasons on occasions to protect some decisions – whether of public bodies or others – from late or frivolous challenges. But it is suggested that consideration can be met in other ways, to which we shall turn later, than the automatic protections for respondents under section 31 of the Supreme Court Act and Order 53 of the Rules of the Supreme Court.

Third, it is notable that similar, statute-based, protections against late or unmeritorious challenges to acts or decisions exist or have existed

13 *R v Barker* (1762) 3 Burr 1265.
14 See chapters 4 and 5.
15 See Annex.

in the past in private law situations where relationships are in issue. There is nothing particularly 'public' about short time limits and discretionary remedies. For instance, an application to an Employment Tribunal alleging unfair dismissal or redundancy or discrimination must in principle be made promptly and in any event within three months of the matter complained of. There were six-month time limits for certain complaints of matrimonial offences under the pre-1969 divorce law. These privileges may be justified in certain circumstances, but should not be awarded in blanket form to particular kinds of respondent as is the case in judicial review.

In short, the present provisions for the application for judicial review, giving procedural protections to respondents in applications for judicial review are not fundamental to that jurisdiction. Many common law jurisdictions – including Scotland – survive without them. Nor are such protections unique to public law, since similar provisions have found a place in private law disputes in the past, and in the case of employment law they still do. It is notable too that before 1954 public authorities enjoyed a special privilege by way of a statutory twelve-month limitation period in civil actions,[16] reduced to six months in 1939.[17] That protection was removed by the Law Reform (Limitation of Actions) Act 1954.[18] The present blanket three-month time limit in the application for judicial review is anomalous.

It is readily understandable that many decisions of public bodies need to be implemented promptly and that it would be contrary to general public interests for projects, for instance for the construction of roads, hospitals and the like to have the prospect of litigation hanging over them on the part of aggrieved neighbours, landowners and the like – especially if the remedy in such litigation, if the applicant were successful, would be the quashing of the order authorising the project, so that it had to be abandoned. Again this is not a problem unique to public law. For instance in the *Wrotham Park Estate* case[19] an estate of houses had been built, sold and occupied, in breach of a restrictive covenant. The court refused an injunction requiring the demolition of the houses because of the detrimental effect on third parties, and awarded instead a sum in equitable compensation. In public law this kind of problem is provided for in planning and compulsory purchase cases by short statutory limitation periods for appeals, but there is no option of an award of compensation. Such protections could be extended to other situations in which public interests or the interests of third parties might be damaged

16 See Public Authorities Protection Act 1893.
17 Limitation Act 1939, sections 21, 34(4) and Schedule.
18 See M Beloff 'Timeliness and public authorities' in C Forsyth and I Hare (eds) *The Golden Metwand and the Crooked Cord* (1998).
19 *Wrotham Park Estate v Parkside Homes Ltd* [1974] 2 All ER 321.

by late litigation and the quashing of orders. It is the blanket protection of respondents under Order 53, regardless of the subject matter of the decision under challenge, and the unavailability of damages, which seem indefensible.

THE CASE AGAINST INTEGRATING PUBLIC AND PRIVATE LAW

Samuel has argued that 'a failure to distinguish between public and private law could be dangerous for the individual in that it could encourage the view that the state is just like a private person entitled to the same rights of privacy, reputation, property and the like – a disturbing tendency for civil liberties.'[20] This objection to the removal of a public-private divide – which rested on decisions such as *Malone v Metropolitan Police Comr*[1] – has been partially overcome by decisions such as *Derbyshire County Council v Times Newspapers*,[2] which denied the council a right to sue to protect its governing reputation. The objection is accommodated in acceptance of the proposition that public bodies have no interests of their own that they may legitimately advance or pursue.[3] But the argument put here has been in favour both of increasing control of state bodies by removing their procedural privileges in judicial review and extending the scope of damage awards, and of increasing the responsibilities of those in positions of power in private law, thus diminishing the attraction to the state of bringing itself within private law rather than public law, as it did in *Malone*. On this line of reasoning there is no implication at all that without a public-private divide the state would enjoy even greater freedom of action than in a divided system. On the contrary, the suggestions are that it should be subject to greater controls by the removal of its procedural privileges, and that private bodies too may be subjected to duties of consideration and altruism in certain circumstances.

Another objection to the idea that the public-private divide should be abandoned or dissolved would be that the rule of law requires certainty. Abandoning the divide will leave it unclear what public or private bodies owe what duties to those with whom they deal. A problem here is that there is no certainty under the present system. The boundaries of the decision in *O'Reilly v Mackman* have been gradually moved since that decision. The scope of duties of considerate action and considerate

20 G Samuel 'Public and private law: A private lawyer's response' 46 MLR (1983) 558, at p 582.
1 [1979] Ch 344, discussed in chapter 5.
2 [1993] AC 534. See discussion in chapter 5.
3 See chapter 3.

decision making in private law will no doubt continue to expand. The Human Rights Act will clarify to some extent the duties of public bodies, whether they are exercising public or private functions. But its application to private bodies is more uncertain.

It is an inevitable consequence of the common law method that doctrines develop and change in response to changing conditions. If we add to the common law method the passing of statutes dealing with public law issues which often introduce new uncertainty, and developments in European Community and European human rights law, desires for legal certainty are never likely to be satisfied in this field. But, it is suggested, if the courts were freed from the procedural exclusivity rule it would be open to them to develop the system along the lines outlined above: then there would in fact be much less uncertainty and more coherence – and justice – in the law in this area.

LAW, POLITICS AND THE ROLE OF THE STATE

An important argument in favour of a public-private divide is that we need a clear idea of the role of the state, and the law should reflect that idea. Allison suggests that without such a concept there is bound to be a lack of systematic principles in our public law.[4] This is a powerful argument, but it does not touch on the case for integrating public and private law being put forward here. Whatever their functions and whether or not the functions fit with any particular concept of the role of the state, it is broadly right that decision makers in positions of power should be subject to duties of considerate decision making on grounds of public policy, especially when their decisions affect the vital interests of individuals. It is wrong that state bodies should as a matter of course enjoy procedural law privileges when their acts or decisions affect identifiable individuals adversely. The notion that we need a clear concept of the role of the state does not affect the argument that private bodies in positions of power in relation to individuals should in principle be subject to duties of considerate decision making.

Allison is correct in asserting that without a set of systematic principles governing the role of the state there will (continue to) be dissatisfaction with judicial procedures and uncertainty about the judicial role; but that consideration of itself does not, it is suggested, undermine the case being put forward here that we should move to an integrated approach to the exercise of power, taking into account all the matters set out above, pending the unlikely emergence of a coherent set of views about the proper role of the state in England. Indeed, it is part of Allison's argument

---

4   J Allison *A Continental Distinction in the Common Law* (1996) chapters 2 and 11.

that a public-private distinction cannot work unless the society has a well-developed theory of the state, which appreciates the distinctness of the state administration and which would therefore justify the application of a special set of rules to the state administration, and special bodies to administer those rules. It may be that the very fact that there is no well-developed theory of the state in England (or, so far, in Scotland[5]) accounts for the present incoherence of the public-private divide.

Allison suggests that 'In the absence of a rough consensus about the state administration, and thus about the scope of public law, the distinction would be reduced to a rhetorical tool.'[6] In conditions in which 'private' bodies exercise many broadly 'public' functions and possess accumulations of power that can affect individuals' interests adversely, and in which there appears to be no interest either among politicians or the general public to think about or agree upon 'the distinctness of state administration' – especially if it implied not subjecting private bodies to controls on the exercises of their power – it is suggested that a public law-private law distinction cannot be workable. The distinction cannot but be a mere rhetorical tool. Allison concludes that 'Those who advocate the distinction's retention should countenance fundamental reforms, reforms that are theoretical, institutional, and procedural.'[7] It seems highly improbable that such reforms will take place, or indeed that they would be appropriate given the reality that many 'private' bodies resemble state bodies, and vice versa. In reality there is no alternative to accepting the process of disintegration of the public-private divide, and adopting instead an integrated approach.

5   See Annex.
6   *Allison* at 38.
7   *Allison* at p 246.

Chapter 12

Towards Democracy and Citizenship in Public and Private Law

In this final chapter we seek to draw some threads together and to relate the material in previous chapters to the theories of government, democracy and citizenship that were sketched in chapter 1. We shall draw out the common theories that link public law and private law, thus seeking to justify in democratic and citizenship terms the claim that the integrated approach to public and private law that was set out in the previous chapter would be consistent with democratic principles.

POWER

In chapter 2 the nature of power was explored. Public and private law have in common both that they constitute power, and that they are frequently engaged in controlling exercises of power. Chapters 5 to 10 contained a number of examples of the kinds of power which the courts have been concerned to control, again on both sides of the divide. Both public and private bodies wield compensatory power or 'dominium' when they have resources at their disposal, whether in the form of property or the right to grant other benefits such as licences, education, employment, membership of important associations and so on. Although in principle only state bodies can wield 'condign' power – the power to punish, and certainly to use physical coercion to enforce their will – nevertheless private organisations have powers that may be equally effective and damaging to the interests of individuals, such as the power to expel a person from membership of a group or association, or to withdraw cooperation. Both public and private bodies have bureaucracies – organisational power – at their disposal which place them at an advantage in relations with individuals.

VALUES

The nature of 'values' was considered in chapter 3, and the particular values which the courts uphold were briefly outlined and their provenances in liberal and social theory were noted. In chapters 4 to 10 examples have been given of how these values are acknowledged as important and given weight in many areas of the law, on both sides of the public-private divide.

The courts have not reflected at any great length on the exact nature of these values; they are in practice fairly simple, undeveloped legal concepts. But drawing on the examples given in previous chapters, the concepts can now be elaborated as follows. Autonomy is associated with physical integrity and freedom of action in relationships, and rights to make one's own decisions about matters such as medical treatment, protection for the real freedom of those entering into contracts in the face of pressure or inequalities of power, freedom of association, and opportunities to earn a living free from arbitrary or capricious obstacles. Dignity is associated with opportunities to participate in and influence decisions that may affect a person adversely, freedom from arbitrary or capricious discrimination or domination – psychological or physical – or exploitation by another, privacy, and the ability to repose trust and confidence in those with whom a person deals. Respect involves being treated with consideration as a fellow citizen and having one's interests taken seriously and weighed in the balance when a possibly adverse decision is under consideration. Thus respect will often be manifested in participatory decision-making processes. Status means a person's reputation, position and standing in civil society and its various institutions – family, church, university, employment, and professional associations, local and functional communities, social groups and associations, and so on. Security is associated with access to income at present and in the future, protection against danger, risk or damaging changes in one's life – for instance in relationships in the family or in employment – and the ability to trust and rely upon others with whom one deals.

THEORIES OF GOVERNMENT AND DEMOCRACY

In chapter 1 four theories of government or democracy, with their parallel theories of subjecthood or citizenship were sketched. Issues to do with the control of power and the protection of individuals' interests arise in relation to each. There are still elements of positivist authoritarianism in public law, as where the courts will not impose duties of fairness or rationality on the exercise of certain discretionary functions on grounds of national security, or where they defer to Parliament when statutory instruments are being challenged. In private law a parallel is found, for instance, in the upholding of the authority of employers over employees. The 'glue' which holds society together under a positivist-authoritarian system is hierarchy and authority, which provide a certain degree of status and security to members of society, but place little importance on the dignity, autonomy and respect of inferiors in relation to superiors. The trend over the last century or so has been against this approach to the exercise of power, and towards the other theories that were sketched in chapter 1.

A liberal-majoritarian approach is reflected in the doctrine of parliamentary sovereignty which the courts use to justify deferring to Parliament. The doctrine operates to legitimise interferences with the interests of individuals. The system is liberal because without parliamentary authority interferences with the civil and political liberties of individuals are not permitted. But this theory does not rule out other interferences with individuals' interests or provide, for instance, protection in the form of duties of considerate decision making when such interests are damaged by governmental decisions.

Cotterrell calls this an 'imperium' model:[1] the image is of individual subjects of a superior political authority. There is a relationship of domination between a political authority (Parliament and the government) and each subordinate person. In our terms this is a combination of positivist-authoritarian and liberal-majoritarian theory. On this model, subordinates do not necessarily hold any values in common, but they do share their recognition of a common superior authority. Cotterrell suggests that the ultra vires rule reflects this imperium image, in justifying judicial review on the basis that the judges are giving effect to the legislative intent of Parliament.[2] But the democratic element in such a system means that the 'glue' which holds both political and civil society together no longer consists only of authority and hierarchy, but includes consent via parliamentary elections and a sense of security in that civil and political freedoms, and thus an individual's autonomy, dignity and respect, cannot be interfered with coercively without the consent of Parliament.

Generally the development of both public and private law have tended to reflect our other two models of democracy more than the liberal-majoritarian or positivist-authoritarian models. Considerate altruism lies behind the development of much of the law of tort. This theory also explains cases on decision making in both public and private law, in

---

1   R Cotterrell 'Judicial review and legal theory' in G Richardson and H Genn *Administrative Law and Government Action* (1994).
2   See discussion of this theory of judicial review in chapter 2.

requirements that decisions be not made arbitrarily or capriciously, or unreasonably or in a discriminatory way, and that decision makers should not act in their own interests, but altruistically. Participative communitarianism is strongly influential in the developments of duties of procedural propriety in judicial review, and also in private law where similar duties are imposed on those in positions of power, as in contractual relationships in membership associations such as trade unions, universities, private regulatory bodies and the like. There is even the possibility that duties of natural justice might be imposed in fiduciary relationships, as in trusts.

For Cotterrell communitarianism involves an image of a morally cohesive association of politically autonomous people. It suggests a horizontal relationship of natural, spontaneous, or freely chosen association between individuals and between social groups on the basis of values held in common, rather than a vertical authoritarian relationship between the individual and the state.[3] This conception effectively merges civic and civil theories of democracy and thus supports the argument for replacing the public-private divide with an integrated approach to public and private law. The glue which holds political and civil society together in these models is the mesh of interdependence, mutual respect, responsibility for the vulnerable, altruism and trust, rather than hierarchy and authoritarianism.

Citizenship theories

These developments clearly have implications for citizenship. With the waning of positivist-authoritarian theory the individual has moved from being a subject towards becoming a citizen. But the kind of citizenship a person experiences depends upon how her interests in the key values are protected and her attitude to the exercise of power both on her part and in relation to her. Allan suggests that the common law embodies, albeit imperfectly, a set of constitutional values transcending the ordinary more transient, and particular, rules enacted by the legislature.[4] He notes equality before the law as 'an aspect of equal citizenship, an ideal of the moral equality or equal dignity or all those subject to governmental power.'[5] People's security and the level of trust in society are enhanced

---

3   R Cotterrell 'Judicial review and legal theory' in G Richardson and H Genn *Administrative Law and Government Action* (1994).
4   T R S Allan 'Fairness, equality, rationality: Constitutional theory and judicial review' in C Forsyth and I Hare (eds) *The Golden Metwand and the Crooked Cord* (1998) at p 17.
5   Allan, op cit.

by requirements of generality and prospectivity in the law. 'And the rules of natural justice ensure not only that statutes and policies are efficiently and accurately applied – the instrumental justification – but also enhance human dignity by acknowledging the respect properly due to those whose liberties and interests are made subject to administrative control.'[6] He suggests also that requirements of procedural fairness acknowledge 'the special dignity of the fellow-citizen, to whom an official or public agency appeals for willing cooperation in a shared endeavour. The citizen is offered a justification for official action, and enabled to participate in official deliberation, on the basis, so far as possible, of a shared understanding of the common good.'[7]

The fact that similar duties of considerate action and decision making are required of private bodies as of state bodies means that citizenship is a civil as well as a civic status. It also serves to undermine the theory that the ultra vires rule and the doctrine of parliamentary intent are the basis of judicial review, and thus the majoritarian view of democracy. Instead it reinforces the view that communitarian and altruistic principles are at work as the law of decision making develops. To the extent that a communitarian view is developing, it should be expected to span public and private law, for it is of the essence of this approach that the state does not have unchallengeable authority to do what it wishes in relations with its citizens, which is what is implied in the majoritarian view, but assumes instead that the state should act cooperatively, and that where power is also held in private hands, the same expectations of respect for fellow citizens on the part of the powerful should come into play.

Thus the abandonment of the public-private divide that has been advocated in the previous chapter would promote the process of extending democracy and citizenship into civil society which has been taking place for over a century as a result of developments in statutes, equity and the common law.

The nature of citizenship in a society is affected by the ways in which power is exercised and controlled, the values which the law upholds, and how it upholds them. These matters in turn affect what people are like and how they behave. If – to use a stereotype – most people are selfish, me-first individualists, lacking in political skills and uninterested in the communities in which or near which they live, or in political processes, then the practice of citizenship in the senses of participation in government and society and acceptance of responsibilities to others and to the public interest will be sparse. Such individuals' views of what citizenship is are likely to be highly individualistic – it is about having rights and freedom of action, and being entitled to freedom from intrusion

6   Allan, op cit at pp 18-19.
7   Allan, op cit.

either by the state or by other individuals or private organisations. This is a passive form of individualism the essence of which is 'being left to go about one's business.'[8] It is also likely to involve a sense of entitlement to exploit others and to take advantage of power imbalances, and rejection of any duties of altruism in relations with others. It will be about power without responsibility, political involvement limited to voting in elections, and a lack of trustworthiness in dealings with others, or of trust in others not to exploit one.

If on the other hand the stereotype is of individuals who enjoy autonomy, dignity, respect status and security and acknowledge that others in their society also have interests in the same values, a different sort of person emerges. One who will not exploit her own autonomy if it involves interfering with others' enjoyment of the key values; one who feels knitted into many organisations and institutions in society, both public and private, because she knows that status is important for social well-being; one who has a sense of security, based on trust in those with whom she deals and in the law and the political process. Such a person will respect fellow citizens equally and will not discriminate against particular groups. She will be alert to the needs of others to have their dignity respected. This sort of person, if in a position of power, will accept that in exercising that power she should give weight to the interests of others, especially those in a relatively vulnerable position. She will accept responsibility and duties of altruism.

Those in relatively powerless positions in such a society, and generally the population at large, will understand that managerial decisions have to be made, both in public and private organisations, which may have negative impacts on individuals. They should experience a sense of security when positive or negative impacts on them are in view, both because their status in society will derive from a range of involvements, in jobs, institutions of civil society, public and political activity, so that their vulnerability is not focused on a single aspect of their lives; and because they will feel that they can trust those in positions of power to respect them and make considerate provision for them so far as it is in their power and compatible with altruistic decision making for them to do so.

In such a Utopia individuals, even in vulnerable positions, will have the political experience, the confidence and self-respect and the understanding to make altruistic judgments about the plans and actions of those in authority, to seek and make inputs into decisions with a sense of proportion and mutual respect. This set of attitudes will derive from

8   See P Cane 'Public law and private law: A study of the analysis and use of a legal concept' in J Eekelaar and J Bell (eds) *Oxford Essays in Jurisprudence* (3rd series, 1987) at p 58.

their sense of being integrated into – included in – society through their status and security, a sense of trust, and confidence in their own dignity and respect and those of the others with whom they deal.

This of course is a highly idealised and simplified picture of what life would be like if the life experience of all individuals was that their interests in the key values were highly regarded and would generally be weighed in the balance when possibly unfavourable decisions were being made by those in positions of power. But this sketch of Utopia seeks to put the key values in a broader social, political and ethical context. What people are like is determined partly by how the law regards them. Discussion in previous chapters has sought to show how both public law and private law give some recognition of the need to promote the interests of individuals in the key values, and to protect the weak from abuses of power, whether in private or public hands.

AND FINALLY..

In summary, then, public and private law have much in common. It is artificial and goes against trends going back well over a century to seek to separate them by substantive, procedural or remedial divides. In effect in both public and private law theories of democracy – civic and civil democracy – and citizenship are influential. These influences emanate from Parliament, from the European Community, from the European Convention of Human Rights, and not least from the common law and equity. They attach increasing weight and importance to upholding the dignity, autonomy, respect, status and security of individuals against exercises of power. These values are at once individualistic and social or communitarian. And the theories of democracy and citizenship which lie behind these values give decreasing weight to the demands of authority and majoritarianism and increasing weight to arguments for consideration for others, altruism, communitarianism and participation. Thus the doctrine of legislative intent and the ultra vires rule become unconvincing as justifications for the jurisdiction in judicial review of statutory discretions. It is coming to be recognised that as a matter of public policy as articulated in statutory provisions, equity and the common law, the courts have undertaken a role in righting wrongs and requiring democratic standards of behaviour of those in positions of power, whether public or private. In effect they have an important role in developing and providing channels for democracy and the practice of citizenship.

A Comparison:
The Scottish Approach

Scotland provides an example of a system closely related to England's which manages without the English privileges for those exercising public or governmental functions in the way of short time limits and requirements for permission for applications for judicial review; nor is there a substantive public/private divide of the kind that is supposed to exist in England.[1] In what follows the focus will be on these two points of comparison between the two systems where decisions are likely to affect adversely individuals' vital interests and where there are imbalances of power. However, a note of caution needs to be sounded: the Scottish system has different roots from the English one, the concepts are different, as is the law of contract – which is on the periphery of many Scots and English cases involving supervisory jurisdictions[2] – and interest to sue.

First, a sketch of the Scottish position on judicial review and the public/private divide. The Court of Session possesses inherent powers of review by way of a supervisory jurisdiction which is not confined to public law cases. (In fact the term 'supervisory jurisdiction' has only recently been adopted in Scottish law, the expressions 'supervisory powers'

---

1   See Lord Clyde 'The nature of the supervisory jurisdiction and the public/
     private distinction in Scots administrative law' in W Finnie, C Himsworth and
     N Walker eds *Edinburgh Essays in Public Law* (1991); W J Wolffe 'The scope of
     judicial review in Scots law' [1992] PL 625; C M G Himsworth 'Judicial Review
     in Scotland' in M Supperstone and J Goudie (*Judicial Review*) (2nd edn, 1997)
     and 'Judicial review in Scotland' in B Hadfield ed (*Judicial Review. A Thematic
     Approach*) (1995).
2   See chapter 1 for explanation of the term 'supervisory jurisdiction'.

of the court, its 'superintending' authority and 'supereminent jurisdiction' having been preferred.[3]) The pre-eminent example of the Court of Session's supervisory jurisdiction operating outside public law is the power to keep arbiters within their powers.[4] The procedure for the exercise of these powers of review is governed by chapter 58 of the Rules of the Court of Session 1994.[5] This provides that:

> 'An application to the supervisory jurisdiction of the court ... shall be made by petition for judicial review ...' (note the mandatory terms of the Rule.)

Appeals or applications for review under enactments are excluded from chapter 58 so that, as in the application for judicial review in England, statutory appeals and review operate outside the 'petition for judicial review' procedure.

The West case

The principles for the exercise of the supervisory jurisdiction in judicial review were set out by the former Lord President, Lord Hope, in the leading case of *West v Secretary of State for Scotland*[6] in terms which sought to clarify confusion caused by previous cases. They are as follows:

1   The Court of Session has power, in the exercise of its supervisory jurisdiction, to regulate the process by which decisions are taken by any person or body to whom a jurisdiction, power or authority has been delegated or entrusted by statute, agreement or any other instrument.

2   The sole purpose for which the supervisory jurisdiction may be exercised is to ensure that the person or body does not exceed or abuse that jurisdiction, power or authority or fail to do what the jurisdiction, power or authority requires.

---

3   See C M G Himsworth 'Public employment, the supervisory jurisdiction and points *West*' 1992 SLT (News) 257 at p 259. A W Bradley in the account of Scots administrative law in *Laws of Scotland*, para 348, defines the supervisory jurisdiction as follows: 'The inherent jurisdiction which the Court of Session exercises in supervising and reviewing the acts or decisions of inferior courts, tribunals, public bodies, authorities and officials on grounds of ultra vires, abuse of discretion, excess of jurisdiction, breach of natural justice and fairness, failure to comply with statutory procedural requirements and failure to perform statutory duties.'

4   See *Forbes v Underwood* (1886) 13 R 465.

5   SI 1994/1443. These were first included in Rule of Court 260B, which was promulgated in 1985: SI 1985/500.

6   1992 SC 385.

3   The competency of the application does not depend upon any
     distinction between public law and private law, nor is it
     confined to those cases which English law has accepted as
     amenable to judicial review, nor is it correct in regard to issues
     about competency to describe judicial review under Rule of
     Court 260B as a public law remedy.'

Lord President Hope than went on to make a number of further
'important points'.

'(a) Judicial review is available, not to provide machinery for an
     appeal, but to ensure that the decision maker does not exceed
     or abuse his powers or fail to perform the duty which has been
     delegated or entrusted to him. It is not competent for the
     court to review the act or decision in its merits, nor may it
     substitute its own opinion for that of the person or body to
     whom the matter has been delegated or entrusted.
 (b) The word "jurisdiction" best described the nature of the
     power, duty or authority committed to the person or body
     which is amenable to the supervisory jurisdiction of the court.
     It is used here as meaning simply "power to decide", and it
     can be applied to the acts or decisions of any administrative
     bodies and persons with similar functions as well as to those
     of inferior tribunals. An excess or abuse of jurisdiction may
     involve stepping outside it, or failing to observe its limits, or
     departing from the rules of natural justice, or a failure to
     understand the law, or the taking into account of matters which
     ought not to have been taken into account. The categories of
     what may amount to an excess or abuse of jurisdiction are not
     closed, and they are capable of being adapted in accordance
     with the development of administrative law.
 (c) There is no substantial difference between English law and
     Scots law as to the grounds on which the process of decision
     making may be open to review. So reference may be made to
     English cases in order to determine whether there has been an
     excess or abuse of the jurisdiction, power or authority or a
     failure to do what it requires.
 (d) Contractual rights and obligations, such as those between
     employer and employee, are not as such amenable to judicial
     review. The cases in which the exercise of the supervisory
     jurisdiction is appropriate involve a tripartite relationship,
     between the person or body to whom the jurisdiction, power
     or authority has been delegated or entrusted, the person or
     body by which it has been delegated or entrusted and the

person or persons in respect of or for whose benefit that jurisdiction, power or authority is to be exercised.'

After West: When is a Scots supervisory jurisdiction exercisable in private law? When is the jurisdiction exercisable otherwise than in a petition for judicial review?

Although, as is indicated by the cases relied on by former Lord President Hope in *West*[7] (which predated the rule change of 1985) the supervisory jurisdiction is said to be available in principle against private bodies exercising private functions, it is not clear what kinds of private bodies are subject to the jurisdiction, and in what situations private bodies are subject to duties, broadly, of legality, fairness and rationality in their decision making; nor is it clear when the jurisdiction must be exercised through the petition for judicial review as opposed to in other actions. Part of the problem is that these points have not always been taken when they could have been.[8]

In *West* Lord President Hope referred to two cases in particular in which the Court of Session had had jurisdiction in private law cases involving duties of considerate decision making. In *McDonald v Burns*[9] the Court of Session accepted that it could have power to exercise a 'supervisory jurisdiction'[10] over the decision of authorities of the Roman Catholic Church to evict nuns from their convent following a dispute about matters of doctrine and church authority. The church authorities had applied to the Court of Session for eviction of the nuns, plus associated remedies of declarator and interdict. The nuns relied on the substantive law applied in the exercise of the supervisory jurisdiction in their defence, alleging that the church authorities were acting ultra vires and in breach

7   *McDonald v Burns* 1940 SC 325; *St Johnstone Football Club v Scottish Football Association Ltd* 1965 SLT 171; *Brentnall v Free Presbyterian Church of Scotland* 1986 SLT 471.

8   For instance in *McDonald v Secretary of State for Scotland (No 2)* 1996 SLT 575, Extra Division, a prisoner raised an action in the Sheriff Court alleging illegal searches. The point was taken that the case should have been brought by way of petition for judicial review and it was held that a question as to the validity of the prison standing orders could only be raised in a petition for judicial review. By contrast in *Tait v Central Radio Taxi (Tollcross) Ltd* 1989 SC 4 the pursuer sued for damages for breach of a contractual duty of natural justice, no point was taken as to whether he should have proceeded by way of petition for judicial review, and the court decided in his favour.

9   1940 SC 325.

10 Using the term 'supervisory jurisdiction' in the sense explained in chapter 1, namely to enforce obligations of conformity with duties of, inter alia, procedural fairness and not exceeding powers in decision making.

of natural justice. The Lord Justice-Clerk said that: 'The internal discipline of any such body is a matter of domestic concern, notwithstanding that status, or civil rights, may be involved, and it is only in extraordinary circumstances that the Courts will regard it as within their competence to intervene.' Those circumstances included where a body has acted clearly and demonstrably beyond its own constitution, and in a manner calculated to affect the civil rights and patrimonial interests of any members; and where, although acting within its constitution, the procedure of its judicial or quasi-judicial tribunals has been marked by gross and fundamental irregularity.[11] The case therefore stands for the proposition that the courts may supervise the decisions of a private body in the narrow circumstances set out in the judgment, and that they may do so when the point is raised by way of defence to an ordinary action. The nuns could of course have initiated the litigation in *McDonald v Burns*, rather than raising the decision making by the Church in their defence. The point is that, whether the points are raised by petitioners for judicial review or by way of defence to an action, the same substantive principles apply.

In *St Johnstone Football Club v Scottish Football Association Ltd*[12] a football club had been summarily fined for breach of the rules of the association, and the club complained of breach of the rules of natural justice. Here the court extended the test beyond that set out in the *McDonald* case, and held that the court may entertain actions arising out of the 'judgments' of the governing bodies of private associations, whether or not the civil rights and patrimonial interests of its members have been interfered with where a gross irregularity, such as a departure from the rules of natural justice, has been demonstrated.[13] In both of these cases, then, the decisions of private governing bodies were held to be subject to a supervisory jurisdiction, in the sense that they were under duties of legality, fairness or rationality. But, as will be shown, it may be that there exist, separately, *the* supervisory jurisdiction referred to in Chapter 58, which is exercisable only by the Court of Session on a petition for judicial review, and other supervisory jurisdictions exercisable by other courts – for instance in relation to trusts – or at the behest of defenders.

In *McDonald v Burns* the relationship between the church and the nuns was, if not exactly contractual, consensual. By becoming members the nuns had voluntarily undertaken to submit themselves to and abide by the constitution of the church, although not entering into any express

---

11 At pp 331-332. For criticism of this decision see Himsworth 'Judicial review in Scotland' in Hadfield ed, op cit.

12 1965 SLT 171.

13 At 174.

contract or covenant to do so.[14] The *St Johnstone* case too was based in contract. In other words these two cases are not unambiguously authorities for the view that there is a private law supervisory jurisdiction in the Court of Session outside contract. Nor can they help on the question whether such points can, since the rule change and since *West*, be raised by way of defence in an ordinary action, or whether, even though a claim may be based in a membership contract, it may or must be brought by way of petition for judicial review.

There are further cases in which duties of legality, fairness or rationality have been found to arise in contractual relationships, so that a supervisory jurisdiction arises *that is exercisable in an ordinary action and not in judicial review*. *Tait v Central Radio Taxi (Tollcross) Ltd*[15] is an interesting example of an ordinary action in contract for breach of contractual duties of natural justice: a taxi-driver raised an action in contract for damages for breach of natural justice when a disciplinary committee of the defenders, of which he was a member, required him to resign or be excluded from membership. In *McMillan v Free Church of Scotland*[16] in 1861, a minister of the Free Church was suspended. In an action in contract alleging breach of the rules of the church, and damage caused by the fact that his character had been injured and his future prospects had been damaged, it was held that a cause of action would lie. Lord President McNeill said: 'I cannot doubt that damages may be claimed, if that is the result of a departure from the agreement between the parties, and a violation of the conditions of the contract which existed between them.'

In some contract-based cases the Court of Session has declined jurisdiction on a petition for judicial review, and in others it has accepted such jurisdiction. It is not easy to reconcile them. The leading case is *Tehrani v Argyll and Clyde Health Board (No 2)*, decided before the decision in *West*. A consultant surgeon employed by the Health Board challenged the way in which the decision to dismiss him had been made, on the grounds that it had been unreasonable of the board to choose a method which deprived him of the right to obtain a review from the Secretary of State. The Second Division held that, although there were statutory elements in the contract of employment, the claim was for breach of the contractual terms of employment and thus the application for judicial review was not competent.[17] This position may be partly explained on

14 At 331.
15 1989 SC 4, First Division.
16 1861 SC 1314, Court of Session.
17 Contrast the position of Lord Weir in the Court of Session in *Tehrani* (rejected on appeal by the Second Division) that this contract of employment had the necessary 'public element' for it to be subject to the supervisory jurisdiction. 'The concepts of natural justice and "unreasonableness" are both aspects of administrative law and properly open to judicial review and cannot be kept apart artificially.' 1990 SLT 118 at 126.

the basis that the contract may provide an alternative remedy – breach of the duties of natural justice may be remedied in ordinary proceedings, for instance. However, it will not always be the case that a contract will include express or implied duties of fairness and rationality. In the absence of such contractual duties it seems that no remedy will be available if the dispute is concerned with 'contractual rights and obligations, such as those between employer and employee', even if the employer is a public body, since, according to *West*, judicial review would not be available.[18]

In *Watt v Strathclyde Regional Council*,[19] another employment dispute, and decided before *West*, in which a council's decision unilaterally to amend the terms and conditions of service of its teacher workforce was challenged, the supervisory jurisdiction under chapter 58 was exercised, broadly on the basis that the issues were not 'purely' contractual but were administrative. It is not clear whether this decision has survived the decision in *West*. In the 1998 case of *Ronald McIntosh v Aberdeenshire Council*[20] Lord MacLean held that a petition for judicial review seeking reduction of an agreement between a developer and the local planning authority and reduction also of the authority's refusal to discharge the agreement was incompetent: the questions raised involved simply a contractual arrangement between the two parties and did not involve an exercise of jurisdiction (in the *West* sense of 'power to decide') on the part of the planning authority.

Let us turn now to Scottish cases based in contract in which the defender was not a public body, and consider how duties of legality, fairness or rationality may be enforced. In some of these cases the Court of Session or Outer House have exercised the supervisory jurisdiction on a petition for judicial review, in others it has been prepared to do so in a contract action. In *Gunstone v Scottish Women's Amateur Athletic Association*[1] the pursuer brought an ordinary action in contract. She was the retiring honorary secretary of the SWAAA and stood for re-election.

18 See *Tehrani*, supra; *Blair v Lochaber District Council* [1995] IRLR 135. The English parallel is *R v East Berkshire Health Authority, ex p Walsh* [1984] 3 All ER 425, CA. Compare *Watt v Strathclyde Regional Council* 1992 SLT 324 in which Lord Clyde indicated that though purely contractual disputes could not be proper subjects for review some individual employment cases might warrant recourse to the supervisory jurisdiction (where for instance there is a public law element) as would cases where the decision at issue is not one affecting a particular contract but a number of contracts and is taken 'as a matter of general decision in the exercise of their administrative function by a local authority' (at 331-332); see also *Naik v University of Stirling* 1994 SLT 449; *Joobeen v University of Stirling* 1995 SLT 120; and discussion by C M G Himsworth in 'Public employment and the supervisory jurisdiction' 1992 SLT (News) 123; 'Judicial review in Scotland' in B Hadfield ed, op cit.
19 1992 SLT 324.
20 1999 SLT 93
1   1987 SLT 611.

The Executive Committee put forward their own nominee, in breach of the rules, and elected her. The action was based on the contract of membership. It was held that the pursuer had title and interest to sue[2] – by implication without having to resort to the petition for judicial review in the Court of Session – through the loss of the undoubted prestige and status the office carried in the world of women's amateur athletics.

The claim in *Brown v Executive Committee of the Edinburgh District Labour Party*[3] was also based in contract – the contract of membership of the party – but the Outer House exercised the supervisory jurisdiction under a petition for judicial review and not in an ordinary contract action. Nine councillors of the City of Edinburgh District Council were subjected to disciplinary proceedings by the Labour Party; they alleged denial of natural justice. The Labour Party argued that it was not competent for the court to intervene in the internal affairs of a voluntary association. The Outer House held that although the court would only interfere in the proceedings of voluntary associations in extraordinary circumstances (echoing the point made in *McDonald v Burns*), where the apprehension of a denial of natural justice might create a suspicion in the mind of a reasonable man about the impartiality of the domestic tribunal, a prima facie case for the exercise of the supervisory jurisdiction was made out. The balance of convenience in this case was in favour of awarding an interim interdict and interim suspension. The fact that the relationship between the petitioners and respondents was contractual was not raised against the exercise of the supervisory jurisdiction by way of the petition for judicial review.

Overall the position, though somewhat uncertain, seems to be that where the terms of a contract involve a supervisory jurisdiction – for instance express or implied requirements of natural justice or reasonableness – there is no requirement to proceed by petition for judicial review, and these duties may be relied on in ordinary actions, either by the pursuer or the defender. But all other cases in which the court has a supervisory jurisdiction (save where a statutory procedure is laid down), whether public or private must be brought by petition for judicial review. If this approach were adopted in England it would mean that cases concerning, for instance, unreasonable restraints of trade or public policy controls on such private activity – as in *McInnes v Onslow Fane* and *Nagle v Feilden* – would have to be brought under the special application for judicial review procedure rather than by ordinary action in the Queen's Bench or Chancery Divisions. But this would not entail that they were public law cases.

---

2   Interest to sue is an element of the cause of action, and is not the same thing as standing in English public law.
3   1995 SLT 985.

On the question whether a supervisory jurisdiction imposing non-contractual duties of legality, fairness or rationality in private law exists in Scots law, the decision in *Lennox v Scottish Branch of the British Show Jumping Association*[4] provides some guidance: a former member of the association, which was a company limited by guarantee, challenged decisions taken by the committee of the association preventing him from standing for election to the branch's council and removing him from office of judge. He complained inter alia of breach of natural justice. His claim was not based on a contract of membership. In the event his action (not by way of petition for judicial review) failed as he had chosen the wrong defender, but the Outer House indicated that if he had chosen the correct defender he would have had title and interest to sue, on the basis that he was alleging breach of natural justice. (The Outer House also held that it was not necessary for him to aver that the matter affected his pecuniary rights or status.)

Grounds for review in Scotland

In *West* the point was made that the grounds for review in Scotland and England are the same. It is not in fact clear that this is true in judicial review.[5] But a significant implication of the position that the grounds for judicial review in Scotland are the same as those in England, coupled with the assertion that there is no public/private divide in Scotland, is that in Scotland the same grounds – in effect illegality, unfairness and irrationality – are available in supervisory jurisdictions in private as in public law. This represents support from another jurisdiction for the argument being advanced in this book that there is no fundamental difference between substantive public and private law where supervisory jurisdictions exist in English law.

Tripartite relationships

The principal difficulty experienced under the Scots system stems from Lord President Hope's focus on tripartite relationships.[6] It is not clear from the way in which Lord President Hope expressed this point whether it was intended to apply solely to employment cases. Given that contractual rights and obligations, including those in employment, were

4   1996 SLT 353.
5   See Himsworth in Hadfield ed op cit, pp 305-306.
6   See Himsworth, op cit; and 'Judicial Review in Scotland' in M Supperstone and J Goudie eds, op cit.

generally excluded from judicial review in Lord President Hope's judgment, the question is whether he was leaving open the possibility of some employment cases being judicially reviewable, presumably on the basis of the case of *Malloch v Aberdeen Corpn*[7] where a statutory element was present. However, that case lacked a tripartite relationship – unless we are to regard Parliament as legislator as sitting at the apex of a triangle, an interpretation rejected in *Blair v Lochaber District Council.*[8] In *Blair* the council's chief executive sought judicial review of his suspension from duties on full pay. Lord Clyde decided that judicial review was not competent on the basis that generally public and private employment cases should be treated in the same way, and if there were no tripartite relationship in private employment cases it would be illogical to find one in public employment cases.[9]

So it may be that the tripartite relationship element was intended as a general indication of the availability of judicial review. If this is the case, it would probably represent a change to the substantive law in Scotland before *West*, and clearly does not apply in all 'supervisory jurisdictions' – for instance in relation to trusts and company directors' duties. Lord MacLean has indicated that he is not persuaded that in every case in which application is made to the supervisory jurisdiction of the court, there must exist a tripartite relationship.[10] Himsworth notes that 'There has been very little sympathy for the prospect of wholesale redefinition of reviewability by reference to elusive and ill-defined inter-institutional triangles'.[11] In practice the test does not seem to have caused problems, outside the field of public employment. One implication might be that it is a requirement only in applications to 'the supervisory jurisdiction' of the Court of Session under RCS, chapter 58, and does not apply to other supervisory jurisdictions.

Let us cast our minds back over the kinds of supervisory jurisdiction exercisable in English law – in relation to the duties of public and private bodies in judicial review under Order 53, of private trustees, and pension trustees, of directors of companies, of trade unions, universities and regulatory bodies in sport in private law proceedings, for instance: it is clear that a definition of a supervisory jurisdiction that requires a tripartite relationship, such as that set out by Lord President Hope in the *West* case, would not reflect the incidence of these jurisdictions in England.

---

7   1971 SLT 245.
8   [1995] IRLR 135, Lord Clyde.
9   See discussion by Himsworth in Hadfield ed at pp 302-305.
10   *Naik v University of Stirling* 1994 SLT 449; *McIntosh v Aberdeenshire Council* 1999 SLT 93.
11   Himsworth in Supperstone and Goudie, op cit at p 19.17.

Procedural contrasts

The Scots petition for judicial review procedure under RCS, chapter 58 does not erect special hurdles for those invoking the jurisdiction, or privileges for respondents, in the way of short time limits and the leave or permission stage such as are required under RSC, Order 53. Indeed, the Scots procedure is particularly attractive to would-be applicants, many of whom seek to bring their cases within the jurisdiction rather than follow other procedures.

Protections for those subject to the Scottish supervisory jurisdiction are provided by the doctrine of 'mora, taciturnity and acquiescence' which permits the court to bar a petition, for instance on grounds of unreasonable delay in commencing proceedings. This power may be exercised, for example, if the petitioner has remained silent despite knowledge of relevant facts, and others have relied upon the decision in question and act upon it to their detriment.[12] However, an essential ingredient for a plea of mora, taciturnity and acquiescence to succeed is prejudice, and this will be a matter of evidence.[13] This doctrine is regarded as on a par with the power of the English court on an application for judicial review to refuse permission to apply after the three-month limit.[14] But if a similar approach were adopted in England in applications for judicial review, applicants would be in a better position than under the present very strict English rules on time limits and leave.

As in judicial review in England, in Scotland in most cases oral evidence is not required and decisions are made on the strength of affidavits. However it is recognised that oral evidence may be necessary for the satisfactory resolution of contentious issues.[15]

Remedies

The remedies available in the exercise of the supervisory jurisdiction in Scotland have strong parallels with those available in England. Reduction[16] resembles certiorari and orders for the cancellation of

---

12 See Himsworth in Supperstone and Goudie, supra, pp 19.27-19.28. And *Hanlon v Traffic Comr* 1988 SLT 802; *Pickering v Kyle and Carrick District Council* 1991 GWD 7-361; *Conway v Secretary of State for Scotland* 1996 SLT 690; *Ronald McIntosh v Aberdeenshire Council* 1999 SLT 93.

13 *Conway v Secretary of State for Scotland* 1996 SLT 690, Outer House.

14 See the analogy drawn by Lord MacLean in *Ronald McIntosh v Aberdeenshire Council* 1998 SCLR 435 at 443, citing with approval the observations of Laws J in *R v Secretary of State for Trade and Industry, ex p Greenpeace Ltd* (14th October 1997) transcript pp 42-43.

15 *Walker v Strathclyde Regional Council (No 2)* 1987 SLT 81.

16 See 1 *Laws of Scotland* para 325.

documents; declarator[17] resembles the declaration; interdict[18] resembles the injunction. There is no direct parallel with orders for mandamus and prohibition in Scotland, though interdicts may achieve equivalent results, and the Court of Session has power to order an inferior court, tribunal or other authority to exercise its jurisdiction or to make a determination which it is required by statute to make.[19] By contrast with the position in English law, where a petitioner's rights have been held to have been infringed, the view is that a remedy should not be regarded as discretionary and refused on the ground, for instance, of great inconvenience or pecuniary loss to another person.[20] The Crown Proceedings Act 1947 gives the Crown similar protections against the award of mandatory remedies in England and Scotland, but the Scottish courts have not followed the English courts after *Factortame*[1] and *M v Home Office*[2] in making interdicts available against ministers, save where European law is in issue.[3]

Petitioners in judicial review cases in Scotland have the possibility of an award in damages by way of remedy under chapter 58.4 of the Court of Session Rules.[4] Some of the cases in which damages have been awarded are akin to English actions in tort.[5] Damages are not available under Order 53 in England, unless the action is also in tort or breach of contract. Himsworth notes that in practice damages are rarely awarded in Scotland.[6] The position of those subject to private law supervisory jurisdictions under present arrangements in England (for instance in restraint of trade and related actions) as far as remedies are concerned may therefore be similar in practice to that of their equivalents in Scotland.[7]

17 See op cit, para 326.
18 See op cit, paras 327-330.
19 See op cit, para 334.
20 See C M G Himsworth in Supperstone and Goudie, op cit at p 19.42, and cases noted there including *Hanlon v Traffic Comr* 1988 SLT 802, at 806.
1   *R v Secretary of State for Transport, ex p Factortame (No 2)* [1991] 1 AC 603.
2   [1994] 1 AC 377.
3   *McDonald v Secretary of State for Scotland* 1994 SLT 692; but see also *Millar and Bryce Ltd v Keeper of the Registers of Scotland* 1997 SLT 1000.
4   See *1 Laws of Scotland* para 333.
5   See for instance *Edwards v Kinloss Parochial Board* (1891) 18 R 867 (power to remove nuisance used to demolish a house); *Sinclair v Middle Ward District Committee of Lanarkshire County Council* 1907 SC 285, 14 SLT 534 (alteration of road without statutory authority, obstructing private access).
6   Himsworth in Supperstone and Goudie, op cit at p 19.44. But see *Kelly v Monklands District Council* 1986 SLT 169; *Mallon v Monklands District Council* 1986 SLT 347; *B v Forsey* 1988 SLT 572.
7   See discussion of remedies in chapter 9.

Summary

Overall, it is suggested, the Scottish approach to the public/private divide and the exercise of supervisory jurisdictions would not transplant readily into the English legal system. It is by no means clear what the extent of the supervisory jurisdiction in private law in Scotland is, nor indeed the extent of the 'public law' supervisory jurisdiction, for instance where public employment cases are concerned. The Scottish exclusivity requirement in chapter 58 of the Rules of the Court of Session could cause problems where the supervisory jurisdiction was relied upon by way of defence (as in the *McDonald* case), and indeed in other situations – as in England at present; the Court of Session's discretion to stop litigation for 'mora, taciturnity and acquiescence' would place parties in private law cases in a worse position than at present in England, where no such doctrine operates except in relation to the discretion whether to award declarations and equitable remedies; the Scottish tripartite relationship rule would simply not fit into the substantive English law of supervisory jurisdictions (it does not fit well into the Scottish system either); as in England, the exclusion of contract from the Scottish jurisdiction can lead to false starts in litigation where the question is whether duties of fairness and rationality derive from contract or not.

On the other hand the Scots arrangement does provide an example of a legal system closely related to our own which survives without a substantive public/private law divide, without special procedural protections for respondents to (public law) applications for judicial review, and which does not include in its remedies certiorari, mandamus or prohibition but achieves equivalent results by ordinary remedies, some of them very close to English equitable remedies.

Bibliography

Alder, J 'Obsolescence and renewal: judicial review in the private sector' in P Leyland and T Woods, (eds) *Administrative Law Facing the Future: Old Constraints and New Horizons* (1997) Blackstone Press, London.

Allan, T R S 'Pragmatism and theory in public law' (1988) 104 LQR 422.

Allan, T R S 'Fairness, equality, rationality: Constitutional theory and judicial review' in C Forsyth and I Hare (eds) *The Golden Metwand and the Crooked Cord* (1998) Oxford University Press, Oxford.

Allen, Sir Carlton 'Status and capacity' (1930) 46 LQR 277.

Allison, J *A Continental Distinction in the Common Law* (1996) Clarendon Press, Oxford.

Arden, Dame Mary 'Codifying directors' duties' in R Rawlings (ed) *Law, Society and Economy* (1997) Clarendon Press, Oxford.

Arrowsmith, S 'Government contracts and public law' (1990) 10 LS 231.

Arrowsmith, S *Civil Liability and Public Authorities* (1992) Earlsgate Press, Winteringham, S Humberside.

Arrowsmith, S *Government Procurement and Judicial Review* (1988) Carswell, Toronto.

Arrowsmith, S 'Judicial review and the contractual powers of local authorities' (1990) 106 LQR, 277.

Arterburn, N 'The Origin and First Test of Public Callings' 75 U Penn LR (1926-27) 411.

Arthurs, H 'Rethinking administrative law: A slightly Dicey business' (1979) 17 Osgoode Hall LR 1.

Atiyah, P S *Pragmatism and Theory in English Law* (1987) (Hamlyn Lectures, 39th series) Sweet and Maxwell, London.

Atiyah, P S *Essays on Contract* (reprinted 1990) Clarendon Press, Oxford.

Austin, J *Lectures on Jurisprudence* (5th edn, 1885) John Murray, London.

Bailey, S 'Personal liability in local government law' [1999] Public Law 461.

Bailey-Harris, R 'Pregnancy, autonomy and refusal of medical treatment' (1998) 114 LQR 550.

Bain, G S (ed) *Industrial Relations in Britain* (1983) Basil Blackwell, Oxford.

Baker, J H *An Introduction to English Legal History* (3rd edn, 1990) Butterworths, London.

Barendt, E *Freedom of Speech* (1985) Clarendon Press, Oxford.

Barendt, E 'Libel and freedom of speech in English law' [1993] Public Law 449.

Barnard, C 'The principle of equality in the Community context. *P, Grant, Kalanke* and *Marshall*: Four uneasy bedfellows' 57 Camb LJ (1998) 352.

Beatson, J and D Friedmann, (eds) *Good Faith and Fault in Contract Law* (reprinted 1995) Clarendon Press, Oxford.

Beatson, J '"Public" and "private" in English administrative law' (1987) 103 LQR 34.

Beatson, J 'Judicial review in contract' in J Beatson and D Friedmann (eds) *Good Faith and Fault in Contract Law* (1995).

Beatson, J and T Tridimas (eds) *New Directions in European Public Law* (1998) Hart Publishing, Oxford.

Beatson, J 'The Courts and the Regulators' (1987) Professional Negligence 121.

Bell, J 'Mechanisms for cross-fertilisation of administrative law in Europe' in J Beatson and T Tridimas (eds) *New Directions in European Public Law* (1998) Hart Publishing, Oxford.

Beloff, M 'Timeliness and public authorities' in C Forsyth and I Hare (eds) *The Golden Metwand and the Crooked Cord* (1998).

Beloff, M 'Pitch, Pool, Rink ... Court? Judicial Review in the Sporting World' (1989) Public Law 109.

Benn, S I 'Human rights – for whom and for what?' in E Kamenka and A E Tay (eds) *Human Rights* (1978).

Bentham, J 'Comment' in J H Burns and H L A. Hart (eds) *A Comment on the Commentaries and A Fragment on Government* (1977).

Bentham, J 'First Lines of a Proposed Code of Law' in P Schofield and J Harris (eds) *'Legislator of the World': Writings on Codification, Law and Education* (1998).

Bentham, J *Official Aptitude Maximized; Expense Minimized* (ed P Schofield) (1993) Clarendon Press, Oxford.

Birkinshaw, P *Grievances, Remedies and the State* (2nd edn, 1994) Sweet and Maxwell, London.

Birks, P (ed) *Wrongs and Remedies in the Twenty-first Century* (1996) Clarendon Press, Oxford.

Birks, P and Chin Nyuk Yin 'On the nature of undue influence' in J Beatson and D Friedmann (eds) *Good Faith and Fault in Contract Law* (reprinted 1995).

Blackstone, Sir William *Commentaries on the Laws of England* (1765) Butterworths, London.

Black, J 'Constitutionalising Self-regulation' (1996) 59 MLR 24.

Black, J and P Muchlinski 'Introduction' in J Black, P Muchlinski and P Walker (eds) *Commercial Regulation and Judicial Review* (1998).

Black, J, P Muchlinski and P Walker (eds) *Commercial Regulation and Judicial Review* (1998) Hart Publishing, Oxford.

Borrie, Sir Gordon 'The Regulation of Public and Private Power' [1989] Public Law 552.

Bowers, J and A Clarke 'Unfair dismissal and managerial prerogative: A study of "some other substantial reason"' (1981) 10 ILJ 34.

Bowers, J and J Lewis 'Whistleblowing: freedom of expression in the workplace' [1996] EHRLR 637.

Bradley, A W 'Administrative law' in *1 Laws of Scotland* (1987) Butterworths, Edinburgh.

Bradley, A W and K D Ewing *Constitutional and Administrative Law* (12th edn, 1997) Longman, London.

Brodie, D 'Beyond exchange: The new contract of employment' (1998) 27 ILJ 79.

Bromley, P *Family Law* (1st edn, 1957) Butterworths, London.

Brown, L N and J S Bell *French Administrative Law* (4th edn, 1993) Clarendon Press, Oxford.

Brownsword, R 'Static and dynamic market individualism' in R Halson (ed) *Exploring the Boundaries of Contract* (1996).

Brownsword, R 'From co-operative contracting to a contract of co-operation' in D Campbell and P Vincent-Jones (eds) *Contract and Economic Organisation* (1996).

Burns, J H and H L A Hart (eds) *Bentham's A Comment on the Commentaries and A Fragment on Government* (1977) Athlone Press, University of London, London.

Butler, A S 'Constitutional rights in private litigation: A critique and comparative analysis' (1993) 22 Anglo-American LR 1.

Cairns, J W 'The contract of employment' 105 LQR (1989) 301.

Campbell, D and P Vincent-Jones (eds) *Contract and Economic Organisation* (1996) Dartmouth, Aldershot.

Cane, P 'Self-regulation and judicial review' (1986) Civil Justice Quarterly 324.

Cane, P 'Public law and private law: A study of the analysis and use of a legal concept' in J Eekelaar and J Bell (*Oxford Essays in Jurisprudence*) (Third series 1987).

Cane, P 'Damages in public law' (1999) 9 Otago Law Review, 489.

Capper, D 'Undue influence and unconscionability: a rationalisation' (1998) 114 LQR 479.

Carnwath, Sir Robert 'The *Thornton* heresy exposed: Financial remedies for breach of public duties' [1998] Public Law 407.

Clapham, A *Human Rights in the Private Sphere* (1993) Clarendon Press, Oxford.

Clapham, A 'A human rights policy for the European Community' (1990) 10 YBEL 331.

Clarke, C and C Otton-Goulder 'The need for wholesale reform on vires issues in public and private law' in J Black, P Muchlinski and P Walker (eds) *Commercial Regulation and Judicial Review* (1998).

Clarke, A 'Property Law: Reestablishing Diversity' in M Freeman (ed) *Law and Opinion at the End of the Twentieth Century* (1997) Oxford, Oxford University Press.

Clyde, Lord 'The nature of the supervisory jurisdiction and the public/ private distinction in Scots administrative law' in W Finnie, C Himsworth and N Walker (eds) *Edinburgh Essays in Public Law* (1991).

Coke, Sir Edward 4 Inst.

Collins, H *Justice in Dismissal* (1992) Clarendon Press, Oxford.

Collins, H 'Against abstentionism in labour law' in J Eekelaar and J Bell *Oxford Essays in Jurisprudence* (Third Series, 1987).

Collins, H 'Market power, bureaucratic power, and the contract of employment' (1986) 15 Industrial Law Journal 1.

Collins, H 'Contract and legal theory' in W L Twining (ed) *Legal Theory and Common Law* (1986).

Collins, H *The Law of Contract* (3rd edn, 1997) Butterworths, London.

Collins, H 'The sanctimony of contract' in R Rawlings (ed) *Law, Society and Economy* (1997).

Coppel, J and A O'Neill 'The European Court of Justice: Taking rights seriously' (1992) Legal Studies 227.

Cotterrell, R 'The Law of Property and Legal Theory' in W L Twining (ed) *Legal Theory and Common Law*, 1986.

Cotterrell, R 'Judicial review and legal theory' in G Richardson and H Genn *Administrative Law and Government Action*, 1994.

Craig, P P 'Compensation in public law' (1980) 96 LQR 413.

Craig, P P *Administrative Law*, (3rd edn, 199) Sweet and Maxwell, London.

Craig, P P 'Constitutions, property and regulation' [1991] Public Law, 538.

Craig, P P 'Ultra vires and the foundations of judicial review' (1998) 57 Camb LJ 63.

Craig, P P 'Competing models of judicial review' [1999] Public Law 428.

Craig, P P and G de Burca *EC Law*, 1995 Oxford University Press, Oxford.

Cretney, S M ' "What will the women want next?" The struggle for power within the family 1925-1975' (1996) 112 LQR 110.

Cretney, S *Elements of Family Law* (2nd edn, 1992) Sweet and Maxwell, London.

Cretney, S and J Masson *Principles of Family Law* (6th edn, 1997) Sweet and Maxwell, London.

Dahl, R 'The concept of power',(1957) *Behavioural Science* 2 201.

Daintith, T C 'The Executive Power Today' in J Jowell and D Oliver, (eds) *The Changing Constitution* (3rd edn, 1995).

Daintith, T C 'Regulation by contract: the new prerogative' [1979] *Current Legal Problems*, 41.

Daintith, T C 'The Techniques of Government' in J Jowell and D Oliver (eds) *The Changing Constitution* (3rd edn, 1994).

Davies, P *Gower's Principles of Modern Company Law* (6th edn, 1997).

De Smith, S A, Lord Woolf and J L Jowell *Judicial Review of Administrative Action* (5th edn, 1995) Sweet and Maxwell, London.

De Smith, S A *Judicial Review of Administrative Action* (4th edn, 1980) Sweet and Maxwell, London.

De Smith, S A 'The Prerogative Writs' (1951) 11 Camb LJ 40.

Deakin, S 'The utility of "rights talk": Employees' personal rights' in C Gearty and A Tomkins *Understanding Human Rights*, 1996.

Deakin, S and G Morris *Labour Law* (2nd edn, 1998) Butterworths, London.

Dicey, A V *Introduction to the Study of the Law of the Constitution* (1885) (7th edn, 1908) (reprinted 1959) Macmillan, London.

Drewry, G 'Judicial review: the historical background' in M Supperstone and J Goudie (eds) *Judicial Review* (2nd edn, 1998).

Dworkin, R *Taking Rights Seriously* (1977) Duckworth, London.

Eekelaar, J 'The emergence of children's rights' (1986) 6 Oxford Jo LS 161.

Eekelaar, J and J Bell *Oxford Essays in Jurisprudence* Third series (1987).

Ellesmere, Lord *Observations* and noted at 77 ER 1278.

Elliott, M 'The demise of parliamentary sovereignty. The implications for justifying judicial review' (1999) 115 LQR 119.

Elliott, M 'The ultra vires doctrine in a constitutional setting: still the central principle of administrative law' (1999) 58 Camb LJ 129.

Ely, J H *Democracy and Distrust. A Theory of Judicial Review*, (1980) Harvard University Press, Cambridge, Mass.

Ewing, K and C Gearty *Freedom under Thatcher* (1990) Clarendon Press, Oxford.

Ewing, K 'Remedies for breach of the contract of employment' 52 Camb LJ 405.

Feldman, D 'Public Law Values in the House of Lords' (1990) 106 LQR 246.
Feldman, D *Civil Liberties and Human Rights in England and Wales* (1993) Oxford University Press, Oxford.
Feldman, D 'Remedies for violations of Convention rights under the Human Rights Act' [1998] EHRLR 691.
Finn, P D 'The fiduciary principle' in T G Youdan (ed) *Equity, Fiduciaries and Trusts* (1989) Carswell, Ontario.
Finn, P D 'Fiduciary law and the modern commercial world' in E McKendrick (ed) *Commercial Aspects of Trusts and Fiduciary Obligations* (1992) Oxford University Press, Oxford.
Finn, P D 'Controlling the Exercise of Power' (1996) 7 Public Law Review 86.
Finnie, W, C Himsworth and N Walker (eds) *Edinburgh Essays in Public Law* (1991). Edinburgh University Press, Edinburgh.
Finnis, J *Natural Law and Natural Rights* (1980) Clarendon Press, Oxford.
Ford, M *Surveillance and Privacy at Work* (1998) Institute of Employment Rights, London.
Forsyth, C and I Hare (eds) *The Golden Metwand and the Crooked Cord* (1998) Oxford University Press, Oxford.
Forsyth, C 'Of Fig Leaves and Fairy Tales: The *Ultra Vires* Doctrine, the Sovereignty of Parliament and Judicial Review' 55 (1996) CLJ 122.
Forsyth, C 'Collateral challenge and the foundations of judicial review: orthodoxy vindicated and procedural exclusivity rejected' [1998] Public Law 364.
Foucault, M 'Disciplinary power and subjection' in S Lukes (ed) *Power* (1986).
Franks Committee Report on *Administrative Tribunals and Inquiries* (1957) Cmnd 218. HMSO, London.
Fredman, S *Women and the Law* (1997) Clarendon Press, Oxford.
Fredman, S and G Morris *The State as Employer. Labour Law in the Public Services* (1989) Mansell, London.
Fredman, S and Morris, G 'Judicial review and civil servants: contract of employment declared to exist' [1991] Public Law 485.
Fredman, S and G Morris 'Public or private? State employees and judicial review' (1991) 107 LQR 298.
Fredman, S and G Morris 'The costs of exclusivity. Public and private re-examined' [1994] Public Law 69.
Freeman, M D A *The Rights and Wrongs of Children* (1983) Pinter, London.

Freeman, M D A 'Family Values and Family Justice' in M Freeman (ed) *Law and Opinion at the End of the Twentieth Century* (1997) Oxford University Press, Oxford.

Freeman, M D A (ed) *Medicine, Ethics and the Law* (1988) Stevens, London.

Freeman, M D A 'Sterilising the mentally handicapped' in M Freeman (ed) *Medicine, Ethics and the Law* (1988)

Freeman, M D A (ed) *Law and Opinion at the End of the Twentieth Century* (1997) Oxford University Press, Oxford.

Fried, C *Contract as Promise* (1981) Harvard University Press, Cambridge, Mass.

Fuller and Perdue 'The reliance Interest in Contract Damages' (1936) 46 Yale Law Jo 52 and 373.

Fuller, L *The Morality of Law* (1969) Yale University Press, London.

Fuller, L 'The forms and limits of adjudication' (1978) 92 Harv LR 353.

Fulton Report, *The Civil Service* (1968) Cmnd 3638, HMSO, London.

Galbraith, J G *The Anatomy of Power* (1983) Houghton Mifflin, Boston.

Galbraith, J K 'Power and organisation' in S. Lukes (ed) *Power* (1986).

Galligan, D J *Due Process and Fair Procedures: A Study of Administrative Procedures* (1996) Clarendon Press, Oxford.

Gearty, C and A Tomkins *Undertanding Human Rights* (1996) Mansell, London.

Gewirth, A *Human Rights: Essays on Justification and Applications* (1982) University of Chicago Press, Chicago.

Gewirth, A 'Are there any Absolute Rights?' in J Waldron (ed) *Theories of Rights* (1984).

Giddens, A *The Third Way* (1998) Polity Press, Oxford.

Glendon, M A *State, Law and Family* (1977) North Holland Publishing Co, New York.

Gower, J *Principles of Modern Company Law* ed P Davies (6th edn 1997) London, Stevens.

Gray, K 'Equitable property' (1994) 47 Current Legal Problems 157.

Gray, K 'Property in thin air' (1991) 50 CLJ 252.

Griffith, J A G *Judicial Politics since 1920* (1993) Blackwell, Oxford.

Griffith, J A G *The Politics of the Judiciary* (3rd edn 1985) Fontana Press, Glasgow.

Haar, C M and D W Fessler *The Wrong Side of the Tracks: A Revolutionary Discovery of the Common Law Tradition of Fairness in the Struggle against Inequality* (1986).

Habermas, J *Between Facts and Norms* trans W Rehg (1996) Polity Press, Oxford.

Hadfield, B (ed) *Judicial Review. A Thematic Approach* (1995) Gill and Macmillan, Dublin.

Hadjiemmanuil, C 'Civil liability of regulatory authorities after the Three Rivers case' [1997] Public Law 32.

Hale, Dame Brenda *Private Lives and Public Duties* (1997) ESRC, London.

Hale, Sir Matthew *An Analysis of the Civil Part of the Law* (4th edn, 1779).

Hale, Sir Matthew *The Analysis of the Law* (1713) Walthoe, London.

Hale, Sir Matthew *Tracts* (ed F Hargrave 1787) Dublin.

Halson, R (ed) *Exploring the Boundaries of Contract* (1996) Dartmouth, Aldershot.

Hanworth Committee *The Business of the Courts* Third Report (Cmnd 5066 1936) HMSO London.

Harden, I *The Contracting State* (1992) Open University Press, Milton Keynes,

Harlow, C '"Public" and "Private" Law: Definition without Distinction' (1980) 43 Modern Law Review 241.

Harlow, C *Compensation and Government Torts* (1982) Sweet and Maxwell, London.

Harlow, C and R Rawlings *Law and Administration* (1st edn, 1984) Weidenfeld and Nicolson, London.

Harlow, C and R Rawlings *Law and Administration* (2nd edn, 1998) Butterworths, London.

Harris, B V 'The "third source" of authority for government action' (1992) 108 LQR 626.

Harris, J W 'Private and non-private property: what is the difference?' (1995) 111 LQR 421.

Hartley, T *The Foundations of European Community Law* (4th edition, 1998) Oxford University Press, Oxford.

Hayek, F *Law, Legislation and Liberty* (1982) Routledge and Kegan Paul, London.

Heater, D *Citizenship: The Civic Ideal in World History, Politics and Education* (1990) Longman, London.

Held, D (ed) *Political Theory Today* (1991) Polity Press, Oxford.

Held, D *Models of Democracy* (1987) Polity Press, Oxford.

Henderson. E G *Foundations of English Administrative Law* (1963) Harvard University Press, Cambridge, Mass.

Hepple, B and S Fredman *Labour Law and Industrial Relations in Great Britain* (2nd edn, 1992) Kluwer, Deventer.

Hepple, B in 'The impact on labour law' in B S Markesinis (ed) *The Impact of the Human Rights Bill on English Law* (1998).

Hepple, B chapter 18 in G S Bain (ed) *Industrial Relations in Britain* (1983).

Himsworth, C M G, 'Public employment and the supervisory jurisdiction' 1992 SLT (News) 123.

Himsworth, C M G 'Public employment, the supervisory jurisdiction and points *West*' 1992 SLT (News) 257.

Himsworth, C M G 'Judicial review in Scotland' in B Hadfield (ed) *Judicial Review. A Thematic Approach* (1995).

Himsworth, C M G 'Judicial Review in Scotland' in M Supperstone and J Goudie *Judicial Review* (2nd edn, 1997).

Hobbes, T *Leviathan* (1651) (R Tuck, ed 1991) Cambridge University Press, Cambridge.

Holdsworth, *History of English Law* (2nd edn, 1937) Little, Brown, Boston.

Home Office White Paper *Rights Brought Home: The Human Rights Bill* Cm 3782 (1997) HMSO, London.

Honore, T *The Quest for Security: Employees, Tenants, Wives* (1982) Stevens. London.

Hood, C 'A public management for all seasons' (1991) Public Administration 3.

Hunt, A 'Fundamental rights and the New Zealand Bill of Rights Act' (1995) 111 LQR 567.

Hunt, M 'The "horizontal effect" of the Human Rights Act' [1998] Public Law 423.

Hunt, M 'Constitutionalism and Contractualisation' in M Taggart (ed) *The Province of Administrative Law* (1997).

Irvine of Lairg, Lord 'Judges and Decision-makers: The Theory and Practice of *Wednesbury* Review' [1996] Public Law 59.

Irvine of Lairg, Lord 'Opening Address' in B Markesinis (ed) *The Impact of the Human Rights Bill on English Law* (1998).

Jaffe, L L and E G Henderson 'Judicial review and the rule of law: historical origins' (1956) 72 LQR 345.

Jaques, E *A General Theory of Bureaucracy* (1976).

James, R *Private Ombudsmen and Public Law* (1997).

Jansen, N 'The idea of the lost chance' (1999) 19 Oxford Jo LS 217.

Jolowicz, J A 'Abuse of the process of the court: handle with care' [1990] CLP 77.

Jowell, J L 'The legal control of administrative discretion' [1973] Public Law 178.

Jowell, J L and A Lester 'Beyond *Wednesbury*: towards substantive principles of administrative law' [1987] Public Law 386.

Jowell, J L and D Oliver (eds) *The Changing Constitution* (3rd edn, 1994) Oxford University Press, London.

Jowell, J L 'Restraining the State. Politics, principle and judicial review' [1997] CLP 189.

Jowell, J L 'Is equality a constitutional principle?' (1994) 47 Current Legal Problems 1.

Justice-All Souls *Administrative Justice. Some Necessary Reforms* (1988) Clarendon Press, Oxford.

Kamenka, E and A E Tay *Human Rights* (1978) Edward Arnold, London.
Kamenka, E 'The Anatomy of an Idea' in E Kamenka and A E Tay *Human Rights* (1978).
Kamenka, E and R S Neale (eds) *Feudalism, Capitalism and Beyond* (1975) Edward Arnold, London.
Kant, I *The Moral Law (Groundwork of the Metaphysic of Morals)* (trans H J Paton, 1965) Hutchinson, London.
Kelly, P J *Utilitarianism and Distributive Justice. Jeremy Bentham and the Civil Law* (1990) Clarendon Press, Oxford.
Kennedy, I 'The fiduciary relationship between doctors and patients' in P Birks (ed) *Wrongs and Remedies in the Twenty-first Century* (1996).
Klare, K E 'The public/private distinction in labour law' (1982) U Penn. LR 1358.

Law Commission Paper: *Administrative Law: Judicial Review and Statutory Appeals* (Law Com no 226) (1994) HMSO, London.
Laws of Scotland (Stair Memorial Encyclopaedia) (vol 1, 1987) Butterworth, Edinburgh.
Laws, Sir John 'Is the High Court the guardian of fundamental constitutional rights?' [1993] Public Law 59.
Laws, Sir John 'Law and Democracy' [1995] Public Law 72.
Laws, Sir John 'The constitution – morals and rights' [1996] Public Law 622.
Laws, Sir John 'Public law and employment law: Abuse of power' [1997] Public Law 455.
Laws, Sir John 'Illegality: the Problem of Jurisdiction' in M Supperstone and J Goudie (eds) *Judicial Review* (2nd edn, 1997)
Lawson, A 'Detrimental reliance in the family home' (1996) 16 Legal Studies 218.
Le Sueur, A and M Sunkin 'Applications for judicial review: The requirement of leave' [1992] Public Law 102.
Levine, J *Needs, Rights and the Market* (1988).
Lewis, D 'Whistleblowers and job security' (1995) 58 MLR 208.
Leyland, P and T Woods (eds) *Administrative Law Facing the Future: Old Constraints and New Horizons,* (1997) Blackstone Press, London.
Locke, J *Two Treatises of Government* (1690) (P Laslett edn, 1960). Cambridge University Press, Cambridge.
Loughlin, M *Public Law and Political Theory* (1992) Clarendon Press, Oxford.
Loveland, I 'The constitutionalisation of political libels in English common law?' [1998] Public Law 633.

Loveland, I (ed) *Importing the First Amendment* (1998) Hart Publishing, Oxford.

Lukes, S (ed) *Power* (1986) Basil Blackwell, Oxford.

Macpherson, C B 'Capitalism and the changing concept of property' in E Kamenka and R S Neale (eds) *Feudalism, Capitalism and Beyond* (1975).

Macpherson, C B *The Life and Times of Liberal Democracy* (1977) Oxford University Press, Oxford.

Maine, Sir Henry *Ancient Law* (1861) (reprinted 1959) Dent, London.

Maitland, F W *The Constitutional History of England* (1908) (reprinted 1974) Cambridge University Press, Cambridge.

Markesinis, B 'Negligence, nuisance and affirmative duties of action' (1989) 105 LQR 104.

Markesinis, B S (ed) *The Impact of the Human Rights Bill on English Law*, (1998) Clarendon Press, Oxford.

Markesinis, B S and S F Deakin *Tort Law* (3rd edn, 199) Oxford University Press, Oxford.

Marshall, T H *Citizenship and Social Class* (1950) Cambridge University Press, Cambridge.

Mason, Sir Anthony 'The place of equity and equitable remedies in the contemporary common law' (1994) 110 LQR 238.

McAllister, Breck P 'Lord Hale and Business Affected with a Public Interest' (1929-30) 43 Harvard LR 759.

McCormick, N 'Jurisprudence and the Constitution' (1983) Current Legal Problems, 13.

McCrudden, C 'Racial discrimination' in C McCrudden and G Chambers (eds) *Individual Rights and the Law in Britain* (1994).

McCrudden, C and G Chambers (eds) *Individual Rights and the Law in Britain* (1994) Clarendon Press, Oxford.

McCrudden, C 'The impact on freedom of speech' in B Markesinis (ed) *The Impact of the Human Rights Bill on English Law* (1998).

McKendrick, E (ed) *Commercial Aspects of Trusts and Fiduciary Obligations* (1992) Oxford University Press, Oxford.

Mill, J S *Utilitarianism, On Liberty and Representative Government*, J M Dent and Sons, (1910) (ed M. Warnock, 1985) Fontana, Glasgow.

Morris, G 'Political activities of public servants and freedom of expression' in I Loveland, (ed) *Importing the First Amendment* (1998).

Morris, G 'The Human Rights Act and the public/private divide in employment law' 27 ILJ 293 (1998)

Morris, G 'Local government workers and rights of political participation: time for a change' [1998] Public Law 25.

Morris, G. 'The political activities of local government workers and the European Convention on Human Rights' [1999] Public Law 211.

Mowbray, A 'The composition and operation of the new European Court of Human Rights' [1999] Public Law 219.

Nafziger, J A R 'International sports law as a process for resolving disputes' 45 ICLQ (1994) 130.

Nardell, G 'The Quantock Hounds and the Trojan Horse' [1995] Public Law 27.

Neill, Sir Patrick 'The duty to give reasons' in C Forsyth and I Hare (eds) *The Golden Metwand and the Crooked Cord* (1998) Oxford University Press, Oxford.

Nobles, R *Pensions, Employment and the Law* (1993) Clarendon Press, Oxford.

Northcote Trevelyan Report 1854, reprinted as an Appendix to the Fulton Report, *The Civil Service* (Cmnd 3638) (1968) HMSO, London.

Oliver, D 'Is the ultra vires rule the basis for judicial review?' [1987] Public Law 543.

Oliver, D 'What is Happening to Relations between the Citizen and the State?' in J Jowell and D Oliver (eds) *The Changing Constitution* (3rd edn, 1994).

Oliver, D 'The underlying values of public and private law' in M Taggart (ed) *The Province of Administrative Law* (1997).

Oliver, D 'Common Values of Public and Private Law and the Public Private Divide' [1997] Public Law 630.

Oliver, D and G Drewry *Public Service Reforms. Issues of Accountability and Public Law* (1996) Pinter, London.

Olowofoyeku, A *Suing Judges* (1994) Clarendon Press, Oxford.

Olowofoyeku, A 'State liability for the exercise of judicial power' [1998] Public Law 444.

Osborne, D and T Gaebler *Reinventing Government: How the Entrepreneurial Spirit is Transforming the Public Sector* (1992) Addison-Wesley, Reading, Mass.

Palmer, G *Unbridled Power* (1987) Oxford University Press, Oxford.

Parry, D H *The Sanctity of Contracts in English Law* (1959) Stevens, London.

Pateman, C *Participation and Democratic Theory* (1970) Cambridge University Press, Cambridge.

Prosser, T *Law and the Regulators* (1997) Clarendon Press, Oxford.

Rawlings, R (ed) *Law, Society and Economy* (1997) Clarendon Press, Oxford.

Rawls, J *A Theory of Justice* (1971) Oxford University Press, Oxford.

Raz, J *The Morality of Freedom* (1986) Clarendon Press, Oxford.

Raz, J 'Free Expression and Personal Identification' (1991) 11 OJLS, 305.

Reece, H 'Losses of chances in law' 59 MLR (1996) 188.

Reeve, A 'The theory of property. Beyond private versus common property' in D Held (ed) *Political Theory Today* (1991).

Reich, C 'The New Property' (1964) 73 Yale Law J 733.

Richardson, G *Law, Process and Custody: Prisoners and Patients* (1993) Butterworths, London.

Richardson, G 'The legal regulation of process' in G Richardson and H Genn *Administrative Law and Government Action* (1994).

Richardson, G and H Genn *Administrative Law and Government Action* (1994) Clarendon Press, Oxford.

Samuel, G 'Public and private law: A private lawyer's response' (1983) 46 MLR 558.

Samuel, G and J Rinkes *Law of Obligations and Legal Remedies* (1996) Cavendish, London.

Samuel, G 'The impact of European integration on private law – a comment' 18 Legal Studies (1998) 167.

Schofield, P (ed) *Bentham's Official Aptitude Maximized; Expense Minimized* (1993) Clarendon Press, Oxford.

Schofield, P and J Harris (eds) *'Legislator of the World': Writings on Codification, Law and Education*, 1998. Clarendon Press, Oxford.

Schwarze, J *European Administrative Law* (1992) Sweet and Maxwell, London.

Scott, C 'Regulatory relations in the UK utilities sector' in J Black, P Muchlinski and P Walker *Commercial Regulation and Judicial Review* (1998).

Sedley, Sir Stephen 'The common law and the constitution' in *The Making and Remaking of the British Constitution* (1997).

Sedley, Sir Stephen 'Public law and contractual employment' (1994) 23 ILJ 201.

Sedley, Sir Stephen 'Public power and private power' in *Freedom, Law and Justice* (50th series of Hamlyn lectures), (1999) Sweet and Maxwell, London.

Shaw, J 'Sterilisation of mentally handicapped people: Judge rules OK?' (1990) 53 MLR 91.

Simpson, A.W.B. *A History of the Common Law of Contract: The Rise and Rise of the Action of Assumpsit*, 1975. Oxford University Press, Oxford.

Simpson, A W B 'The common law and legal theory' in W L Twining (ed) *Legal Theory and Common Law* (1986).

Smillie, J A 'Fundamental rights, parliamentary supremacy and the New Zealand Court of Appeal' (1995) 111 LQR 209.

Smith, S 'Future freedom and freedom of contract' (1996) 59 MLR 167.

Spry, I C F (1997) *The Principles of Equitable Remedies* (5th edn) Sweet and Maxwell, London.

Sunkin, M, L Bridges and G Meszaros *Judicial Review in Perspective* (1993) Public Law Project, London.

Supperstone, M and J Goudie (eds) *Judicial Review* (2nd edn, 1997) Butterworths, London.

Supperstone, M 'The ambit of judicial review' in Supperstone, M. and J. Goudie (eds) *Judicial Review* (2nd edn, 1997).

Swainston, M 'Court procedures and remedies in the context of commercial regulation' in J Black, P Muchlinski and P Walker (eds) *Commercial Regulation and Judicial Review* 1998.

Taggart, M *Corporatisation, Privatisation and Public Law* (1990) Legal Research Foundation, New Zealand.

Taggart, M 'The province of administrative law determined?' in M Taggart (ed) *The Province of Administrative Law* (1997).

Taggart, M (ed) *The Province of Administrative Law* (1997) Hart Publishing, Oxford.

Turpin, C C *Government Procurement and Contracts* (revised 1989) Longman, Harlow.

Twining, W L and D Miers *How to do Things with Rules* (3rd edn, 1991) Weidenfeld and Nicolson, London.

Twining, WL (ed) *Legal Theory and Common Law* (1986) Blackwell, Oxford.

Vickers, L 'Whistleblowing in the public sector' [1997] Public Law 594.

Vickers, L *Protecting Whistleblowers at Work* (1995) Institute of Employment Rights, London.

Wade, H W R and C F Forsyth *Administrative Law* (7th edn, 1994) Oxford University Press, Oxford.

Waldron, J (ed) *Theories of Rights* (1984) Oxford University Press, Oxford.

Walker, P 'Irrationality and commercial regulators' in J Black, P Muchlinski and P Walker, (eds) *Commercial Regulation and Judicial Review* (1998).

Walker, P 'Unreasonableness and proportionality' in M Supperstone and J Goudie (eds) *Judicial Review* (2nd edn, 1997).

Weber, M *Law in Economy and Society* (1954) Harvard University Press, Cambridge, Mass.

Weber, M *Economy and Society* (trans G Roth and C Wittich, 1978).

Weir, T 'Complex Liabilities' Int Encl Comp L (1976) 5.

Wightman, J *Contract, A Critical Commentary* (1996) Pluto Press, London.

Wilson, G (ed) *The Making and Remaking of the British Constition* (1997) Blackstone Press, London.

Wintemute, R *Sexual Orientation and Human Rights* (1995) Clarendon Press, Oxford.

Wolffe, W J 'The scope of judicial review in Scots law' [1992] Public Law 625.

Woolf, Sir Harry 'Public law – private law: Why the divide?' [1986] Public Law 220.

Woolf, Lord 'Droit public – English style' [1995] Public Law 57.

Wyman, B 'The Law of the Public Callings as a Solution of the Trust Problems' XVII Harvard Law Review (1903-1904) 156.

Youdan, T G (ed) *Equity, Fiduciaries and Trusts* (1989) Carswell, Ontario.

Index